Language Learner Strategies
Thirty Years of Research anc

D0800611

Published in this series

Language Learner Strategies:
Thirty Years of Research and Practice

Edited by

ANDREW D. COHEN and ERNESTO MACARO

OXFORD
UNIVERSITY PRESS

OXFORD
UNIVERSITY PRESS

Great Clarendon Street, Oxford OX2 6DP

Oxford University Press is a department of the University of Oxford.
It furthers the University's objective of excellence in research, scholarship,
and education by publishing worldwide in

Oxford New York

Auckland Cape Town Dar es Salaam Hong Kong Karachi
Kuala Lumpur Madrid Melbourne Mexico City Nairobi
New Delhi Shanghai Taipei Toronto

With offices in

Argentina Austria Brazil Chile Czech Republic France Greece
Guatemala Hungary Italy Japan Poland Portugal Singapore
South Korea Switzerland Thailand Turkey Ukraine Vietnam

OXFORD and OXFORD ENGLISH are registered trade marks of
Oxford University Press in the UK and in certain other countries

ISBN: 978 0 19 442254 3

Printed and bound by Eigal S.A. in Portugal.

Contents

Foreword

PETER YONGQI GU

Few people would accept a theory of human learning as nothing but stimulus-response and feedback. We agree that human agency means more than a hyphen between S and R, or a black box beyond scrutiny. So long as we accept the importance of human agency in learning and agree that, besides individual differences such as aptitude and motivation, what learners choose to do also makes a difference in the learning process, we should give learners' strategic behaviors the rightful place they deserve in a theory of learning in general and in L2 acquisition in particular.

Language learner strategy research focuses on the learner's decision-making process and the behaviors involving learning decisions aimed at maximizing results. Since the publication of Rubin (1975) and Stern (1975), learner strategy research has gained vibrancy in applied linguistics enquiry. Indeed, the theoretical breadth and depth and empirical scope and rigor of this volume reveal the maturity and vitality of this confident and self-reflective field.

Yet many both inside and outside the learner strategy tradition feel we have reached a crossroads. Since we have already established that frequent use of a large repertoire of strategies is positively related to learning results, we need more research investigating the real picture, which is more complex. For example, there is still lack of consensus as to what constitutes a language learner strategy. We also need more rigorous research designs and practices, and more tangible and useful applications for teachers and learners.

While I appreciate critiques of learner strategy research, some of the more radical solutions offered—discussed evenly and lucidly in Chapter 1—do not seem plausible and viable, such as that of dismissing a line of robust research simply because a central concept is not clearly defined. While Pluto was recently removed from the list of planets because astronomers voted for a new definition of 'planet', no one is dismissing astronomy because astronomers can't agree on what a planet is. Likewise, 30 years of research has told us that language learner strategy is a multidimensional and elusive moving target, not a straightforward construct to conceptualize and operationalize. None the less, learner strategy researchers came together and had another hard look at the issues. These efforts are well reflected in this book.

This volume is therefore a link between the past and the future, marking the end of an exploratory era and ushering in a new era of theoretical depth, empirical rigor, and practical utility. In this sense, this book is a landmark and a monumental collection—an orchestrated attempt by leading researchers in the field to reflect on 30 years of research and outline a research agenda. This kind of collective self-reflection is not often seen in SLA research communities. I urge all doubters to take a closer look at the chapters in this book, and all interested parties to think about where the field should go from here.

Acknowledgements

The editors would like to acknowledge the effort and contributions of all the researchers and teachers who came together in Oxford for three days in June of 2004 without whose initial impetus this book would not have been possible.

Introduction

ERNESTO MACARO and ANDREW D. COHEN

One day very many edited books will be written like this!

The above comment from one of the authors of this book was meant to be neither flippant nor self-congratulatory. It heads this introduction because we genuinely believe that the book seeks to be different from the many other edited books on a given research area of applied linguistics. It is different because:

1 The language learner strategy research area has a long, multifaceted, and controversial history that this book seeks to document, describe, and resolve.

2 The book brings together the top international researchers in the field not only to celebrate 30 years of research and practice but also to provide an introspective and highly self-critical account of three decades of research endeavour, and it spells out the areas and issues that future research will need to address.

3 The book is not merely a series of unrelated chapters or personal accounts by authors in the field, nor a collection of conference papers. Rather, the topic of each chapter was conceived by the editors in collaboration with the team of authors in order to provide a coherent story of 30 years of theory-building and of empirical research, and to offer readers a landmark publication in the field.

4 All but one chapter is at least co-authored. Dialogue is thus encouraged, with possible disagreement and, we hope, a relatively unbiased synthesis of argument.

5 Each chapter has been extensively and anonymously peer-reviewed and several drafts have resulted from this process.

6 In the chapters where a review of empirical research is offered (Part Two of this book), the authors adopted systematic review guidelines in order to maximize the scope of the review and to minimize reviewer selectivity and bias. A summary of the systematic review process is provided in the Introduction to Part Two and a full account can be found at www.oup.com/elt/teacher/lls along with a comprehensive keyword mapping of the studies reviewed.

7 The concluding chapter was first written separately by the two editors. It was then compared, discussed, and the conclusions synthesized thereby,

once again, minimizing editorial bias. It was then commented on by the team of authors.

The book then should be seen as the product of a collective: in essence a multi-authored book. It is intended first and foremost to appeal to experts in the field in that it represents cutting-edge thinking. The level and style should also be appropriate for postgraduate students and teacher-researchers who are interested in learner strategy research.

Now for a brief description of the contents of the book.

Part One

Chapter 1 (by Mike Grenfell and Ernesto Macaro) outlines problematic theoretical areas. It narrates in some detail how the concept of language learner strategies began with publications by Joan Rubin, by David Stern, and by Neil Naiman and his associates. This was probably the first time that researchers really began to take an interest in the language learners themselves. The chapter outlines the claims made by language learner strategy research and traces the development of strategy research. It then documents the critiques that have been levelled at this research, and identifies ways that, over the past 30 years, strategy research has evolved. This chapter, then, sets the stage for Part One of the book which is intended to provide the historical and theoretical background to the field.

Of course, strategies were not called 'language learner strategies' in the beginning but 'learning strategies' or 'learner strategies' or even 'language learning strategies' and the search for an uncontested terminology is part of the story that this book narrates.

The term 'language learner strategies' (LLS) was probably never used before June 2004. It was then that 23 international scholars, who were significantly involved in the field of 'strategies', came together at the University of Oxford for three days to work together on crucial issues relating to strategies for language learning and for language use following planning meetings in Singapore, at the AILA Congress, December 2002, and in Oxford, December 2003. At this series of meetings issues which had been exercising the minds of participants were identified and problematized:

1 *defining LLS*—why did there continue to be the problem of what actually constitutes a strategy? Why had so many different definitions been used hitherto?
2 *relating LLS to learners' short- and long-term goals*—why was it important to map out strategy use not only against the immediate tasks that language learners were engaged in but also their own long term objectives?
3 *relating strategies to individual and situational differences*—with regard to strategy use, what did we know and what more did we need to find out about the interaction among individuals, the group that they might belong to, and the learning situation that they might find themselves in?

4 *demonstrating and communicating the importance of strategies to the end-user*—why was it that, despite the obvious practitioner interest in LLS, and despite many authors' valiant attempts to bridge the gap between strategy theory and classroom practice, was there still little sign of a concerted inclusion of strategy instruction in second language programs worldwide?

A major outgrowth of the meeting in June 2004 was to plan out the current volume in which each of these themes would get rigorous treatment. Another outgrowth was a consensus that a survey questionnaire be constructed and circulated among these experts to find out how they conceptualized and used theory and terminology in LLS research; the results of that survey are summarized in Chapter 2 by Andrew Cohen. The survey is probably the first in applied linguistics to seek openly, amongst a group of researcher practitioners, the areas of consensus and the areas for which there remain a wide range of views.

Chapter 3 (by Rebecca Oxford and Karen Schramm) continues the theme of introspection and auto-critique. It discusses strategy theory not only from the much more common perspective of psycholinguistics but also from the socio-cultural perspective. It argues that both these over-arching theories need to interact in order that we might arrive at a clearer understanding of strategic behavior. In addition, it illustrates this interaction by projecting its combined spotlights on a number of relationships, such as strategies and metacognition, strategies and aptitude, and strategies and motivation.

The challenges set by both Chapter 3 and the issues problematized at the June 2004 meeting, begin to be taken up in Chapter 4. Firstly, the authors (Osamu Takeuchi, Carol Griffiths, and Do Coyle) review the strategies literature by investigating variables such as age, gender, career orientation, and personality type. The chapter then provides an insight into such individual and group differences though a small-scale study of language learners in New Zealand, and finishes with a study which, taking sociocultural theory as its framework, explores how strategic behavior might be encouraged and shaped by the environment in which the learning is taking place.

The critiques of LLS research documented in Chapter 1, particularly relating to a strategy as the 'unit of analysis' are addressed in Chapter 5 through a discussion of LLS research methods in general and of 'think-aloud protocols' in particular. The authors (Cynthia White, Karen Schramm, and Anna Uhl Chamot) argue that we understand better the introspective learner reports of strategic behavior if we researchers, in turn, understand the context in which that behavior is taking place and if the processes for eliciting and analyzing strategies are finely tuned and draw on research methods in other disciplines. They then explore the methodological implications of emerging language learning contexts such as online learning, and they call for a broadening of research techniques, ones which place practitioners and learners more at the center of the research.

The chapter on grammar strategies (by Rebecca Oxford and Kyoung Rang Lee with Gloria Park) covers an area that has not been explored from a strategy point of view. It discusses grammar development theories, explores the way that learners might be dealing with morphosyntax strategically, and relates this to theories of implicit and explicit learning. The chapter highlights the areas of research that are desperately needed and questions whether we can use existing research methods to explore them.

Part One of the book concludes with Chapter 7, on LLS interventions. Whereas other second language acquisition areas (for example the area of 'language aptitude') examine attributes which their proponents claim are relatively stable, it has always been a major claim of LLS that strategies are susceptible to instruction—that intervening in learners' strategic behavior can improve learning processes and ultimate attainment. These interventions are not simple, however, nor can they be prescribed without involving the learner and without referring to the context in which the learning is taking place. The authors of this chapter (Joan Rubin, Anna Uhl Chamot, Vee Harris, and Neil Anderson), therefore, divide their analysis of and practical strategy instruction for LLS into two broad phases—younger learners and older learners—seeing this distinction as posing the greatest challenge to would-be researchers or teachers.

Part Two

Part Two of the book reviews the research literature as applied to specific learning tasks and skills. Each chapter refers the reader to where a full account can be found of how the review process was operationalized, and validity and reliability issues addressed. Underlying models of learning related to tasks and skills are presented briefly in all these review chapters before diverging according to what the authors consider to be the emerging themes.

Ernesto Macaro, Suzanne Graham, and Robert Vanderplank (in Chapter 8) identify three themes: the relationship between listening success and strategy use, the relative effectiveness of prior knowledge in listening, and the effectiveness of listening strategy instruction. In Chapter 9, Lynn Erler and Claudia Finkbeiner focus on the interaction between first language (L1), second language (L2), the reader, and reading strategies before reviewing research into reading strategy instruction. They find that factors influencing the activation and use of reading strategies during an L2 reading event include aspects of the text at all levels from pre-lexical to contextual, and learner factors including L1 linguistic and cultural background, L1 and L2 proficiency levels, interest, and motivation.

Yasuo Nakatani and Christine Goh in Chapter 10 observe that it is possible to classify the research on oral communication strategies into two broad categories: interactive strategies, in which there is the obvious and crucial presence of an interlocutor, and psycholinguistic strategies, which are concerned with the cognitive and metacognitive processes involved in producing meaning within the limitations offered by the learner's interlanguage.

In Chapter 11, the authors (Rosa M. Manchón, Julio Roca de Larios, and Liz Murphy) provide a critical account of writing strategy research by challenging previous conceptualizations and the research methodology used. The review findings are grouped under four themes: the strategies that L2 writers use, variables influencing the L2 writer's selection of strategies, whether first language writing strategies can be transferred to second language writing, and the influence of instruction on strategy use.

Whereas other chapters in Part Two of the book have reviewed research on strategies according to different language skills, Chapter 12 reviews strategy research on vocabulary acquisition, which cuts across the various language skills. This chapter examines the vocabulary learning strategies (VLS) of learners at varying proficiency levels, with emphasis on the learners' report of their perceptions regarding strategy use. They look both at strategies which decontextualize the vocabulary (for example, mnemonics) and strategies based on the context (for example, context clues in inferencing), as well as look-up strategies involving dictionaries. They also review strategy instruction studies, but again with an emphasis on studies involving the learner's voice in the vocabulary learning process. They find that integration of VLS into instruction appears to be more effective than non-integration and that significantly better vocabulary performance is possible with VLS instruction.

It will be up to the reader to judge whether the book represents a coherent auto-critique and theoretical synthesis that points the way to the future of LLS research. We as editors would maintain that this innovative approach to an edited book indeed provides the opportunity for such desired outcomes to be facilitated. It is for this reason that we have allowed ourselves the self-indulgence of a comprehensive concluding chapter—'LLS and the future: resolving the issues'—where we attempt to draw together the threads of critique and to suggest ways to resolve outstanding issues. Regardless of whether it truly resolves some of the issues in the field, this book is intended to promote a cutting-edge to future research efforts in LLS and thereby ensure that efforts continue to be made to improve opportunities for all language learners.

PART ONE

Issues, theories, and frameworks

I

Claims and critiques

MICHAEL GRENFELL
and ERNESTO MACARO

Introduction

In this chapter we examine the various claims that have been made regarding language learner strategies (LLS). We adopt a chronological perspective in order to give a sense of the unfolding debates surrounding this area of research. We track LLS research from its inception in the 1970s and early studies, through to its more developed forms in the last decade of the twentieth century and to the present day. Interwoven with this historical overview is an account and an assessment of the critiques of strategy research which have appeared in the literature. We end at the point we have reached in the debate as to the desirability of strategy research and a series of challenges facing future researchers.

The background: research on the language learner

As will be noted elsewhere in this book (for example, Chapter 2), definition and terminology are major issues in LLS research. We do not attempt to resolve these issues in the present chapter. Rather we examine in some detail the problems they have posed. Nevertheless, we suggest that these issues are not exclusive to LLS but are indicative of the way second language acquisition research in general developed in the second half of the twentieth century.

In retrospect, we can see that the arrival of LLS research formed part of a fundamental shift of perspective in thinking about the processes of language learning. Until the 1970s, language learning was seen essentially as a psychological phenomenon. Behaviorist theories, which gave birth to the ubiquitous language laboratory of the 1960s, approached the problem of learning a language as a question of manipulating the psychology of the individual; hence the practice of phrasal drilling, learning through repetitions, and stimulus-response. Here, grammar was learnt as an individual habit essentially devoid of social context.

The Chomskyan revolution, stemming from the 1950s, seemed to do little to alter this asocial view of language learning. Universal Grammar, after all, deals with an ideal speaker and a perfect competence. What Dell Hymes did when he stipulated that 'there are rules of use without which the rules of grammar would be useless' (1972: 278) was to provide a new paradigmatic perspective to language teaching and learning, one which focused much more on social context. Of course, the rules which Hymes had in mind were vastly different from the universal grammatical rules which were beginning to dominate thinking in linguistics in the 1960s. Indeed, what Hymes really intended when he wrote of the need to take account of socially conditioned aspects of language—feasibility, possibility, potentiality, and appropriacy—is probably better understood as patterns rather than fixed rules *per se*.

It is in this context that the word 'strategy' gained increasing prominence as a concept, one which could capture a wide range of linguistic behavior in second language learning. For Hymes, communicative competence distinguished itself from Chomskyan competence because he conceived any effective linguistic behavior as being determined by more than deep innate structures.

Further conceptual and theoretical development led to major statements about what communicative competence was. By 1980, the seminal article by Canale and Swain (1980) posited strategic competence as one of the four components of communicative competence. Strategic competence was the practice individuals adopted to hold conversations and repair breakdowns in communication. Ten years later, Bachman (1990) also argued that strategic competence was a part of linguistic competence. The issue here is the extent to which such strategic linguistic behavior is an integral part of language learning; indeed, whether it is coterminus with psychological factors of linguistic processes in operating language, and how far it is complementary or is additive to such processes. Nevertheless, despite such implicit questions, increasingly, during the 1970s the notion of 'strategy' established itself as part of the conceptual vocabulary of applied linguistics. Even Krashen who, with his Monitor Model, probably took as far as anyone the notion of first and second language competences developing from similar natural processes, argued that 'adults therefore use common strategies for second language learning' (1984: 238). Researchers such as Færch and Kasper (for example, 1983a) investigated the strategies those involved in developing a second language activated in the course of their learning. In particular, they targeted communication strategies, or those strategies that learners employ to better manage their communication.

What these various approaches to strategic linguistic behavior implied was that second language learning is inherently problematic. A strategy is therefore some form of activity that is used in response to problems when and where they arise. These problems might be found within discourse, within the social context, or inside the head of the learner—or all three. Consequently, attention to 'strategic behavior' does present us with fundamental questions concerning the relationship between the psychological and the social context. The initial impetus for LLS research, however, came from a different direction, and it is to this which we now turn.

The birth of strategy research: the 1970s and 1980s

If there is one article which can be seen to have announced the birth of language learner strategy research, then it was: 'What the "Good Language Learner" Can Teach Us' by Joan Rubin in 1975. Her answer (1975, 1981) was to set out techniques and approaches employed by successful language learners:

I Processes which may contribute directly to learning:
    A   Clarification and verification
    B   Monitoring
    C   Memorization
    D   Guessing/inductive inferencing
    E   Deductive reasoning
    F   Practice.

II Processes which may contribute indirectly to learning:
    A   Creates opportunities for practice
    B   Production tasks related to communication.
(Rubin 1975: 124–25)

This list includes social strategies and techniques under II A, where all those activities related to and involving seeking opportunities for interaction, both with other students and with fellow learners, are listed. The list can be seen to be weighted in terms of what might be termed academic or study skills. Such skills include the repertoire of what a learner might go through in order to deal with the very wide range of demands with which they are confronted in learning a second language.

Others researchers were working along similar lines. For example, Stern (1975: 31) listed the top-ten strategies of the good language learner (GLL):

1 A personal learning style or positive learning strategies.
2 An active approach to the task.
3 A tolerant and outgoing approach to the target language and empathy with its speakers.
4 Technical know-how about how to tackle a language.
5 Strategies of experimentation and planning with the object of developing the new language into an ordered system and/or revising this system progressively.
6 Constantly searching for meaning.
7 Willingness to practise.
8 Willingness to use language in real communication.

9 Self-monitoring and critical sensitivity to language use.

10 Developing the target language more and more as a separate reference system and learning to think in it.

This list is conceptual and speculative (rather than being based on empirical investigation) in that Stern's main source for these strategies was his own experience as a teacher, together with a review of relevant literature. However, it began to offer the systematization referred to above. 'The Good Language Learner' (Naiman, Fröhlich, Stern, and Todesco 1978/1996) took this list as its *point de départ*. 'What makes good language learners tick?', the authors ask at the outset of the book, and 'What do they do that poor learners don't do?' They go on to ask: 'Could we help the poor learners by teaching them some of the good learners' tricks?' (Naiman *et al.* 1978/1996: 1–8). The pedagogical intent behind the book is clear, then, from the start. They argue that good language teachers have an intuitive understanding of language learning. What they do not have is a systematic understanding. The book sets out to provide such an understanding. LLS, they claim, are useful for pedagogical purposes in that they allow us to pass on the behaviors of good learners to less good learners, assuming that such transfer is possible. For the purpose of matching their data with Stern's list in order to provide exemplification of their empirical investigations, Naiman *et al.* (1978/1996: 30–33) distilled it down to five major strategies. They proposed the following:

1 Active task approach
  GLLs were active in their response to learning situations; they intensified efforts where necessary; they practiced regularly; they identified problems; they turned everyday life experiences into learning opportunities.

2 Realization of language as system
  GLLs referred to their own native language 'judiciously' and made comparisons; made guesses and inferences about language; responded to clues; systematized language.

3 Realization of language as means of communication
  GLLs often concentrated on fluency rather than accuracy (especially in the early stages of learning); looked for communicative opportunities; looked for sociocultural meanings.

4 Management of affective demands
  GLLs realized that learning a language involves emotional responses which they must take on board as part of their learning.

5 Monitoring of L2 performance
  GLLs reviewed their L2 and made adjustments.

Even though this is not a comprehensive list, it is difficult to imagine any one learner doing all these things all of the time. Moreover, it is unclear whether there is an implicit assumption that the actual strategic dimension of individual language behavior varies according to the particular context and the actual stage of any one learner's linguistic competence. We might argue that this assumption, if true, itself casts some doubt on the teachability of learning strategies. Moreover, we can surmise that teaching a strategy is just as problematic as teaching grammar and vocabulary, in that what has been taught still has to be learnt and used. Strategies, some might suppose, are just as prone as any other aspect of language to the influence of such factors as level of competence, cognitive style, gender, and motivation. Furthermore, it might seem to the reader that what is listed above varies so widely, in terms of what is actually involved in deployment, that to group them under the common title 'strategy' is rather misleading.

These issues, as we shall see, took on greater significance as the research field developed. Some strategies could even conflict with each other. For example, willingness to be active and communicative might inhibit monitoring language and developing a systematic understanding in comparison with the first language (L1) if insufficient mental space is available to do both at the same time. In this case, the learner risks being pulled in different directions—one outer and social, the other inner and psychological. Naiman *et al.* (1978/ 1996: 33ff) also offered a list of what they called techniques to complement these strategies. Such techniques included a further comprehensive list of what a learner might do to learn language with regard to particular skill areas such as grammar, vocabulary, listening, writing, speaking, and reading. Examples were: repeating words; reading a dictionary; following the rules as given in grammar books.

In a sense, what we see in these seminal studies are issues concerning the epistemological core of LLS research in terms of its social and psychological aspects. Other work in the 1970s and 80s underlined its dual nature.

Wong-Fillmore (1979) stressed the social dimensions of language learning. Her research was more in the area of communication strategies than within the broader definition of LLS. The logic, as argued by such writers as Long (1983), was that discourse is an important source of comprehensible input and thus incorporated language learning potential. However, the strategies proposed by Wong-Fillmore appear more like social-psychological identity management than directly related to learning *per se*: join a group; give the impression you understand; count on your friends. She argued that the actual cognitive strategies behind these social strategies include the use of stock phrases, or formulaic language in order to get the conversation started and keep it going. Once discourse gets going, we might conclude, natural language learning strategies are activated in developing competence.

What was intended by strategy in these early stages of LLS research, then, covered a wide range of linguistic behavior and included techniques, tricks, tactics, attitudes, exercises, and learning activities before converging on the term 'strategies'. Similarly, both the terms learner strategies and learning strategies were used at this stage in a fairly interchangeable way (cf. Tarone 1983). As we have seen, the term 'communication strategies' was also used referring to discursive events. One would conclude, therefore, that such linguistic behavior overlaps with 'learning strategies', in that social interactive contexts are an important source of strategic activity and, therefore, communication strategies complement and form a part of LLS.

Even from the limited range of literature so far reviewed we can see, in the distinction between 'learning' and 'learner', a further fundamental issue of definition in LLS research. In their most narrow sense, the term 'strategies', as used in the research literature, might refer to nothing more than study skills and repetition techniques. On the other hand, 'strategy' can also refer to quite sophisticated cognitive skills such as inferencing and deducing grammar in a generative way. Further to these issues is the question of the 'problematic' character of strategy use. Should we see strategies as a means of dealing with and/or avoiding problems? Or, as we suggested above, should we see all language learning as inherently problematic—both are implied in the research at this time. We detail the developments in this research field in the next sections when we look at its claims and criticism to the present day. For the moment, it is worth adding that the popularity of LLS research was the potential it held for affecting learning, both in and outside of the classroom. Firstly, it offered information that was clearly useful to both teachers and learners of a second language. Secondly, it systematized this information in a way which could be integrated with pedagogical methods. Thirdly, it led to the realization that if strategies can be taught, they could enhance the processes of language learning. (See G. Ellis and Sinclair 1989.)

So far, most of what we have presented has been predicated on a fairly simplistic and homogeneous sense of the language learner. Individual differences in strategy use were slowly acknowledged in this early research but were hardly exemplified and certainly not integrated into a coherent model of language learning. Other work in the 1970s and 80s extended this early but seminal work and it is that which we now address.

Shifting perspectives in early LLS research

Early claims for LLS also related to the psychological character of the learner; what later came to be referred to as their 'psychotypology'. Reiss (1981), for example, examined the way strategy use varied with cognitive style, arguing that there is considerable variation in language processing, and this variation depended on the cognitive character of learners. One test of this style was the distinction between 'field independence' and 'dependence' based on individuals' innate ability to separate figures out from background information; an important skill in, for example, phonemic coding ability where, in order for learners to decode aural material, they must first be able to distinguish its patterns and sounds. Cognitive style goes back to general work on cognitive psychology in the early 1960s (for example, Witkin 1962). Not only are field-independent people able to separate figures from a background field, they are also said to be analytical and object-orientated. Field-dependent individuals, on the other hand, see the field as an unanalyzed whole, but they are also more person-orientated and sensitive. Reiss (1981) argued that the 'good/not good language learner' could be studied in terms of these cognitive differences.

The suggestion in this area of enquiry was that teachers could exploit actual language teaching materials to take account of these differences in cognitive processing. Failure in the language classroom might thus be avoided through greater degrees of differentiation, and by implication autonomy. Similarly, Wesche (1981) argued that we might enhance language learning by matching teaching methodology to cognitive type. For example, a more person-orientated approach might best suit a field-dependent individual, whilst for the field-independent person, a more analytical approach might be best.

Along with these differences in cognitive style, a range of other variables began to be linked to strategy use. Among these were proficiency level, affect and motivation. O'Malley, Chamot, Stewner-Manzanares, Russo, and Küpper (1985), for example, reported that 'higher' level students used more strategies and employed more sophisticated strategies. Alvermann and Phelps (1983) and Padrón (1985) similarly concluded that students in lower grade classes used 'less sophisticated' and more inappropriate strategies. Jones, Palinscar, Ogle, and Carr (1987) concluded that motivation was an important aspect of self-regulation. Therefore, successful and highly motivated learners adopted more strategies, especially those involving planning, evaluation, and monitoring. Poorly motivated pupils, on the other hand, employed a limited set of strategies and were less ready to act strategically.

In much of this early research, the good language learner was often used synonymously with the advanced language learner; that the former *was* the latter. Intermediate to advanced adult learners were often the subjects of empirical studies on LLS. Yet, as we shall argue, it is theoretically possible to be a 'good' beginner language learner and a 'poor' advanced learner.

It was also now observed that there might be considerable variation in strategy type. Chesterfield and Chesterfield (1985) took up this issue with regard to so-called 'easier' and 'harder' strategies. We noted above the range of difficulty and different levels of sophistication between strategies. These authors claimed that easier strategies are learnt and employed earlier whilst harder ones are employed at a more advanced level. Connected with this issue of strategy difficulty is both the number of strategies particular learners have at their disposal and the frequency of deployment. As noted above, some 'good language learner' research claimed that successful learners have a wide range of strategies, including 'difficult' and sophisticated ones, which they use frequently. The opposite was true for the 'unsuccessful learners'.

Such levels of cross-correlation between learners opened the door to comparing any learner variable with strategic behavior for example, according to variations in age, gender, first or second language, level of competence, instructional methods, degrees of natural exposure. Notwithstanding the methodological problems in successfully eliciting and recording strategy use (see Chapter 5, this volume), there was no theoretical reason why any kind of strategic variability could not be examined in relation to any other variable.

Much of the research literature in the 1970s and 80s can be understood as representing a growing level of sophistication in conceptualizing LLS together with methodological advances leading to further empirical studies to test emerging hypotheses. Increasingly, in this early work, it becomes evident that a clear and precise theoretical framework was needed which would take strategy research beyond the utilitarian and pragmatic. This theory was to come from the cognitive psychology of John Anderson (1983, 1985).

O'Malley and Chamot (1990) set LLS research within a cognitive framework derived from Anderson's work, and this provided a theoretical background to much LLS research in the 1980s. (See Chapter 3.) In brief, Anderson had posited a fundamental dichotomy between two sorts of information processing—declarative and procedural—which might best be summed up respectively as knowledge *of* and knowledge *how*. In other words, declarative knowledge is about facts; procedural knowledge is about how to perform actions. O'Malley and Chamot offered a list of reasons for using Anderson's work:

1 It integrates numerous concepts from prevailing notions of cognitive processing that give the theory generality and currency with regard to existing views in the field.
2 The theoretical developments in production systems cover a broader range of behavior than other theories, including comprehension and production of oral and written texts as well as comprehension, problem solving, and verbal learning.
3 The theory distinguishes between factual knowledge and procedural skills in both memory representation and learning.
4 The theory can be expanded to incorporate strategic processing as part of description of how information is learned.
5 The theory has been continually updated, expanded, and revised in a number of recent publications.

(O'Malley and Chamot 1990: 19)

The theory at least offered the possibility of an approach which might integrate the neurological, cognitive, emotional, and behavioral. Allport (1985) put forward an explanation of the storage and operation of language as a part of neurological modular subsystems. Words (the declarative), he argued, were not stored in specific neural hardware but were in fact distributed over broader 'concept domains'. Such domains constituted the sum knowledge of the world—declarative and procedural—gained from experience. Many words, and many processes, shared features between and across declarative and procedural knowledge. For Allport, they formed part of a matrix linking up concepts, propositions, and predictions about language. Retrieval was activated by the firing of appropriate associations. This 'firing' was conceptualized as 'cognition in action', as the information (both declarative and procedural) was processed. This theoretical framework suggested that a distinct approach to understanding second language acquisition was being offered by LLS research.

O'Malley and Chamot (1990) claimed, on the basis of Anderson's theory, that there was a further fundamental distinction among strategies: meta-cognitive, cognitive, and social. The social referred to all those means of dealing with affective and social aspects in language learning situations, the cognitive was the actual processing of language in the brain, and the metacognitive dealt with planning, monitoring, and evaluating those cognitive processes. The whole, it was claimed, amounted to a coherent theory of practice of LLS use against which the various individual and contextual differences discussed above could be set.

One further salient claim was that it was possible to observe, record, and classify LLS. (See for example Cohen and Hosenfield 1981; Ericsson and Simon 1987; O'Malley, Chamot, and Küpper 1989.) Oxford (1990a) also provided a classification scheme for strategies. For her, strategies could be divided into direct and indirect. The latter supported and managed learning without involving language *per se*. The former involved direct manipulation of the target language. Indirect strategies included metacognitive, affective, and social strategies; direct strategies involved memory, cognitive, and compensatory strategies. We can see how this taxonomy had much in common with that of O'Malley and Chamot (1990) without necessarily being based on an explicit learning theory. It was also used to construct the *Strategy Inventory for Language Learning* (SILL) (Oxford 1986, 1990a). This questionnaire set out to measure a learner's frequency of strategy use (see Chapter 5). The SILL's fundamental claim was that strategies were identifiable and quantifiable. The SILL had an enormous impact and, by the mid 1990s, it was estimated that it had been used to assess the strategy use of more than 10,000 learners worldwide.

Early criticisms of language learner strategies

Despite the enthusiasm which greeted the initial publication of work on LLS, already, by the early 1980s, there was disquiet that the developing field held inherent structural difficulties. For example, Seliger (1983: 180) argued against the assumption that 'the verbalizations of learners represent some form of internal reality'. In other words, he questioned the claim that it was actually possible to find out what strategies learners were using because they were so deeply ingrained in the psychological mechanisms of the individual learner.

In 1986, R. Ellis contributed a whole chapter of a book to 'learner strategies' and indeed proposed his own categorization system. However, he admitted his system might not 'represent psychological reality' as such but was to be considered 'a heuristic device for coping with the lack of precision which characterizes discussions of learning strategies' (Rod Ellis 1986: 167). This lack of precision was associated with a number of unresolved issues, prevalent in the emerging research field, which provided a concatenation of theoretical problems. For Ellis, these originated from a twofold dilemma. The first was the inability to enter the workings of the mind (like 'stumbling blindfold around a room to find a hidden object'; Rod Ellis 1986: 188). As we have seen, the second was the imprecision of the metalanguage available to researchers. The latter problem led researchers not only to use 'strategies', 'tactics', and 'processes' interchangeably, but also to describe LLS as sometimes 'general mental operations' and sometimes specifically as 'operations involved in language processing' (Rod Ellis 1986: 166). Similar concerns with theoretical problems were raised by Stevick (1990). He developed Ellis's argument by proposing firstly that there was the problem of what he classed as the 'size-abstractness dilemma' (Stevick 1990: 144), which perceives that some strategies refer to phenomena which are larger than others and that some strategies refer to phenomena which are more abstract than others. This led to imprecision and confusion. Secondly, for Stevick, there was the 'outside-inside' issue which resulted from his belief that 'no clear relationship exists between external acts and the mental constructs to which they are attributed' (1990: 144). In other words, the link between cognitive behavior (action in the mind) and overt motor behavior (actions of the body) was far too tenuous and atheoretical to be simply assumed. Citing Wenden (in Wenden and Rubin 1987), he also alluded to the problem of incorporating into the construct of strategies what 'learners know about the strategies they use', making the construct both wider and even more ambiguous. Stevick asked, therefore, if the problem did not lie in the use of the term 'strategies' itself which had been appropriated to define 'something new in our world of experience', rather than the other way around—researchers coining a new word to describe something newly discovered.

By the last decade of the twentieth century, therefore, at the very time when two of the most influential LLS books (O'Malley and Chamot 1990; Oxford 1990a) were hitting the market, there was already considerable unease at the theoretical underpinnings of LLS research and particularly with the concept of a strategy itself. This unease led Kellerman (1991: 20) to argue that most attempts at setting up taxonomies of (in his case, communication) strategies were based on conflicting and inexplicit criteria and thus had doubtful psychological validity. In addition, he dismissed LLS instruction as irrelevant on the basis that learners had already developed strategic competence in their first language (L1) and could therefore simply transfer it to their L2.

However, the enthusiasm of LLS researchers, and the positive reactions of many practitioners to its applicability in the classroom, led most commentators to look upon strategy research as embryonic. The field, some assumed, was in the process of ironing out these complexities and contradictions. For example Skehan (1989: 98), in a chapter which acknowledged LLS as an individual difference alongside aptitude, motivation, and personality, remained optimistic as to its usefulness as an avenue for exploring the language learner, and recommended further efforts despite arriving at the conclusion that the field was 'dealing with a clear example of a research-then-theory perspective'.

By 1992, some of the researchers in the field, sensitive to these criticisms, began to attempt to provide solutions to the problems defined above. Oxford and Cohen (1992: 1) addressed 'crucial issues of concept and classification'. Firstly, they reformulated the claims that had been made about LLS: strategies had the power to 'increase attention essential for learning a language, enhance rehearsal that allows linkages to be strongly forged, improve the encoding and integration of language material, and increase retrieval of information when needed for use'. Having re-established the potential of LLS they acknowledged that 'strategies and tactics become confused' and that there were too many 'fuzzy synonyms'. However, they decided to reject distinct classifications of 'strategies' and 'tactics' because this would produce strategy lists that would be overly long, atheoretical, and filled with mixed levels of behavior. They also acknowledged that there was little clarity about what made a strategy conscious in some instances and unconscious in others. They therefore proposed that all strategies be regarded as conscious. They also ventured that the highest learning performance was 'associated with congruent, well-integrated packages of learning strategies along with personality-related factors including learning style' (Oxford and Cohen 1992: 24). This argument is one of the first allusions to strategies being 'only effective' or 'more effective' if they are used in combination. Very importantly, the authors advocated that rather than avoiding discussion of the problems associated with LLS research (and thus exacerbating them), investigators should come to grips with them.

One of the researchers working in the field who attempted to come to grips with these difficulties was LoCastro (1994), who argued that large and general LLS inventories (such as the SILL) were not transferable across sociocultural domains and that their results and conclusions, therefore, might be less valid than claimed. She cited the example of research findings outside mainstream school or university settings and suggested that these might not equate with large classes and that strategies developed by learners under a grammar-translation method were not the same as those developed under a communicative approach. In other words, strategy use might well be influenced by the learning environment (see Chapter 4, this volume), a notion which echoed the work of Wesche (1981) cited earlier. She made these observations after comparing Japanese students' data from the SILL with interviews, observations, and group discussions, and where she detected some discrepancies in their answers. Indeed, she claimed that students in this particular context found the SILL inappropriate, suggesting that the extent to which they used the strategy depended on the situation in which they found themselves. Although Oxford and Green (1995) provided a riposte to these critiques, LoCastro's concern with the SILL has remained and has been taken further in the literature (see over).

With this background of critique of LLS research, it was inevitable that there should be concerns connected to LLS instruction, sometimes referred to in early literature as 'strategy training' or 'learner training'. If the fundamental claim was that the good strategies used by good students could be adapted and taught to less successful students, then the effectiveness of that teaching would have to be put to the test. However, by 1993, Rees-Miller was claiming that, although there was some correlational evidence, there was no empirical evidence 'to show that awareness of strategies (was) a *causal* factor in L2 learning success' (our emphasis), and that to dedicate as much as 20 per cent of teaching time (as recommended by G. Ellis and Sinclair 1989) was therefore highly risky. Rees-Miller (1993: 681) also alluded to the possibility that strategies could not easily be transferred from one person to another. Nor could they easily be provided as exemplars by the teacher, and she doubted whether teachers could actually observe a student performing the strategy once it had been taught. Lastly, she cited evidence (Porte 1988; Vann and Abraham 1990) that poor language learners often have all the manifestations of being strategy users but with little success. A riposte to these charges was provided by Chamot and Rubin (1994) who argued that the effective management of strategies was useful for all learners and that some indicators of what constituted effective strategy instruction were already available in the literature. However, the charge that causality had not been proven remained (Rees-Miller 1994).

Another critique came from Sparks and Ganshow (1993), who took LLS theory to task in a quite unexpected way. They too agreed with earlier criticisms that LLS were too global and not sufficiently refined. However, they argued that this very broad approach, if adopted in the context of L2 learners with learning difficulties, was counterproductive. Far from being potentially beneficial to such learners it would, paradoxically, condemn them as poor strategy users 'generally deficient in dealing with cognitive tasks of all types' (Sparks and Ganshow 1993: 291). Instead, they argued for a much more fine-grained etiology for low achievement, for example, by examining the link between poor phonological decoding and poor reading skills.

In sum, the early critiques of LLS research centered around the lack of consensus as to the nature of a strategy, its size and location, whether external learner behavior could correctly predict cognitive operations, how they could be described and classified, whether they applied to all groups of learners and to all aspects of a learner's performance, and whether, given this lack of consensus, time dedicated to learner training was justifiable. We will now return to the claims being made about LLS by authors operating in the later 1990s and up to the present day.

Modifications to earlier claims

Despite the concerns expressed above about the location of strategies, a number of researchers continued to assert that both what went on inside the brain and certain external behaviors could be classified as strategies. (See, for example, Chamot and El-Dinary 1999.) However, it was clear that other researchers were aware of the problem of so doing. Nyikos and Oxford (1993: 12–13) explained that 'information processing and social psychological approaches were chosen as theoretical frameworks through which to interpret the present study' but that ... 'a few language learning strategies are overt and observable (for example, taking notes). Most, however, seem to be covert and unobservable (for example, creating mental images, rehearsing silently)'. On the other hand, there remained a determination that strategies should encompass more than mental operations. Oxford and Burry-Stock (1995: 18) argued strongly that 'language researchers must conceptualize LLS in a way that includes the social and affective sides of learning' and that language learning ... was 'an adventure of the whole person, not just a cognitive or metacognitive exercise'.

Post-1990 LLS research also continued to posit the importance of approaching second language learning problems from the perspective of the individual learner. Cohen (1998: 21) argued that 'language learning and language use strategies can have a major role in helping shift the responsibility for learning off the shoulders of the teachers and on to those of the learners'. Grenfell and Harris (1999: 50) proposed that the 'emphasis on learning to learn marks an intention to approach language learning from a different direction: rather than a perfect method, it focuses on the learner—their particular competence profile, learning styles and developmental stage ...'.

Although the concept of a good language learner persisted, many of these authors now duly acknowledged that different learning contexts might indeed affect the strategies that learners were using. McDonough (1995: 122) proposed that:

> If we can get learners to reveal their learning processes and strategies in language skill areas and tests, then we can also get them to reveal their reactions to the techniques which are used to teach them and perhaps glimpse their processing of these. A skilled language learner possesses skill in coping not only with problems of language but with the context of learning—and for large numbers of learners this context is the classroom.

If the learning environment affected strategy use, the important issue became whether students had any choice in the strategies they deployed. Nyikos and Oxford (1993: 20) strove to strike a balance, seeing certain cognitive processes as innate and therefore common to all:

> ... the ways learners choose to learn are related, at least in part, to the internal cognitive requirements of information processing ... (although)

choice of strategies also depends on existing (institutional) reward systems.

For Grenfell and Harris (1999) teaching approaches had to be in harmony with what could be discovered about learning processes. The problem, however, was to what extent these processes were innate and common to all. If only a small proportion were innate, then teachers would find it very difficult to accommodate all the 'optional processes'. This argument brought the discussion back to the nature of strategies themselves, the unresolved issue of whether good strategies were used by good language learners, good language learners used only good strategies, or strategies were used by all language learners but some used them ineffectively.

Despite the lack of resolution of these issues, we see during these years a growing awareness of the need to contextualize LLS in an environment that facilitated strategic growth on the part of the learner. This realization connected with another issue that had been emerging since the 1980s: the extent to which differences in LLS use was an individual or a group phenomenon. McDonough (1995), reviewing the individual differences literature, proposed that differences could be of two kinds: (a) those individual differences which correlate with measures of proficiency; and (b) individual differences which are simply an individual's different approaches to solving the same language problem. Graham (1997: 81), on the other hand, argued that her research showed that 'across all tasks, there was in indication of a more careful, planned approach on the part of girls …'. Other authors also increasingly emphasized the importance of group differences. Oxford and Burry-Stock (1995: 19) concluded that it was important to have more 'information on how students from different cultural backgrounds and different countries use language learning strategies' and how they prioritized strategies differently. It would appear then that the modified claims being made, during the 1990s, were that, although there existed a fixed number of strategies, different students used them in different ways and circumstances led to different prioritizing. For Hsiao and Oxford (2002), strategies were not inherently good or bad, but had the potential to be used effectively. For Cohen (1998), more effective learners intentionally and systematically selected and combined strategies relevant to the language task. McDonough emphasized this notion: 'strategies are not necessarily good in themselves' (1995: 81). Any strategy could lead to failure if used inappropriately. Macaro (2001) went further by suggesting that one cannot simply study good language learners and then propose that the behavior observed should be the behavior adopted by low achievers in order to make them high achievers. One had to observe how low achievers within a context were operating and then ask why they were operating in this way.

This shift in beliefs about strategies, away from a rigid 'good or bad' learner dichotomy, occurred in the field of L2 comprehension more than in any other. Graham (1997) argued that many authors had referred somewhat prematurely to the superiority of top-down processes over bottom-up processing (for example, Hosenfeld 1984) in both reading and listening comprehension. However, there was a body of writing which suggested that the tendency to emphasize top-down processing was not without dangers, in that in some cases the role of bottom-up, decoding strategies was ignored altogether. (See Eskey 1988.) Graham (and others) advocated an 'interactive approach' (a combination of both top-down and bottom-up strategies) and recognized a need for some ineffective learners to move away from 'an almost exclusive reliance on inferencing from context, and towards checking initial prediction ... in the light of how the text progresses ...' (Graham 1997: 160).

We thus observe two dimensions to the way that claims about LLS were being modified. The first is a move away from a general profile of the good language learner to an individual's strategic reaction to a contextualized task or series of tasks. The second is a shift away from an interest in the quantity of strategy use to an interest in the quality of strategy use. Both these shifts brought with them an increasing interest in metacognition as the orchestrating mechanism for combining strategies effectively in any given situation. Macaro (2001: 269) proposed that 'although it is the range and combinations of all strategies that ineffective learners lack, it is the metacognitive ... strategies which seem to be the strategy types most lacking in the arsenal of less successful learners'. Grenfell and Harris (1999: 39) claimed that it was now generally known that a good language learner was one who took personal decisions, in an implicit or explicit manner, regarding what to do to facilitate learning in the context they found themselves. Some authors went further, proposing that good learners would consistently monitor and adapt strategies, whereas poor learners would cling to ineffective strategies. (See for example, Chamot and El-Dinary 1999: 20.)

The question remained as to *why* some learners were able to combine strategies effectively thanks to metacognition. One answer to why this question does not seem to have been explored may lie in the very nature of the research questions themselves. As we shall see in other chapters in this book (for example, Chapter 8), LLS research has overwhelmingly examined the relationship between strategy use and achievement at the level of correlation rather than pursuing the direction of causality. There has been insufficient interest in whether strategy use leads to higher achievement or whether proficiency levels dictate particular kinds of strategy use. As a result, the research question 'why do certain learners behave in certain ways?' has rarely been asked. A second answer is to do with level: although some research has been carried out with younger learners (see for example in this volume the cited work of Chamot, of Vandergrift, and of Macaro), overwhelmingly the set of research outcomes that have been considered have been those obtained at the tertiary level; here the margins of failure are less marked, these being students who have already reached a certain standard of academic performance in general.

The complex relationship between strategy use and achievement remained unresolved throughout the 1990s and beyond. Grenfell and Harris (1999: 70) in their case studies of three students concluded that proficiency levels did not necessarily determine the use of strategies, and that learning style, as well as the nature of the task, might be significant factors.

None the less, learner strategies were firmly linked to achievement and proficiency continued to be the major claim made by some authors, despite the above arguments. (See for example, Vogely 1995.) Hsiao and Oxford (2002: 369) claimed that strategies were linked to proficiency or achievement, although an explanation of how strategies operate differently with these two factors was not provided. This distinction is crucial in our view. For example, let us take three students. Student A is a low achiever by the end of his first year of language learning, compared to his peer group. Student B is a high achiever by the end of her first year of language learning compared to her peer group; Student C is an average achiever by the end of her fifth year of language learning compared to her peer group. When we ponder this scenario, it becomes clear that the link among proficiency, achievement, and strategies needs to be more carefully examined. Macaro (2001: 264) suggested, moreover, that successful and unsuccessful strategy deployment may be linked to other things than stage of learning and proficiency level. Firstly, working memory limitations may have an influence on deployment in that the learner simply cannot do enough cognitive processing at the same time. Secondly, the learner may not have enough linguistic resources to be able to deploy certain strategies. Thirdly, they may not have the motivation to deploy a full range of strategies in combination.

To sum up, the claims made by LLS researchers in the 1990s and up to the present day were:

1 that strategies could continue to be identified under broad categories, despite the difficulties this entailed;
2 that strategy research offered a radical new conceptualization of the language learning process, shifting the emphasis onto the individual learner;
3 that the learning context, nevertheless, was a major influence on the way that individuals and groups used strategies;
4 that strategies were value-neutral, not in themselves good or bad, but were used either effectively or ineffectively by individuals and by groups;
5 that strategy research continued to offer insights into the complex operations that constituted the process of language learning; and
6 that strategy use and achievement were inextricably linked.

None the less, there continued to be a debate as to the relationship between success at learning and strategy deployment, and between proficiency levels and strategy deployment. Increasingly, there was a call to find out more about the reasons for the different strategic behaviors observed in learners.

Most recent critiques of LLS research

In this last section we will examine the critiques of LLS made by authors more recently and, in particular, in the last few years before the publication of this book. These come from a surprisingly small number of individuals, given the controversies outlined above—or, at least, the *published* critiques are few in number. Indeed, a brief glance through the content sections of the major L2 journals shows that LLS-type publications are still featuring significantly, as other chapters in this book will show.

We will limit ourselves to the critiques of two authors in particular: Zoltán Dörnyei and Peter Skehan. In the last five years, these authors have moved on from their early position of 'sceptical but supportive', with regard to the value of pursuing LLS research, to a position of 'sceptical and dismissive'. This scepticism is essentially based on what they perceive as the lack of consensus regarding the unit of analysis, the construct of a strategy itself. In their brief review, Dörnyei and Skehan (2003) examine definitions of strategies and argue that a strategy cannot be at the same time cognitive, emotional, *and* behavioral. They insist that a strategy needs to be defined either as a neurological process, or as a cognitive operation, or as a behavioral act involving motor skills. They also appear highly sceptical that a strategy can have the dual function of contributing both to linguistic knowledge and to language skills. They therefore conclude that a theoretical basis for the concept of LLS is still unavailable. Their most pessimistic conclusion, however, is that, to provide a scientifically rigorous definition of a strategy, researchers would have to provide a coherent neurological and biological account of learner behaviors, something they appear to consider impossible.

In his most recent writing on the topic, Dörnyei (2005) in fact asks whether LLS actually exist as a psychological construct given their persistent ambiguity. For Dörnyei, the most fundamental problem is the literature's inability to explain the difference between 'engaging in an ordinary learning activity and a strategic learning activity' (2005: 164). He concludes on this point that it is this lack of watertight definition which has led a number of scholars to leave the field and switch to the broader and more versatile notion of 'self-regulation'. The second most important problem for Dörnyei is the search for taxonomies of LLS. His fundamental criticism here is that the best known of these (O'Malley and Chamot 1990; Oxford 1990a) include categories in which individual items clearly overlap—for example cognitive strategies and memory strategies. In other words, classification continues to be miscellaneous and *ad hoc*.

Dörnyei's third criticism, and one clearly related to the first two, is that the most used strategy inventory (the SILL, Oxford 1990a) is seriously flawed in its design. The design problems include the adoption of frequency-of-use scales with highly specific items of a different nature. These items, rather than tapping into a general trend, attempt to reveal actual specific behaviors whereby a linear relationship between item scores and total scale scores becomes invalid. In other words, the scales in the SILL are not cumulative and computing mean scores 'is psychometrically not justifiable' (Dörnyei 2005: 182). Surprisingly, Dörnyei brushes all these doubts aside when it comes to the issue of strategy instruction. Whilst having a highly sceptical attitude to the value of LLS research, he roundly supports continuing with teaching about strategies in the classroom, thus marginalizing the whole field to an area of acceptable but unproven pedagogical activity—a sort of 'it can't do any harm' approach.

The above critiques by Dörnyei are certainly pertinent to the ongoing debate about whether or not strategy research is a worthwhile enterprise. Whilst acknowledging their significance for future strategy research, it is clearly not within the scope of this chapter to refute them—even were that possible. However, our own conviction is that Dörnyei may be setting up a straw man in order to knock him down. For example, while recognizing the development over the years (as this chapter has done) from quantity of strategy use to quality and combination of strategy use, Dörnyei attributes to the whole field the claims of individual authors past and present. An obvious example is the case of the SILL which, at the time of writing, is more than sixteen years old. Yet one gets the impression from Dörnyei that everyone is using this inventory, which later chapters will show is not the case. Another example is his unattributed use of phrases such as 'it does go against the standard view in the field' (Dörnyei 2005: 166) when, as has been shown in this chapter and will be taken up again in the next, there are relatively few standard views in the field. Similarly, he claims that 'learning strategies are related to the broad process of learning' (and does not provide a reference) whereas in fact a number of researchers in the field (for example, Hsiao and Oxford 2002; Macaro 2001) have called for a much more fine-grained association between strategy use and specific tasks. In other words, whilst on the one hand pointing to the contradictions, lack of consensus, and ambiguities in the field he, on the other, lumps together all the research endeavour of the last 30 years and presents it as if it were the work of a single research team. The editors of this volume return to this tension within the 'community of practice' in their concluding chapter.

Conclusions

In this chapter we have attempted to provide an historical account of the claims made by authors working in the field of language learner strategies, by tracing the development of these claims from the early works by Rubin and by Naiman and his associates, through a number of well known books of the early 1990s, through to the present day. In so doing we have situated LLS research in an overall historical perspective of language teaching and learning which shifted from an interest in the mechanisms of language to an interest in the mechanisms of the language learner. It is within the latter theoretical framework that the claims of LLS research should be considered. It is what the learner *does* rather than what the language *is* which has remained central to the investigative efforts of LLS researchers.

LLS research began with the basic assumption that an L2 learner, unlike his/her first language counterpart, would find the endeavour problematic. However, since some learners found the endeavour less problematic than others, it was worth finding out what they did. This remains to the present day the fundamental mission of LLS research. The original mission has diversified, however, and gone on to explore a range of logical extensions to the early lists of strategies: the range and extent of strategy use; individual differences; their link with autonomy and competence; task specificity; relationships with achievement over time and with proficiency at specific points in time.

The broad claims made by authors in the field can be summarized as follows:

1 The strategies that learners use are accessible and can be documented.
2 A strategy is a construct that can be defined, and what it is and what it does can be described in practical terms.
3 Strategies are important because they are associated with successful learning.
4 Some learner types are more likely to use strategies or use them more successfully than other learner types.
5 Strategies can be taught and learners, as a result, can develop more effective strategic behavior.

We have also examined the literature for critiques of learner strategies research and found these to be centered around issues of construct validity, the lack of consensus as to the unit of analysis, and whether strategies are extra things that learners do, in addition to the learning process, or part of the learning process itself. The issue, therefore, for us as authors in concluding this chapter, is whether LLS research has developed over the past 30 years, in part but not exclusively, in order to address some of the critiques and problems it has encountered and to propose how it might continue to address these issues in the future.

Continuing the development of LLS research

The first major development in LLS research has been in the perspective adopted to discover what more successful learners do. In the 1980s and early 1990s the perspective swung between two ends of a continuum. At one end, researchers were describing general patterns of desirable behavior with, possibly, high levels of within-subject variation. At the other end, researchers were eliciting specific examples of behavior, with little or no scope for within-subject variation, *but* still related to no specific task. More recent work has focused on specific examples of strategic behavior but *in the context of* specific tasks and skills. We believe that future research will need to build on this development in a methodical way and begin the slow process of mapping scientifically specific strategies to specific tasks, carefully investigating the cognitive response of learners to task demands.

In order for the mapping to become scientific, researchers will need to operate with a much more coherent research agenda and greater consensus as to the location, size, and effects of a strategy. LLS research has often proceeded in an *ad hoc* style with researchers providing their own particular definitions. We have highlighted the objections that strategies cannot be cognitive, behavioral, and emotional. In one sense, of course, they can, as long as they simply remain aids to pedagogy. LLS research, however, claims to be underpinned by a credible learning theory and ambiguities will need to be resolved.

The second major development has been in the shift from the notion of quantity to that of quality. Whereas earlier work suggested that the successful language learner had a vast repertoire of strategic behaviors, more recent work has attempted to identify localized sophisticated strategic behavior. There is still, however, considerable uncertainty as to the nature of sophisticated strategic behavior. There is a growing consensus that it is in the combination or strategies selected for a task and their orchestration through metacognition that sophistication lies. Future research will need to map these combinations but, more importantly, will need to begin to ask the question 'why?' Why is it that certain learners are able to combine strategies more effectively than others?

The third development can be detected in a recognition, if not a solution, of the problem of linking strategy use with achievement. Whilst early theorizing made a fairly unproblematic causal relationship between strategic behavior and success, more recent theorizing has led to a realization that independent variables of stage of learning, time of beginning learning, rate of progress, achievement level relative to peers, and absolute proficiency levels all have to be carefully disentangled in order to see their associations and effects on the dependent variable of strategy deployment. This third development presents a major challenge for LLS researchers.

It may seem surprising that, after 30 years, we (as authors of this chapter) should conclude that LLS research is still quite an immature field. Perhaps this is to do with the huge scope of its undertakings: on the one hand to identify how learners learn; on the other to throw a spotlight on the interrelationship between teaching and learning. Both of these undertakings present researchers with an enormous challenge and, with this background of aspiration, it is understandable if the field is still working to define its parameters. Yet it is because of the importance of our aspiration that it feels to us almost a duty to continue to rise to the challenge.

Acknowledgements

We would like to thank the two anonymous reviewers of this chapter together with the anonymous reviewers of this volume as a whole for their helpful reactions, insights, and suggestions.

2

Coming to terms with language learner strategies: surveying the experts

ANDREW D. COHEN

Introduction

Chapter 1 dealt briefly with the issues of strategy terminology, the linking of specific strategies to specific tasks, individual differences in strategy use, and strategy instruction, and reviewed some of the critiques of language learner strategy (LLS) approaches. The current chapter takes up the issues of definition and rubric, and explores the construct 'language learner strategies' by reporting on the results of a survey questionnaire administered to an international group of strategy experts to find out how they conceptualize and use the terminology in language learner strategy research and practice. This is one of the first surveys of its kind in the SLA field.

This chapter will first briefly describe how the survey questionnaire was constructed and administered, and how the data were analyzed. Then key findings from the survey will be presented in the following order: emergent themes in strategy description, views concerning purposes for LLS, and treatment of constructs regarding learners' use of strategies, including both areas of consensus and where it is lacking.

The construction of a language learner strategy survey

As a co-organizer of the Oxford University meetings[1] described in the Introduction to this volume, I designed a questionnaire to collect views of respected strategy experts about terms and issues in the LLS field. I identified key terms and issues in position papers, PowerPoint presentations, discussions, and other products posted on the closed University of Oxford website for our International Project on Language Learner Strategies (IPOLLS). I subsequently prepared in draft form a questionnaire covering these key issues, plus others that were not in those papers but worthy of consideration. Next, this draft questionnaire was circulated to IPOLLS participants for feedback. Then the questionnaire was revised and posted on the IPOLLS website. It had

11 sections. (See Appendix 2.1 on the website www.oup.com/elt/teacher/lls for a copy of the instrument.)

Data collection and data analysis procedures

In September of 2004, the 23 colleagues who had attended the University of Oxford meeting the previous July were asked to respond to the IPOLLS survey questionnaire. Altogether, 18 of those who were at the meeting as well as one who was unable to attend, responded to the questionnaire.[2] Given the questionnaire's length and the difficulty of the issues addressed, it took six months to obtain the complete set of 19 responses.

In the first stage of analysis the questionnaire responses were entered into a data base of 60 pages of text. In the second stage, these responses were read carefully and those which seemed to best represent one or another position were grouped under the respective question. In addition, if the question called for a yes/no or agree/disagree response, then a numerical tabulation was also made as to how many respondents used the terms or concepts relating to strategies in a given way, or agreed or disagreed with a given statement. In the third stage of the analysis, an effort was made to summarize key statements in order to arrive at the findings presented below. Rather than giving a long string of quotes, an effort was made to paraphrase the respondents' comments accurately and succinctly. In the fourth stage, key findings from the survey were identified and integrated into this chapter, while the complete survey was posted on the IPOLLS website as 'Coming to Terms with LLS' on May 5, 2005 (https://www.weblearn.ox.ac.uk/site/socsci/edstud/langforum1/).

Results from this survey underscore the paradox of LLS research. On the one hand, the field fascinates researchers and teachers alike, perhaps because there is a sense that the answer to language learning is bound up in the successful use of strategies. On the other hand, the field is still lacking consensus on a unified theory, with agreement by learner strategy experts on some concepts and definitions and not on others. The goal of the chapter is to demonstrate how this kind of survey can help identify the points of agreement and disagreement, which can serve to move the action along, and ideally bring about greater consensus among international experts as well. The key findings from the questionnaire will now be presented, except for responses to items dealing with research methodology and with strategy instruction, which are covered by Chapters 5 and 7 respectively.

Results

Before getting into the specific findings, it is important to note that the experts reported consulting a wide range of fields when making a case for the theoretical underpinnings of the LLS work (Question 3). The most cited fields were educational psychology, cognitive psychology, and cross-cultural psychology. In addition, information-processing theory, sociocultural theory, and social constructivist theory were mentioned. The field of neurolinguistics (for example, neural functioning, associative memory, and brain chemistry studies) was mentioned not so much as a field of current study, but rather one that strategy experts would probably want to consult. Respondents also made more general reference to the fields of applied linguistics and its sub-branches. So there was a fair degree of consensus here, with psycholinguistics serving as the 'base' discipline that most respondents seemed to turn to, applying it to divergent areas of interest. That experts consult different research literature helps explain why at times they espouse differing terminologies in their LLS work.

The exercise of having the experts react to the same description of LLS provided an opportunity to see the level of consensus regarding the features of these strategies. The questionnaire offered the following definition (Question 4):

> Strategies can be classified as conscious mental activity. They must contain not only an action but a goal (or an intention) and a learning situation. Whereas a mental action might be subconscious, an action with a goal/intention and related to a learning situation can only be conscious.

The responses to this item illustrate why there is no popularly-accepted definition. While three respondents accepted the definition fully, one agreed but felt more was needed. Others were not in agreement with most parts of it. With regard to strategies being 'conscious', one view was that strategies have developed into routines at high levels of competence and are no longer conscious. Another view was that consciousness is not just one thing but actually involves intentionality, attention, awareness, and control (after Schmidt 1994a), and so the level of strategic involvement would vary.

With regard to 'mental activity', some asserted that strategies are not always mental, but rather may be manifested in a physically observable form (for example, 'eating a rich dessert as a reward for studying hard for a language test'). Also, some argued that not all strategies must contain an action, but could just be mental (for example, thinking about doing something but not actually doing it). In addition, a few did not feel that all strategies had to have a goal.

The next section will look in turn at survey results for the seven major themes associated with efforts to define LLS: level of consciousness, degree of mental activity, extent of describable actions, degree of goal orientation, strategy size, amount of strategy clustering, potential for leading to learning.

Major themes in the description of strategies

1 Level of consciousness

The majority of respondents agreed that any given strategy has to have a metacognitive component whereby the learner consciously and intentionally attends selectively to a learning task, analyzes the situation and task, plans for a course of action, monitors the execution of the plan, and evaluates the effectiveness of the whole process (Question 5.4). The strong view was that overall metacognitive control must be present for a mental action to be 'strategic' and that metacognitive strategies are the overarching strategies determining the cognitive strategies the learner will deploy. Nonetheless, there was a rather robust group of undecided and dissenting respondents as well. One of the undecided respondents noted that ideally every strategy should have a metacognitive component, but that in actuality this is not necessarily the case as less effective language learners use strategies repetitively, inflexibly, and inappropriately.

One of the dissenting respondents suggested there may be metacognitive moments, however fleeting. Thus, if learners did metacognitive stocktaking, they might be unable to reconstruct a description of their attention level, the nature of the analysis, the exact plan intended, or the nature of the monitoring and evaluation. Another suggested that highly intuitive students may not need to go through a highly analytic sequence, but could consider the task (not analytically), instantly select the necessary strategy, and sense its effectiveness.

Whereas four respondents categorically accepted that strategies could be situated along a continuum regarding the necessary degree of *planning* involved in their use, others felt that there were invariably a number of unplanned strategies (Question 7.1). While these respondents would consider a degree-of-planning continuum as irrelevant to the description of the strategy, it could be argued that being 'unplanned' is a useful descriptor for a strategy. The view was expressed that some intuitive learners instantly know the strategies to use with the given task.

While there was relative consensus that the metacognitive function of *monitoring* is a prototypical feature of a strategy, the extent of monitoring likely to be found in actual strategic behavior was questioned (Question 7.1). While one view was that monitoring is a necessary dimension for a strategy, another was that its extent would depend on the activity and for some tasks, it might not take place at all (for example, when engaging in monitoring on that particular task would detract from task performance, such as in certain speaking tasks). Another view was that the extent of monitoring depended on the learner's style preference. The respondent felt that since monitoring implied learners were conducting an analysis of the effectiveness of a strategy while using it, this might apply more to concrete-sequential learners than to intuitive learners, who might simply sense whether the strategy was working.

While some respondents recognized the metacognitive function of *evaluation* as a necessary dimension for a strategy, they felt that in reality learners do not often reflect on the effectiveness of a strategy (Question 7.1). Turning to the style preference literature, one respondent noted some students perform end-of-task evaluation, while others rely on an ongoing, intuitive sense of strategy effectiveness.

Two-thirds of the respondents indicated making a distinction between *strategic knowledge* and *strategic action* (Question 1.9). Several of the experts pointed out that metacognition was comprised of two components: *declarative knowledge* and *procedural knowledge*. Another respondent added that procedural knowledge drew from four general sources: knowledge about the tasks (their purpose, their type, the demand), oneself (learning styles, multiple intelligences, and motivation), background knowledge (about the domain, the culture, the language, the context, the given language text, and the world), and beliefs (about learning and about language learning). (See Rubin 2005.) Several other respondents pointed out that having strategic knowledge does not guarantee that the learner can mobilize those strategies, especially if they are not part of their own 'culture of learning'.

Finally, there was some disagreement regarding the level of consciousness necessary for a process to be considered as strategy. Some felt strongly that once a process is automatic, it can no longer be a strategy since in this context 'automatic' means habitual and unconscious (Question 6.5). Others felt that various phases of strategy deployment could be at differing levels of consciousness. Taking this view, then, the execution phase of a strategy could, for example, be less conscious and more automatic.

2 Extent of attention

The questionnaire also focused separately on that part of consciousness represented by *attention* (Question 7.1). There was relative consensus that attention can be viewed on a continuum from full focus on the strategy at one end to only minimal attention at the other. In contemplating this continuum, one respondent pondered the issue of just how much attention was necessary for a process to make it strategic. In the view of another respondent, we need to allow for the level of attention to shift during the strategic process. In other words, at the beginning of the process, the strategy might be at the center of attention, but as the plan is carried out, the strategy is reduced to peripheral attention, then to a standby mode, and perhaps ultimately to a 'no attention' mode. So that would give this feature a potentially fluctuating nature, depending on the strategy being used by a given learner.

3 Explicitness regarding 'action'

There was a range of reactions to the statement that the action component in a given learning situation needs to be explicit (for example, what is meant by 'rereading a text' or 'rehearsing and memorizing' a dialog) (Question 5.2). Some felt that since strategies are conscious, the learners should be able to state explicitly what a strategy such as 'rereading a text' actually entailed. Then there were those who, while being in agreement with the intent of the statement, felt it was the job of the researcher eliciting strategy data to find out what 're-reading a text' actually means since the action could have various possible goals. One respondent noted that while he had not in the past taken this kind of fine-tuned tack in his own investigations, the result had been the collection of fuzzy data where it was not exactly clear what the learner had actually done or why.

Among the undecided regarding 'action', the opinion was voiced that whereas it is better if learners can articulate their strategic action since it enhances their awareness and consciousness, this may require strategy instruction and then practice. One of these respondents questioned what was meant by 'explicit'. She felt that while learners need to know what they are doing, the degree of explicitness required depends on the learner. For instance, if the strategy is, 'I will ask myself questions while reading to improve my comprehension', numerous students could leave it at that, others who are more detail-oriented or who need more structure, might take the strategy to the level of specifying that they will ask themselves at least three factual questions per page and will look in the text for answers to them, while yet other students might break it down at a one-step-at-a-time level (processing the text on a paragraph-by-paragraph basis). Those disagreeing with the statement felt that learners are unlikely to make explicit statements to themselves about the strategies that they use, partly because they lack the metalanguage to do so.

So what emerges from the survey relating to the explicitness of the action is the conceptualization of a 'strategy' as being a behavior which may change according to the given learner. Whereas some respondents seemed happier with 'fixed concepts', others were happier with more fluid concepts.

4 Degree of goal orientation

Most respondents agreed that strategies have a goal (Question 5.1). Whereas a teacher or a researcher may be able to identify this goal, various respondents were not sure whether learners would be able to articulate the goal, either because they may never have been conscious of their strategy use at that level of specificity or because they were no longer conscious of it. Those who disagreed with the statement did not interpret this feature as allowing for the teacher or researcher to be the one identifying the goal, and that despite the learners' lack of awareness of goals, they would often use strategies none the less. It was felt that especially the less successful learners may not have a clear goal for specific tasks or have very general goals (for example, 'to finish the book by English class').

Most of those responding supported the notion that any given strategy can be situated on a continuum from more to less goal-oriented (Question 7.1). They felt they could make this distinction because it was easy to decide if a process was motivated by a purpose. Purposefulness was viewed as the intentionality aspect of consciousness. All the same, several were in doubt, such as one who said he could envision strategies where the learner could not articulate a clear goal for using them.

5 Strategy size

While the majority of the respondents tended not to make the distinction between macro- and micro-strategies, even some of those not making the distinction could see the advantages of doing so (Question 1.2). One said that she could see some strategies as 'umbrella' strategies that incorporate smaller ones. Another felt that person-related strategies tended to be more macro than task-related strategies, and that within task-related strategies, some tasks were more macro than other tasks. Still another respondent felt that the macro-micro strategy distinction could be related to the distinction that was once made between 'strategies' and 'tactics'. So whereas note-taking could be viewed as a macro-strategy, using outline form to take notes could be seen as a micro-strategy.

6 Amount of strategy clustering

There was general consensus among respondents that strategic behavior could fall along a continuum from a single action to a sequence of actions (Question 7.1), with only one or two dissenting voices. Respondents generally felt that depending on the task at hand, sometimes one strategic action (for example, 'selecting a keyword mnemonic to remember a difficult vocabulary word') would be enough to handle the task, but for more complex tasks (for example, 'looking up a new word in a dictionary') a cluster of strategies would be needed.

Taking this strategy clustering notion further, there was relatively strong agreement with the statement that for a strategy to be *effective* in promoting learning or improved performance, it must be combined with other strategies either simultaneously in *strategy clusters* or in sequence, in *strategy chains* (Question 5.5). The experts generally felt that no single strategy can function well in isolation. One respondent felt that while the notion of strategy combinations sounded sensible, the field had tended to describe strategies as isolated phenomena rather than as existing in clusters. Several of the respondents were quick to point out that the use of strategy clusters would depend on the nature of the task. One of these respondents contrasted a complex reading comprehension task, where a series of strategies would be needed to interact successfully with the text, with a less complex decoding task, which could conceivably be completed with the strategy of 'finding/ applying patterns'. But that respondent was quick to note that a strategy such as 'using prior knowledge' would most likely be needed for virtually any learning task. Another respondent considered this clustering of strategies to be an irrefutable reality if we take a close look at the task-specific or situation-specific research. She drew upon her recent research with beginning French students in suggesting that strategies do not simply increase as a result of instruction, but rather that clusters of them change over time.

Among the undecided, one respondent did not feel that strategy clusters were always essential. Another felt that although strategy combinations are often used for even the simplest of tasks, the use of strategies in combination is not a necessary precursor to success. Finally, a dissenter insisted that learning is neither black nor white, and that some strategies work more effectively when combined with others into strategy clusters or chains, but that other strategies can work well without clustering.

There was also relatively strong agreement with the statement that strategy clusters include and are evaluated via a metacognitive strategy or series of metacognitive strategies (which monitor and evaluate them) (Question 5.6). One respondent commented in agreement that strategy clusters are complex and involve adding and shedding strategies often from moment to moment, in line with ongoing monitoring and evaluation. In her view, the bringing together of strategy clusters involves a high level of planning and orchestration which is the result of metacognitive strategies. Another respondent said that such strategy orchestration is what enables learners to distinguish the best strategies from the rest. Others were keen to point out that while metacognition may play a beneficial role, only some of the strategies in sequences or clusters receive metacognitive scrutiny and that not all learners monitor or evaluate their use of strategies, whether singly or in clusters.

7 Potential for leading to learning

The majority agreed that included in a description of a strategy would be its potential for leading to learning, even if only expressed at the level of an hypothesis (Question 5.3). So, if 'putting a word into a sentence so as to remember it' is to be considered a strategy, then it must be made clear how doing this action would lead to learning. Several even felt that it was 'vital' to specify the relations between a certain strategy and its consequences in learning. One respondent noted that while we can only propose that the use of a given strategy will lead to learning in combination with other strategies, a hypothesis needs to be provided regarding how a given cognitive action in combination with others in working memory can lead to (a) long-term memory development and (b) the development of a skill in the long term. He offered 'advance organizers in French L2 listening' as an example of the development of a skill over time. He noted that these advance organizers constitute a strategy cluster (for example 'predict content', 'identify possible French words that might come up', 'beware of any *liaisons* which might derail you', 'prepare to visualize certain parsed bits of language') + metacognition ('stay calm', 'think about how you coped last time'). He stated that eventually this cluster would become relatively automatic and if the hypothesis were correct, should lead to improved listening.

One undecided respondent felt that including 'potential for learning' as a feature would eliminate numerous behaviors which traditionally have been considered strategic but which do not involve making an effort to learn anything (for example, using the cover strategy of 'laughing at a joke that was not understood'). Another respondent interpreted this feature as referring more to how a *teacher* rather than a learner might view a strategy, yet she agreed that at some level it could be beneficial for learners to consider the appropriateness of a strategy for a given task, goal, and purpose.

Among those who disagreed with the statement, one respondent noted that especially less successful learners might choose a strategy for the sake of comfort rather than because of its effectiveness in learning—for example, purposely committing only enough effort to language learning so as to get just a passing grade. Another felt that instead of loading a strategy description with details such as how a strategic action might work cognitively, we need to go for simplicity and clarity. In addition, she felt that a strategic action might lead to learning in different ways for different learners.

Strategy selection and effectiveness

The survey also included items dealing with the source for language learner strategies, the learner's choice of strategies, and the effectiveness of strategy deployment for the given learner. With regard to the source for strategies, respondents saw this feature as being in flux, with the source sometimes being the teacher, sometimes a peer, and sometimes themselves (Question 7.1). Several respondents posited that there was likely to be a gradual movement from initially looking elsewhere for strategies to use and then eventually generating their own strategies. While respondents saw as potentially difficult identifying the actual strategy source, tracking the types of strategies learners used and their source might none the less provide useful insights about the value of strategy instruction.

With regard to the effectiveness of the strategies deployed (Question 6.6), respondents were asked to react to the following statement:

> The strategies a learner uses and the effectiveness of these strategies very much depend on the learner him/herself (for example, age, gender, language aptitude, intelligence, cognitive and learning style preferences, self-concept/image, personality, attitudes, motivation, prior knowledge), the learning task at hand (for example, type, complexity, difficulty, and generality), and the learning environment (for example, the learning culture, the richness of input and output opportunities). We must view strategies within this larger framework to properly interpret their role in the language learning process.

Perhaps not so surprisingly, this statement received almost uniform support. Those who have worked in the language learner strategy field as long as many of these experts have seen firsthand the impact of learners' background, task, and context on strategy use and effectiveness. None the less, one respondent, speaking for himself but probably on behalf of others as well, admitted that he rarely considered all these factors while conducting a given study or while engaged in strategy instruction since it would be 'mind-boggling'. Another stressed that we need more research into the learners' own prior knowledge base in order to understand the extent to which their strategy use reflects group behavior or individual patterns.

Now that we have looked at results on views about language learner strategies and how they function, let us consider what the experts considered their purpose to be.

The purpose of language learner strategies

1   To enhance learning

There was general agreement that learner strategies have as a purpose the enhancement of learning (Question 8.1). In addition, one respondent stated that without strategies, conscious learning cannot take place. Another respondent commented that if we accept the distinction between language learning and language use strategies (Cohen 1998), then learner strategies should be aimed at enhancing both the learning and the use of an L2.

2   To perform specified tasks

Most respondents were in agreement with the statement that learner strategies have as their purpose to perform specified tasks (Question 8.2), even though until now numerous strategies have been stated in broad, general, and even fuzzy terms. Several respondents noted that the selection of strategies depends upon the task, with some strategies being appropriate for more than one task. Finally, one respondent felt that it was inappropriate to assume that learner strategies had as their predetermined purpose the performance of specific tasks, but rather the individual learner had to make that determination.

3   To solve specific problems

Most respondents agreed that a purpose for strategies is to solve specific problems (Question 8.3). One respondent gave the example of how a series of listening strategies might be used when a learner is having difficulty perceiving and correctly parsing an L2 phrase. In this case, he felt it would take other strategies to show that this first strategy was not useful in making sense out of the utterance. A dissenting voice commented that strategies are not necessarily aimed at solving problems and gave as an example the strategies for using filled pauses which, in his view, may not be intended to solve a problem at all.

4 To make learning easier, faster, and more enjoyable

While most respondents agreed with the notion that strategies serve to make learning easier, faster, and more enjoyable (Question 8.5), they sometimes did so with reservations. On the positive side, strategies were seen to allow learners to develop more knowledge of themselves and of language learning. This self-awareness aspect was what made learning for them more satisfying and enriching. Another respondent pointed out that at the beginning stages of strategy instruction students may (and usually do) perceive that incorporating new learning strategies into task completion takes more time and effort than just working on a task in their accustomed way. But then when the learning strategy pays off in greater success on the task, the students begin to find that use of this strategy with the given task makes for truly easier, faster, and more enjoyable learning. On the more negative side, it was felt that overusing strategies or using them too much in isolation rather than in meaningful combinations could prove unhelpful and might lead to slowing down the learning process. It was also pointed out that there are strategies used in self-defense, which do not make learning easier, faster, or more enjoyable. It was felt, in fact, that some strategies end up making learning more tedious, more complex, and slower (for example, 'finding L1 equivalents for all unknown words in a text before answering the reading comprehension questions').

5 To compensate for a deficit in learning

The notion of 'compensating for a deficit' (Question 8.4) drew a range of responses with half disagreeing, some of them strongly. As one respondent put it, it depends on what we mean by 'deficit'. He noted that if someone were to give him an advanced text in Spanish to read (and he had only received a few hours of Spanish instruction), then he would compensate for his extreme language deficit by using everything at his disposal such as other Romance languages, common sense, and any prior topic knowledge. However, if he encountered phonological problems while attempting to understand spoken Spanish after only minimal instruction in the language, the use of compensatory strategies might not help him identify and distinguish the Spanish sounds.

Among the numerous dissenters, one commented that given the way she interpreted the notions of 'compensate' and 'deficit', the terms were a bit loaded for her, and did not capture the extent to which strategies can facilitate future learning. She did not view the use of strategies as a stopgap measure, especially since she viewed learners as continuing to develop and refine their strategy use throughout their language learning experience, an aspect which the statement did not reflect. Another respondent felt that for years we have been trying to avoid operating from a deficit mentality or a medical model (i.e. to cure the sickness of ignorance). Finally, a respondent speculated that whereas many people would probably relate to strategy use in terms of deficit (for example, ESL students need strategies to help with their 'problems' in learning to speak, write, etc.), learners can be highly strategic in an area where they do not have a deficit or problem.

Finally, let us take a look at survey results dealing with the opinions of the experts regarding areas related to language learner strategy use.

Concepts related to learners' use of strategies

1 Autonomous language learning

While the clear majority used the concept of 'autonomous language learning' (Question 2,3), there was some diversity in terms of how the concept was applied. Generally, respondents reported using it to refer to learning which has as its ultimate goal to produce self-motivated students who take control of the 'what, when, and how' of language learning and learn successfully, independently of a teacher, and possibly outside of the classroom without any external influence.

One respondent saw the value of defining 'autonomy' at three different levels—(1) 'autonomy of language competence': the threshold level at which learners can say or write what they want to say or write, (2) 'autonomy of language learning competence': the level at which learners can deploy cognitive and metacognitive strategies consistent with or in place of the teacher's teaching approaches, and also without the immediate presence of a teacher, and (3) 'autonomy of choice': the learners' role in determining personal language goals, the designated purposes for learning the language and proficiency goals, and the extent to which the learner has input into the content and modality of the language curriculum.

With regard to problems encountered in using the term, a respondent noted that while 'autonomy' (from the ancient Greek) literally means 'self-regulation', the phrase 'autonomous language learning' has over time gathered many new accretions of meaning, some of which are mutually exclusive (for example, autonomy from a technical, psychological, socio-cultural, or political-critical perspective—Oxford 2003). In addition, 'autonomous language learning' was sometimes understood (or maybe misunderstood) to be counter to the values of certain cultures. As a case in point, another respondent indicated that the term 'autonomous' was not amenable to the EFL context in Japan in that teachers regarded it as an excuse for abandoning teaching. A third respondent noted that while the field of language autonomy had turned to learners' narratives as a source of insights, she was not sure how having learners go through the process of telling their stories about language learning actually improves the product, namely, their language proficiency. Finally, a fourth respondent pointed out that 'autonomous learning' is not the same as 'strategic learning' in that a learner can work independently in a rote, non-strategic manner. She also noted that learners who are not effective autonomous learners may be very effective (and strategic) learners in a supportive group setting. (See Chapter 4 for more on this issue.)

2 Self-regulation

The majority of respondents reported using the term 'self-regulation' (Question 2.2). One identified the term as that used in the educational psychology literature and as synonymous with 'self-management'—see below. Another said if she used it, it was referring to Vygotsky's concept of self-regulation, with his theoretical and practical focus on specific sets of learning behaviors that would be recognized today as cognitive, metacognitive, and social strategies. She added that various experts see general learning strategies as what students use to become more self-regulated in their learning. A third respondent indicated that grounding learner strategies in cognitive psychology does not allow for the recognition of the affective side of learning. He views 'self-regulation' as a broader term that allows for both the cognitive and the affective side of strategic learning.

Various respondents alluded to a major difficulty in using this term, namely, that it is difficult to distinguish 'self-regulation' from 'autonomy'. In fact, two respondents indicated that they used 'self-regulation' synonymously with 'autonomy', with 'autonomous' being used as an adjective to describe the self-regulating person or group. One respondent pointed out that for some scholars, 'self-regulation' is now being used to more or less replace 'strategy' as a term, but that doing so leaves unanswered the obvious next question, 'What do learners *do* to self-regulate? (which is to use strategies)'. Another respondent picked up on this same use (or misuse) of the term and viewed this use of self-regulation as being in conflict with the research and theory on learner strategies from cognitive and educational psychology.

3 Self-management

As with self-regulation, the majority of respondents indicated that they used the term 'self-management' (Question 2.1). For one respondent, learner self-management was the combination of procedures and knowledge. Another reported using the term to refer to learners who (a) use metacognitive strategies extensively to monitor, plan, and evaluate their strategy use, and (b) are able to control their own learning and seek/find solutions to problems in their learning. A third respondent similarly reported using self-management as a metacognitive strategy which can be applied to any learning task. She saw four components to the concept of self-management which included having learners (1) determine how they learn best, (2) arrange conditions that help them learn, (3) seek opportunities for practice, and (4) focus attention on the task.

Various problems were raised with regard to the use of the term. One respondent felt that while in her view all strategies reflect a form of learner self-management, some researchers in the field have used the term 'self-management' to refer only to metacognitive strategies (as noted in the previous paragraph). In the strategy instruction sessions that she has led, this usage (limiting 'self-management' to metacognitive strategies) has been confusing to the participants, especially to those teachers among them who were using the term more broadly. Another respondent saw self-management as a necessary but not sufficient prerequisite to strategic behavior. She viewed the concept as having some overlap with self-regulation, but she thought that the self-regulation was more inclusive of the range of strategic behavior—including both the *will* (i.e. the motivation to use self-management) and the *skill* (i.e. the ability to deploy both metacognitive and task-specific learning strategies).

4 Independent language learning

The term 'independent language learning' (Question 2.4) drew a mixed response. Half of the respondents reported that they used it and half not. Six of those indicating that they used it tended to use it as a synonym for 'autonomous language learning', which also says something about how they relate to the term 'autonomous'. Another respondent said that she uses this term when she wants to focus on learners who are taking responsibility for their learning through independent study (for example, in self-access centers).

As to problems with the term, one respondent felt that the term interfaced with autonomous language learning in sometimes ambiguous ways. Another respondent indicated that it was a problematic term in distance education because it was associated with a perception that learners can and should be independent, without sufficient attention being paid to issues of learner proficiency or support. In her view, independence needs to be balanced with an awareness of the abilities and competencies of the learner and with concern for the support available to learners to ensure successful learning experiences. A third respondent commented that while for some learners there is language material which is best learnt independently, there is also material which certain learners best learn in an interactive social context.

5 Individual language learning

Most of the respondents reported not using the term 'individual language learning' (Question 2.5). Two of those who reported using it, indicated that it serves for them as synonymous for 'independent language learning'. According to one respondent, what makes the term problematic is the lack of clarity in comparing it to 'independent' and 'autonomous' language learning. Another respondent gave an interesting spin to the notion of 'individual' language learning, suggesting that it could refer to personal or even quirky approaches to language learning. She was thinking of how some good language learners she has encountered are reluctant to share their strategies with others out of a belief that their strategies are not good for anyone else because they are highly personalized.

Discussion

This survey is perhaps the first of its kind in the area of language learner strategies, so for that reason alone, it constitutes a valuable undertaking. By probing the strategy construct among learner strategy researchers engaged both in theory building and in the practice of strategy instruction, it is possible to determine just how much consensus exists. It is of course natural to find disagreement in any academic field. In fact, disagreement in academia is perhaps more of an indication of vitality than is seemingly uniform conformity. In any event, it would appear overall that the areas of consensus outweighed those of disagreement.

This rather unusual survey questionnaire produced a number of insights. The first was that strategy experts are generally accessing psycholinguistics as the 'base' discipline, but then they apply that discipline to a number of divergent areas of interest which are reflected in the professional literature from different fields. Accessing divergent research literature can help to explain some differences in approaches and perspectives.

Secondly, it is still a matter of debate as to how conscious of and attentive to their language behaviors learners need to be in order for those behaviors to be considered strategies. While there was consensus that learners deploy strategies in sequences or clusters, there was some disagreement as to the extent to which a behavior needs to have a mental component, a goal, an action, a metacognitive component (involving planning, monitoring, and evaluation of the strategy), and a potential that its use will lead to learning in order for it to be considered a strategy.

So, in essence, two contrasting views emerged, each with its own merits. On the one hand there is the view that strategies need to be specific, small, and most likely combined with other strategies for completing a given task; there is, on the other hand, the view that strategies need to be kept at a more global, flexible, and general level. What would lead an expert to favor one or the other of these conceptualizations would be a topic for future investigation. Notwithstanding these differing views, there was enthusiastic agreement for the view that strategy use and effectiveness will depend on the particular learners, the learning task, and the environment.

With regard to the purposes for language learner strategies, there was consensus that strategies enhance performance in language learning and use, both in general and in specific tasks. There was also consensus that strategies are used to help make language learning easier, faster, and more enjoyable. The experts were found to be less likely to see strategies as compensating for a deficit, so the deficit notion of language strategy use seems to have fallen a bit out of favor. This finding is paradoxical in that while experts may wish to play down the deficit compensatory model of strategies, this model still plays a significant role in many of the learner strategy studies described in Part Two of this volume.

Again on the side of consensus, there was general consensus that terms like autonomy, self-regulation, and self-management, independent and individual language learning related in systematic ways to a learner's use of strategies. For example, the respondents generally felt that whereas the use of learner strategies can lead to enhanced autonomy, being an autonomous learner does not necessarily imply that the learner is drawing selectively and effectively from a refined repertoire of strategies. There was, however, less consensus concerning the interrelationship of these concepts to one another. Autonomy and self-regulation were reportedly used either synonymously or in a similar fashion. Self-management appeared a useful term but overlapped with self-regulation. Independent language learning was used by some of the respondents but was also seen to overlap with autonomous language learning, and individual language learning was not reported to be used much by this group.

A few limitations of this study should be noted. One limitation was that given the nature of the survey instrument, this chapter reports on 'sub-beliefs' from given respondents on specific issues on the questionnaire, and thus does not reflect the whole picture of how these issues interrelate for those respondents. Another limitation is that it was not always perfectly clear whose perspective was being represented in the various questionnaire statements—whether it was that of the learner, of a teacher, of a teacher educator, or of a researcher. One such example was with item number 5.3, which dealt with hypothesizing about a strategy's potential for leading to learning. (See Appendix 2.1 on the book's website.) A third limitation was the challenge of using general education terminology (for example, terms like 'learning context' and 'task') across such a wide educational spectrum as that represented by the experts participating in this survey. An additional limitation was that since seven of the 19 respondents were non-native speakers of the language used for the questionnaire, this could have influenced respondents' reactions to the terminological issues. A native Chinese-speaking respondent, for example, commented that she did not find it easy to locate equivalent terms for 'tactic' and 'technique' in Chinese.

In conclusion, conducting this survey brought numerous issues to the attention of the expert respondents, and in the process of completing the questionnaire the respondents identified lines of investigation that would need to be pursued to gather the kinds of information that could help resolve some of the issues raised. In various instances, experts noted that they simply had not considered some of the issues raised. So, including them in the questionnaire served the important purpose of consciousness raising. The next step would be to investigate some of the debated strategy features to determine more rigorously the extent of their role in language learning.

Notes

1 Along with Ernesto Macaro, Anna Chamot, Cathy Keatley, Vee Harris, and Do Coyle.
2 The respondents included (in alphabetical order) Neil Anderson, Anna Chamot, Andrew Cohen, Do Coyle, Claudia Finkbeiner, Christine Goh, Suzanne Graham, Carol Griffiths, Peter Gu, Veronica Harris, Ernesto Macaro, Martha Nyikos, Rebecca Oxford, Joan Rubin, Osamu Takeuchi, Larry Vandergrift, Qiufang Wen, Cynthia White, Lawrence Zhang.

3

Bridging the gap between psychological and sociocultural perspectives on L2 learner strategies

REBECCA L. OXFORD and
KAREN SCHRAMM

... [T]he ontological conflict in SLA between cognitive and sociocultural orientations ... seems irreconcilable.
Canagarajah 2006: 28

... [U]se of multiple paradigms contributes to greater understanding of the phenomenon under study.
Teddlie and Tashakkori 2003: 22

Introduction

This chapter examines language learner strategies (LLS) from two perspectives: the psychological and the sociocultural. These perspectives have often conflicted with each other in the second language (L2) field. We respectfully attempt to break down boundaries by noting important theoretical contributions from each perspective and indicating how each perspective can learn from the other. Regarding LLS, we encourage greater, more positive interaction between different camps, a real dialogue (Bakhtin 1984: 293). The L2 field will understand strategies in more encompassing, more useful ways only when multiple viewpoints are honored, when theorists and researchers representing different perspectives communicate productively, and especially when they plan joint research studies.

The dual purpose of the current chapter then is to explore LLS deeply from two vantage points, which we call *psychological* and *sociocultural*, and to point out in detail what each perspective can contribute to the other. The difference in the perspectives lies in the focus, individual versus group. As we show in this chapter, it is not essential to consider only one of the two foci; both are valuable and, in fact, essential for a better understanding of how languages are learnt.

From the psychological perspective, we define an L2 learner strategy as being a specific plan, action, behavior, step, or technique that individual learners use, with some degree of consciousness, to improve their progress in developing skills in a second or foreign language. Such strategies can facilitate the internalization, storage, retrieval, or use of the new language and are tools for greater learner autonomy (adapted from Oxford 1999: 518). Internalization and storage relate directly to learning. Retrieval and use of the language indirectly foster further L2 learning, because learners can discern whether their L2 speech or writing is understandable to others and whether they need to improve it, and they can elicit input and negotiate meanings. A given strategy is useful only when the strategy addresses the L2 task at hand (that is, the relevance of a strategy depends on task demands) and when the learner employs the strategy effectively and links it to other relevant strategies.

The sociocultural perspective starts with society (its culture), not the individual, as the fundamental unit. This perspective explores material tools, such as hammers, and non-material tools, such as language, that are handed down from ancestors and that contain societal knowledge, from which individuals can learn. In fact, the underlying process in the sociocultural perspective is the ongoing mediation of the social to the individual. The sociocultural perspective contains several definitions of L2 learner strategy, the most general being a learner's socially mediated plan or action to meet a goal, which is related directly or indirectly to L2 learning. Vygotsky's (1978, 1979) dialogic model, explained later, suggests that an L2 learner strategy can be a higher order mental function, such as analysis, synthesis, planning, or evaluation, which the L2 learner develops with the help of a more capable person in a sociocultural context. Within sociocultural action theory, also detailed later, the definition of an L2 learner strategy is a socioculturally based action pattern that aims to reach an L2 learning goal. In the critical-sociocultural framework, issues of power, oppression, imperialism, and resistance are applied to the teaching and learning of L2 learner strategies, as indicated later in this chapter.

The organization of this chapter is as follows: in the first section we describe the two viewpoints and their historically contested relationship inside and outside the L2 field. In sections two to five we present LLS from the two perspectives in relation to the following themes: (a) self-regulation, (b) motivation and volition, (c) aptitude, and (d) aspects of 'activity' and 'action'. In the sixth section we conclude the chapter with reference to the need to increase positive dialogue between the two perspectives.

The two perspectives: irreconcilable or complementary?

The *psychological* perspective in the L2 field is sometimes called 'cognitive', 'mentalist', 'psycholinguistic', 'individual(ist)(ic)', or 'individual-difference'. We use the term 'psychological' because it is broader than 'cognitive', additionally includes metacognitive (regulation and control) and affective (emotion- and motivation-related) aspects, and is more descriptive than terms like 'individual-difference'. The psychological perspective is primarily associated with quantitative research. The ontological (reality-related) and epistemological (learning-related) roots are rationalist, that is, they are concerned with a quest for certainty through exacting, precise, rational, logical methodology based on objective observations of empirical data.

The *sociocultural* approach is linked with qualitative research. In this perspective, conceptions of reality and knowledge are relative to and constructed subjectively by those who hold them or interpret them, so this approach is sometimes called 'interpretivist', 'constructivist', or 'relativist'. The sociocultural approach involves 'thick description', i.e. detailed information gathered by participant observers in specific sociocultural settings. The sociocultural approach has a number of branching domains, such as dialogism, communities of practice, and critical theory.

In the L2 field, Zuengler and Miller (2006) have described the psychological and sociocultural perspectives as 'incommensurable' and 'parallel worlds' (pp. 35, 50), on the assumption that the ontological and epistemological underpinnings of the two are 'irreconcilable' (Canagarajah 2006: 28). This is the *incompatibility thesis*, which—in the L2 field—was at its most heated in the 1990s and is still accepted by some L2 theorists. However, we respectfully disagree with the incompatibility thesis and support the *compatibility thesis*, which has been widely supported outside the L2 field since the beginning of the 1990s (Creswell 1994, 2002; Guba and Lincoln 1994; Newman and Benz 1998; Tashakkori and Teddlie 1998, 2003; Lincoln and Guba 2000). Newman and Benz (1998) demonstrated that qualitative (often but not always sociocultural) and quantitative (often but not always rationalist) approaches are on a continuum and that the two ends of the continuum actually meet to create a complete research cycle. Brown (2004, 2005) underscored the usefulness of this continuum for L2 research. Larsen-Freeman (1997, 2000) proposed that psychological and social perspectives on second language acquisition could be linked in a single framework. Oxford and colleagues[1] used sociocultural and psychological approaches to investigate LLS and learning styles in many locations around the world.

In the L2 field, an ongoing psychological-versus-sociocultural paradigm war is unnecessary and could deny opportunities for synergy that might lead to more powerful and useful theory and research on learner strategies. We offer the current chapter as an example of the potential compatibility and complementarity of the two perspectives. We honor both approaches and attempt to show here how they can enrich and be enriched by the other. We begin by presenting themes of self-regulation and strategy instruction as viewed from the two perspectives.

Self-regulation from both perspectives

Both psychological and sociocultural perspectives have focused on self-regulation and its corollary, strategy instruction. However, the two perspectives' treatments of these themes are very distinct.

Psychological views of self-regulation

According to Zimmerman (2000; see also 2001), psychologically-based self-regulation models typically include (a) strategies, (b) a feedback loop by which learners consciously monitor the effectiveness of their strategies and make changes, (c) motivation for students to self-regulate (for example, achieving a goal or feeling good about themselves), and (d) deeper reasons why students might want to self-regulate (for example, attitudes, beliefs, and self-perceptions). Psychological self-regulation models (see Zimmerman, Bonner and Kovach 1996; Boekaerts, Pintrich and Zeidner 2000; Zimmerman and Schunk 2001) often include strategies for setting and adjusting goals, planning approaches to tasks, evaluating progress, assessing the utility of strategies, controlling the physical and social environment, using analysis and synthesis, applying inference, and dealing with motivation and emotion.[2]

Within the L2 field, a predominantly psychological approach to self-regulation is that of O'Malley and Chamot (1990). This model, which emphasizes cognitive information processing, includes three broad strategy categories: (a) cognitive strategies for controlling the processing of L2 information; (b) metacognitive strategies for managing the L2 learning process in general; and (c) socioaffective strategies for managing emotions and motivations and for learning with others. This last category acknowledges the role played by the individual as part of a collective but does not theorize it, as is the case with 'socioaffective strategies' or 'social strategies' in most LLS taxonomies. O'Malley and Chamot (1990) asserted that knowledge of strategies, like L2 knowledge itself, moves from declarative to procedural through practice by the learner. 'Declarative knowledge' is defined more fully as conscious, fact-oriented, effortful knowledge of static, discrete data points or facts, such as definitions of words, the conventions of punctuation, or grammar rules. 'Procedural knowledge', on the other hand, is knowledge that is unconscious, automatic, habitual, effortless, and implicit, for example, understanding a word without thinking of its definition, using correct punctuation habitually, or using grammar automatically. At the procedural stage, what were once strategies are no longer conscious. By definition strategies must be at least somewhat conscious. Strategies that have become 'proceduralized' or automatic are known as 'processes' (Cohen 1998). Chamot and O'Malley (1987, 1994b, 1996) created the Cognitive Academic Language Learning Approach (CALLA), in which declarative knowledge about strategies is taught, practiced, transferred, and evaluated so that it gradually becomes procedural knowledge. In CALLA, strategy instruction is combined with L2 instruction and content teaching (math, science, and so on). CALLA has become popular as a model for L2 strategic self-regulation in many parts of the world.

The most effective strategy instruction appears to include demonstrating when a given strategy might be useful, as well as practicing how to use and evaluate it and how to transfer it to other related tasks and situations. So far, research has shown the most beneficial strategy instruction to be woven into regular, everyday L2 teaching, although other strategy instruction modes are possible (Oxford and Leaver 1996; see also Chapter 7, this volume). Oxford (2006a) presented the following suggestions for strategy instruction:

a Choose strategies to teach based on specific L2 tasks and learners' needs.
b Use easy-to-remember strategy names and descriptions, and ask students to call strategies by name, for example, 'underlining key points in the text'.
c Explain that strategies help learners do a language task more effectively and efficiently.
d Demonstrate how to use a relevant strategy while doing a language task.
e Ask students to demonstrate strategies that work for them.
f Encourage students to share useful strategies with each other with reference to specific tasks.
g Once every few weeks, ask young students to decorate a 'strategy bulletin board' that shows their favorite strategies.
h Weave strategy instruction into regular language teaching, and always refer explicitly to the strategy, so that students will not think it is an additional task.
i Give students opportunities to practice strategies in class and at home to make their learning easier, and ask how well the strategies worked for them.
j Remind students to transfer a given strategy to a new language task to which the strategy is relevant, and if necessary demonstrate how. Later ask how successful the transfer was.
k Explain that although certain strategies are more comfortable (i.e. related to a student's preferred learning style), it is good to try less comfortable strategies if they aid in completing the task.

The above list exemplifies many psychological learning principles, so some readers might believe it reflects a purely psychological approach to strategy instruction. However, this approach is also intentionally imbued with a major sociocultural learning principle: mediation of learning by the 'more experienced other' (Vygotsky 1978, 1979). Mediated learning occurs when the teacher or other competent person helps students learn by offering scaffolding (assistance that is offered until it is no longer needed). Through interactive dialogue, the teacher models and teaches higher-order cognitive skills, discussed later. The dialogue is gradually internalized, helping the learner become increasingly self-regulated.

Research using strategy instruction techniques such as the ones above showed significant, positive effects on proficiency in speaking (O'Malley, Chamot, Stewner-Manzanares, Küpper, and Russo 1985a, 1985b; Dadour and Robbins 1996) and reading (Park-Oh 1994). In addition, L2 strategy instruction was related to greater strategy knowledge and L2 motivation (Nunan 1997) and to increases in strategy use and self-efficacy (Chamot, Barnhardt, El-Dinary, and Robbins 1996).

Bandura's (1986, 1997) 'social cognitive model' of self-regulation, despite its title, is mostly individual and centers on 'self-efficacy', the person's self-perception (belief) about his or her ability to take action leading to a desired performance level, goal, or attainment. Self-efficacy predicts choice of tasks, persistence, effort, and skill acquisition. Three aspects of self-regulation (self, environment, and behavior) and three phases (forethought, performance, and self-reflection) exist in this model. During *forethought*, the learner sets goals. (Goal-setting is viewed as a strategy in most strategy taxonomies.) During *performance*, the learner verbalizes and uses learner strategies to meet the goals, considers whether the ongoing performance reflects his or her ability (attribution), and compares the performance to others' anticipated performance (social comparison). In the *self-reflection* stage, according to Bandura's model, the learner uses strategies such as self-monitoring, i.e. recording and giving feedback on performance; self-evaluating, i.e. comparing observed performance with goals; and reacting with satisfaction or dissatisfaction, self-reward, or some other way.[3] All of these strategies are learnable and teachable.

As we have seen in this section, various psychological views of self-regulation have social or in some instance sociocultural elements. We now turn to more explicitly formulated sociocultural vistas of self-regulation.

Sociocultural views of self-regulation

Here we present learner strategies and strategy instruction in relation to three sociocultural models: the dialogic model, the communities of practice model, and the social autonomy model.

The dialogic model The best-known sociocultural model of self-regulation and 'strategy instruction' is Vygotsky's dialogic model (Vygotsky 1978, 1979; Kozulin, Gindis, Ageyev, and Miller 2003), which has been cited in writings about L2 learning and language learner strategies. (See Scarcella and Oxford 1992; Chamot, Barnhardt, El-Dinary, and Robbins 1999; Oxford 1999.) Vygotsky (1978, 1979) did not use the term 'strategies' but instead discussed a number of higher order functions that we would call strategies. (See Oxford 1999, for the first linking of higher order functions with L2 strategies.) For example, Vygotsky's higher order functions of analyzing and synthesizing are known to us as 'cognitive strategies', while his higher order functions of planning, monitoring, and evaluation are known to us as 'metacognitive strategies' (Oxford 1999). To Vygotsky, these functions are internalized through social interaction in the form of dialogues, which necessitate *social* strategies, such as asking questions and seeking help, and *affective* strategies for controlling emotion and motivation (Oxford 1999). To McCaslin and Hickey (2001), Vygotsky's model contains four categories of strategies: (a) *task*-involved strategies, including cognitive and metacognitive; (b) *self*-involved strategies, including volitional-motivational and emotion-control strategies, all of which are what we call affective strategies, plus some metacognitive strategies for refining goals; (c) *other*-involved strategies, which we call social strategies; and (d) *setting*-involved (environment-organizing) strategies, which we view as a segment of metacognitive strategies.

In Vygotsky's view, learning takes place through (in his terms, is 'mediated by') dialogues with a 'more capable other', that is, a teacher, parent, or more advanced peer.[4] These problem-solving processes verbalized or mediated in the dialogues become part of the learner's thinking (Berk and Winsler 1995). The learner's cognitive development and self-regulatory competence are aroused when he or she appropriates (actively internalizes and transforms) the essential features of the dialogues that occur with the more knowledgeable person (Kozulin *et al.* 2003). Dialogues become internalized and transformed by the learner through several stages: first, the social speech occurring in the dialogue; second, private or egocentric speech; and finally, internal speech. Learning starts out as 'other-regulation' (regulation by another person) but, through a series of dialogues with more capable people, becomes self-regulation. (See, for example, Berk and Winsler 1995; Kozulin *et al.* 2003.) The more knowledgeable person helps the learner traverse the 'zone of proximal development', the area of potentiality made possible through help (or scaffolding), and removes the help or scaffolding when it is no longer needed.

Elements of Vygotsky's dialogic model are reflected in the 'self-regulation strategy development model' of Graham and Harris (1996). This model, which emphasizes children's self-regulation through social interaction within the L1, is also applicable to L2 learning, especially if the learners have a common L1 background and if strategy instruction occurs in the L1. In this model, structured strategy instruction generally occurs in a group, with the teacher explaining and modeling specific strategies and providing useful mnemonics, such as acronyms, for remembering the strategies. Slower students receive individual strategy coaching, in which a more capable person models strategy use and provides help for internalizing strategies. The model requires children to collaborate on a learning task, especially a writing task. Students write collaboratively until they are ready to work on their own, so there is a movement from social to self, just as in Vygotsky's model. The Graham and Harris model involves socially interactive strategies (for example, writing with others and applying what is learnt co-operatively to independent writing) and individual strategies (for example, goal-setting, monitoring progress, talking oneself through frustrations, assessing whether a given strategy works effectively, reinforcing one's own progress).

Situated cognition in communities of practice A different sociocultural emphasis involves situated cognition in communities of practice (Brown, Collins, and Duguid 1989). Situated cognition means learning in a particular sociocultural context. Communities of practice are authentic, meaningful communities centered on specific practices in particular areas of life and learning. (See Lave and Wenger 1991; Rogoff 1994; Wenger 1998; Wenger, McDermott, and Snyder 2002.) 'Old-timers' (the term often used for masters), whose esteemed status is related to knowledge and position, are central to the community. Old-timers model strategies simply by doing their usual tasks. If permitted to enter a particular community of practice, newcomers at first 'participate peripherally' in the community as 'apprentices'. They learn from old-timers or from other apprentices, or from both (Lave and Wenger 1991), as in Vygotsky's description of 'more capable others'. Those already in the community must be willing to provide to apprentices insider knowledge, cultural understandings, practices, and what we might call 'master-strategies'.

In their attempt to understand the situation, roles, and discourse of the community, apprentices observe or infer strategies of old-timers, and they also occasionally ask the old-timers about the strategies used to accomplish the crucial work of the community. Apprentices' strategies are thus observing, inferring, and questioning, on the basis of which apprentices can learn to imitate the master-strategies of more capable members of the community. The success of relatively new apprentices depends partly on the old-timers' and other apprentices' willingness to provide access to opportunities to observe, infer, question, and imitate—all of which we view as an indirect, socially controlled form of 'master-strategy instruction'. In other words, in the sociocultural perspective the individual is not all-powerful; the social environment can either restrict or facilitate individuals' efforts to learn the strategies of the old-timers. The power of the sociocultural setting is thus reflected well in this perspective. Paris, Byrnes, and Paris (2001) offer their own viewpoint on strategies in situated cognition and communities of practice. A very different model follows, one that focuses on recognizing students' existing autonomy.

The social autonomy model In Holliday's (2003) social autonomy model, students share their strategies and academic perspectives with each other and with teachers. Students already have viable, inbuilt, socially relevant forms of autonomy. Through informal sharing and close observation, learners and teachers can understand, support, and strengthen one another's versions of autonomy. Teachers do not judge students' strategies according to their own experiences or values.

In the field of L2 learning, students' strategy-sharing has been fostered for almost 20 years through informal strategy discussions, strategy bulletin boards, and students' demonstrations of strategies to each other (Oxford 1990a). One group of Asian graduate students took strategy-sharing and social autonomy to new heights. In 1999, while discussing their own vocabulary-learning strategies, these students brought up the subject of non-Asian professors' ethnocentric judgments that their strategies were 'rote', uncreative, and not useful for long-term learning. This chapter's first author encouraged the students to investigate systematically their own vocabulary-learning strategies and those of other Asian graduate students. This resulted in a study of the vocabulary-learning strategies of approximately twenty Asian EFL learners enrolled in several graduate programs. Results demonstrated the complex, creative, idiosyncratic mental associations embedded in many Asian vocabulary-learning strategies that non-Asians often mistook as purely 'rote'. This is an example of how learners' strategy-sharing helped destroy a misleading cultural stereotype.

Holliday (2003) criticized teachers who provide imperialistic strategy instruction based solely on their own alien cultural values ('native speaker-ism'). Such an approach ignores the students' autonomy to evaluate and choose strategies according to their own personal goals. He likewise criticized those who refuse to teach *any* strategies out of fear of seeming culturally imperialistic or inappropriate ('critical linguists', 'cultural relativists'). Such an approach withholds from students strategies valuable for entering new communities; under the pretense of tolerance, it actually prevents students' access to potentially relevant parts of the target culture.

For self-regulation or strategy instruction to be successful, learner motivation and volition are essential. The next section explores these topics.

Strategies, motivation, and volition

Motivation and volition are highly related to L2 learner strategies. 'Motivation' is an inner drive, intention, or impulse to do something. 'Volition' literally means the general capability of making a conscious choice or decision. For self-regulation or strategy instruction to be successful, learner motivation and volition are essential, as shown below.

Psychological views of strategies, motivation, and volition

L2 learner strategies and motivation have been approached in two ways in the psychological perspective: (a) relationships among strategy use, strategy instruction, and motivation; and (b) specific strategies for managing motivation and emotion.

Relationships among strategy use, strategy instruction, and motivation
Psychologically-oriented L2 researchers have explored relationships between L2 motivation, measured by various means, and use of a variety of L2 learner strategies, measured by questionnaires, think-aloud protocols, and other means. In descriptive studies motivation, among all learner variables, often had the strongest relationship to L2 strategy use. (See Oxford and Nyikos 1989; Ku 1995; Okada, Oxford, and Abo 1996; Wharton 2000.) Greater strategy use at high school, university, and adult levels was linked with

motivation to use the L2 *outside* of class (Oxford, Park-Oh, Ito, and Sumrall 1993; Oxford and Ehrman 1995) and with other types of motivation (Schmidt, Boraie, and Kassabgy 1996). In these particular studies, it could not be discerned whether high motivation led to high strategy use or vice versa. The likelihood is that these factors are truly interactive. Other studies showed a significant increase in motivation and self-efficacy following strategy instruction (Chamot, Barnhardt, El-Dinary, and Robbins 1996).

Specific strategies for controlling motivation and emotion Other strategies are of little use if not supported by strategies for controlling motivation and emotion. In Oxford's (1990) taxonomy, affective strategies for motivation- and emotion-control include: (a) strategies for lowering anxiety, such as using progressive relaxation, deep breathing, music, or laughter; (b) strategies for encouraging oneself, including making positive statements, taking risks wisely, and rewarding oneself; and (c) strategies for taking one's emotional temperature, such as listening to the body, using an emotional checklist, writing in a diary, or discussing feelings. Affective strategies such as these were among the most frequently used strategies in a Canadian ESL children's study (Gunning, Oxford, and Gatbonton, forthcoming). Affective strategies had the highest correlation with proficiency among all strategy categories in a Taiwanese EFL children's study by Lan and Oxford (2003).

Wolters (2003, cited by Dörnyei 2005) identified eight strategies for self-regulating motivation: (a) self-consequating, i.e. identifying and using extrinsic rewards and punishments; (b) goal-oriented self-talk; (c) enhancing interest to increase intrinsic motivation; (d) structuring the environment; (e) self-handicapping, i.e. making the task more difficult before or during the task to increase challenges and provide excuses; (f) attributing control differentially to affect motivation; (g) managing self-efficacy through goal setting, self-talk, and defensive pessimism; and (h) regulating emotions.

Rheinberg, Vollmeyer, and Rollett (2000) presented an expectancy-value model involving (a) expectancy that the learning activities will improve the outcome and that the outcome will have the desired consequences (for example, contentment, pride, praise, instrumental use of the knowledge, decreased need to study) and (b) the incentive value of having a good result. For these authors both expectancy and value must be present. When students face aversive or difficult learning situations, volitional control strategies help them continue working toward the desired outcome. Examples of volitional control strategies in this model are: (a) attention control—paying attention to why the learning is important; (b) emotion control—blocking emotions that undermine volition; (c) manipulating the environment to help control emotion and motivation, such as by making social commitments to create social pressure that might help maintain an intention; (d) halting any thought that would undermine the power of the intention; and (e) if no positive incentives emerge, maintaining the learning activity continually with volitional control strategies.

The volitional model (Corno 2001) is even broader, including strategies for all aspects of learning, including cognition (attention, encoding, processing), emotion, motivation, task, setting, and even peers and teacher. Similarly, Dörnyei (2005), synthesizing the work of several other theorists, listed five broad classes of strategies for promoting self-motivation. We summarize these classes below.

a Commitment control strategies for preserving or increasing learners' original goal commitment, for example, keeping in mind favorable expectations, incentives, or rewards; focusing on what would happen if the commitment failed.
b Metacognitive control strategies for controlling concentration and halting procrastination, for example, identifying distractions, developing defensive routines, focusing on first steps to take.
c Satiation control strategies for eliminating boredom, for example, adding a twist or fantasy.
d Emotion control strategies for managing disruptive emotional states or moods and generating productive emotions, for example, self-encouragement, relaxation, or meditation.
e Environmental control strategies for eliminating negative environmental influences and using positive environmental influences, such as eliminating distractions or asking friends to help.

Dörnyei (2005) emphasized that the motivational power of the 'possible self' (the learner's desired, imagined end-state) will have an impact on behavior only if the individual can personalize it in terms of concrete, relevant strategies, scripts, and action plans. In other words, the possible self is most meaningful and motivating when the learner possesses strategies to bring that self to life.

We have discussed psychological stances on strategies, motivation, and volition. Next we examine sociocultural views.

Sociocultural views of strategies and motivation

Levine, Reves, and Leaver (1996) compared the strategies of recently-immigrated ex-Soviet EFL learners (newcomers) in an Israeli university with the strategies of earlier-immigrating ex-Soviet peers ('old-timers') in the same setting. Compared with old-timers, newcomers were particularly motivated to prove themselves in the Israeli university system because of the high need for achievement, willingness to work hard, and powerful instrumental motivation to learn English. However, as compared to old-timers' strategies, newcomers' strategies were more rigid, less creative, and more strongly influenced by the recency of their educational experiences in the Soviet educational system. As they became apprentices in the Israeli community, newcomers gradually relaxed, became more flexible and creative in their strategy use, and were increasingly comfortable with learning in Israel.

This section is inevitably brief, because little research exists on the linkage between strategies and motivation within the sociocultural perspective. This perspective is the home of interesting, important theories concerning L2 motivation as 'investment' (see, for instance, Norton 2000a, 2000b[5]), and we advocate intensive sociocultural research on relationships between LLS and investment in L2 learning. We now turn to aptitude and strategies from psychological and sociocultural perspectives.

Aptitude and strategies from the two perspectives

Language aptitude has been researched for many years within the psychological perspective, but it is little discussed in the sociocultural perspective.

Psychological views: strategies within the L2 aptitude domain

The most recent synthesis of views on the topic of aptitude is by Dörnyei (2005), who describes the long history of aptitude research and raises key issues. Here we share some key points from Dörnyei, combined with our own strong recommendation for dynamic-strategic assessment of L2 aptitude—a major departure from current modes of aptitude testing.

MLAT and other related measures The main initial development was Carroll and Sapon's (1959) Modern Language Aptitude Test (MLAT), containing four elements: (a) phonemic coding ability, the capacity to code sounds so that they can be retained for more than a few seconds; (b) grammatical sensitivity, the capacity to identify the functions that words fulfill in sentences; (c) inductive language learning ability, the capacity to take a corpus of material in a target language and make extrapolations (i.e. generalizations) from that material; and (d) associative memory, a capacity to form links between native and foreign language words. Strategies relevant to the MLAT are mainly cognitive (analytic, detail-oriented, inductive and deductive grammatical, inductive and deductive phonemic, and associational) and metacognitive (selective attention). Though the MLAT was originally a major method of assessing language aptitude, it is now rarely used. Other aptitude batteries, for example, the Pimsleur Language Aptitude Battery (PLAB) and the Defense Language Aptitude Battery (DLAB) are more often used today, and their items and sections are, perhaps unwittingly, also related to strategies. These measures are all traditional, static assessments of purportedly innate, but actually learnable and teachable, language abilities. The presence of strategies in L2 aptitude tests could become important in dynamic-strategic aptitude assessment (see later).

CANAL-F The Cognitive Ability for Novelty in Acquisition of Language, as applied to foreign language (CANAL-F, Grigorenko, Sternberg, and Ehrman 2000; see also description in Dörnyei 2005), is a theory-driven rather than purely psychometrically-based aptitude measure and is therefore different from most L2 aptitude tests. CANAL-F is based on Sternberg's triarchic theory of human development with analytical, creative, and practical metacomponents (Sternberg 2002), operationalized at four language levels (lexical, morphological, semantic, and syntactic) and in two modes of output (visual and oral). The CANAL-F contains nine sections related to aptitude for learning an artificial language, 'Ursulu'. Key tasks on this test include learning meanings of neologisms from context, understanding the meaning of passages, continuous paired-associate learning, sentential inference, and learning language rules.

Five specific language acquisition processes are measured in the CANAL-F: (a) selective encoding, (b) selective comparison, (c) selective transfer, (d) selective combination, and (e) accidental encoding. In our analysis, the first four are actually metacognitive strategies related to the metacognitive macrostrategy of selective attention (O'Malley and Chamot 1990; Oxford 1990a). These four embedded (CANAL-F) strategies, like all strategies, are learnable and teachable. See the opportunities posed under dynamic-strategic aptitude assessment later.

Skehan's acquisitional-stage approach In Skehan's (2002) approach to L2 aptitude, each putative acquisitional stage is linked with proposed aptitude constructs. In our interpretation (or extension) of this model, specific strategies are associated with every stage. (See Table 3.1.)

Elements missing from L2 aptitude to date As seen in the note appended to Table 3.1, Skehan (2002) contended that L2 aptitude assessment (and theories) does not yet address certain important aptitude constructs, such as attentional control, working memory, automatization, chunking, integrative memory, and retrieval memory. We similarly assert that L2 aptitude assessment and theories, no matter how successful in particular ways and for specific purposes, have not yet come to grips with still other crucial aptitude constructs. For instance, missing are the aptitude constructs of L2 self-awareness (knowledge of one's own styles, strategies, and motivation), ability to handle L2 interpersonal interactions, and ability to understand how culture and, more generally, context influences linguistic aspects, such as pragmatics. These constructs are part of personal, interpersonal, and social-cultural competencies that are necessary for learning more effectively, understanding and applying pragmatics, learning idioms, understanding culturally embedded meanings, and communicating effectively with native speakers. More than 15 years ago Oxford (1990b) urged theorists to expand L2 aptitude theories and assessment to include such aspects, as well as retaining the very important cognitive and metacognitive aspects that were already included by L2 aptitude specialists. Many existing ways of looking at L2 aptitude still do not include the constructs called for by Skehan (2002) and Oxford (1990b). Expansion of the components of L2 aptitude theory and assessment needs to progress still further.

Skehan's name for this stage	Skehan's corresponding aptitude constructs	Samples of L2 learner strategies we believe are related to this stage
1 Input processing strategies, such as segmentation	*Attentional control* *Working memory*	Distinguishing between focal (selective) attention and global (general) attention Using focal (selective) attention to get information into working memory (e.g. attending to differences between interlanguage and the L2) Using global (general) attention to get information into working memory
2 Noticing	Phonetic coding ability *Working memory*	Using focal (selective) attention to get information into working memory (e.g. attending to differences between interlanguage and the L2) Using global (general) attention to get information into working memory
3 Pattern identification	Phonetic coding ability *Working memory* Grammatical sensitivity Inductive language learning ability	Reasoning from the specific to the general Noticing pattern-generating features like repetition and difference both aurally and visually Comparing patterns (between the interlanguage and the target language, and between earlier-encountered patterns and newly-encountered ones) Sustaining attention by noticing the most interesting or most frequent patterns
4 Pattern restructuring and manipulation	Grammatical sensitivity Inductive language learning ability	Identifying differences and similarities Reasoning inductively Reasoning deductively Transforming linguistic data
5 Pattern control	*Automatization* *Integrative memory*	Practicing often Moving from massed practice to spaced practice Synthesizing information Integrating new information
6 Pattern integration	*Chunking* *Retrieval memory*	Chunking (categorizing relevant data) Drawing on already-learned patterns Using memory hooks to retrieve material from long-term memory

Note: First two columns summarized from Skehan (2002). Third column original (by authors of current chapter). Skehan (2002) notes that aptitude constructs in italics have not been explicitly addressed in language aptitude tests. (See also Dörnyei and Skehan 2003; Dörnyei 2005.)

Table 3.1 Skehan's componential approach to language aptitude with our extension (learner strategies related to different stages)

Sociocultural views: potential of L2 dynamic assessment

In addition to the components mentioned above for expanding L2 aptitude, Vygotsky and other Soviet theorists provided ideas that could make L2 aptitude assessment more comprehensive and authentic than is usually the case in psychological forms of L2 aptitude assessment. As socialists, they were motivated to construct a theory showing how learning creates new potentials for still further learning, possibly so that the ruling class could no longer continue its oppression based on claims about inherent inadequacies and weaknesses of the working class. Vygotsky's dialogical model involves a dynamic, not static, concept of aptitude. The model views aptitude as dynamic, that is, aptitude depends not just on what is in the individual's head but also on social interaction with a 'more capable other'. Specific strategies are 'mediated' during the interaction; that means the person being addressed is helped to identify and use optimal strategies for doing the learning tasks that measure aptitude. Based on Vygotsky's concepts, we suggest that aptitude assessment should not be merely a measure of a person's *current* competence for figuring out and employing elements of an artificial language. Instead, it should predict how competent the person *could become* if, in the future, he or she encounters the proper socially-mediated learning conditions and has help in discovering the most useful strategies for specific learning tasks. Accurate prediction can be made only if the aptitude assessment includes an opportunity for interactive, socially mediated learning to occur at the very time the person is being assessed. In this view of aptitude assessment, aptitude is not a stable trait. It is susceptible to instruction and environmental stimulation and can be improved.

Israeli sociocultural theorist Reuven Feuerstein believed that 'anyone can become a fully effective learner' (Williams and Burden 1997: 41) because, as he contended, mental structures are infinitely modifiable. Aptitude is not established at birth or in the early years of life but is instead changeable. Such 'structural cognitive modifiability' allows a person's capacity (aptitude) to expand cumulatively throughout the lifespan with the proper assistance and stimulation. Feuerstein's program for teaching people to 'learn how to learn' is known as 'instrumental enrichment', or IE (Feuerstein, Rand, Hoffman, and Miller 1980; Feuerstein, Klein, and Tannenbaum 1991). IE is associated with a twin concept, 'dynamic assessment' (Feuerstein, Rand, and Hoffman 1979), which involves a dialogue between the learner and a more competent person, who assesses the learner's current level of performance, teaches ways (strategies) for improving performance, and assesses again (the test–teach–test paradigm described by Kozulin and Garb 2001). By assessing learning potential instead of just current ability, dynamic assessment holds great promise for L2 aptitude measurement. Unlike dynamic assessment, static assessment, including virtually all L2 aptitude testing as currently employed, measures only the current level of ability and is woefully 'insufficient for estimating students' *learning potential* ...' (Kozulin and Garb

2001: 4, emphasis added). Though current L2 aptitude assessment is based on the assumption that L2 aptitude is a static quantity, not subject to further development, dynamic assessment would view L2 aptitude as a capacity open to lifelong development. For more information on dynamic assessment, see Lidz (1987), Lidz and Elliott (2000), and Minick (1987).

Strategies as related to 'activity' and 'action' from psychological and sociocultural perspectives

This section deals with strategies as related to 'activity' and 'action' from both perspectives. In the psychological perspective, this theme focuses on two general aspects of mental activity: metacognition and cognition (including metacognitive and cognitive strategies). In the sociocultural perspective, the theme concerns strategies as action patterns in the broader context of Activity Theory.

Psychological views of two key types of mental activity

From the viewpoint of psychology, we now discuss strategies as related to two broad aspects of mental activity: metacognition and cognition, with an emphasis on the former. Cognition involves the mental process of knowing, including aspects such as awareness, perception, reasoning, and judgment (and strategies related to those aspects). Metacognition means 'beyond cognition'. It is generally viewed as encompassing strategies for regulating and controlling one's own cognition.

Metacognition has been among the most influential constructs in research on language learner strategies and learning in general, established initially and primarily in the field of psychology. Aspects of metacognition can be traced through centuries, all the way back to Hegel and Spinoza (Fischer and Mandl 1981; Brown 1984). Flavell's (1971) work inspired a vast body of research on the subject. By the mid-1990s, the discussion of how to define metacognition as opposed to cognition had led to consensus within the information processing paradigm (Flavell 1978, 1979, 1984; Fischer and Mandl 1981; Kluwe 1981; Brown 1984; Chi 1984).

Metacognition is related to declarative and procedural knowledge, which were mentioned and defined under the psychological perspective on self-regulation. As noted earlier, declarative knowledge is effortful and static, whereas procedural knowledge is automatic and smoothly operating. Cognition in a declarative form ('cognitive declarative knowledge') involves topic-specific data, or conscious facts, while cognition in a procedural form ('cognitive procedural knowledge') involves problem-solving skills that operate automatically. Metacognition in a declarative form ('metacognitive declarative knowledge') involves knowledge about one's own cognition, for example, learning, or thinking, whereas metacognition in a procedural form ('metacognitive procedural knowledge') involves automatic, executive processes of regulation and control.

Let us take a closer look at metacognitive procedural knowledge, which both regulates and controls cognition and thus also strategy use. According to Kluwe and Schiebler (1984), the process of regulation in metacognitive procedural knowledge has four aspects (also see Anderson forthcoming; Wenden 2001):

a 'capacity regulation': decisions about how many resources someone puts into a task and how to allocate these resources—for example, 'I will put all of my energy into this tonight, and then briefly go over it tomorrow in the office where I won't be able to concentrate that well';
b 'intensity regulation': decisions on frequency, duration, and perseverance of operations—for example, 'I will do this for ten more minutes';
c 'object (focus) regulation': decisions about what is to be processed or focused upon—for example, 'I will go back to the figure';
d 'speed regulation': decisions about how quickly a piece of work is to be done and whether certain mental operations are necessary or not—for example, 'I have to pay close attention, so I should go slowly'.

Control (or monitoring) also has four aspects:

a 'identification': learner identifies what he or she is doing, or has just done—for example, 'I am rereading this sentence for the third time';
b 'analysis': learner analyzes how he or she is doing it—for example, 'I am doing this pretty superficially';
c 'evaluation': learner evaluates the quality of cognitive processes—for example, 'It's not good for me to be stuck on this point for so long';
d 'prognosis': learner considers and assesses probable outcomes of alternatives—for example, 'rereading this will probably not help, but if I try to map this out on paper, I will understand it'.

These eight executive processes are metacognitive strategies that control or regulate one's use of cognitive strategies. The combined use of cognitive and metacognitive strategies in an L2 learning activity often not only results in new cognitive knowledge, but—so to speak as a by-product—also in new metacognitive declarative knowledge about cognition that can be used to regulate and control cognition in the future.

We have just discussed strategies related to two crucial aspects of mental activity in the psychological perspective: metacognitive and cognitive. Next we portray strategies as 'action patterns' in sociocultural activity theory.

Sociocultural views of strategies as action patterns

In the Soviet school of psychology, thinkers such as Vygotsky (1978, 1979), Leont'ev (1974a/1984, 1974b/1984), and Gal'perin (1976/1980) viewed themselves as psychologists whose work was thoroughly sociocultural; they did not make any artificial separations between the psychological and the sociocultural. One of their main contributions was Activity Theory, which distinguished processes on three levels: activities, actions, and operations.

According to Leont'ev, '[h]uman activity exists as action and action chains' (translated from Leont'ev 1974a/1984: 22). The defining characteristic of an 'activity' is that it serves to satisfy a human need and is thus based on a motive. The co-operation in a legal system to produce security, a human need, can serve us as an example of an activity. 'Actions', on the other hand, are defined by goals. Within the larger context of legal activity, a specific individual's goal might be to prosecute a person. His or her corresponding action cannot satisfy the human need for security by itself, but only as part of an action chain (including, for example, actions of attorneys, judges, jurors, or prison staff) that ultimately serves to establish security. (Also see Leont'ev 1974a/1984: 22; Rehbein 1977: 105–109.) On the next lower level, actions are composed of 'operations'. Characteristic of operations, according to Leont'ev, are the conditions under which they are employed. 'Actions [...] relate to goals; operations [relate] to conditions', he stated (1974a/1984: 24). For example, a person who reads a foreign language text in a legal action context usually does not pursue the goal of processing graphemes or relating text information to figures. For the experienced reader, these are merely operations that he or she employs under certain conditions.

This action-theoretical approach has been explored with respect to native language reading by Schnotz, Ballstaedt, and Mandl (1981), with respect to foreign language reading by Schramm (2001) and Stiefenhöfer (1986), and with respect to language learning in general by Baur (1979), Baur and Rehbein (1979), Lantolf and Pavlenko (2001), and Wendt (1993, 1997). Lantolf and Pavlenko's (2001) concept of 'SLA agency' is among the most recent contributions. Based on Taylor's (1985) work, these authors identified 'significance' as a central characteristic of human agency. With this term, they stressed that it is not the mere performance of an action (or 'doing') that matters for human agency, but instead the meanings and interpretations assigned to these actions by the acting person and others who are involved in this action. (See Lantolf and Pavlenko 2001: 146.) According to their view, '[i]t is agency that links motivation [...] to action [...]. Agency, in turn, is socially and historically constructed and is part of a person's *habitus*' (p. 146; italics in original). With respect to language learning in particular, they considered the 'significance languages and language study have for the individuals in their lives as humans' (p. 146) as central for the motives and thus pointed out that language study does not matter to everyone to the same degree and in the same way. Instead, Lantolf and Pavlenko (2001) described L2 learners as agents whose actions (a) occur in specific sociocultural environments and (b) are affected by learners' dynamic identities, which are related to nationality, ethnicity, class, educational experience, gender, age, and so on.

Unlike the constructs of activity, action, operation, and agency, the construct of 'action pattern' does not stem from the field of learning theory, but from linguistics. Based on the philosophical work of Wittgenstein (1958/ 1971), Austin (1955/1999), and Searle (1969, 1979), pragmatics has evolved as a field of linguistic research that inquires into the question of how we *act* with language. The functional pragmatic approach of Ehlich and Rehbein (Rehbein 1977; Ehlich and Rehbein 1979a, 1986; Ehlich 1991), a linguistic approach based on Western philosophical tradition and Soviet sociocultural-psychological tradition, has theoretical potential for the discussion of learner strategies.

According to Ehlich and Rehbein (1979a, 1986), an 'action pattern' is a socially shared, abstract ensemble of mental, interactional, and physical action-steps to achieve a recurring social purpose. When concrete persons perform concrete actions, their actions are based on socially shared knowledge of how to do this, i.e. on the corresponding action patterns. This concept is thus an abstraction of individual mental representations of actions at the social level. Inherent in these forms is their particular social purpose, and it is the social category of *purpose* that primarily defines a specific action pattern. Members of a society can use the collectively developed patterns of actions with their inherent social purposes to pursue their concrete individual *goals*. For example, a bilingual speaker of Japanese and German can make use of two different (abstract) action patterns for (concretely) apologizing to a German or a Japanese person. Both apologies will be different not only in language, but also in performance because they will be based on two culture-specific action patterns.

Schramm (2001) and Kameyama (2004) have established an interesting link between this functional pragmatic approach and strategy research. Their analyses of (mental) reading strategies (Schramm 2001) and (interactional) communication strategies (Kameyama 2004)[6] is based on the linguistic action pattern of 'giving reasons for an action' (Ehlich and Rehbein 1986). This means that their empirical data on L2 repair strategies conform to the pattern of social interaction between two or more people in giving reasons. Schramm's (2001) study might thus be of interest for future research on learner strategies because it empirically shows how individual mental action is related to socioculturally determined social interaction.

In a different research project on elementary school children's LLS employed during second language classroom storytelling, Schramm (2006) outlined a relational databank-design that combines (psycholinguistic) profile data (Clahsen 1985; Grießhaber 2005; Pienemann, Keßler, and Roos 2006) of individual learners with (sociocultural) classroom discourse analysis based on detailed transcripts of videotaped classroom storytelling interaction in grades 1–4. Her analyses (also see Schramm forthcoming) demonstrated how specific kinds of teacher scaffolding allow students to use communication strategies in order to venture beyond their current language level and thus provide them with access to second language acquisition opportunities, whereas other specific kinds of teacher scaffolding correlate with stories that fall behind the students' individual interlanguage potential, or even worse, that disorient and silence them. On this basis, Schramm (2005b) recommended explicit teaching of active listening comments and questions to young learners, whose interaction with the storytelling child can provide valuable scaffolding to their peer.

We have discussed the two perspectives—psychological and sociocultural— with reference to the relationship between strategies and the following: (a) self-regulation; (b) motivation and volition, (c) aptitude, and (d) concepts related to 'activity' and 'action'.

Conclusion: why the two perspectives need positive communication

> A resolution of paradigm differences can occur only when a new paradigm emerges that is more informed and sophisticated than any existing one. That is most likely to occur if and when proponents of these several points of view come together to discuss their differences.
> *Guba and Lincoln 1994: 116*

However, proponents of the two perspectives, psychological and socio-cultural, have been discussing their differences for years with few positive results. The real problem, it seems to us, is that representatives of the two sides have not systematically, constructively discussed their differences in specific areas of mutual interest, such as the areas explored in this chapter: self-regulation, motivation, aptitude, and aspects of activity. If such a discussion could be established, advocates of each viewpoint would likely start to respect each others' work more deeply and might even discover reasons to expand or modify their own theoretical categories on the basis of information from the other viewpoint. For example, sociocultural and psychological theorists in the L2 field could learn from each other new methodologies for inculcating strategic self-regulation and increasing students' motivation and volition. Aptitude theorists from the two camps could start talking to each other with the goal of retaining the precision of existing L2 aptitude testing while including key aspects of dynamic aptitude assessment. Psychological theorists could teach sociocultural theorists about mental activities such as metacognition and cognition, while sociocultural theorists could teach psychological theorists about strategies as action patterns within Action Theory. If a series of productive talks were held, proponents of both perspectives could make joint research proposals and plans, with each side focusing on the same variables but in distinct ways, thus making the results richer and more meaningful for the entire L2 field.

It is disappointing that when theorists have compared the two perspectives, they have generally shone a spotlight on differences, making these seem as sharp as possible, while ignoring potential synergies. A few notable ex-ceptions exist, such as Larsen-Freeman (1997, 2000) and Brown (2004, 2005), who were cited in the introduction. Their recommendations about seeing the complementarity of the two perspectives should be implemented. One could argue that deeply seated ontological and epistemological differences will never allow such learning, sharing, or theory-development across these two perspectives. With all due respect to ontological and epistemological differences, we nevertheless believe that it is unwise to use such differences as a reason to cut off theory-building across perspectives.

We close with some thoughts from Bakhtin (1984, 1986, 1998) about the nature of and need for communication. He revealed that any language is 'heteroglossic', that is, filled with a multiplicity of voices, dialects, jargon, styles, tones, contextual nuances, subcultural vocabulary, idioms, and slang (Bakhtin 1998; see also Oxford, Massey, and Anand 2005). We might call the psychological and sociocultural perspectives two 'voices' or 'dialects' in the current world conversation about LLS. Despite these different voices or dialects, it is possible to have an ongoing *dialogue*, which involves responding to, relying on, supplementing, presupposing, refuting, or affirming others in an open interaction (Bakhtin 1984, 1986, 1998). Dialogue also involves looking forward to responsive reactions from others and listening to the other from the other's perspective in order to negotiate differences (Bakhtin 1986, 1998). As Bakhtin opined, 'To live means to participate in dialogue: to ask questions, to heed, to respond, to agree ...' (1984: 293). As yet, few in the L2 field have availed themselves of positive, constructive dialogues aimed at in-depth mutual understanding, theory-building, and joint research across psychological and sociocultural perspectives. The area of LLS is a clear example of this lack. We hope this chapter will help create a true dialogue in which researchers, theorists, and practitioners on both sides, psychological and sociocultural, can talk productively and positively with each other about LLS, starting with themes such as self-regulation, motivation, aptitude, and activity. If this occurs, the ultimate goal, bringing about richer and more effective L2 learning and teaching, has a better chance of being achieved.

Acknowledgements

We are very grateful to an anonymous reviewer, who suggested that strategies for intercultural communication could be beneficially analyzed through our double perspective, sociocultural and psychological. We believe that this is an excellent suggestion for future research.

Notes

1 See, for example, Nyikos and Oxford 1993; Ehrman and Oxford 1995; Oxford 1996b; Oxford, Tomlinson, Barcelos, Harrington, Lavine, Saleh, and Longhini 1998; Lan and Oxford 2003; Yamamori, Isoda, Hiromori, and Oxford 2003; Oxford, Massey, and Anand 2005.

2 The fact that self-regulation theory and research have always been rich with references to LLS contradicts Dörnyei and Skehan's (2003) declaration that in the 1990s educational psychologists abandoned the term or construct of 'strategy' and replaced it by 'self-regulation'.

3 In our view, self-reflection can occur at any stage, but in Bandura's model it comprises a separate stage.

4 According to this theory, additional mediators can include (a) symbolic tools, such as letters, numbers, and language itself, and (b) formalized learning activities.

5 Though Norton (2000a, 2004b, 2001) did not focus on relationships between L2 learner strategies and motivation, her work in sociocultural motivation—viewed as 'investment'—is important to mention.

6 Note that these authors, for theoretical reasons, do not use the terms strategies, but instead analyze actions and action steps within the presented theoretical perspective.

4

Applying strategies to contexts: the role of individual, situational, and group differences

OSAMU TAKEUCHI, CAROL GRIFFITHS, and DO COYLE

Introduction

The purpose of this chapter is twofold: (a) to review the literature investigating the influence of such variables as age, gender, motivation, career orientation, personality type, nationality, proficiency, and learning situation on strategy use; and (b) to show how the literature review applies to individuals and groups in specific situations. The first section provides a review of empirical studies dealing with each of the variables, and indicates what we know so far concerning the influence of these variables on strategy use. The second section provides an example of a qualitative study conducted in New Zealand, which focused on individual variables in language learning. The relationships among strategy use, age, gender, motivation, career orientation, personality, nationality, and proficiency are examined. The third section looks at the situational variables conducive to the development of strategies among learners in a classroom group—hence, the name 'strategic classrooms'. It provides a macro view of contextual variables leading to the development of certain learner strategies. The final section stresses the importance of taking both individual and situational variables into consideration. It concludes that whilst the relationship between individual differences and learner strategies is both psycholinguistic and sociocultural in nature, group differences and learner strategies are essentially symbiotic and sociocultural.

There is an appendix (Appendix 4.1) on the website (www.oup.com/elt/teacher/lls) which lists the studies we reviewed and summarizes our analysis of them.

Review of studies focusing on individual, group, and situational variables

What variables are related to the choice and the use of learner strategies? How strong is the influence of a certain variable? These are questions that have been asked in the 30-year course of strategy research. A rationale behind this inquiry is that strategy instruction should be geared to learners' individual and situational or group needs. Hence, there is justification for studying the effects of individual, group, and situational variables on strategy use. In this section, we first review empirical studies dealing with the influence of variables such as age, gender, motivation, career orientation, personality types, and nationality. Then we look at studies investigating the relationship between strategy use and proficiency. Finally, we turn our attention to studies examining the influence of situational variables on the choice and use of learner strategies.

Age

Only a handful of studies have been conducted so far to examine the influence of age on strategy use. One of them was the study by Griffiths (2003a), which involved a total of 348 students aged 14–64. In this study, the effect of age, course level, nationality, and gender were examined quantitatively. While neither age nor gender were significantly related to strategy use, she did find differences according to nationality. Peacock and Ho (2003), on the other hand, found that older students (aged 23–39; N = 112) used four of Oxford's six strategy categories—memory, metacognitive, affective, and social—significantly more often than did younger students (aged 18–22; N = 894). The use among the older students was higher for 13 individual strategies and much higher for seven other strategies. In a study by Victori and Tragant (2003) involving 766 participants from three age groups (10-, 14-, and 17-years-old), the mean obtained by the youngest group of students varied significantly from that of the other two groups: the older two groups reported significantly higher use of cognitively complex strategies than the young learners, whereas the young learners reported higher use of social strategies.

One of the reasons behind the mixed findings presented above may be that the contexts where these three studies were conducted were appreciably different. Griffiths' study was conducted in the New Zealand ESL context with a variety of ethnic backgrounds and student learning goals. The study by Peacock and Ho was carried out in the Hong Kong EFL context with a highly homogeneous population and relatively uniform learning goals. The study by Victori and Tragant was conducted in the Spanish primary/high-school EFL context with a relatively homogeneous population and diverse goals for learning. These contextual differences might have exerted some influence on the relationship between age and strategy use.

Gender

Early work on the role of gender in learner strategy use was conducted primarily by Oxford and colleagues, as reviewed by Oxford (1993a, 1993b,

1994) and by Oxford and Green (1995). They note that one of the very first empirical studies was conducted by Politzer (1983), who examined 90 American college students learning foreign languages and found that female students used social/interactional strategies more frequently than their male counterparts. Then, in their study of strategy use by various occupational groups, Ehrman and Oxford (1989) found a much more frequent use of four strategy categories (general learning, functional, searching for/communicating meaning, and self-management) by females. Oxford and Nyikos (1989) examined 1,200 US college students and found a greater use of three strategy categories (formal practice, general study, and input elicitation) by female students. These studies consistently showed that females made a greater use than males of social/communicative/interactional strategies. Oxford, Nyikos, and Ehrman (1988) attributed this to women's greater (a) desire for social approval, (b) willingness to accept existing norms, and (c) verbal ability.

More recently, in a South African study with 179 females and 126 males, Dreyer and Oxford (1996) reported that, overall, females used strategies more often than males and that females used social and metacognitive strategies more frequently. In a larger-scale study with 1,006 Chinese EFL students (of whom 51 per cent were male and 49 per cent female), Peacock and Ho (2003) found that females had reported a significantly higher use of all six categories on the *Strategy Inventory for Language Learning* (SILL) than did males. In addition, they found a much higher use of nine individual strategies by females, 78 per cent of which were from the memory or metacognitive categories.

It is noteworthy, however, that some studies reported markedly different findings from those in the studies presented above. Hashim and Sahil (1994), for example, found that, apart from affective strategies, which women used significantly more frequently, no difference was observed in the other SILL categories. Wharton (2000), in a study involving 678 university students learning Japanese and French in Singapore, reported that men used a significantly greater number of strategies than women. Griffiths' (2003a) New Zealand study with 234 females and 114 males found no statistically significant difference in strategy use by gender. Furthermore, Nisbet, Tindall, and Arroyo (2005), in a Chinese study with 139 females and 29 males, found no significant difference among males and females in the use of SILL strategies. Nisbet *et al.* attributed the discrepancy described above to the effect of the specific cultural contexts of learning.

Motivation

There is a general consensus among researchers that learners who are more motivated tend to use a wider range of learner strategies and to use these strategies more frequently. Oxford and Nyikos (1989), in a large-scale study of US college students, found that highly motivated learners used four (out of five) categories of strategies significantly more often than did less motivated learners. A study by Okada, Oxford, and Abo (1996), conducted with 36 learners of Japanese and 36 learners of Spanish, found very strong relationships between metacognitive/cognitive/social strategy use and several motivational aspects in both language groups. Mochizuki (1999), along with Wharton (2000), also found that highly motivated Asian university students used learner strategies more frequently than less motivated students in all six categories of SILL strategies.

The question prompted by these results concerns causality: whether motivation spurs strategy use or, conversely, strategy use leads to better language performance, which in turn increases motivation and thus leads to increased strategy use (Okada *et al.* 1996). Few studies, however, have been conducted so far to ascertain causality.

Career orientation/reason for study

The influence of career orientation on strategy use was first pointed out empirically by Politzer and McGroarty (1985); they compared 26 engineering students with ten humanities majors learning English. Results showed that humanities majors made a greater use of individual study strategies than engineering students. In this study, however, the influence of ethnic background was confounded with that of career orientation, and thus it was difficult to separate the effects of these two variables clearly. Oxford and Nyikos (1989), in a study of 1,200 US college students, found that humanities majors used functional practice strategies and strategies grouped in a factor referred to as 'resourceful, independent strategies'[1] more frequently than technology majors. In a Japanese study of 44 English majors and 113 non-English majors, Mochizuki (1999) reported that English majors used compensation strategies, social strategies, and metacognitive strategies more frequently than the non-English majors. In addition, Peacock and Ho (2003), in a large-scale study with Hong Kong ESL learners across eight academic disciplines, found that (a) English majors reported a much higher use of three strategy categories—cognitive, metacognitive, and social—than did students from other disciplines, and (b) computer studies students reported a much lower use of metacognitive strategies. English majors in this study, moreover, reported a higher use of 26 strategies than students from other disciplines.

Personality types

Some researchers have investigated the effects of personality types measured by the Myers-Briggs Type Indicator (MBTI) on strategy use. Ehrman and Oxford (1989), for example, conducted a survey exploring the relationships between personality types and strategy use on the SILL. Extroverts in the survey were found to use two categories of strategies (affective and visualization) more frequently than introverts. Introverts, on the contrary, made a greater use of strategies for searching for/communicating meaning than did extroverts. They also indicated that (a) intuitive people used four strategy categories (affective, formal model building, authentic language use, and searching for/commutating meaning) more frequently than sensing people, and that (b) feeling-type people, compared with thinkers, showed a greater use of general study strategies.

A study by Ehrman and Oxford (1990) conducted with 20 adults learning Turkish in the US found that extroverts preferred social strategies and functional practice strategies, while introverts in contrast preferred learning alone the most, so as to avoid social contact and surprises. In a US study with 520 participants, Oxford and Ehrman (1995) reported that overall strategy use measured by the SILL was related to extraversion on the MBTI. Wakamoto (2000), in a study conducted on 254 Japanese college students, also found that extroversion on the MBTI was significantly correlated with functional practice strategies and social-affective strategies, while, unlike the Ehrman and Oxford's studies, introversion was not correlated with any preferred use of SILL strategies.

The aforementioned studies seem to concur that extroversion is a factor promoting the use of certain strategies. This consensus is consistent with earlier studies such as that by Rubin (1975), in which extroversion represented by lack of inhibition was observed to be a characteristic of successful learners. Reiss (1985), however, argued that successful learners were not always so uninhibited, and thus implied that the trait might be situational or subject to the influence of the learning contexts.

Nationality/ethnicity/culture

One of the earliest efforts to investigate the effect of nationality was a study by Politzer and McGroarty (1985). In this study, Hispanic students were found to use the various strategy categories under investigation more frequently than their Asian counterparts. In terms of progress in English, however, the Asians made more progress than did the Hispanics. Based on these results, the authors speculated that what constitute 'good' strategies, as identified by researchers, might indeed be ethnocentric.

Bedell and Oxford (1996), in a study of 353 mainland Chinese EFL university students, revealed that compensation strategies were the highest-ranking category. According to the researchers, this was also true with Chinese students studying in Taiwan and the US. In contrast, the Puerto Rican and Egyptian students reported only a moderate use of compensation strategies. Based on these findings, they argued the higher use of compensation might be typical of Asian students. Memory strategies, contrary to the popular belief, were ranked low in their study. This infrequent use of memory strategies by Asian students was also confirmed in Mochizuki's (1999) study on Japanese EFL students. Grainger's study (1997) with 133 learners of Japanese with various ethnic backgrounds found no significant differences in overall SILL scores among native English speakers, those from European backgrounds, and those students from Asian backgrounds. The study, however, revealed that Asian-background students were better at managing their affective state, remembered more effectively, and compensated better than students with English-speaking backgrounds. Griffiths (2003a) furthermore reported that European students used SILL strategies more frequently than did students from other backgrounds. These studies seem to suggest that nationality is a major factor influencing the use of learner strategies.

Proficiency/achievement

A major reason to investigate strategy use in language learning has been to determine the relationship between strategies and proficiency. One of the first attempts to clarify this relationship was a study conducted by Bialystok and Fröhlich (1978). In their study of 157 high school students learning French as a second language, they found that the combined use of three learning strategies (practicing, inferencing, and monitoring) was responsible for their achievement in reading, listening, and grammar tests.

Takeuchi (1993), in a study conducted with 78 Japanese college English majors, reported that some 60 per cent of the variance in the Comprehensive English Language Test (CELT) scores was associated with reported strategy use on the SILL. He also found several significant relationships between the subscales of the CELT and strategy use as determined by the SILL. Dreyer and Oxford (1996) found that 45 per cent of the variance in the Test of English as a Foreign Language (TOEFL) scores was predicted by the use of SILL strategies of university ESL learners in South Africa. Also reported in this study was a correlation of .73 between English proficiency scores and strategy use. A study by Park (1997) conducted with 332 Korean university students found a significant linear relationship between SILL learning strategies and English proficiency measured by a practice version of the TOEFL. In addition, results indicated that cognitive and social strategies were more predictive of TOEFL scores than other strategy categories, and that these two categories jointly accounted for 13 per cent of the total variance on the TOEFL.

In contrast to these studies, a study of 36 Asian and Hispanic graduate-level students in an intensive English course (Politzer and McGroarty 1985) did not yield such positive relationships. Three tests of language ability were administered twice at an eight-week interval, and the gain scores on the tests were related to results of a self-reported strategy inventory. While there was a relationship between the test of communicative ability and reported strategy use, it was weak. In addition, the correlation between the test of communicative ability and the reported use of individual strategies was not significant. Similarly, in an intensive foreign language program in the US, Oxford and Ehrman (1995) reported low correlations between the strategies on the SILL and proficiency ratings. Mullins' (1992) study in Thailand reported few significant relationships between SILL strategies and the following measures of university EFL students' proficiency/achievement:

entrance examination, placement test, and GPA. Furthermore, in a study conducted on 168 university English majors in mainland China, Nisbet *et al.* (2005) found that only one category of SILL strategies, i.e. metacognitive strategies, was significantly correlated with the TOEFL scores and that the strategies accounted for just four per cent of the variance in the scores.

We might ask why some studies yielded significant relationships between strategy use and proficiency while others did not. One possible explanation is that other variables overshadowed strategy use, such as tolerance of ambiguity, self-esteem, risk-taking, field dependence/independence, and motivation (Scarcella and Oxford 1992). Another possible explanation for the weak relationships observed was the type of instrument selected to measure language proficiency. The TOEFL, for example, is designed to assess cognitive/academic language proficiency, and does not include any direct measures of interactive/communicative skills (even in its most recent internet format). It is thus possible that learner strategies would correlate more strongly with other, more communicative measures of proficiency (Nisbet *et al.* 2005). Thirdly, learners may have used strategies other than those reported on the SILL or other similar inventories based mainly on North American strategy research (Nisbet *et al.* 2005). In fact, several researchers in Asian EFL contexts have reported that their EFL students have used both strategies included in the SILL and those that are not (LoCastro 1994; Takeuchi 2003a). The last explanation is that what determines learning outcomes is not the frequency with which strategies are used, but the flexibility of strategy use in a specific context. As several researchers have argued (Cohen 1998; Gu 2002), measuring strategy use in terms of a frequency count only furnishes part of the picture, and serious consideration needs to be given to the appropriateness of strategy use for the given context.

Learning situation

Some studies indicate that situational variables exert a substantial influence on the use of strategies, or at least confound the relationships among individual variables and strategy use. Ikeda and Takeuchi (2000), for example, investigated the effect of a situational variable, i.e. task difficulty, on the reported frequency of strategy use in a study with 192 university-level EFL learners in Japan.

In an effort to replicate and expand Ikeda and Takeuchi's study, Oxford, Cho, Leung, and Kim (2004) reported a complex picture of how task difficulty and proficiency level affected the reported frequency of strategy use by ESL students. Based on the findings of their study, they argued that task-based strategy assessment was useful because it anchored strategy use within the context of a particular language task, thus allowing for more contextualized and detailed analysis of strategy use. The article also noted that there continues to be an important role for non-task-based strategy questionnaires that assess 'typical' strategy use of individuals. The two types of assessment serve different, complementary purposes.

Several studies reported the influence of ESL versus EFL differences on strategy use. For example, Riley and Harsch (1999) compared 28 Japanese ESL students attending two language programs in Hawaii with 28 Japanese EFL students attending a university in Japan, and found the two groups used different strategies. The researchers maintained that the environmental differences could play an important part when learning another language. Likewise, the relatively scarce opportunity for input and output in a study of Japanese EFL students resulted in student report of a pattern of strategy use characterized by special emphasis on certain metacognitive strategies, as well as certain cognitive strategies such as reading aloud (Takeuchi 2003a, 2003b).

Recently, researchers (for example, Donato and McCormick 1994; Lantolf and Appel 1994; Norton and Toohey 2001; Gao 2006), influenced by the work of Vygotsky and others, have asserted that the development of learner strategies is highly affected by the social context in which they occur. From this perspective, strategies are linked both to specific cognitive activities and also to the social communities in which they occur. According to Lave and Wenger (1991), activities, tasks, functions, and understandings do not exist in isolation, but are built on complex systems of relationships developed within social settings. The individual learner is defined by, as well as defines, these relationships. Understanding the development of learner strategies from this perspective extends beyond the individual learner and focuses on the classroom and the interactions that constitute it.

Section summary and directions for further research

The literature review presented above has shown that individual, group, and situational variables have an influence on learners' use of strategies. The review has also indicated the value of strategy research that takes account of individual learner differences anchored within specific learning situations. In the following sections, we present two separate illustrative studies, one which focuses on the development of language learner strategies by individuals, and one which looks at strategy development by a group of learners in a specific sociocultural learning situation.

Individual learner variables in context

This section of the chapter will look at LLS use in the context of individual learner variables. The effect of learner variables is a complex issue since the variables are in many ways intertwined. If, for instance, a young woman is a successful language learner, might this be related to her age or to the fact that she is female, or might there be some other factor altogether, such as motivation, personality, or nationality which explains her success? While conclusive answers to these multifaceted questions have proven to be elusive, they are, nevertheless, important questions with implications for teaching practice, as the study to be described below illustrates.

A study of learner variables

The data reported in this study were part of a larger study involving a series of interviews conducted in a private language school in Auckland, New Zealand. From among the students studying at the language school, 26 were selected to be interviewed. These interviewees were chosen to be as representative as possible of the student population, especially in terms of age, gender, nationality, and level of proficiency—the variables which were the main focus of the study at this time. The basic instrument was the 50-item version of the SILL (Oxford 1990a) designed for speakers of other languages learning English, which was used to obtain basic quantitative information about students' reported strategy use. An interview guide was also used, consisting of three main questions which dealt with the learners' key strategies, their learning difficulties, and the effects of learner variables on their success. Since it will not be possible to deal with all of the interviewees from the larger study within the space of this chapter, readers who would like more details are referred to Griffiths (2003b).

Although Griffiths' (2003b) study focused on the variables of age, gender, nationality, and proficiency, in the course of some of the interviews, insights also emerged as to the effects of other variables, including apparent level of motivation, reason for study, and personality—variables which have been examined in the literature review section above. In particular, there were five interviewees whose data provided insights regarding all of these variables. (See Table 4.1.) So, these five interviewees (Nina, Kira, Mikhail, Yuki, and Kang) are the focus of this chapter which will examine the relationship between learner variables and strategy use.

Nina

At 19, Nina had already passed the Cambridge First Certificate (FCE) examination in Germany when she arrived at the school where she planned to study for the Cambridge Advanced English (CAE) and the Cambridge Proficiency in English (CPE) examinations. After her exams, Nina planned to return to Germany to study English at a university to equip herself for a career involving English. According to the SILL, Nina used strategies at a high-frequency rate (Oxford 1990) (an average of 3.5 out of 5).

Although she allowed herself some time to go out with other students and socialize, Nina was focused on her studies. During the interview, Nina said that a key strategy she used was to always write down everything she learnt since this helped to fix it in her mind and also meant that she could revise and learn it later. With her somewhat shy personality, she had found making a conscious effort to talk to people in English the most useful strategy as a

	Nina	Kira	Mikhail	Yuki	Kang
Age	19	28	24	44	41
Gender	F	M	M	F	M
Apparent level of motivation	Strong	Strong	Weak	Weak	Strong
Reason for study	Further study/job	Job/ creative	Study/ social	Children's education	Job
Personality	Shy	Outgoing	Sociable	Unclear	Kept to himself
Nationality	German	Japanese	Russian	Japanese	Korean
Achievement	A passes in CAE & CPE	6 levels in 3 months	6 levels in 10 months	3 levels in a year	7 levels in 7 months

Table 4.1 Individual variables and achievement for the five interviewees

means of improving speaking skills, an area in which she lacked confidence. Her strategy for maximizing opportunities for practice was to live in an English-speaking environment, with a native-speaking family.

As a native speaker of German, Nina felt that she had an advantage over students from some other backgrounds because of the similarities of the languages, which made strategies such as 'relating new knowledge to what was already known' easier to deploy. Since she believed that women were more likely to study languages than men, who were more likely to be expected by others to study something practical, she felt that it was an advantage for herself to be doing something others accepted as 'normal'. When she took the CAE and CPE examinations, Nina achieved A passes in both, indicating near-native level proficiency.

Kira

Although he did not take an examination to provide an external measure of success, 28-year-old Kira from Japan made the fastest rate of progress among the interviewees in terms of moving through the levels of the school. The school operated seven levels: elementary, mid-elementary, upper elementary, pre-intermediate, mid-intermediate, upper intermediate, and advanced. Of the interviewees, Kira reported the highest average frequency of strategy use (average = 3.8). When he started his English language course, Kira was placed in a mid-elementary class. He said that he wanted to learn English in order to obtain a new job and to satisfy a creative urge to write lyrics for songs. Like Nina, Kira was focused: he knew what he wanted and he worked hard. He made excellent progress, moving through six levels (mid-elementary to advanced) in a mere three months, a remarkable rate of promotion.

During his interview, Kira was very definite and specific about his key strategies. He said that he watched television to practice listening and that he read newspapers. He spent two-to-three hours a day, working on his grammar in the self-study room. In class he always sat next to the teacher so that it was easy to ask questions, or next to the best speaker in the class so that he could use the other student's knowledge to expand his own. He did homework and lesson revision every day and talked with his host family in the evenings. With his outgoing personality, Kira used every opportunity to converse with native speakers and he kept a special notebook in which he wrote sentences. In order to give himself a break from study, on the weekends he played sports as a deliberate strategy to 'refresh himself'.

Mikhail

Compared with Nina and Kira, who both gave high-frequency ratings to numerous strategies and who achieved excellent results, Mikhail's average reported frequency of strategy use (average = 3.2) was below the high-frequency threshold of 3.5 (Oxford 1990a) and he progressed through only 0.6 of a level per month during the ten months he was at the school. Mikhail was a 24-year-old Russian who, like Kira, was initially placed in a mid-elementary class. Although managing to become fluent over the months, Mikhail's utterances included various irregular structures such as 'twenty-oneth of January', 'one month and half of holiday' and so on.

When asked about his key strategies, Mikhail said that he felt that watching television (especially American comedy) and talking to friends (especially Kiwi friends) were more important than formal study. He complained of the difficulties of English grammar, especially the tense system. As for strategies he might use to overcome the problem, he said he would more likely consult with a friend than check a grammar book.

Ostensibly, further education was Mikhail's main reason for learning English, as he was studying to be a lawyer, but he was doing it mainly to please his parents. His personal motivation for learning English was social, for the purpose of drinking and going to parties. His linguistic deficiencies suddenly became vividly apparent when he had to take the qualifying examination for law school, on which he scored well below the level he needed to pursue his (or his parents') ambitions—a failure which he himself attributed in part to his neglect of formal study strategies.

Yuki

Yuki, who was even less successful than Mikhail at being promoted in her studies (0.25 of a level per month), reported the lowest average frequency of strategy use (average = 2.1). When 44-year-old Yuki started her English language course, she had already been in New Zealand with her children on a visitor's visa for one year. Wanting to stay in New Zealand, rather than return to Japan and leave her children, she applied for a student visa, obliging her to attend school. On the *Oxford Placement Test* (Allan 1995) she scored 81, which categorized her as a 'minimal user' and she was placed in the lowest class.

Her attendance was erratic, in part because she moved four times and in part because she or her children were often sick. After being warned about breaching visa conditions, she became more regular. After four months she was moved to a mid-elementary class, and three months later to an upper-elementary class. Her ability to communicate remained low, however, and the results of the monthly tests were also unspectacular. After nearly a year at the language school, and after nearly two years in New Zealand, she was still only in the upper-elementary class.

Yuki was not easy to interview because she found it difficult to understand the questions, and, when she understood, found it difficult to express herself in English, especially in speaking and writing. While she thought that using the telephone and writing long sentences might be useful strategies to help with these difficulties, she admitted that she did not actually use either of these. As a Japanese speaker, she found English grammar difficult, but was unable to suggest strategies for dealing with the difficulty. The only key strategy she was aware of using was 'reading easy books in English'. Yuki thought English was difficult to learn because, as she put it, 'my mind is blank', a condition which she attributed to her age. Her motivation for coming to New Zealand was her children's education and she attended an English language school to obtain a student visa.

Kang

Like Yuki, Kang was in his forties, but apart from their age, they could hardly have been more different. Kang's reported strategy use was on the low side (average = 3.2) and yet he still managed to make good progress (one level per month). When the 41-year-old Korean first arrived he was initially placed in the lowest class (elementary). Despite leaving a wife and young children in Korea and obviously missing them, Kang focused single-mindedly on the task of learning English.

Notwithstanding the low-frequency ratings he gave to SILL items, Kang nevertheless mentioned a long list of key strategies during his interview, including listening to radio, watching television, and going to the movies. Kang said he consulted a textbook for vocabulary, sentence structure, and grammar, and used a notebook to write down language he picked up from signs, notices, and advertising. He kept a dictionary with him at all times and listened to people talking around him. Like Kira, he spent long hours in the self-study room revising lessons, doing homework, and listening to tapes, especially pronunciation tapes, which was the area he found most difficult. An interesting theory that he had was that pronunciation is affected by food, because different foods require different movements of the mouth and tongue. Accordingly, while in New Zealand, he purposely eschewed his Korean diet and ate Kiwi food instead.

Although being older may be disadvantageous in learning a language, Kang was more successful than many of his younger peers. Asked why he thought he had made such good progress, Kang replied, 'My heart is one hundred per cent want to learn'. Unlike Kira, Kang did not socialize a great deal with others, apparently preferring individual study strategies.

Summary of learner variables

The results of the SILL questionnaire for these five interviewees are set out in Table 4. 2 below:

	Nina	Kira	Mikhail	Yuki	Kang
SILL average	3.5	3.8	3.2	2.1	3.2
SILL items rated 5	14	19	9	0	3

Table 4.2 Strategy use for the five interviewees

Although care needs to be taken when trying to generalize from just five individuals, a comparison of the quantitative results from the strategy questionnaire above with the qualitative data summarized in Table 1 above suggests some interesting possible conclusions and some potentially useful areas for further research.

Age

Insofar as the youngest learner among the five described in this report (19-year-old Nina) was the most successful, achieving a near-native level of proficiency, the data reported here is consistent with the view that younger is generally better as held by a number of applied linguists (such as Dulay, Burt, and Krashen 1982; Harley 1986; Singleton, 1989). However, it should also be pointed out that the next youngest (Mikhail) did not achieve his learning goals, while two of the older learners (Kira and Kang) managed to make good progress. So, the results from this small set of learners do not reflect a decline in language learning ability with age, leaving 'optimism for older learners', as Ehrman and Oxford (1990: 317) put it. The possibility that older learners such as Kang tend to develop their own idiosyncratic strategy patterns which are not reflected on surveys such as the SILL (a tendency which was also displayed by 64-year-old Japanese student Hiro in the larger study by Griffiths 2003b) might form the basis of an interesting question for further research.

Gender

With regard to the view that females are better language learners than males (Ellis 1994) and the finding that they use strategies more frequently than males (Green and Oxford 1995), Nina did fit that pattern but Yuki did not. Nina did well with her studies and reported high-frequency strategy use, while Yuki did poorly and reported the lowest frequency of strategy use. Although we cannot, of course, make substantial claims from only two cases, Yuki's poor performance and infrequent use of strategies does at least indicate the need for caution when claiming any superiority for females as language learners.

Motivation

Motivation is considered by many to be a major, if not the most important, learner variable relating to success in language learning (for instance, Dörnyei 2001), and an examination of the five cases reported here seems to support this position. Nina was highly motivated to pass her exams so that she could carry on with her studies and build her career. The same focus and determination to succeed was evidenced by both Kira and Kang, and all three reported extensive strategy use (although Kang's strategy use was not reflected in high-frequency ratings on the SILL). Mikhail, however, was not really interested in his studies: he just wanted to socialize and have a good time. And Yuki had almost no interest in learning English: it was merely something she had to do in order to qualify for her student visa and stay in New Zealand with her children. This lack of motivation appeared to be reflected in Yuki's and Mikhail's reported low frequency of strategy use and slow rate of progress. In the larger study (Griffiths, 2003b), Fernando and Kim also appeared strongly motivated throughout, and both did well. In contrast, May, who took a more relaxed approach to her studies and did not want to be pressured, moved through only three levels in almost a year.

Career orientation

Of the five interviewees highlighted in this chapter, those who made faster progress were those who wanted to learn English to further their careers. Although their career goals were different, Nina, Kira, and Kang all appeared highly motivated and reported large strategy repertoires, suggesting that, for these three at least, the exact nature of the career orientation might not be as important as the existence of a career goal. Although Mikhail's parents had ambitions for their son to become a lawyer, Mikhail himself was not interested in a legal career, while Yuki was not interested in a career at all, only in her family. Mikhail's and Yuki's lack of career motivation may well have been reflected in their non-strategic approach to their learning and in their slow progress. Another possible example of language learning influenced by a lack of career motivation might be that of May from the larger study (Griffiths 2003b). The reasons for May's studying English were rather amorphous, expressed rather vaguely in terms of wanting to 'change my life'. The possibility that lack of clear goals may be related to lesser achievement might be worthy of further research with larger numbers of participants.

Personality

This study did not use a measure of personality such as the Myers-Briggs Type Indicator, and so the variable was only able to be used as a basis for comments as to the personalities of the interviewees in the most general terms. However, the data obtained from the interviews reported in this chapter would not seem to support the common belief that extroverts are better language learners. While both Kira and Nina reported frequent use of strategies and did well in their studies, the former had an outgoing personality and the latter was rather shy and spoke of needing to make a conscious effort to interact with others. Kang was more like Nina in preferring to keep to himself, while highly sociable Mikhail, who appeared to have an extroverted personality, reportedly used strategies infrequently, and made slow progress in his studies. The data therefore seem to suggest that there was no clear pattern for these five learners as to the relationship between the extraversion/introversion dimension of personality and language learning success.

Nationality

According to Griffiths (2003b), European students reported higher average frequency of strategy use than non-European students, and they were also working at higher levels of English. Explanations given for this finding included similarities in educational systems and in culture, as well as similarities in graphic systems, lexical patterns, and grammatical structures. The results from this sub-sample of five learners highlights the fact that while Nina from Germany was the best student with a reportedly high frequency of strategy use, the other European, Mikhail from Russia made slower progress and used strategies less frequently than Kira from Japan and Kang from Korea. Other successful Asian students in the larger study (2003b) include Kim from Korea and Hiro from Japan. Thus, it would appear that, although Europeans may have certain advantages when learning English, non-Europeans can learn successfully, especially with the judicious use of strategies.

Proficiency

The interview data generally supported the findings from the studies by Green and Oxford (1995) and by Griffiths (2003a) that more proficient students tend to make frequent use of a large number of strategies. This was especially true of Nina and Kira, both successful students who made frequent use of a large repertoire of strategies. Mikhail and Yuki, on the other hand, were both relatively low-frequency strategy users, and both made relatively slow progress in learning English. At first glance, the statistics on strategy averages seem to indicate that Kang was an exception to this trend since he made good progress in spite of a relatively low frequency of reported strategy use. Yet the interviews tell a different story, since it became clear that, like another learner, Hiro, described in the full study (Griffiths 2003b), Kang actually had a large number of frequently employed strategies of his own which were not included on the SILL.

Summary and directions for further research

The finding regarding the patterns of Kang's strategy use underlines the importance of triangulation and of using more than one method to approach a research question, since the real extent of his strategy use was not apparent from the questionnaire alone. Kang's case also seems to indicate that, although younger may generally be better in language learning, older learners can be successful language learners. In addition, motivation, especially in the form of career orientation, does seem to be related to both strategy use and the development of proficiency. It must be stressed that, focusing on just five of 26 students makes any conclusions simply suggestive. While the study described in this section of the chapter has focused on individual variables, it has become increasingly evident that we also need to consider the *situation* in which the individual operates in order to better understand the relationship between language learner strategies and learning outcomes (for instance, Norton and Toohey 2001). Individual differences may be either psycholinguistic or sociocultural, but group differences are inevitably sociocultural. Thus, in the final section of the chapter, the sociocultural learning situation will be explored.

Strategic classrooms—a macro view

This final section of the chapter considers how the social setting for learning, i.e. the classroom, can foster the development of language learner strategies. Inspired by the early work of Donato and McCormick (1994: 462) where 'the classroom culture was itself strategic', this approach provides an exploratory lens through which language learner strategies can be studied within the social context of the classroom.

In the first section of this chapter, research findings were presented (Reiss 1985; Scarcella and Oxford 1992) which suggest that teaching methods and the learning context can significantly influence learner strategies. Moreover, a study by Anton (1999) demonstrated how the social setting of the classroom encourages learners to try new strategies and use other learners as resources. Breen (1985) also advocated that classrooms should be studied as complex activity systems in their own right.

The study

The study reported on here foregrounds contextual factors and discursive practices as a catalyst for strategic activity. The study was predicated on two premises drawn from sociocultural theory:

1 Language learner strategies potentially lead to effective learning. Effective learning involves the learner being in control (i.e. using self-regulation).
2 Effective learning also involves assistance or scaffolded guidance (Wood, Bruner, and Ross 1976). For learners to progress they need assistance in the learning zone by objects, symbols, peers, and teachers (i.e. through mediated activity).

This research explores socially-constructed learning within a classroom community which promotes the development of emergent strategic events. It analyzes classroom interaction involving mediated activity, self-regulation, and other observable strategic behaviors in order to conceptualize further the construct of 'strategic classrooms' (Coyle 1999). The data from this study will be used to define 'strategic classrooms' towards the end of this chapter.

The classroom as a 'learning community'

Drawing on sociocultural theory, a learning community is the locus of learning comprising a physical, cognitive, and social space. A 'learning community' in this study explores the classroom as an interpersonal space where 'minds meet and new understandings can arise through collaborative interaction or inquiry' (Cummins 2005: 105). It refers to the social settings of the classroom, its ethos and culture, and the relationships within it which impact on learning. The study is based in a class of 11-year-old beginner learners of German in a secondary school in the UK. The class had 28 students in a 'mixed-ability' group. There were seven lessons per 2-week block, each lesson lasting 55 minutes.

The school was selected for three reasons. First, the teacher had already started building a 'learning community' with the researchers through previous pilot work and was willing to participate in the study. Second, the foreign language department had an excellent reputation, with early high-level student achievement. And finally, the learners were taught in a mixed-ability setting and would continue to be grouped accordingly for the following three years, which enabled longitudinal study into the development of a strategic classroom.

Design of the study

The following data were collected over the period of one year:

- video-recorded lesson observations complemented with field notes by 'insider' researchers (six cycles of three consecutive lessons involving interactions between teacher, learners, and researchers, producing 16½ hours of data)
- audio-recorded teacher–researcher reflective conversations (pre-, mid-, and post-research cycles)
- audio-recorded learner–researcher interviews: a random sample of students selected for one-to-one reflective interviews conducted in English about strategic learning towards the end of the year
- an audio-recorded interactive speaking task in German to facilitate comparison of the learner cohort with national norms as a measure of effective learning.

Data analysis

Data collected were analyzed using grounded techniques to lead to a clearer definition of 'strategic classrooms'. This meant that any significant inter-actions and events during a lesson were collated in a series of clips. The clips were analyzed in order to investigate the occurrence of different types of strategic behaviors which would lead to a deeper understanding of strategic classrooms. The analytic tool used to select the clips was an adaptation of Tripp's (1994) 'critical incident' (CI) technique. CIs are significant incidents which occur in everyday events. They provide evidence of learning goals shared between the teacher and learners—i.e. the construction of strategic learning. CIs are selected using pre-negotiated criteria, in this case capturing short classroom 'events' which the person/s making the choices believe/s impacted on or contributed to successful learning and teaching. CIs are usually no more than a few minutes in duration.

A practical issue in this study was that the teacher did not have the time to revisit all 18 recorded lessons to select and edit CIs from the videos. Therefore, the two researchers selected the CIs independently and then negotiated these during the second and third reflective conversation cycles (RCs) with the teacher. Subsequent coding of CIs led to an edited and manageable catalog of strategic classroom events which allowed interpretation, reflection, and discussion by teachers, researchers, and learners. A rich co-constructed picture of learner and teacher classroom behaviors emerged.

In terms of measurable outcomes with respect to 'effective learning', student oral skills were recorded using an interactive speaking task. An eight-level National Curriculum scale is used to measure attainment during the first five years of secondary education in England. While the national expected range for German speaking skills would be levels 1 to 3, the levels within this mixed-ability class after just one year of learning the language ranged between levels 3 and 5. The aim here is not to justify a causal link between achievement and classroom behaviors, but rather to provide a deeper understanding of strategic activity and its potential impact on learning, i.e. to understand better the development of language learner strategies as a classroom by-product (Donato and McCormick 1994).

Findings

Three strands emerge from the data which appear to impact on the develop-ment of classroom interaction—the core of socially strategic activity.

1 Impact of teacher goal-orientation on creating learning contexts

Here is an extract from the first reflective conversation before the start of classes between the teacher (T) and researcher (R):

Extract T1.1

T I think I respond according to a set of goals which I have in my head and which are (a) you've got to get as much out of each kid as possible without giving it to them, and (b) you've got to encourage them and help them …

R So would you say that those were the two main principles …?

T Getting them to say what they want … and I think the scaffolding comes from the encouraging principle … I suppose it's getting maximum output from them out of minimum input from me and getting them used to it in as many different ways as possible…

In defining her goals, the teacher reveals her high expectations of students. She makes subtle reference to challenging learners to think for themselves and to achieve self-regulation whilst working towards learner independence.

Here is an extract from the second reflective conversation between teacher and researcher midway through the cycles:

Extract T2.3

T … the further you get through the year … you're building a wall and then it starts building itself in a way. You've given them a few bricks and I'm just building one little bit of the wall, but they are building bits of it over here and over here as well.

… I'm certainly helping them put the bricks on. I'm kind of putting my hand in now and again and saying this is where it goes, but I think a lot of the stuff, I think maybe it's with giving them the freedom to do the building themselves.

The second principle clearly frames her understanding of mediated activity in supporting and encouraging learners to achieve the above. CI data confirmed that these behaviors and their consequences were played out constantly during lessons and are transparent in the ways learners and teachers interact.

Here is an extract from the third reflective post-cycles discussion:

Extract T3.7

T When you first start off it's kind of everything—it's language awareness, it's talking strategies, it's the confidence thing …

2 Impact of shared/negotiated goal-orientation between learners and teachers in co-constructing the learning context

The following data, extracted from CIs, summarize classroom expectations which were co-constructed by the teacher and learners. These expectations were not presented to the learners as a set of rules. Instead they emerged, were discussed and constructed during the first few months, and were revisited as appropriate during the year. They not only reflect the importance of teacher goals, but also indicate how these must become shared goals if they are to impact on the ways in which learners learn to interact in the classroom:

- We can all use German as our language of communication
- We will help each other in different ways to use German
- We can interrupt the teacher whenever we like, provided it is in German
- Individual problems are shared problems
- Be patient and help other people to work out what they want to say or write
- We are expected to ask questions or discuss things with the teacher as well as each other
- *Warum?* 'Why?' is one of the most important words. Use it.

Here are a series of extracts involving students (S).

Extract S1.3

S1   Miss helps us to work out what we want to say us selves (sic.).

R   How exactly?

S1   It depends, but we learnt immediately how to ask for explanations and meanings in the first lesson so that everyone could start off until we got stuck. Then we knew to ask stuff like *Wie sagt Man auf Deutsch*.

Extract S2.6

S2   She encourages us to start off without knowing how we'll finish, and that was scary at first but I got used to it, and now it doesn't matter coz it's the same for everybody.
I like speaking in German and inventing things. We use the back of our vocab books for our own personal vocab, and we sometimes play word games to see if we can guess other people's words. I remember things because we use them and the phrases on the wall are always there ... or we hear Miss or our friends using the words we need. It just goes in because we talk a lot in German.

Extract S3.2

S3   We are encouraged to interrupt her whenever we wanted to speak, so that made us all want to speak out. We do it all the time. It's normal.

R   So what happens when you don't understand?

S3   Miss helps us when we are stuck—she gives us advice about how we might learn our homework then we try to find someone else who does it in the same way. We also tell her if we don't understand and say something like *Ich habe ein Problem* or something, and then she helps us but she doesn't tell us straight.

Extract S3.7

S3   We do lots of role-plays and little discussions. We know about *why?* Someone is meant to lead ... we sometimes discuss with Dr W [one of the researchers accessible via video conferencing] about our progress ... .We get merits for asking questions too, so some people do it all the time.

Extract S6.2

s6 We get used to talking German in front of the class. We sometimes have to give presentations or teach other members of the class about something we want to ...

R So what do you do to prepare for this?

s6 We work in groups and decide what we want to say we ask Miss or Dr W for words we don't know ... or ... we look them up in the dictionary or we use the wall. Sometimes we are allowed to write down key prompts, but that is all.

The significance of co-constructing or 'living' these goals is very different from more traditional classroom rules fixed to the wall. The almost exclusive use of the target language by the teacher is matched by the expectation that the students and researchers will also use German. However, with beginning learners this meant that the students needed to develop a range of strategies (communication, cognitive, metacognitive, social) to construct meaning. Again this underlines the importance of the context in determining the type of learner strategies developed and used. Extensive use of the target language required effective scaffolding techniques to be used not only by the teachers but also by her learners with each other. To respond to the dynamic nature of linguistic progression in the mixed-ability setting, mediation took on different forms according to individual needs. Encouraging students to self-regulate also required the teacher to exercise judgment in sharing the 'control' of linguistic direction—for example, student interruptions, student initiation of conversation, and discussion with each other and herself.

3 Impact of emerging activity patterns (interaction, mediation, and self-regulation) by individuals contributing to the learning context

From the CI analysis and subsequent reflective conversations between teacher and researcher, three significant categories of activities emerged, which were substantiated by regular occurrences during lessons and confirmed by the participants. These are the development of a range of learner strategies by a range of learners, systematic mediated learning and scaffolding, and progression in working towards self-regulation. Each of these categories will now be illustrated by data extracts.

a Development of a range of learner strategies by a range of learners such as using limited language to express genuine messages
  Lesson Cycle 1.3.7 (September 1st month)
  L *Ich habe ein Problem.* [I have a problem.]
   Äh, nein Buch. [Errr, no book...]

  т *Du hast das vergessen.* [You've forgotten it.]
  ʟ *Ja.* [Yes.]
  т *Aber das ist dein Buch.* [But that's your book.]
  ʟ *Ja,ähm...* [Yes, errr, ...] *für deutsch ja, für alles ... nein.* [for German yes, for all ... no.]

b Systematic mediated learning and scaffolding by the teacher and the learners for the learners
  Lesson Cycle 5.1.4 (March 7th month)
  ʟɪ *Indie Wochenende mein deutsches Freund Vater kommt aus England.* [On the weekend, my German friend's father came from England.] *aeh, fuer ein ... wie sagt man 'conference'?* [errr, for a ... how do you say 'conference'?]
  т *Konferenz. Konferenz.* [Conference. Conference.]
  ʟɪ *Fuer ein Konferenz...* [For a conference ...]
  ʟɪ *MeinFreunds Vater ... wie sagt man 'gave me' auf deutsch?* [My friend's father ... how do you say 'gave me' in German?]
  т (to rest of class) *Wie koennte man das sagen? Ja?* [How could you say that? Yes?]
  ʟ3 *Gegeben mich.* [Me given.]
  т *gegeben. In der Vergangenheit.* [Given. In the past.]
  ʟɪ *Er ist...* [He is ...] (making drinking action)
  ʟ5 (other) *Er hat ...* [He has ...]
  т *Milch? Zum Trinken?* [Milk? For drinking?]
  ʟɪ *Aeh,nein. Wie sagt man 'glass' auf deutsch?* [Errr, no. How do you say 'glass' in German?]
  т *Oh, das haben wir gelernt.* [Oh, we have learned that.]
  ʟ3, 5, 7 (others) *Tasse.* [Cup.]
  т *Eine Tasse oder ein Glas.* [A cup or a glass.]
  ʟ *Aeh... ein Glas ...* [Errr ... A glass ...]

c Progression involved working towards self-regulation
  By the ninth month linguistic progression was marked by learner strategies based increasingly on self-regulation as well as other-regulation. Self-regulation strategies included self-correction, independent dictionary use, self-expression, use of argument, use of other students, and circumlocution.

Implications

The study set out to understand better how the classroom setting might impact on learning and in particular 'strategic learning'. It would appear that shared goals have an impact on classroom interaction where the classroom is seen as a learning community and learning is valued. Data in this study included examples of learners' strategic use of language both for and with others. Since goals are socially-constructed, this research concurs with that of Gillette (1994) suggesting that the classroom context has a crucial role to play in learner strategy use. The teacher encouraged learners to talk about the problems they were experiencing and to share learning strategies that work for them with each other.

The following types of mediation strategies were in evidence, enabling learners to 'piece together' or construct what they wanted/needed to express:

- The scaffolding of utterances by the teacher and peers to empower learners to say what they wanted to
- The occasional use of English (the mother tongue) to support learning
- The encouragement of self-regulation through an expectation that students would initiate utterances. (This was more important as the year progressed, and there was a fine balance between teacher-led and learner-led utterances.)
- Learning to respond and initiate dialog centered on the question 'why?'
- The operationalization of different types of peer support to assist learner strategy development.

These features when woven together form the foundations of a learning community—with shared goals and transparent strategic activity.

The strategic classroom: the construct

The findings of this study suggest that by considering macro- as well as micro-perspectives, i.e. by exploring not only individual learner strategies but also the classroom as a learning community, the resulting 'strategic classroom' has a contribution to make to understanding effective learning. The data analyzed in this case study are not intended for making exaggerated claims, but simply for attempting to explore how social settings impact on strategic activity.

Strategic learning contexts make maximum use of affective, cognitive, metacognitive, and social learner strategies to influence effective learning communities. Strategic classrooms therefore have a genuine contribution to make to a wider understanding of learner strategy research since learning is both individual and social (Wegerif *et al.* 1999):

> From a socio-cultural perspective, the classroom culture can be designed to move students beyond thoughtful consumption to reflective construction of language learning strategies.
> *Donato and McCormick 1994: 463*

Summary of strategic classroom study and directions for further research

Focusing on the social setting, the strategic classroom study was built on a transparent understanding between learners and teachers of ways in which, for example, learners self-regulate, tasks become co-constructed activities, the target language is used strategically, and interaction is perceived as pivotal to learning by both teachers and learners. In such contexts learners develop strategies which involve co-operation, meaning making in a collaborative environment, understanding how to scaffold others and how to be scaffolded, and how to become independent language users. Learner strategies from this perspective are inextricably linked to learner variables such as age, gender, motivation, personality, nationality/culture/ethnicity, and level of proficiency, since these factors all influence the way individuals interact in a given situation. It would seem to be self-evident that future research, rather than trying to isolate these many variables from each other as much previous research has done, needs to develop methods for including consideration of the multiple factors which affect the ways that individual learners learn in specific situations.

Conclusion

This chapter has looked at language learner strategies in the context of both individual learner variables and the learning situation. The learner variables considered were age, gender, motivation, career orientation, personality, nationality/culture/ethnicity, and level of proficiency/achievement. Although this is not an exhaustive list of all possible factors which make one learner different from another—other possibilities might include, for instance, aptitude, learning style, or beliefs—the individual variables dealt with in this chapter represent some of the most commonly researched. The exploration of the learning situation, meanwhile, has led to the conclusion that learners learn best in an environment where students are supported, where goals are shared, and where strategic activity is transparent.

Overall, the findings from the two empirical studies reported on here would seem to suggest that the individual and situational context in which a learner operates is complex. Learners bring to the learning situation their own individual set of characteristics which influence the outcomes. The aim of strategic classrooms is to foster the development of strategies which will help learners to manage the contextual complexities and achieve a successful outcome given their personal language learning goals. Research to determine how these successful outcomes might best be managed in the context of a wide range of individual and situational variables remains an ongoing challenge for the future.

Note

1   i.e. listing related words, using mechanical tricks to aid memory, making up sentences and exercises on one's own, elaborating sentences, outlining main ideas, using a tape recorder, planning on a daily or weekly basis, writing summaries, highlighting while reading, and testing oneself.

5

Research methods in strategy research: re-examining the toolbox

CYNTHIA WHITE, KAREN SCHRAMM, and ANNA UHL CHAMOT

Introduction

In the 30 years of investigation of language learner strategies (LLS), attention has been directed towards developing and refining tools to investigate the mental processes of learners in understanding, remembering, and using a new language, in both descriptive and intervention studies. As Breen (2001a: 175) observes, researchers have found 'diverse' and 'imaginative' ways to gain access to learners' accounts of the means they use to learn the target language. At the same time new standards of research have developed based on experience with different kinds of data and data-gathering methods (McDonough 1999). An ongoing concern has been to acknowledge the limitations of self-report instruments used to access learners' mental processing (for example, Cohen 1998; Grenfell and Harris 1999), while continuing to refine instruments and the ways in which they are used in order to minimize such limitations.

Problems inherent in strategy research are also common to the study of such areas as learner motivation and beliefs, and can be seen as relating to two broad areas. Firstly, strategies are, for the most part, not directly observable since they refer to internal, mental processes, and researchers must rely on learner accounts as indirect indicators of these mental processes. Verbal reports have emerged as one of the key ways of accessing strategy use, and methodological developments and issues in relation to obtaining and transcribing verbal report data are discussed in the chapter. Secondly, strategy use is not a fixed attribute of individuals, but changes according to the task, the learning conditions, and the available time. The challenges associated with acknowledging and capturing the variable and dynamic nature of strategy use are also examined.

With major advances in quantitative research methodology made in the field of language learner strategy research (for example, Hsiao and Oxford 2002; Vandergrift, Goh, Mareschal, and Tafaghodtari 2006), an extensive coverage of the methodological refinement of strategy research is beyond the scope of this chapter. We therefore focus on emerging qualitative data-collection procedures and context-sensitive research approaches that enlarge the methodological toolbox of strategy researchers and might strengthen their endeavors in future strategy studies involving mixed-methods designs. In the early part of the chapter we provide a general, brief overview of the main research traditions in LLS research as a background for a more detailed analysis of issues in think-aloud studies, and recent methodological refinements. Following on from this we argue for the value of a contextual approach to developing an understanding of learner strategy use, how it relates to students' experiences and the actions they take as learners. We then consider methodological applications in two relatively new research contexts—online language learning and the learning of heritage languages. The final section of the chapter points to the value of widening research methods to include action research approaches. It is argued that collaborative action research has much to offer in extending and illuminating our understanding of learner strategies, in strengthening the often tenuous links between theory, research, and practice, and in demonstrating the ongoing relevance of language learner strategy research.

Research tools and practices

As described through overviews of research methods for investigating LLS (for example, Cohen and Scott 1996; Macaro 2001; Mackey and Gass 2005), methods to investigate strategies include oral interviews, questionnaires, observation, verbal reports, diaries and journals, and recollection studies. In this section we highlight research tools and practices as background to a more detailed examination of verbal report methods. While we consider the methods individually, it should be noted that researchers generally combine methods to investigate and analyze strategy use in order to provide interpretive clarity and to avoid the criticism that the method predetermines the results obtained.

Retrospective interviews were among the earliest techniques used to investigate LLS (for example, Rubin 1975; Naiman, Fröhlich, Stern, and Todesco 1978/1996), and have remained an important tool largely because of the flexibility they afford the interviewer to seek clarification and elaboration from learners. As the field moves towards a deeper understanding of strategy use influenced by particular cultural, contextual, and individual factors (discussed later as the contextual turn in strategy research), retrospective interviews re-emerge as an important tool providing opportunities for exploration and elaboration of aspects of strategy use.

The most frequently used and efficient method for ascertaining learner strategies is through self-report questionnaires (Cohen 1998; Oxford 1996a). The *Strategy Inventory for Language Learning* (SILL) developed by Oxford (1990a) has been deployed extensively to measure perceived strategy use and its relationship to other variables such as learning styles, gender, proficiency level, culture, and task (Oxford and Nyikos 1989; Nyikos and Oxford 1993; Green and Oxford 1995; Bedell and Oxford 1996; Wharton 2000; Bruen 2001). With more than 30 doctoral dissertations (Oxford, personal communication) and a number of refereed articles based on the SILL, it is without doubt the most widely used instrument in language learner strategy research. Oxford and Nyikos (1989: 292) as well as Nyikos and Oxford (1993: 14) provide evidence for the SILL's reliability and validity:

> Internal consistency reliability using Cronbach's alpha is .96 based on a 1,200-person university sample (in the current study) and .95 based on a 483-person Defense Language Institute (DLI) field text sample (…). Content validity is .95 using a classificatory agreement between two independent raters who blindly matched each of the SILL items with strategies in the comprehensive taxonomy (…). Concurrent, and to some extent construct, validity can be assumed based on the demonstration of strong relationships between SILL factors and self-ratings of language proficiency and language motivation, as reported in this article. Additional evidence supporting validity is found in a different study by Ehrman and Oxford (…) [i.e. 1989] in which more highly trained linguists, in contrast to less highly trained linguists, predictably reported significantly more frequent and more wide-ranging use of strategies on the SILL.
>
> *Oxford and Nyikos 1989: 292*

The SILL evolved to include versions for English as a Second Language (ESL) and a variety of foreign languages, as the scope of research into strategy use expanded. With the ESL/EFL version of the SILL Cronbach alphas within the range of .91 to .95 were found when the SILL was used in translation among different populations of EFL learners in Taiwan (Yang 1992), Japan (Watanabe 1990), and Korea (Oh 1992). More recently classification theories of language learner strategies were compared in a study by Hsiao and Oxford (2002). Using confirmatory factor analysis on results from the ESL/EFL version of the SILL given by 517 college EFL learners, Hsiao and Oxford found that Oxford's taxonomy of six strategy factors provided the most consistent fit with learners' strategy use.

Generally, self-report questionnaires are seen to have three potential limitations: learners may not understand or interpret accurately the strategy description in each item, may claim to use strategies they do not use, and may fail to recall strategies they have used in the past. An important development in addressing these methodological concerns has been to base the questionnaire on a task students have recently completed. (See Chamot and El-Dinary 1999; National Capital Language Resource Center [NCLRC] 2000a,b; Fan 2003; Vandergrift, Goh, Mareschal, and Tafaghodtari 2006; Cohen and Weaver 2006.) Accordingly, Oxford and co-researchers foreshadow the development of a task-based questionnaire to complement the SILL, arising out of the rationale they outline for task-based strategy assessment. A valuable element in any task-based questionnaire, they suggest, is to allow learners to identify their own strategies not captured by the researcher-provided or teacher-provided items (Oxford, Cho, Leung, and Kim 2004).

The *Language Strategies Survey* (LSS) developed by Cohen, Oxford, and Chi broke new ground as a skill-based means of researching strategy use (Cohen, Oxford, and Chi 2003). In a study of the impact of strategy instruction on language and culture learning during study abroad, the LSS was revised to consist of 89 items covering skills of listening, speaking, reading, writing, vocabulary, and translation (Paige, Cohen, and Shively 2004). Confirmatory factor analysis was performed on the LLS with a sample of 300 tertiary students in French and Spanish classes. Results indicated that the model was a 'fair, if not robust, fit with the data' (Paige, Cohen, and Shively 2004: 264). The five factors (Learning Structure and Vocabulary, Speaking, Listening, Reading, and Asking for Clarification) had reliability coefficients ranging from .67 to .85. The LSS together with the *Strategies Inventory for Learning Culture* were both found to be reliable and valid measures of strategy use in a new domain, namely study abroad, providing 'strong initial support for the integrity of these instruments as measures of the underlying theoretical models upon which they are based' (Paige *et al.* 2004: 273).

Three other examples of questionnaire refinement come from the fields of reading and listening. The *Metacognitive Awareness of Reading Strategies Inventory* (MARSI) developed by Mokhtari (1998–2000) was validated using a large native speaker population (N = 825) and tested for its internal consistency reliability which was .92 on the metacognitive subscale, .79 on the cognitive subscale, and .87 on the support strategies subscale; reliability for the overall scale was .93. (See Sheorey and Mokhtari 2001: 435.) This measure was adapted for non-native speakers of English by eliminating two redundant items and by modifying the wording of some items. The revised *Survey of Reading Strategies* (SORS) was then pilot-tested on ESL students (N = 147) and its overall reliability was established with a Cronbach's alpha of .89. (See Sheorey and Mokhtari 2001: 436.)

Another instrument, the *Metacognitive Awareness Listening Questionnaire* (MALQ), was developed by Vandergrift *et al.* (2006). The MALQ is designed to assess listeners' metacognitive awareness and perceived use of strategies while listening to oral texts, and can be used for self-assessment, diagnosis, and research purposes. The instrument was trialed and validated with approximately 1,000 learners in different countries and learning contexts. The 21-item questionnaire has high internal validity and does not aim to include all possible listening strategies, but those relating to the five distinct factors which emerged: problem-solving, planning and evaluation, mental translation, person knowledge, and directed attention. Vandergrift *et al.* (2006: 446) report respectable Cronbach's alpha reliabilities ranging from .68 to .78, and they submitted their five-factor model to confirmatory factor analysis. They established a significant relationship between the reported listening strategies and actual listening performance, and interpreted their regression analysis to verify a meaningful relationship between metacognition and listening comprehension success (Vandergrift *et al.* 2006: 452).

Finkbeiner's (2005) recent study on reading comprehension was also based on newly developed questionnaires for measuring interest in EFL text comprehension (ITEF), EFL learner strategies for text comprehension (LEFT), and EFL text comprehension (CTEF). Finkbeiner based the ITEF on various interest questionnaires that have been extensively researched with regard to their reliability and validity such as, for example, Schiefele, Krapp, Wild, and Winteler's (1992, 1993) 'Study Interest Questionnaire', and she adapted the metrologically best items to English classroom learning. She provided a detailed literature review and discussion of operationalization issues as a theoretical validation for item construction. For internal consistency on the ITEF, she reported Cronbach's alphas ranging from .66 to .88 (Finkbeiner 2005: 335); and for the LEFT, she reported Cronbach's alphas ranging between .55 and .85 (Finkbeiner 2005: 332).

Besides questionnaires, during the past decades written diaries, logs, and journals have secured a place as 'important introspective tools in language research' (Nunan 1992: 118) and as a means of tapping into students' perspectives on how they learn. In some cases the diary is an open-ended instrument in that writers note down anything that comes to mind in reaction to learner strategies. In others, more guidelines are given. (See, for example, Nunan 1996.) Halbach (2000) argued that one of the advantages of using diaries to investigate learner strategies is that the texts can be analyzed in different ways, from different perspectives: in her study they were used to shed light on learners' strategy use, to provide evidence of the impact of strategy training, to note changes in strategy use, and for developing a seven-item rating scale to evaluate strategy use. While diaries and reflective journals may not provide fully accurate or complete insights into learner strategies, they may have another important function of raising students' metacognitive awareness of themselves and of their language learning (Riley and Harsch 1999; Rubin 2003).

A further development in research methodology is the use of e-journals as a means for learners to reflect on their strategy use while involved in language learning in areas and contexts remote from those of the researcher. Paige, Cohen, and Shively (2004) included e-journals to assess the impact of a strategy-based curriculum on language and culture learning in the context of study abroad. They were used as an open-ended means of collecting data at regular intervals (twice a week) requiring students to reflect on assigned sections of the guide entitled *Maximizing Study Abroad: A Students' Guide to Language and Culture Strategies and Use*. In addition, they were asked to reflect on their own experiences, and their experiences in relation to the assigned reading. The e-journals were complemented by interviews, question-naires, and profiles. Preliminary analysis of the e-journals suggests that students valued the way in which the journaling enabled them to make links between the world of learning in the guide, and their experiences during study abroad. Thus the e-journaling was useful in accessing students' reflections in the field, as well as in structuring their reflections and use of the guide. (See Cohen, Paige, Shively, Emert, and Hoff 2005, for the final research report on this study.)

A recurrent argument in language learner strategy research is that observation is a limited research tool since it does not capture mental processes (Rubin 1975; Naiman *et al.* 1978/1996; O'Malley and Chamot 1990; Wenden 1991; Cohen 1998). In a study of the range of note-taking strategies used in language learning, White (1995a) commented that observation used in conjunction with verbal report procedures while learners complete a task can reveal further complexities about strategies which function as traces of cognition as in noting down, writing out, listing, and underlining. More recently Macaro (2001) revisited the place of observation in strategy research and highlighted the contributions it could make to classroom-based research. Teachers, for example, may observe the extent to which students are 'buying processing time' through the use of discourse markers such as 'uh' and 'mmm' for holding their place in the discourse, rather than yielding their turn. Other examples given by Macaro (2001: 66) include teacher awareness of how students approach a task—whether they begin directly or spend time planning, the extent and frequency of dictionary use in relation to particular tasks, the use of peer support, and the use of compensation strategies such as circumlocution. While there are limits on what can be inferred from such observations, within the paradigm of classroom-based action research on LLS, for example, observation holds an important place. We return to this theme later in the chapter.

Think-aloud protocols, a specific type of verbal report, have been used extensively in strategy research projects, and, arguably, developments in the use of verbal report measures represent one of the main methodological contributions from strategy research to the field of second language (L2) acquisition.[1] This is the subject of the next section.

General issues in introspection

Introspection usually involves the researcher asking the subjects to verbalize their thoughts, feelings, motives, reasoning processes, and mental states (Nunan 1992: 115). This method of data collection can be used in experimental as well as non-experimental settings and the data collected in verbal reports can be analyzed statistically or interpretively (Grotjahn 1987).

Introspection has had a long and controversial history. (See Ericsson and Simon 1984/1993, 1993.) The strong reliance on classical introspection during the early days of psychological research became the object of major criticism from behaviorists. (See, for example, Watson 1930: 6.) Consequently, psychologists hardly used introspection for decades until cognitive science emerged. Ericsson and Simon (1984/1993: 61) summarized the criticism of the few authors who discussed the method in this anti-introspective context (for example, Verplanck 1962; Nisbett and Wilson 1977) as

1 the *effect-of-verbalization argument* (i.e. that verbalization changes cognitive processes),
2 the *incompleteness argument* (i.e. that protocols are incomplete and therefore do not reveal the cognitive processes completely), and
3 the *epiphenomenality* or *irrelevance argument* (i.e. that subjects report parallel activities that are independent of the actual mental processes, and that are therefore irrelevant).

In their detailed discussion of these arguments Ericsson and Simon (1980, 1984/1993, 1987) refute such general rejection of introspective methods. (See also Deffner 1984, 1987, 1988; Ericsson 1988; Garner 1988; Pritchard 1990b; Howe 1991; Jourdenais 2001; Aguado 2004; Leow and Morgan-Short 2004; Heine 2005.)[2] They come to the conclusion that reliable data cannot be gathered when subjects are asked to give reports on information that they usually do not pay attention to (for example, causes) or when they are asked to give generalized reports after several performances. However, two kinds of verbal report emerge as strong research tools from their analysis: concurrent reports, and retrospective reports of specific cognitive processes (Ericsson and Simon 1984/1993: 30). We will use the example of think-alouds—that is the simultaneous verbalization of thoughts during a specific task—to discuss methodological refinement and issues in the elicitation and transcription in some detail.

Issues in eliciting think-aloud data

Our discussion of issues in eliciting think-aloud data will focus on how to train and prompt subjects, especially young learners, in thinking aloud, on what to consider when choosing a language for think-aloud, and finally on how to integrate data collection unobtrusively into an authentic context (see also Heine and Schramm 2007).

1 Training and prompting

Much of the research in both first and second or foreign language contexts using verbal reports such as think-alouds has provided little information about key aspects of this methodology, such as the tasks and directions given to subjects (Afflerbach 2000). Since both the type of task and how students are asked to respond can influence the kind and quality of their thinking aloud, an understanding of the specifics in past research can assist in the development of research methodology that is consistent across studies and therefore useful for purposes of comparison. This is particularly important when studying younger learners whose metacognitive processes guiding their ability to report on their own thinking are in the process of development (Dominowski 1998).

Techniques adapted to the ages of the subjects were used in a six-year study of English-speaking children (aged 6–10) in foreign language immersion programs in the United States (Chamot, Keatley, Barnhardt, El-Dinary, Nagano, and Newman 1996; Chamot 1999; Chamot and El-Dinary 1999). An important first step was to select materials and tasks that would be interesting to children of these ages. Teachers from the immersion classrooms identified authentic children's literature unfamiliar to the children and ordered them according to reading difficulty in each of the target languages: French, Japanese, and Spanish. In addition, teachers helped researchers identify a set of six colorful pictures, also from children's books, that could be used as writing prompts. Finally, the teachers identified a simple logic problem that could be used for think-aloud training purposes.

Before each interview four small paper cups containing prizes such as erasers, stickers, pencils, and toy animals were placed upside down (to hide the contents) on the desk where the child would sit. In addition, puzzle pieces were placed upside down in front of the researcher. Children were interviewed individually, and the interviewer used both English and the target language, telling the children that they could do likewise. After preliminary discussion explaining that the researchers wanted to find out about the kinds of things they thought about while learning, the actual training was divided into four segments. The interviewer said: 'We will do four different things: a puzzle, a problem, a little reading, and a little writing. After each activity I'll ask you to turn over a cup and you'll find a little prize. This is to thank you for helping us' (Chamot *et al.* 1996: A17). The interviewer then modeled thinking aloud with the puzzle, turning over puzzle pieces and explaining his or her reasoning for determining where to place each puzzle piece. The script for this modeling was memorized by each interviewer to maintain consistency across interviews. After about five minutes, the interviewer stopped, asked the children to tell what they remembered about what the interviewer had said while modeling, and reinforced the children's responses. Then the children were asked to select and turn over one of the paper cups covering the small prizes.

In the second activity, the children practiced thinking aloud with a logic problem consisting of drawings of T-shirts of different colors and patterns. The interviewer said, 'There is a boy named Gus. He likes *this* T-shirt [pointing to it], but he doesn't like *these* T-shirts [pointing to them]. Can you figure out which ones he likes? Before you start, what are you thinking?' (Chamot *et al.* 1996: A18). Throughout this and subsequent parts of the interview, prompts like 'What are you thinking?' 'What's going through your mind?' were used. After about five minutes the children were praised, thanked, and told to select another cup with prizes under it.

With the third activity the children began to think aloud while reading part of a story with lines marked for each segment of the oral reading. The children were prompted to think aloud after each segment, and uncovered the third cup and prizes after about ten minutes of reading and thinking aloud.

Similar procedures were followed for the writing task. In this task the children selected one of six pictures to write a story about in the target language, were prompted to talk about their thoughts during the planning and composing process for about ten minutes, and then received the final small prize (Chamot and El-Dinary 1999).

In another study of young L2 learners' learner strategies, researchers focused on listening strategies of primary school students in Singapore (Gu, Hu, and Zhang 2005b). As in the study of immersion children, teachers were enlisted to help in selecting the materials for the think-aloud interviews. These consisted of two narratives appropriate for the children's grade level, one easy and the other more challenging. The narratives were then recorded by a researcher who had been a primary school teacher. The think-aloud interviews began with a general discussion as a warm up, followed by a training activity in which the children were asked to guess what was inside a bag by touching the objects inside with their eyes closed. Then the child was asked to continue thinking aloud as the taped narrative texts were played. The tapes were stopped at meaningful breaks and children were encouraged to describe their thoughts.

The findings of both studies revealed strategic differences between more and less effective and younger and older L2 learners in the areas of listening, reading, and writing. Taken together, these two studies seem to indicate that think-aloud tasks and protocols with younger learners need to be carefully planned so as to be engaging to the children. Engaging in some kind of game that stimulates the children to begin talking about their thoughts served as an effective form of practice for children in these studies. Both studies report considerable variation in young children's ability to verbalize their thoughts, with some children, especially the younger ones, not able to easily describe their thinking. This is understandable, given the fact that the ability to monitor (see Flavell 1992) and metalinguistic awareness (see Bialystok 2001) are developmental processes. What is of particular interest is that some of the children, especially the better learners, were able to describe their thinking about the task and expressed awareness of their own mental and linguistic processes.

The challenges encountered in conducting think-aloud interviews with young children in language immersion programs were mostly related to their age (Chamot 1999). In a study of Singaporean lower primary school children learning English, a number of challenges were identified by the researchers (Gu *et al.* forthcoming). Problems were encountered in communication between the researcher and the child, in the process for eliciting strategies, in dealing with children's silence or soft voices, and in recording and transcribing the data. In spite of these problems, the researchers suggest that '... think-aloud is a feasible data collection method to use with lower primary children' (Gu *et al.* 2005a: 295).

2 Language choice

Another important aspect to consider with respect to think-aloud elicitation is the question of language. Subjects can report their thoughts in their first or their second (third, fourth, etc.) language, or they can mix languages during their verbal reports. Little methodological research has been done on the influence of language choice on think-alouds. The only study that we are aware of is Heine (2005). In this study, she varied languages in her piloting of think-alouds with bilingual (German-English) high school students. She reports that, without exception, her 13 subjects dominantly used the language that the researcher had employed for explaining and for practice in the think-aloud task, even though the subjects were explicitly told that they could choose, and also go back and forth between languages.

In the ESL context, researchers have often asked subjects to think aloud in English as their second language (L2) on the basis of the argument that these subjects were sufficiently proficient in English (for example, Block 1986, 1992). This procedure is usually motivated by the fact that translations from various first languages (L1s) into English as the language of analysis are time-consuming and costly. However, Anderson and Vandergrift (1996: 5) raise doubts that think-alouds in an L2 provide as much information as those done in an L1. (See also Anderson 1989, 1992; Devine 1987.) Furthermore, it is also an important question whether verbal reporting in an L2 alters thought processes.

At least two potential problems emerge as topics for future methodological investigation. One is the possibility that reporting in an L2 requires more cognitive capacity than reporting in an L1 and that it thus limits the cognitive capacity available for the task. Similarly, Aguado (2004: 30) points out that some subjects might concentrate on speaking correctly and thus operate under additional cognitive demands. Heine (2005) draws attention to the fact that L2-related verbalization problems can result in an increased number of inferences and associations and thus a deeper level of processing. A second problem is that culture-specific action patterns (Ehlich and Rehbein 1979a, 1986) may constitute a source of interference with the task. In other words, subjects might approach tasks differently according to the language they are asked to use. It is plausible that both aspects might play a role at different levels of language proficiency, but the problem of cognitive capacity seems to be especially relevant to examine in further research on the think-alouds of lower-proficiency subjects. It may be that higher-proficiency subjects have greater cultural flexibility regarding their action patterns.

Thinking aloud in an L1 may be easier for many subjects and thus allow more processing capacity for the task. However, the question of whether the language induces subjects to choose certain culture-specific action patterns is just as relevant for the L1 as it is for an L2. Also, the use of the L1 might have detrimental effects on the performance in the L2 (Færch and Kasper 1987:

19). Clearly, these are issues that future methodological research on the use of verbal reports in language learner strategy research needs to address.

It is interesting to note that subjects who are free to choose a language for their verbal report may make use of their first language as well as their L2. Schramm (2001) reports a functionally different use of the native language German and the target language English in a study of German undergraduate EFL readers. Her subjects used their native language German for most of their verbal reports, but included English terms at several points. Schramm (2001: 312) characterizes such functionally motivated use of English terms in the German think-aloud as 'L2 labels', a term taken from Grießhaber, Özel, and Rehbein (1996: 11–12). These L2 labels facilitate the construction of thematic plans and, in particular, the comparison of incoming text information with the constructed thematic plan. Her analysis indicates that readers' knowledge structures are composed of mental representations that are partly accessible in German and partly in English.

On the basis of these insights, it seems helpful for many analytic purposes to give students the opportunity to think aloud in any language(s) that they wish to use. Heine's (2005) report suggests that researchers need to go even further and actually use different potential think-aloud languages when they explain the tasks and conduct the training. Future studies will hopefully shed more light on these questions. In the meantime, however, when researchers ask their subjects to think aloud in a specific language, their reasons are of interest to the academic public.

3 Contextualization

Besides providing practice for subjects, prompting, and offering choice of language for responses, the issues of contextualization and intrusiveness have emerged as major concerns in the use of think-alouds during the past two decades. Language learner strategy research has increasingly recognized the action context in which the strategies are used. Because strategies are goal-oriented and the action context has influence on these goals, the use of strategies varies greatly according to the action context. This fact has strongly encouraged strategy researchers to conduct their studies in authentic contexts that allow subjects to pursue real goals.

Studies of the L1 reading process of Norwegian law students (Bråten and Strømsø 2003; Strømsø, Bråten, and Samuelstuen 2003) illustrate three important points of such action integration. Firstly, these researchers embedded their investigation into the everyday, normal studying of their participants. During the investigation, their subjects attended lectures, received instruction in seminar discussions, studied independently, and received feedback on voluntary written assignments. Secondly, these researchers had their subjects read self-selected texts. This ensured not only the pre-knowledge and interest of the readers, but also authentic goals for their reading. The researchers encouraged their subjects to use any kind of supporting materials that they normally would, such as codes of laws, accounts of legal cases, and their own lecture notes. Thirdly, these authors collected think-aloud data from their subjects at three sessions with intervals of approximately four weeks. They thus captured reading at different points during the semester and observed differences in reading towards the end of the semester when students prepared for the final examinations. These three points illustrate not only how research on LLS can be integrated into authentic contexts, but also that studies conducted in unauthentic contexts may well yield differing results with regard to reading strategies.

A helpful theoretical distinction is made concerning the action context based on the 'criterion of perspective' (Huber and Mandl 1982: 18–19, 22). On the basis of the temporal relationship between cognition and corresponding action, pre-actional, peri-actional, and post-actional cognition are differentiated from one another. In language learner strategy research, peri-actional cognition has so far received most attention from researchers, and questions of strategy use have prevailed. With theoretical progress in the field, attention is now turning towards the role strategies play in the actual learning process. With this emerging research focus, pre- and post-actional think-alouds can provide important data on what strategies learners plan to use before they start a language task and how they evaluate these strategies after the completion of the task when they return to superordinate actions.

Because the action context is so important in the study of LLS, great care needs to be taken to avoid intrusiveness and this remains an ongoing challenge for the field. Our discussion turns to the transcription of think-alouds next and focuses on the documentation of features of oral speech, non-verbal communication, and physical action.

Issues in transcribing think-aloud data

While data transcription is an important stage in strategy research, the actual transcription principles and procedures have received relatively little attention. As Mishler (1991: 259) points out, transcription is 'not merely a technical procedure but an interpretive practice'. (See also Redder 2001.) For some research goals, rough think-aloud protocols produced with word-processing software and a transcription ratio of about 1:10 (i.e. one minute of data corresponds to ten minutes of transcription) may suffice, but more detailed transcriptions modeled on discourse-analytic approaches require transcription ratios of 1:50 to 1:200 as well as two different transcribers to increase reliability. They are thus much more labor-intensive to produce. With regard to the transcription of authentic data in empirical linguistics or discourse analysis, Redder (2002: 118) considers a transcription based on a ratio of 1:80 an adequate example of contemporary documentation. Whereas think-aloud data in cognitive psychology is rarely transcribed in such detail, research on language learning gains its insights from the detailed linguistic analysis of think-aloud data and therefore often requires such detailed transcription (Dechert 1987).

For such purposes, various convention systems such as CHAT (CHILDES, no year given), GAT (Selting, Auer, Barden, Bergmann, Couper-Kuhlen, Günthner, Meier, Quasthoff, Schlobinski, and Uhrmann 1998), and HIAT (Ehlich and Rehbein 1976, 1979b, 1981a, 1981b; Ehlich 1993; Rehbein 1995; Rehbein, Schmidt, Meyer, Watzke, and Herkenrath 2004) as well as diverse software such as CLAN,[3] EXMARaLDA,[4] syncWRITER (Becker-Mrotzek, Ehlich, Glas, and Tebel 1989; Grießhaber 1992; Grießhaber and Walter 1993), and TRANSANA,[5] to name only a few examples,[6] have been developed in discourse analysis and language learning research over the past decades.

1 Documentation of features of oral speech

Transcriptions of think-aloud data in strategy research, first of all, document verbalizations of the study participants. As scholars like Afflerbach and Johnston (1984) or Dechert (1987) pointed out in the 1980s, it is also essential to include in the transcripts features of spoken discourse.

In the course of giving verbal reports, subjects make great use of spoken discourse features that may be lost in a transcription. The range of these features is wide, including intonation, inflection, pauses, and variation in the rate of speech. Thus, there is the need to account for features of spoken discourse when transcribing and analyzing verbal reports. Utterances using sarcasm, rhetorical questioning, and the like need to be adequately accounted for (Afflerbach and Johnston 1984: 315).

Besides the features of oral speech mentioned by Afflerbach and Johnston (1984) above, Schramm (2005a) also suggests noting non-verbal sounds like sighing or swallowing in the transcript, as well as the transcriber's interpretation of emotional states deduced from voice quality. This information, combined with facial gestures and other information, often allows for interpretation of the subjects' decision-making processes, even when their verbalizations do not completely reveal their thoughts. (See Figure 5.1 and Table 5.1.)

2 Documentation of non-verbal communication

It can be helpful to document non-verbal communication in think-aloud data as well. Of particular relevance for strategy research are pointing and gesturing. Pointing to textbook elements, dictionaries, notes, computer screens, and objects in the study area occurs frequently in think-aloud data. Its documentation allows the researcher to understand a deictic expression such as 'this' or 'here' more reliably and to use this information in the analysis.

Subjects use gestures in think-alouds to differing degrees. Hands, for example, are often used to externalize aspects of mental models as well as increased attention. Facial gestures include—among others—pursed lips, frowning, smiling, nodding, shaking of the head, cocking the head to the left

| 65 | Jörg | ((schluckt, 1s)) "The image projected on our retina" • "is a |
| | IL-Jörg | *((swallows, 1s)) "The image projected on our retina" • "is a* |

66	Jörg	[m:osaic] ", ja, "mosaic" • "of varying brightnesses" • "and
	IL-Jörg	*[m:osaic] ", yes, "mosaic" • "of varying brightnesses" • "and*
	NVC (HAr)	--------- lF moves --------

| | Comm | *[hesitant rising intonation]* |

67	Jörg	colors." • "Somehow" • "our perceptual system"... • Brightness
	IL-Jörg	*colors." • "Somehow" • "our perceptual system"... • Brightness*
	NVC (HAr)	--------- moves ---------
	NVC	--- HE l-r-l ---

68	Jörg	and colors ähm ((--------------------- 2s---------------------)); (hm hm)
	IL-Jörg	*and colors um ((--------------------- 2s---------------------)); (hm hm)*
	NVC (HAr)	-- moves ------------------------
	NVC	--- HE l-r-l --- '------- pursed Ll, swallows, nods slightly------ ' '--- HE r-l-r –

69	Jörg	das äh kommt mir bekannt vor aus dem vorigen Kapitel grad
	IL-Jörg	*I think I've seen this uh before in the last chapter*
	NVC (HAr)	----------------------- moves ---
	NVC	---------------------- HE r-l-r ---

70	Jörg	über • • ähm • • Stäbchen und Z/ (hm, hm) und Zäpfchen (im,)
	IL-Jörg	*about • • um • • rods and c/ (hm, hm) and cones (in the,)*
	NVC (HAr)	---------------------------- moves ---------------------------------
	NVC	--------- '

Figure 5.1 Sample transcript documenting features of oral speech (based on Schramm 2005a)

(or, less frequently, to the right), and blinking. Gestures of the torso frequently observed in think-alouds are sitting up straight as an expression of increased attention and relaxing the torso as an expression of decreased attention.

3 Documentation of physical action

Besides features of oral speech and non-verbal communication, researchers can also decide to transcribe physical action steps. For example, subjects take notes, underline, write notes in the margin, use dictionaries, go to other sources, and turn pages. If we consider note-taking as an example, it is clear that the documentation of the product itself cannot help the researcher

Comm	external comment line
HE	head
IF	index finger
IL	interlinear translation line
l	left
LI	lips
NVC (HAl)	non-verbal communication of the left hand
NVC (HAr)	non-verbal communication of the right hand
NVC	all remaining non-verbal communication
r	right
Single brackets	parts of utterance are not clearly audible or non-verbal communication is not clearly visible
Double brackets	non-phonological, acoustic information and pauses (in seconds)
Underlining	marked emphasis on the syllable
Slashes	repairs
...	abortions of utterances
Up to three • symbols	short, medium, and long pauses under one second

Table 5.1 Key to transcription conventions in Figure 5.1

reconstruct the process. The transcription of the videotaped physical action steps, however, documents the order in which a subject produced notes and the precise timing of specific note elements as related to verbalized thoughts. It is certainly not a trivial matter to transcribe handwritten texts of subjects, especially those produced by young learners (Smith, McEnery, and Ivanic 1998), and the integration of scanned representations of the handwritten texts into think-aloud transcripts can therefore be very helpful for future studies that inquire into the knowledge structures that subjects construct during think-alouds.

The 'contextual turn' in language learner strategy research

To date the means used to investigate LLS have drawn mainly on a view of strategies as relatively stable mental processes within the minds of learners, with relatively little attention given to the influence of the situated experience of learners. An alternative approach—a contextual approach—is to view strategy use as the result of not only learners' cognitive choices but also of the mediation of their particular communities. While such an approach has not been applied within many learner strategy studies to date, it has been applied to investigate other aspects of SLA such as attitudes, motivation, and beliefs. Methodologies used include diaries, case studies, observations, and ethnographic methodologies, as well as interviews and focus groups—all of which aim to access students' strategies through their own interpretative meanings and perspectives.

The aim of a contextual approach is to gain a better understanding about strategies in specific contexts, or strategy instruction in particular contexts. Important questions include: Why do students use particular strategies? How do students use strategies to help them interpret different aspects of language learning and learning tasks? How is their interpretation of tasks constrained by the specific repertoire of strategies that they have available based on their past experiences? How do they view strategy instruction? What does it change for them? How do they see it influencing their language learning?

The value of a contextual approach is to reveal the extent to which LLS are part of students' experiences, interrelated with their environment, and also to reveal how strategies function in different aspects of language learning. A contextual approach is also a useful lens to apply to understanding how strategy use relates to students' experiences and the actions that they take as learners both inside and outside the classroom. At a time when criticisms have been leveled at the whole basis of strategy research (see for example Dörnyei 2005)—including questions as to whether the notion of strategy has any basis in reality—accessing and understanding learners' strategies through the accounts that they give of their experiences and perspectives is viewed as beneficial.

The move towards a more situated approach to understanding LLS has also been foreshadowed by a number of researchers who suggest that different repertoires of strategy use may occur in different environments. Hsiao and Oxford (2002), for example, identify the influence of the learning context on strategy use as an important topic for future research using the SILL. In a discussion of new directions for strategy research, Anderson (2005) underlines the need to explore how strategy use changes when the conditions for language use change as in academic versus social language use contexts. And Chamot (2004) focuses on the context of learning, the goals of learners, and teachers' instructional goals as important factors which have not generally been taken into account in naming, describing, and classifying LLS. Learners' goals vary according to the general purpose of learning, such as whether it is to develop academic English at different educational levels, to focus primarily on listening and speaking skills for adult refugees, or to develop translation/interpretation skills. At the same time, the context of learning (including class size, access to target language resources, and assessment formats) and the learners' goals may jointly determine how learners will deal with particular tasks and the strategies that they will use. A combination of qualitative methodologies is needed to allow a more situated understanding and interpretation of learner strategy use in particular contexts.

One example of a contextual approach to understanding learner strategy use comes from Gao (2003) in a longitudinal interview enquiry into Chinese students' strategy use as they move from an EFL (China) context to an ESL (UK) context. An important focus in Gao's study is to provide insights into learners' strategy use from their own perspectives, to focus on changes in strategy use, and to uncover explanations for changes. Retrospective interviews are used, revealing learners' efforts to 'designate, diagnose, evaluate, self-analyze, and theorize' their learning behaviors (Wenden 1986: 189). Gao argues that taking a process approach to strategy research which includes acknowledgement of the sociocultural background of learners and contextual influences permits researchers to better understand the reasons for strategy selection and to understand the dynamic and evolutionary nature of learners' strategy use.

Methodological approaches in new research contexts

L2 acquisition research in the last two decades has extended its focus beyond conventional face-to-face classrooms to encompass the range of contexts in which language learning takes place. Formal and informal contexts for learning, study abroad, self-access learning, and tandem partnerships are just some of the learning environments included in L2 acquisition studies. Strategy research has also extended its boundaries and its methodological tools, most notably in the area of study abroad (Paige, Cohen, and Shively 2004; Cohen, Paige, Shively, Emert, and Hoff 2005). In this section we consider two relatively new research contexts—online language learning and the learning of heritage languages—in terms of the methodological shifts which are required in order to research strategy use in these areas.

Online language learning includes the use of internet technologies to access information and course content, and to interact and collaborate with other learners and teachers online. One of the earliest studies into strategy use in online environments was carried out by Meskill (1991) focusing on learner-content interaction. Using observation of student responses, the tracking of navigation and time on task, individual student interviews, and an attitudinal questionnaire to measure satisfaction with the online session, she studied the effects of online advice messages suggesting learner strategies to students.

In a more recent study Ulitsky (2000) explored the strategies used by experienced foreign language learners in a multimedia online environment through interviews, questionnaires, and journals. Mostly qualitative methods provided insights as to how experienced language learners approached learning in an unfamiliar environment, modified their learner strategies, and found ways to learn from tasks in the new environment. White (1995b, 1997) designed a comparative study of students in face-to-face and distance/online learning environments to explore the effects of mode of study on learners' choice of strategies, using questionnaires and a verbal report procedure termed the 'yoked subject technique' completed in relation to a unit of the course materials. A methodological challenge in the study was that students following the distance/online course appeared to feel somewhat insecure in relation to their learner strategies, due to their unfamiliarity with the learning environment and the absence of ongoing, direct mediation by a teacher.

To overcome this problem, the yoked subject technique was deployed whereby students were asked to imagine that they were talking about their strategy use to another hypothetical student new to the course and about to embark on the section of course materials. The technique follows many of the guidelines for verbal report (for example, the use of a warm-up procedure) and has something of the ingredients of peer tutoring method to externalize the strategic repertoires of 'expert' learners. While in practice it functioned more as a retrospective procedure, it allowed learners to reflect on aspects of their strategy use that they considered significant. The yoked subject technique represents an attempt to find a data-gathering tool which fits the particular requirements of learners in a relatively new learning environment.

Research into strategy use and strategy training in distance and online environments is an important area given the increasing emphasis placed on access to just-in-time learning opportunities and lifelong learning (Harris 2003). Tools such as computer tracking and think-alouds, as students work online, can provide insights into how students choose to interact with the target language and to manage their learning in contexts where the teacher is often remote from the sites of learning. Sociocultural approaches to understanding strategy use online are also valuable (White 2003), given that we know relatively little about how learners' strategy use is linked with the way they perceive, interpret, and derive meaning from online learning experiences.

The learning of heritage and indigenous languages has received increasing research attention over the last two decades, and a key concern is to enhance language maintenance and language learning, while recognizing the particular position and status of those languages for learners and their communities. In terms of LLS, much attention has been paid to finding appropriate ways of assisting learners to develop their language skills. Hancock (2002), for example, calls for more research into the learner strategies of heritage Spanish speakers and focuses on two methods which can be used to explore strategy use and for strategy training: scenarios and strategy inventories. Scenarios have been widely used where learners in groups discuss particular learning scenarios together and exchange ideas about the strategies which would be helpful in those contexts. Hancock argues that this approach fits well with the preferred learning approaches of heritage Spanish speakers, and notes that it allows students to increase their awareness of the social issues involved in learning their language, gives them ideas as to how they can use strategies they are comfortable with, and exposes them to new strategies suggested by other heritage speakers.

New Zealand has seen a resurgence in attempts to preserve the indigenous language, Maori, and to increase the number of speakers particularly within the indigenous population. Approaches to researching strategy use have for the most part included a combination of interviews and questionnaires, supplemented more recently by ethnographic methodologies and narrative enquiry. The Ministry of Maori Development has developed an online guide entitled *Kei te Ako Tonu Au, Strategies for Second Language Learners of Te Reo Maori*, based on learners' accounts of strategy use explored from narrative and biographical perspectives.

As these new avenues of enquiry emerge, questions about language learner strategy use can be posed as a way of coming to know more about language learning and teaching in the new environments. Moving into new contexts of enquiry requires methodological shifts, particularly if the means of investigation are to fit with the background and experiences of learners. At the same time those shifts can be a means of widening the repertoire of tools and practices for strategy research which may, in turn, prove useful in more mainstream contexts.

Action research

Over the last three decades, theory, research, and pedagogy have all influenced what we know about learner strategies, how we get learners to enquire into and develop their strategy use, and how we approach strategy instruction. Strategy researchers have endeavored to provide both teachers and learners with various means of learning about strategy use and strategy development, and a number of instructional frameworks have been developed (see Table 5.2), with attention placed on the role of the teacher in strategy instruction (Cohen 1998; Grenfell and Harris 1999). Important questions remain, however, concerning how such frameworks and approaches are actually implemented in classrooms and incorporated into existing practice, and how enquiry at the chalk face can contribute to our knowledge of LLS and strategy instruction.

The extension of LLS research methods to include action research approaches would provide answers to these questions in line with a broader move within L2 acquisition research to include exploratory practice (Allwright 2003) and practitioner research (Allwright 2005).

While in traditional research approaches the implementation of research is left up to the practitioner, within action research paradigms putting research findings into practice is fundamental to the research process and is subject to ongoing scrutiny. Action research primarily uses methods common to qualitative research, including observing and recording actions, events, behaviors, and reflections which are collected and analyzed systematically. Collaborative action research is a particularly promising approach for learner strategy research since it is essentially participatory, and can involve different combinations of researchers and teachers working as pairs or groups enquiring into a common research problem (Burns 1999).

O'Malley and Chamot (1990)	Oxford (1990a)	Chamot (2005a); Chamot, Barnhardt, El-Dinary, and Robbins (1999)	Grenfell and Harris (1999)
1 Students identify their current strategies	Learners do a task without any strategy instruction	*Preparation* Teacher identifies students' current learner strategies for familiar tasks	*Awareness raising* Learners do a task 'cold'
	They discuss how they did it and the teacher asks them to reflect on how their strategies may have facilitated their learning		They brainstorm the strategies used. Class shares strategies that work for them
2 Teacher explains additional strategies	Teacher demonstrates other helpful strategies, stressing the potential benefits	*Presentation* Teacher models, names, explains new strategy; asks students if and how they have used it.	*Modeling* Teacher demonstrates new strategies, emphasizes their value and draws up a checklist of strategies for subsequent use
3 Teacher provides opportunities for practice	Learners are provided with opportunities to practice the new strategies	*Practice* Students practice new strategy; in subsequent strategy practice, teacher fades reminders to encourage independent strategy use.	*General practice* Learners are given a range of tasks to deploy new strategies
	Learners are shown how the strategies can be transferred to other tasks	*Self-evaluation* Students evaluate their own strategy use immediately after practice	
	Learners are provided with further tasks and asked to make choices about which strategies they will use	*Expansion* Students transfer strategies to new tasks, combine strategies into clusters, develop repertoire of preferred strategies	*Action planning* Learners are guided to select strategies that will help them address their particular difficulties. Further practice and fading out of reminders to use strategies
4 Teacher assists learners in evaluating their success with the new strategies	Teacher helps learners to understand the success of their strategy use and assess their progress towards more self-directed learning	*Assessment* Teacher assesses students' use of strategies and impact on performance	*Evaluation* Teacher guides learners to evaluate progress and strategy use and to set themselves new goals

Table 5.2 A comparison of strategy instruction steps (Chamot 2005a; Harris 2003)

Here we discuss the potential contribution of action research into strategy instruction in two contexts. The first example addresses the concerns of secondary foreign language teachers in the United States wanting to use strategy instruction to help students attain the goals of the five Cs of the Foreign Language Learning Standards i.e. Communication, Cultures, Connections, Comparisons, and Communities using the National Capital Language Resource Center's (NCLRC) learner strategy resource guides. The proposed research cycle consists of six interrelated phases:

Stage 1: Professional development and planning

Teachers meet during the summer prior to the beginning of the project for a professional development summer institute that includes instruction in strategy teaching techniques, principles and methods of action research, and how to integrate learner strategies into the five Cs. (See NCLRC 2004.) Equally importantly, teachers discuss their particular classes and how they anticipate incorporating strategy instruction so as to support foreign language learning and the curricular goals of the five Cs. The teachers collaborate with each other and the NCLRC research staff to decide upon a research focus, the strategies they will teach, and the means they will use to collect and analyze the data.

Stage 2: Collecting data

Teachers collect data as their classes use the strategy instruction program in various activities during the fall semester, and stay in touch with other teachers and the NCLRC researchers through online discussions and telephone contact.

Stage 3: Analysis and reflection

During the break between semesters, teachers meet again with researchers to provide a preliminary report on their classes, their response to the strategy programme, and emerging issues based on the data they gathered. They learn from each other about strategies learners have found useful and how these relate to the five Cs. The researchers then select data from each class for further analysis and reflection, and the teachers go over these data as a group. Hypotheses are formed based on the analysis of data and reflection on results to date, and the enquiry is refocused on specific research questions that have emerged from the preliminary data.

Stage 4: Intervening

Teachers return to the classroom with modified approaches or practices based on the hypotheses made and plans drawn up by the group. Teachers continue to observe, reflect, and carry out data-gathering procedures during the spring semester as in Stage 2.

Stage 5: Reporting and evaluation

Teachers come together for a second summer institute to report to the group on the findings that have emerged through the action research process. The researchers reflect on the findings within the group, and report on the implications they see for theory, research, and practice. Teachers provide individual reports which include their critical reflections on the degree of usefulness of the NCLRC learner strategy resource guides (NCLRC 2003, 2004) for conducting classroom-based action research.

Stage 6: Dissemination of results

The results of the action research project are disseminated through a variety of channels, including the NCLRC newsletter, conference presentations, collaborative articles authored by teachers and research staff, and other appropriate means of dissemination decided by the group as a whole.

Another type of action research involves a partnership between researchers and teachers who share a common goal for improving the L2 acquisition development of a particular group of students. In this type of collaboration it is important that teachers participate as equal partners in the research endeavor, rather than as individuals who merely agree to carry out the plans of the researchers. A research project that implemented this collaborative ideal was *Project Accelerated Literacy*, in which researchers and teachers worked together to increase the literacy of secondary school Hispanic students (ages 13–19) in the United States who had limited literacy in their L1 and who were recent immigrants to the United States without English proficiency (Chamot, Keatley, Mazur, Anstrom, Marquez, and Adonis 2000). Strategy instruction for reading and writing tasks was incorporated into the curriculum and developed collaboratively by the teachers and researchers. Teachers decided on whether and how they could introduce strategies to their students. Bilingual teachers effectively taught strategies in Spanish, then helped students transfer the strategies to English literacy tasks. Most of the monolingual English-speaking teachers decided that it was impossible to teach learner strategies to beginning-level ESL students because of students' limited English proficiency, but some managed to provide this instruction adequately through extensive modeling of the strategies. What can be concluded from this research study is that in action research teachers can be expected to diverge from goals held by their researcher partners and that these differing adaptations of research goals need to be respected and reported as important aspects of the research findings.

Conclusion

Research into LLS is now into its fourth decade. In this chapter we have focused on the ongoing development and refining of selected existing research methods and approaches, as well as the process of developing instruments appropriate for particular groups of learners in new and emerging contexts for research. After a brief, rather general overview of the main research traditions, we provided a critical analysis of elicitation and transcription issues in the use of arguably the most complex method for data collection on LLS, think-alouds. With examples from recent studies, we have argued for three points in the elicitation of think-alouds: (a) careful orientation, practice, and prompting, (b) multiple language use, and especially (c) the integration of think-alouds into an authentic action context. We have also argued for detailed transcriptions of think-aloud data that document not only verbalizations, but also features of oral speech, non-verbal communication, and physical action steps if these aspects facilitate analyses.

The value of a contextual approach to investigating strategies explored here is based on a view of strategy use as the result of learners' cognitive choices, mediated by their particular communities. The kinds of methodological shifts required for conducting strategy research in relatively new contexts, namely online learning and heritage language use, have also been explored together with the possibility of incorporating collaborative action research approaches into strategy instruction. Action research is not without its critiques, and issues concerning the legitimacy of action research and debates over what constitutes knowledge in our field are likely to remain contested for some time. Nevertheless, it represents an important means of strengthening the often tenuous links among theory, research, and practice, and of demonstrating the ongoing relevance of language learner strategy research. Looking ahead, we hope that future learner strategy studies will not only be able to live up to the methodological challenges presented in this chapter, but will contribute to further refinement of research tools, methodologies, and approaches, as well as to our understanding of how learners, teachers, and researchers can come to learn more about language learner strategies.

Acknowledgements

We would like to thank two anonymous reviewers and Rebecca L. Oxford for extensive, insightful feedback on an earlier version of this chapter.

Notes

1 Beyer (2005: 20) highlights five areas of language learning research that introspective methods are particularly suited for: (1) strategies in solving tasks, (2) direction of attention and awareness of specific structures, (3) metalinguistic knowledge of language learners, (4) validation of tests, and (5) learner profiles.

2 We would like to highlight some particularly interesting points of four of the most recent of these studies. Jourdenais (2001: 372–5) discusses in light of Swain's output hypothesis the possibility that verbalizations could act as an additional form of linguistic input for the learner. (Also see Chi, de

Leeuw, Chiu, and LaVancher 1994.) Aguado (2004: 29) points out the fact that the ability to think aloud varies inter-individually as well as intra-individually. Heine (2005) distinguishes different types of think-aloud and other verbal protocols, indicates the research interests for which these types are especially appropriate, and provides prototypical stimuli for each type. Leow and Morgan-Short (2004) compare a group of participants who think aloud during a foreign language reading task and a group of participants who do not, on the basis of pre- and post-test assessment tasks. They conclude that thinking aloud, in their study, was non-reactive.

3 For information and free download, see http://childes.psy.cmu.edu.
4 For information and free download, see http://www1.uni-hamburg.de/exmaralda/index-en.html.
5 For information and free download, see http://www.transana.org.
6 For an overview of tools for transcribing audio and video data, see the 'Link catalogue' on the EXMARaLDA website at http://www1.uni-hamburg.de/exmaralda/index-en.html.

6

L2 grammar strategies: the Second Cinderella and beyond

REBECCA L. OXFORD and
KYOUNG RANG LEE
with diary contributions by GLORIA PARK

Introduction

L2 researcher Larry Vandergrift (1997a) called listening strategies the 'Cinderella of strategies', because other L2 researchers had not given them the same attention as reading, writing, and speaking strategies. However, times have changed, and, thanks to Vandergrift and others, Cinderella has escaped the dinge and anonymity she once faced. (See Chapter 8.) However, a 'Second Cinderella' remains as yet unexplored: grammar strategies. Like many types of L2 strategies, grammar strategies are actions or thoughts that learners consciously employ to make language learning and/or language use easier, more effective, more efficient, and more enjoyable. Of course, consciousness is a continuum, not a mere 'on-off' switch. In this chapter we call all grammar-related or grammar-learning strategies 'grammar strategies'. The reason is twofold. First, for many learners the main interest is not grammar learning *per se* but rather L2 learning or L2 communication. Second, it is difficult to classify those strategies that are only for learning or only for communication, because any opportunity for communication demonstrably provides further opportunity for learning, and any instance of learning could theoretically lead to communication (except in some instances of purely rule-oriented learning).

In the mid-1970s, learner strategy research spread to the L2 field. Rubin's (1975) early work on 'the good language learner' emphasized that such a learner was concerned about and interested in grammar. Unfortunately, most researchers who have become well known in the L2 learner strategy area, perhaps influenced by the low profile of grammar in the communicative language teaching approach, have either ignored grammar strategies or slid them into the more general 'cognitive strategy' category, thereby unwittingly hiding these strategies from view. This trend of not carefully considering grammar strategies has continued to the present among those who have made their reputations as L2 learner strategy experts, but we hope to change that situation.

Here we mention an important, albeit very tightly focused, line of grammar strategy research not discussed in most L2 strategy books. (An exception is Stevens' 1984 volume.) The research concerns strategies used for assigning gender to nouns in either one's own language or an additional language. Examples of such strategy studies abound (for example, Tucker, Lambert, and Rigault 1977; Karmiloff-Smith 1979; Stevens 1984; Cain, Weber-Olsen, and Smith 1987; Oliphant 1997). They fall into three general categories associated with individuals' sensitivity to various cues: morphophonological (for example, word endings), semantic (natural gender of the referent), and syntactic (for example, derivational suffixes). L2-specific studies suggest that learners' use of strategies for assigning L2 noun gender depends on factors such as age, stage of L2 development, nature of the L2, nature of the L1, and relevant discrepancies between the L2 and the L1. For multilingual learners, additional factors yet to be studied might be how many other non-native languages they have already learnt and the nature of those languages. Most learner strategy experts have tended to ignore such sharply focused grammar strategy studies, or, for that matter, *any* grammar strategy research. By the same token, investigators and theorists actively involved in work on highly specific grammar-strategy topics in second language acquisition have tended not to cite broader areas of learner strategy research. This is a serious cause for concern.

To bring grammar strategies into view, let us look at how two students, Kai and Andy, use them. Kai and Andy, like many other successful L2 students, often employ some kind of grammar strategies. Kai's favorite strategies are shown in Strategy Chart 1. Note that in this chapter, the terms 'forms' and 'structures' both refer to any grammatical elements.

Andy, in a more informal setting, learns Spanish grammar with a range of different strategies, including the ones in Strategy Chart 2. Several of his

---

STRATEGY CHART 1
Kai's favorite grammar strategies

- preview a lesson to identify the key structures to be covered
- make visual aids, like a chart or 'tree', to help me remember grammatical structures
- memorize paradigms from grammar books
- write grammar rules and examples on note cards
- review grammar note cards on the subway on the way to the university
- repeat new grammar points before going to bed

(Source: discussion with student)

---

strategies in Strategy Chart 2, form a 'strategy chain', a sequence of coherent, mutually supportive strategies that he uses to improve his grammatical understanding and use through listening and speaking. He also improves his listening and speaking as he increases his grammatical knowledge.

Any type of L2 oral communication, such as asking, 'Would you mind my sitting here?', involves at the very least a combined emphasis on vocabulary,

---

STRATEGY CHART 2
Andy's favorite grammar strategies

- I eavesdrop on conversations to see if I understand
- If I hear a new structure that keeps me from understanding, I write it down
- I look up the new structure as soon as I can
- I review the whole conversation in my mind to see if I understand it more fully now
- I try out new structures in my own conversations

(Note: The five strategies immediately above are a 'strategy chain', i.e. a set of linked, sequentially used strategies)

- I jot down new structures that I pick up when watching TV
- I use a grammar book to find out what the structure is and what it means

(Source: discussion with student)

---

pronunciation, pragmatics, and grammar. Grammar strategies relevant to this example might include noticing the order of the words, noticing the possessive 'my' before the gerund 'sitting', pondering why so many people mistakenly say *me* instead of *my* in such a construction, and practicing the form in speaking and writing.

Before we can talk about grammar strategies or even grammar learning, however, it is essential to offer an overview of four instructional modes teachers employ for dealing with grammar in L2 classrooms. That is the theme of the first section. In the second section, we explore diverse types of grammar strategies in connection with different kinds of grammar learning. In the third section, we quote from a teacher's diary about grammar instruction and grammar strategies and add our own suggestions, comments, and insights. The final section contains implications for theory and research. We begin below with types of grammar instruction.

Four instructional modes teachers use for dealing with grammar in the L2 classroom

One reason for presenting the current section separately from grammar learning is that no matter what teachers do in the L2 classroom, grammar learning might or might not occur for a particular student. At heart, learning depends on the student. Another reason is that no matter what type of grammar instruction, if any, is employed, certain learners might choose to learn grammar in a totally different way; their strategies might or might not be what the teacher wants, expects, or recognizes.

Instructional modes for dealing with grammar in L2 classrooms can be either implicit or explicit. Language pedagogy experts' descriptions of implicit and explicit instruction[1] are varied and can become rather complex. However, it is possible to categorize the most frequently discussed modes and reveal some of their basic features in a table such as Table 6.1 below.

Characteristics	Instructional Modes			
	Implicit Mode		Explicit Mode	
	Focus on meaning (FonM) —avoidance of grammar in the classroom	Focus on form (FonF)	Inductive	Deductive
Primary focus on meaning	Yes	Yes	No	No
Target form made explicit	No	No	No	Yes
Target form enhanced or otherwise made noticeable	No	Yes	No	N/A (rule already explicit)
Grammar rule supplied	No	No	No	Yes
Learners directed to induce grammar rule	No	No	Yes	N/A (rule already explicit)

Table 6.1 Characteristics of four instructional modes for dealing with grammar in L2 classrooms (Source: Robert DeKeyser [personal communication, May 2006], adapted with additions)

As Table 6.1 indicates, implicit instructional treatment of grammar includes two modes: (a) 'focus on meaning' (FonM) with no attention paid to grammar and (b) 'focus on form (FonF)—implicit' with occasional attention paid to grammar. Explicit instructional treatment of grammar has two possible manifestations, each dealing with grammar in a different way: (a) 'focus on forms (FonFs)—explicit-inductive' and (b) 'focus on forms (FonFs)—explicit-deductive'. These are the most frequent ways of delineating the treatment of grammar in L2 classrooms, but they are not the only ways. Doughty (2003) mentions two additional instructional modes under the rubrics of implicit and explicit.

Implicit instructional modes for dealing with grammar in L2 classrooms

Here we describe two implicit treatments of grammar in L2 classrooms: 'focus on meaning' (FonM) (see 1 below) and 'focus on form' (FonF) (see

2 below). These differ greatly in terms of the underlying construct of how language competence develops. As seen below, questions have been raised about whether FonM deserves to be called an 'instructional mode', but we include it here as such for parallelism and completeness.

1 Focus on meaning (FonM)

Doughty (2003) contends that the focus on meaning (FonM) mode is not instruction at all but instead merely classroom L2 exposure. Proponents of the FonM mode would likely disagree with that assessment. At any rate, on theoretical grounds FonM deals with grammar by exclusion and avoidance. In a FonM classroom, 'Learners are presented with gestalt, comprehensible samples of communicative L2 use, for example, in the form of content-based lessons in sheltered subject-matter or immersion classrooms, lessons that are often interesting, relevant, and relatively successful' (Option 2, Focus on Meaning in Long 1997: 2) from the point of view of communicative fluency. Krashen's (1996) Natural Approach is the quintessence of the FonM. Krashen contends that structures are acquired through natural, developmental processes only, not through attention or awareness. With such an assumption, it is not useful to point out, discuss, or analyze forms or encourage learners to do so. In FonM classrooms, teachers do not push learners to attend to any forms and certainly not to induce any underlying grammar rules. This mode is 'based on the conviction that learners (including classroom learners) would automatically proceed along their built-in syllabus as long as they had access to comprehensible input and were sufficiently motivated' (R. Ellis 2006: 85).

In contrast, Ellis (1999, 2002a) defines acquisition as a state in which the target language feature has been truly internalized and has entered into the learner's interlanguage and long-term memory for communicative use. He contends that the FonM mode's exposure to input is insufficient for acquisition and that understanding is also necessary. In addition, the FonM approach has been criticized for producing an unacceptably low level of formal accuracy (R. Ellis 2006: 86). However, FonM still has its adherents.

2 Focus on form (FonF)

In contrast with FonM, in which grammar is ignored, 'focus on form' (FonF) is defined as '... meaning-focused activities in which learners are preoccupied with the process of understanding, extending or conveying meaning and cope with language forms incidentally and as demanded by that process' (Kumaravadivelu 1993: 78). The significance here is that language forms are, in fact, coped with or attended to. FonF is the centerpiece of Long's (1985, 1987, 1997) model of task-based language teaching. Long (1985) proposes that the most important goal for a language task is to confront learners with certain language problems (communication breakdowns or difficulties) in completing the task. This would lead learners to identify gaps in their language and take action to solve these problems, so that they might negotiate appropriate meaning in interaction with others. (See also Foster

1998.) Focus on form refers to how attentional resources are allocated, and involves briefly drawing students' attention to linguistic elements (words, collocations, grammatical structures, pragmatic patterns, and so on), in context, as they arise incidentally in lessons whose overriding focus is on meaning or communication. (Option 3, Focus on Form in Long 1997: 1).

When a communication breakdown occurs, many techniques can be used to help learners shift their attention to form. One of the best known is a 'recast', that is, a corrective reformulation of the learner's incorrect production or understanding. With a recast, the learner must discern the difference between the original form and the correct form in context. Other ways that learners' attention is diverted to form at the point of a breakdown include the following (Doughty 2003): input enhancement (the form in the text is underlined, circled, color-coded, starred, given greater oral emphasis, or otherwise highlighted), input flood (the number of times the form is used in the text is dramatically increased so that it is impossible not to notice), and form-experimental, as in anagrams, i.e. words or phrases are formed by reordering the letters of another word or phrase. In this mode, '... [T]hree major components define ... [this type of] focus on form ... [:] (a) it can be generated by the teacher or the learner(s), (b) it is generally incidental (occasional shift of attention), and (c) it is contingent on learners' needs (triggered by perceived problems)' (Salaberry 2001: 105).

More technically expressed, FonF has the following characteristics (as summarized from Doughty 2003: 267). First, there is neither rule explanation nor any direction to figure out rules, although tasks do draw learners' attention to form as part of meaning. Second, any of the following might be involved:[2] (a) tasks that promote meaning prior to form; (b) naturalness of L2 forms, that is, specific forms must be essential for the task, rather than the task being contrived as an example of the forms; (c) unobtrusiveness of attention to forms; (d) 'noticing' of a form by the learner because of an instructor-assisted attention shift at the point of a communication breakdown; (e) selection of target forms through analyzing learners' communicative needs; and (f) consideration of the constraints that the learner's interlanguage place on understanding and production of forms.

We have discussed two implicit ways of dealing with grammar in L2 classrooms. We now turn to two explicit treatments of grammar in L2 classrooms.

Explicit instructional modes for dealing with grammar in L2 classrooms

The two explicit instructional modes discussed here are very different from each other. The first, 'FonFs—explicit-inductive' (1 below) is characterized by encouraging learners to induce (i.e. figure out) the grammar rule for themselves. The second, 'FonFs—explicit-deductive' (2 below), features direct presentation of the grammar rule, which learners are supposed to apply. Brown (1994), R. Ellis (2002a, 2002b, 2006), Hinkel and Fotos (2002), and DeKeyser (2003) support the role of explicit grammar instruction, particularly for adult learners.

1 Focus on forms (FonFs)—explicit-inductive mode

This mode involves indirect but explicit teaching, in which the teacher does not present the rules but instead establishes conditions in which the learners discover the rules for themselves. In explicit-inductive instruction, learners are overtly told to pay attention to forms and work out the rules for themselves. Although the teacher avoids rule presentation, students might talk about grammar as a subject of conversation in the L2 itself (R. Ellis 2002a), or students might discuss it in the L1.

In this mode, the ways that instructors help learners attend to form can become obtrusive (Doughty and Williams 1998: 258, in Doughty 2003: 266) and are not always part of a meaningful task. Some techniques used to stimulate learners' attention to form include: input practice involving forms, metalinguistic feedback, output practice (forms-focused interaction in pairs or groups), and the garden path technique in which the teacher leads learners to make overgeneralization errors and then points out the overgeneralization as soon as the error is made, giving corrective feedback. Doughty and Williams (op. cit.) rate the garden path technique as perhaps the most obtrusive mechanism for helping students to attend to the target structure, although it can be useful under certain circumstances.

2 Focus on forms (FonFs)—explicit-deductive mode

This is the strongest version of the focus on forms. In this mode, the teacher presents rules and their associated structures, and learners must apply what they are learning to specific instances. Learners are expected to deal with a vast array of grammatical items and rules. Lessons are rarely oriented toward communication.

R. Ellis (2002a) notes that the grammar-translation method, which embodies explicit-deductive instruction, is still the most widely used language teaching method around the world today. One of this method's major drawbacks is that many learners, after years of instruction, do not feel competent to say more than a few sentences in the L2. The standard complaint is: 'After three years of studying Spanish with this method, I still can't order a cup of coffee in Spanish'. However, this depends very largely on the instructor; certain teachers are able to incorporate communicative practice into this instructional method. It also depends on the learner. We have encountered learners from various countries who have learnt languages expertly with this method, but these learners developed competence in the language by dint of their own passionate, autonomous efforts at learning.

We have just discussed four ways in which teachers deal with grammar in the L2 classroom: two implicit and two explicit. The first of these modes, as we have seen, excludes grammar from classroom activity, while the other three deal with grammar in a variety of ways. The next section presents the Second Cinderella, i.e. grammar strategies, in the context of L2 learning. Grammar learning modes are also divided into implicit and explicit, although they are not directly mapped on to implicit and explicit L2 instruction modes for reasons discussed below.

Modes of L2 learning and associated grammar strategies

In this section we present implicit and explicit L2 learning, with which we link particular kinds of grammar strategies and argue that learning and instruction cannot be considered merely 'flip sides' of each other; the instructional mode does not control learning. We then present a model for understanding consciousness, the key to the distinction between implicit and explicit L2 learning. Grammar strategies associated with implicit L2 learning are explored, and lastly those linked with explicit L2 learning are discussed.

Why instructional modes do not control L2 learning

We mentioned that L2 learning is the purview of the learner; that no matter what the teacher does, learning is not guaranteed, and that a given L2 instructional mode does not necessarily predict a given student's way of learning. We elucidate further here:

Cognitive and linguistic developmental stages Adult learners and younger learners often have different ways of approaching L2 learning based on cognitive and linguistic developmental stages. DeKeyser (2003) and others indicate that adults in particular require explicit learning, so their grammar strategies will be oriented toward paying attention to target forms and inducing the underlying rules—no matter what happens in the classroom setting. However, developmental stages are not the only determiners of grammar strategies, as we have just seen.

Learning style preferences These (general approaches to learning, such as visual, auditory, and hands-on, reflective or impulsive, extroverted or introverted) strongly influence the ways different students learn grammar.

Factors influencing learning styles and indirectly influencing choice of grammar strategies Learning style is related to a variety of factors: age, gender, ethnic or racial background, linguistic background, education level, socioeconomic status, sociocultural community of practice in or outside the classroom (Rogoff 1990; Lave and Wenger 1991; Wenger 1998), language proficiency level, and experience in learning other languages. All these factors might influence a learner's grammar strategies more than the type of instruction.

Beliefs, goals, and values of the institution and the teacher The education- and language-related beliefs, goals, and values of the institution and the teacher influence how the teacher deals with grammar in the L2 classroom, but these influences might or might not significantly shape learners' choice of general L2 learning modes or specific grammar strategies. Learners' own beliefs, goals, and values are often stronger influences.

Thus, a given type of instructional mode, even one that does not seem to offer many strategic options, does not necessarily limit or confine grammar strategy use. By the same token, the presence of rich strategic options in a given instructional mode does not mean that a given learner will take advantage of them. To understand L2 learning, particularly the development of grammatical skill and the use of grammar strategies, we turn to a model of consciousness developed for L2 learning.

Modeling consciousness

Schmidt's (1990, 1994a, 1994b, 1995) model of consciousness, translated into visual form in Figure 6.1, posits that consciousness consists of four major parts: attention, awareness, control, and intention. 'Attention' is the most fundamental element. It comprises 'alertness', 'orientation', and 'detection'[3] of the stimulus, i.e. of a particular grammatical form. Detection of the stimulus without awareness is called 'registration'. 'Awareness' is knowledge or subjective experience of either 'noticing' (detection + awareness) the stimulus, a low-level type of awareness, or 'understanding' the stimulus, a high-level type of awareness (Schmidt 1995). 'Control' refers to 'cognitive effort', ranging from great control (much cognitive effort) to spontaneous (little cognitive effort). 'Intention', means 'purpose' or 'goal'. If the individual has a purpose or goal connected to the learning that is occurring, the learning is 'intentional'; if not, it is 'incidental' (unintentional). According to DeKeyser (personal communication, May 2006), incidental learning can be either (a) learning something while not intending to learn anything or (b) learning 'A' unintentionally while intending to learn 'B'.

According to Schmidt (1995: 1), noticing 'seems to be associated with all learning', a statement suggesting that learning does not occur without at least low-level awareness. 'The "noticing hypothesis" states that what learners notice in input is what becomes *intake* for learning' (Schmidt 1995: 20). 'Noticing refers to surface level phenomena and item learning, while understanding refers to [a] deeper level of abstraction related to (semantic, syntactic, or communicative) meaning, system learning ... [and] implies recognition of a general principle, rule or pattern' (Schmidt 1995: 1). However, adherents of the 'most implicit' type of implicit learning argue that such learning occurs without noticing structures at all, as discussed later.

In a nutshell, implicit learning is considered to be primarily unconscious learning, while explicit learning is viewed as conscious learning, although it is not quite that simple. Nevertheless, Schmidt's model above can help us explore implicit learning and associated strategies, to which we now turn.

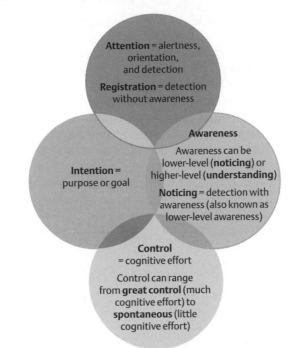

Figure 6.1   One view of Schmidt's four dimensions of consciousness (Content source: Schmidt [1995], visual interpretation by R. Oxford)

Implicit L2 learning and associated strategies

Implicit L2 learning involves learning grammar patterns in the language without any direction to pay attention to form and without any rule explanation. Theoretically speaking, students develop competence without any awareness of linguistic targets or metalinguistic information (DeKeyser 1995; Hulstijn 2005; Robinson 2005). It also occurs without *intention* (goal or purpose), so it is incidental learning (Winter and Reber 1994), and it does not involve *control*, i.e. discernable cognitive effort.

Some believe that implicit learning occurs totally unconsciously, without any attention to form at all. In essence, this is learning by osmosis, exposure, and interaction. However, others believe that implicit learning does involve an element of attention and possibly even noticing (low-level awareness). According to Nick Ellis (1994, 1995), the only aspect of attention that is necessary for implicit learning is detection, specifically detection without awareness (registration). As we have seen, Schmidt argues that for any type of L2 learning, there is a need for learners to notice surface elements.

Some theorists discuss implicit learning in quantitative terms, with a focus on detection of the frequency (statistical regularity) of occurrence of a given form,[4] while others view implicit learning in a more qualitative way (N. Ellis 1994, 1995). Doughty (2003: 291) offers some key assertions about implicit learning. First, '*complex* L2 knowledge is primarily acquired implicitly'. Second, implicit learning is the default mode in second language acquisition. These and other theories about implicit learning are still under debate.[5]

1 Strategies in purely meaning-oriented, implicit learning situations

In implicit, completely meaning-oriented L2 learning, there is theoretically little or no place for grammar strategies, because the theory suggests that learners should not be focusing on form in this type of learning. (Of course, what learners do and what theories say can be different.) The only strategies that would, theoretically, seem to go along with the goals of such learning would be behaviors for increasing exposure or interactions in the L2: 'I read the newspaper in my new language', 'I watch television in my new language', or 'I talk with native speakers of my new language'. However, as intentional behaviors, even these strategies might be considered by some theorists to be 'too strategic'.

2 Strategies in implicit learning that includes form

In a different, less extreme kind of implicit L2 learning, the learner concentrates powerfully on meaning but, when encountering a roadblock in understanding or producing the L2, shifts attention temporarily to grammar in order to move past the roadblock. This attention to form is *part of* the strong emphasis on meaning, rather than totally separate from it (Doughty 2003). Theoretically speaking, this genre of implicit L2 learning has many more strategic possibilities than the genre of implicit L2 learning that is purely meaning-oriented. Strategy Chart 3 displays some strategies that learners use to help them notice forms within implicit L2 learning.

Implicit L2 learning affords possibilities to use grammar strategies such as those in Strategy Chart 3. Explicit L2 learning offers even more strategic possibilities.

Explicit L2 learning and associated strategies

Explicit L2 learning involves awareness, at least at the level of noticing a target structure (lower-level awareness). As we noted earlier, two types of explicit L2 learning are 'explicit-inductive' and 'explicit-deductive'.

1 Explicit-inductive L2 learning

This type of L2 learning involves starting with a specific fact or instance and moving toward a general principle (rule). DeKeyser (2003: 214) terms this 'rule discovery'. This form of learning is similar to Hulstijn's (2005) description of learners processing the L2 input with the conscious intention to find out whether the input contains regularities. In attempting to find out whether the input contains regularities and how those regularities work, conscious and intentional hypothesis formation and testing are essential (Winter and Reber 1994). Put differently, learners use conscious operations to make and

STRATEGY CHART 3
Strategies used by learners who are oriented to meaning but occasionally shift attention to form

- I notice (or remember) structures that cause me problems with meaning or communication
- I notice (or remember) structures that are highlighted in the text by italics, boldface, underlining, starring, circling, color-coding, etc.
- I notice (or remember) structures that are repeated often in the text
- I notice (or remember) structures that are emphasized orally, through pitch, loudness, or repetition
- I notice (or remember) structures that are repeated extremely frequently in a short time period (input flooding)
- I notice (or remember) a structure which, when I encounter it, causes me to do something, like check a box or underline the structure
- When I don't know the gender of a noun, I quickly consider clues like sound, meaning, and form
- I pay attention to how more proficient people say things and then imitate
- I work with others to reconstruct the input text in a 'dictagloss' activity
- I keep a notebook of new structures that seem very important or frequent
- I notice when someone gives me a corrected version of what I said, listen to how that version differs from my own, and try to improve what I said
- I compare my speech or writing with that of more proficient people to see how I can improve

(Source: various learners)

STRATEGY CHART 4
Strategies used by learners who are oriented to explicit-inductive learning

- Based on all possible clues, I try to discover the underlying rule
- I participate in rule-discovery discussions in class
- I write down structures on note cards so that I can think about how they work
- I keep a notebook of examples of any structure for which I am trying to discern the rule
- I create my own hypotheses about how target structures operate and then check my hypotheses
- I notice when the teacher leads me into an overgeneralization error, and then I think about what went wrong (garden path technique)
- I participate in written brainstorming about possible underlying rules
- I check with others who are more proficient to make sure my rule interpretation is correct
- After discovering a rule, I try to apply it as soon as possible in a meaningful context
- I listen carefully for any feedback the teacher gives me about structures I use (metalinguistic feedback)

(Source: various learners)

test hypotheses in a search for an understanding of structure (N. Ellis 1994, 1995). Strategies relevant to this type of learning are included in Strategy Chart 4.

2 Explicit-deductive learning

This mode of explicit grammar learning involves learning a rule that is supplied by the book, the teacher, or by some other means—DeKeyser (2003) calls this 'rule delivery'—and then applying the rule to specific instances. This is the most overt illustration of the rule-oriented approach to language learning. Strategy Chart 5 contains examples of explicit-deductive grammar strategies. This is the most populous category of grammar strategies.

STRATEGY CHART 5

Strategies used by learners who are oriented to explicit-deductive learning

- I preview the lesson to identify the key structures to be covered
- I pay attention to the rule that the teacher or the book provides
- I try to apply the rule carefully and accurately in specific sentences
- I make up new sentences using the rule
- I check my new sentences (or ask for help) to see if I understand the rule
- I memorize rules about frequently used linguistic forms/structures (for example, verb endings, singular/plural, noun–pronoun agreement, subject–verb agreement)
- I memorize how structures change their forms (for instance, from a noun to an adjective, from an adjective to an adverb)
- I color-code different grammar categories in my notebook
- I work with a study partner to apply grammar rules
- I schedule my grammar reviews by massing them closely at first, then spreading them out
- I paraphrase rules I am given, because I understand them better in my own words
- I make grammar charts
- I remember grammar information by location on a page in the book
- I use newly learnt rules/structures in context as soon as possible

(Source: various learners)

This section has presented grammar learning and the grammar strategies associated with it. We have repeatedly argued that learning does not always follow the path intended by an instructional mode or by the teacher; and learners' grammar strategies frequently appear independently of the goals and beliefs of the teacher. However, some learners tend to follow their teachers' or institution's instructional designs and goals in ways that shape their grammar strategies. The next section shows how an ESL teacher has taught grammar strategies to her adult students.

How one L2 teacher taught a range of grammar strategies

This section comes from an ESL teacher's 'instructional diary' about teaching grammar strategies to adult community college students in the US as part of her regular, multiskill instructional assignment. We have added our own comments, suggestions, and further interpretations. The material comes directly from the teacher, Gloria Park. The class appeared to be primarily of the traditional format: presentation, practice, and production. Gloria noticed and built on her students' grammar strategies and also taught them new ones as part of regular instruction. A strategy that she noticed was: 'I explain the grammar points to other students during group-work'.

GLORIA: I saw students using this strategy during their group-work sessions. As I was walking around the classroom to observe them in group interactions, I noticed some of the high-level students explaining the grammar structure to the other students. As this became more apparent, I instituted more group-work during the elicitation-of-grammar-structure part of the lesson. I grouped my students so that there was at least one high-level grammar student and one low-level grammar student in each group.

Our comments: Gloria noticed the grammar strategy her students were already using and built upon it, giving more opportunities for group-work and student-to-student grammar explanations. She also took advantage of the multiple levels of students in her class by having the more advanced learners explain grammar structures to less advanced learners. This is the mode Vygotsky (1986) has encouraged: the more competent person helps the less competent person via an in-person dialogue, and the less competent person can use the assistance to move further through his or her 'zone of proximal development' (the area of potential growth).

A strategy that Gloria encouraged was: 'I create my own sentences so I can use the new grammar structures and remember them'.

GLORIA: After the language presentation, eliciting grammar structure, and controlled exercises, we do 'personalization' sentences. Students are given a situation where they would need to use the structure in sentences. For example, when we did modals related to giving advice ('should', 'ought to', 'had better'), students used the modals to give advice related to different situations (i.e. giving advice to a classmate who is about to fail a course, giving advice to someone who has accepted a dinner invitation from an American friend, etc.).

Our comments: Gloria encouraged her students to make up their own sentences in order to incorporate the particular modal forms. This was part of a sequence that started with the teacher's overt grammar presentation and led to application by students (explicit-deductive instruction). If Gloria emphasized that students can always create new sentences in order to apply and practice rules, the students would gain increasing 'ownership' of the strategy. Instead of being just a teaching strategy, it would then become the students' *own* grammar strategy, which they could use with any new forms or rules. It is very important for students to realize that (a) they are the agents of their own grammar development and (b) they can use strategies without being told or reminded.

Figure 6.2 is a diagram that might be a helpful reminder to teachers. This figure shows how the instructor's strategy for teaching grammar can become, through learner practice, a strategy that the learner 'owns' and employs to learn or use grammar. Teachers can simplify the diagram in any way necessary to make it understandable to students. We have found that talking about strategies openly and saying 'this is a strategy you can use on your own' gives students a new sense of power and competence. Naturally, the teacher can continue using the strategy in class for instruction but can also help learners recognize that many of the in-class strategies can be used equally well at home.

More practice with strategy,
more learner self-direction

Teaching strategy ⸺⸺⸺⸺⸺⸺⸺⟶ The learner's own grammar strategy

Figure 6.2 How a grammar-teaching strategy becomes the learner's own grammar strategy

In addition, we suggest that the particular strategy above, 'I create my own sentences so I can use the new grammar structures and remember them', can be employed in an inductive-learning situation. Without any explanation of the grammar rule, students can consider the forms in context and induce the underlying rule, after which they can create their own sentences using the forms. In the next example Gloria created a learning context for the development of the strategy: 'I apply grammar rules to new situations'.

GLORIA: After I introduced the request modals ('could', 'would', etc.) and how they worked, students were given a pair-work situation in which to apply the modals. For example, Student A was absent from class for the past two days and would like to get someone's notes. Student B is very helpful and always willing to help his classmate. With the above background situation, students were to work in pairs to create a dialogue with at least two exchanges.

Our comments: Gloria had given a situation appropriate for what students had learnt so that they could apply the new rule about request-type modals. She had explicitly presented the rule and given examples of structures (modals) in context, and then she asked students to create their own dialogue. However, this process could work more inductively. The teacher could avoid presenting the rule, and students could induce the rule from the forms in context. The teacher could verify their understanding of the rule before the students apply the rule in creating and acting out a dialogue. Next we see

Gloria promoting the strategy: 'I check and revise my writing (or peer-editing) by paying attention to just one feature: tense of verbs'.

GLORIA: When we were doing the simple past tense, the class was divided into five groups of three or four students per group. Each group was given the beginning of a story (each group was given different beginnings), and their task was to complete the story using the past tense. It was called a 'Chain Story'. For example, the following were some beginnings: 'It snowed for two days …', 'My boy/girlfriend and I had a big argument …'. Each group was given about 10–15 minutes to complete the story. After 15 minutes, each group was given a different story to start the peer-editing process. They were given specific directions to only look for the tense mistakes.

Our comments: Gloria showed the students how to focus on just one major grammar element in peer-editing these stories. She can help students expand this strategy by suggesting a sequence of several key grammar points to check in their own written work. Another strategy she encouraged was: 'I make grammar summary charts'.

GLORIA: In the beginning of a new unit, students were given a table for them to complete as they learnt the grammar structures. For example, in the beginning of this class, I introduced the simple present tense and the present progressive at the same time, so that the students could understand the differences in structure, use and the example sentences. I used a chart like the one below to guide the students in learning grammar. They completed the table.

Simple present	Present progressive (continuous)
When do you use this?	When do you use this?
What is the structure?	What is the structure?
Write two sentences using this structure:	Write two sentences using this structure:

By filling out a chart like this, students became more aware of the use, form, and meaning of the grammar points. Chart format was also used for simple past/past progressive, future, present perfect/present perfect progressive, modals of ability, permission, requests, and modals of advice. I noticed that when they were engaged in controlled and less controlled and free-writing exercises, they always referred to their self-created charts.

Our comments: This type of chart gives learners more autonomy than a chart that is already completed by the teacher or printed in the textbook. It causes learners to pay more attention to forms and create their own sentences using the forms. It is a very powerful tool in terms of getting material organized in a succinct, clear way and helping students practice and remember it. The fact that students like to refer often to such charts means that this format is particularly useful.

However, two issues must be noted. First, someone needs to check what the students write in their charts to ensure its accuracy. Students might insert incorrect information and then practice it until the incorrect information is fully learnt, making it hard to extinguish the mistake later on. Perhaps peer correction would help here. One way might be to provide a jigsaw activity in which students receive different parts of the correct information, and each student serves as an 'expert' on his or her part. In small groups, every student provides the correct information for his or her part, and all students in the group check their own grammar charts against the correct information. This way, the teacher will not have to check all the charts, and students are empowered to serve as experts on certain aspects of the grammar.

Second, students must eventually be able to wean themselves away from the charts in order to use the target forms orally; they cannot pull out their charts every time they need to say something. They can realize that certain grammar strategies are useful for particular situations and skills but not for other situations and skills. Gloria then developed the strategy: 'I circle or highlight the structure being presented in the unit'.

GLORIA: As a part of the controlled exercises in the textbook, students were given exercises where they had to either circle or highlight the structure being presented in that unit.

Our comments: Because it is presented in the book, it is an instructional strategy. However, when the students start doing the same thing on their own because it helps them notice key grammar points, it becomes their own grammar strategy.

In addition, students can be asked to infer what the underlying rule of the highlighted expressions is. This strategy will help students notice the enriched input and discover the underlying rules. Again, when the teacher asks them to do it, it is an instructional strategy, but when students use it on their own, it becomes a grammar strategy that they 'own' and can use at other times.

Gloria also encouraged: 'I try to notice and learn from my grammar mistakes'.

GLORIA: Throughout this course students were given journal topics (two per week). In addition to their daily written homework assignments, the journal was a big part of their writing component. Journals were collected every Friday, so that I could correct some grammar errors. (I didn't want to correct everything, but at the same time, I wanted to help them become better writers.) Students always referred to the previous journal entry to see what types of mistakes they had made, and they tried not to make the same mistakes.

Our comments: Teachers might encourage students to have a column at the right side of the page of the journals, so that students can make a list of their incorrect expressions and the correct versions. A strategy that might follow this could be: 'I think about how much grammar knowledge was improved'.

GLORIA: Through corrective feedback on daily written assignments (from the grammar text) and the weekly journals, students think about how they are progressing in this class.

Our comments: Monitoring and evaluating their own progress is very helpful for students. Teachers might encourage students to give themselves a grade before teachers do, so that they can reflect on their grammar learning. A connected strategy might be: 'I study grammar even when there isn't a test'.

GLORIA: My class begins at 9:30 am and ends at 11:30. I noticed many students coming to class early to study the grammar. Some were trying to finish their homework, but most were reviewing. As noted earlier, they also get together after class to use the language in more informal settings.

Our comments: It is very helpful to encourage students to study grammar even when there is no immediate test. To get this started, teachers might need to say that they will give unannounced quizzes from time to time. After a few unannounced quizzes, students will be in the habit of studying grammar regularly. Moreover, if grammar is needed for meaningful class activities, students will be motivated to pay attention to structure. Another way to pay such attention is the strategy: 'I ask questions to get a grammatical explanation'.

GLORIA: This class has been asking me a lot more questions related to grammar structure than any other classes that I have taught at _____ College. I realized through these question-explanation interactions that my students were actually thinking about the grammar structure, and trying to find ways to help them understand it better. Their metalinguistic awareness has improved.

Our comments: Teachers could model for their students how to ask grammar-related questions. For example, teachers might say, 'If you don't understand this clearly, you can ask me like this: Would you please explain it again? I don't understand it completely'.

We have just presented a teacher's largely successful efforts to teach grammar strategies to her adult students and have provided our own ideas for making such attempts even more effective. The next section unites the whole chapter by presenting elements of a theory of grammar strategies.

Some perspectives from our observations and from research: elements of a theory of grammar strategies

The general statements in this section can serve as anchor points for a theory of grammar strategies. They are based on our own observations and the sparse research on the topics available in the L2 field. They are also founded on a wider understanding of how learning occurs in general. What follows are theory-making avenues that encompass sociocultural and psychological areas of interest regarding grammar strategies.

In this chapter, we have presented four rather distinct instructional modes, two implicit and two explicit, that can serve as part of a theoretical framework for studying grammar strategies. Some learners prefer to go along with whatever grammar instruction mode they encounter. They adapt themselves to the different instructional goals and beliefs of their teachers and institutions and use grammar strategies reflective of the instructional mode in a given cultural setting. Yet a theoretical framework consisting of instructional modes is only the beginning. This is because learners create and use grammar strategies that fit their own beliefs and perceived goals, which might be influenced by sociocultural and psychological variables other than those embodied in the instructional mode. Learners' own language learning goals and beliefs frequently guide their strategy use more than do the goals and beliefs embedded in specific instructional methodologies.

Strategies that learners use in one classroom setting often overlap with those that other learners use in very different classroom settings, no matter what the instructional modes, because the learners are frequently driven by their own desire to understand forms and rules as part of language learning. Many learners, even if in instructional settings that offer very implicit grammar instruction, develop and use grammar strategies that do not fit the instructional mode they face in class. They consciously or unconsciously question, along with DeKeyser, whether 'anything abstract [such as a systemic regularity or grammar rule] is learnt implicitly' (2003: 319) and whether it is possible to experience 'implicit learning of abstract structure' (2003: 321). Not everyone agrees with this questioning stance, but numerous learners seem to.[6] This is congruent with the research that suggests that explicit learning often has an advantage over implicit learning (Schmidt 1995; Norris and Ortega 2000; DeKeyser 2003).

Adult learners and younger learners have different ways of approaching L2 learning. DeKeyser (2003) and others indicate that adults in particular require explicit learning. This suggests that their grammar strategies will be oriented toward paying attention to target forms and inducing the underlying rules—no matter what happens in the classroom setting. For example, Yasushi, a university learner of EFL, has a highly visual, analytical learning style. His teacher provides extensive, rich, auditory, meaning-based communication activities but with no textbook or analytical grammar charts. Each class is frustrating to Yasushi, who immediately goes back home, looks up as many grammar structures and rules as possible, and makes grammar-analysis charts to tape all over the inside of his apartment. His teacher suggests that this will get in the way of developing fluency, but Yasushi does it anyway, knowing—or at least believing—that it is how he learns best. Learners have many such ways to subvert the goals of the classroom to fit their own goals and belief systems.

The role of grammar strategies in the L2 learning of younger learners must be part of any theory of grammar strategies. This raises many other theories and issues, such as 'critical periods' for language learning (Birdsong 1999), what young learners learn during such critical periods, the extent to which L2 grammar learning is implicit during such periods, and changes in learning processes after those critical periods are past.

Holding age constant, the interplay of implicit learning and explicit learning deserves further theorizing. We propose that this interplay operates differently across individual learners because of differences in cognitive style, educational experience, and cultural background. The degree to which L2 grammar (as compared to L1 grammar) can be learnt implicitly might differ, depending on many factors.

The contrasting 'small cultures' of classrooms—the sociocultural 'communities of practice' created there (Rogoff 1990; Lave and Wenger 1991; Wenger 1998)—have much to do with grammar strategies. Many students share grammar strategies among each other and believe that their peers are the ones most qualified to help them learn grammar. In some classrooms, learners bind together with other learners in overt or covert resistance to instructional modes of the teacher (see, for example, Canagarajah 2003) and create their own undiscussed but enacted way of dealing with grammar and the L2 as a whole.

Even if a learner wishes to follow the teacher's instructional processes, sometimes he or she is not cognitively or physically capable of doing so. For instance, some learners, including those with language learning disabilities and some with other cognitive problems, have great difficulty inducing grammar rules on the basis of multiple instances of a structure, while others have problems taking a given rule and applying it to new instances. Some students, when given a recast of their own incorrect output, do not recognize the difference between the recast and their erroneous original version. This is especially true in an oral exchange if a learner lacks auditory discrimination acuity or does not have the necessary sound for the structure in his or her native language.

For cultural reasons, some students might not recognize certain types of instruction as being 'real teaching'. In many cultures (and here we are talking about 'large cultures', not the small cultures of classrooms), implicit instruction does not count as teaching because the rule is not given and is not readily understood, so the learner does not believe he or she is being 'taught' grammar. In other cultures, role-playing is considered literally playing, and it is not part of serious language instruction. In still other cultures, or rather academic subcultures, memorizing grammar rules is considered passé and not viewed as part of modern language instruction.

Beliefs about the role of grammar in language instruction differ. Some teachers believe that it is the central core of language and must be drilled repeatedly each day; other teachers feel that meaning is the lifeblood of language, so grammatical competence should not be the focus of instruction; and still others contend that meaning and form must be in balance in language instruction. There are also different opinions among students about the role of grammar in language instruction.

In an evolving theory of grammar strategies, it will be essential to maintain the distinction between grammar learning and grammar instruction for the reasons noted earlier. It will also be helpful to recognize that grammar knowledge (implicit versus explicit) is yet a separate theme (R. Ellis 2002a), leading to theoretical questions about strong-, weak-, and no-interface positions that are not covered in this chapter.

Interested parties are urgently needed to follow up these divergent leads in order to develop a theory of grammar strategies. From the 'anchoring ideas' above can come a variety of theoretical discussions and research studies (ethnographic, survey, quasi-experimental, and experimental). We hope these ideas and the whole chapter can propel the grammar strategy field from its hidden nook and into the light. The Second Cinderella should not toil namelessly in a patched dress in a dank, dark basement. Our intent has been to provide insights and a theoretical framework so that grammar strategies can emerge as an important theme for theory and research. We hope that many people will take the proffered challenge to enable grammar strategies and grammar learning in general to become a priority. The area of grammar strategies specifically offers L2 learner strategy researchers and linguistically-oriented L2 acquisition specialists many opportunities to engage in debate and collaborative research. Though these two groups have traditionally kept their distance, they can and should work together to investigate strategies used by L2 learners in developing grammatical competence. Collaborative, interdisciplinary research on grammar strategies will benefit learners everywhere, as well as facilitating the work of L2 teachers and helping us all understand better how people learn another language.

Acknowledgments

We wish to thank Rashi Jain for her excellent editorial assistance. We are indebted to Robert DeKeyser and an anonymous reviewer for their very useful suggestions.

Notes

1 Language pedagogy experts' views about implicit and explicit treatment of grammar differ from those of cognitive psychology researchers. The latter describe '*implicit* grammar instruction' as first presenting learners with sentences that model a specific grammar rule and then asking learners to read or memorize the sentences (without telling them the sentences illustrate a specific rule). Cognitive psychology researchers describe '*explicit* grammar instruction' as first presenting learners with sentences that model a specific grammar rule, then telling learners that the sentences model a rule, and finally asking learners to work out the rule (Robert DeKeyser, personal communication, May 2006). In neither case does the researcher provide the rule to the learners.

2 These are our own interpretations of Doughty's (2003) words.

3 According to Schmidt (1995: 19–20), 'alertness' is a general readiness to deal with incoming stimuli; 'orientation' is specific aligning of attention to form or meaning; and 'detection' is the cognitive registration of sensory stimuli, with or without awareness.

4 This comes largely from cognitive psychologists who work in the area of implicit learning (for example, Reber 1976; Lewicki 1986; Hayes and Broadbent 1988; Perruchet and Amorim 1992).

5 Another assertion that stimulates debate is Winter and Reber's (1994) statement that implicit learning is an *inductive* process. But we question whether induction (as a type of logical reasoning) can occur implicitly, i.e., without awareness, intention, or control. With regard to grammar, *induction* involves arriving at rules by inducing them (figuring them out) from specific grammatical forms. Induction typically involves cognitive effort and awareness, so implicit grammar learning cannot be inductive by this definition. (Few would be likely to say that implicit grammar learning can be *deductive*, either. With regard to grammar, 'deduction' means applying a rule to new instances, with the rule either provided externally or figured out by the learner—not usually feasible without some cognitive effort).

Yet another interesting assertion comes from DeKeyser (2003), who suggests that although two dichotomies, (a) implicit and explicit and (b) inductive and deductive, are clearly independent in principle, they appear to coincide in practice. He notes that the pairing of explicit and deductive is common, because explicit learning is virtually always the result of deductive instruction. However, explicit and deductive do not always go together (within learning, within instruction, or across what could be called the 'learning-and-instruction gap'), nor do implicit and inductive always coincide. DeKeyser (2003) mentions the possibility of implicit-deductive learning, in which learners unconsciously deduce specifics from Universal Grammar parameters. Thus, it is often best to keep the two—(a) implicit and explicit and (b) inductive and deductive—separate.

6 DeKeyser (2003: 319) asserts, 'Implicit learning is at its best only when concrete and contiguous elements are involved'.

7

Intervening in the use of strategies

JOAN RUBIN, ANNA UHL CHAMOT,
VEE HARRIS, and NEIL J. ANDERSON

Introduction

This chapter summarizes current practice in implementing instruction in language learner strategies (LLS) which we refer to as strategy based instruction (SBI). Part Two of this book reviews studies into the effectiveness of SBI in relation to different skill areas. Here the focus is on the nature and purpose of SBI itself, although the chapter also offers a brief overview of this research. Four teacher educators describe SBI at two education levels: elementary and secondary (younger learners) and university, adult, and self-access centers (older learners). The purpose is to identify particular constraints at each level, whilst also highlighting a shared underlying pedagogical approach. Since the successful integration of SBI into the curriculum depends in no small part on the knowledge, understanding, and skill of the teacher, the chapter concludes by discussing obstacles faced and the implications for teacher education.

What should a program of SBI look like?

A major outcome of the research into the strategies used by successful language learners is the conclusion that learners should be taught not only the language but also directed toward strategies they could use to promote more effective learning. As Rubin (1990: 282) points out:

> Often poor learners don't have a clue as to how good learners arrive at their answers and feel they can never perform as good learners do. By revealing the process, this myth can be exposed.

Initial debates (O'Malley and Chamot 1990) focused on whether SBI should be a separate course or integrated into the usual language lessons, embedded in the materials or made explicit. Since that time, there has been an increasing consensus that a fundamental goal of SBI is to promote the development of learner self-management since research has shown that, unless learners select strategies in the service of some task, skill, and goal, they will not easily find the most appropriate strategies and be successful (Gu 2003b; Oxford, Cho, Leung, and Kim 2004; Rubin 2005). Hence the explicit development of metacognitive strategies, alongside cognitive strategies, is considered essential (Wenden 1999; Anderson 2002, 2005). For the same reason, although SBI has been presented separately from the language course itself, all evidence points to greater effectiveness when promoting process (learning) and product (the target language) is done in an integrated fashion. In that way, the development of strategic knowledge and skills can be motivated by a specific learning concern which students have and can foster their ability to select appropriate strategies and be more successful in their learning.

What are the essential requirements of SBI?

A number of models for teaching LLS in both first and second language contexts have been developed. (See, for example, O'Malley and Chamot 1990; Oxford 1990a; Pressley, El-Dinary, Gaskins, Schuder, Bergman, Alma, and Brown 1992; Cohen 1998; Chamot 1999; Chamot, Barnhardt, El-Dinary, and Robbins 1999; Grenfell and Harris 1999; Macaro 2001; Graham and Harris 2003; Harris 2003; National Capital Language Resource Center 2003, 2004.) The Cognitive Academic Language Learning Approach (CALLA) is one such model designed to increase the school achievement of students who are learning through the medium of a second language. The CALLA model fosters language and cognitive development by integrating content, language, and SBI (Chamot and O'Malley 1994b; Chamot 2005a). School districts in the United States that have implemented the CALLA model have focused on preparing and encouraging teachers to teach learner strategies to their students.

Common to all the models of SBI is a sequence of four steps so that, although initial instruction is heavily scaffolded, it is gradually lessened to the point that students can assume responsibility for using the strategies independently (Chamot *et al.* 1999):

1 raising awareness of the strategies learners are already using;
2 teacher presentation and modeling of strategies so that students become increasingly aware of their own thinking and learning processes;
3 multiple practice opportunities to help students move towards autonomous use of the strategies through gradual withdrawal of the scaffolding; and
4 self-evaluation of the effectiveness of the strategies used and transfer of strategies to fresh tasks.

The four steps are illustrated in the descriptions of SBI for younger and older learners that follow. The division into two age-related levels serves to highlight that SBI is not a mechanistic experience, neither for the learner nor for the teacher, but requires reflection and evaluation. Hence it is influenced by the learning context, the nature of the task, and each learner's style, goals, and background knowledge.

Facilitating effective use of strategy knowledge in younger learners

The learning context

This section focuses on the teaching of strategies to school-aged students aged 6–17, whether learners of English or languages other than English, and as second or foreign languages. These two contexts are, of course, quite different in terms of cultural and linguistic background, goals and needs for learning a second language, and motivation.

In the United States, learners of English as a second language comprise both immigrants and children born in the US of immigrant parents. They come from diverse linguistic and cultural backgrounds, with the majority (about 80 per cent) having Spanish as their home language. Most of these learners are highly motivated and their educational goals are to be successful in school. Thus, their need is for academic language, especially literacy, to enable them to achieve academically in the content subjects of the curriculum.

As Dörnyei and Csizér (2002: 455) point out, in England and the United States, the world domination of English has resulted in 'motivationally speaking, a losing battle' for the study of foreign languages such as French and German. A large national survey of foreign language teaching in England conducted by the Nuffield Foundation (2000) notes that nine out of ten pupils drop second languages post-16 and motivation dwindles long before that. (See Graham 2004 for a full discussion.) At the beginning levels, the greatest challenge for foreign language students is to develop proficiency in social language, though at more advanced levels they also need academic language for reading, discussing, and writing about literary and informational texts in the target language.

Language learners in both second and foreign language contexts can benefit from using learner strategies, but they may need different strategies for achieving their learning goals.

Ways to raise younger learner's consciousness of learner strategies

Learner strategy instruction begins with helping students become aware of what strategies are and which strategies they are already using (Cohen 1998; Chamot *et al.* 1999; Grenfell and Harris 1999; Macaro 2001; Chamot 2004). This consciousness-raising helps students begin to think about their own learning processes.

Teachers first elicit students' prior knowledge about strategies and then help them identify their current learner strategies for different tasks. In order to address the issue of motivation, they also explore their students' beliefs about learning and whether they believe that learning occurs as a result of effort, native intelligence, luck, or the systematic application of strategic techniques.

One effective way to find out what strategies students are already using is to ask them. The teacher initiates class discussions about strategies (perhaps defining strategies as 'special techniques for learning') that students use for typical assignments such as learning new vocabulary, understanding what is read, or remembering how to make a request. As students describe their special techniques for learning, the teacher lists their contributions, then identifies and names the strategies, and asks the class how many students use each strategy. Students are often amazed to discover the variety of strategies used by their classmates, and this can motivate them to try out new strategies. It is often helpful to ask students to complete a learning task first, then discuss the strategies they used for it (see Grenfell and Harris 1999), while it is fresh in their minds.

For students who do not share the main language used in the classroom, the teacher needs to teach special vocabulary that will assist them in discussing their strategies. For example, words like 'think', 'strategy', and 'learn' may require native language translation or the assistance of a peer who is relatively proficient in both languages. Giving priority to these vocabulary words and concepts will help students begin to discuss their own strategies and approaches to learning.

Of particular relevance to younger learners are two of the options for awareness raising proposed by Macaro (2001). In the first, students are asked to recall the strategies they so recently used to learn to read and write their L1 and to relate them to the strategies used to learn French. The second draws on adolescents' curiosity about their peers by inviting them to compare their strategies to those drawn up by students of a similar age group learning English as L2.

Initial learner strategy questionnaires were directed at the older learner (Cohen, Oxford, and Chi 2003; SILL in Oxford 1990a; Chamot *et al.* 1999) and it is only more recently that more accessible questionnaires for younger learners have been developed such as Cohen and Oxford's *Young Learners Language Strategy Use Survey* (2002). Their (2001) *Learning Style Survey for Young Learners* uses a range of visual resources and practical exemplifications to enable learners to understand their own preferred ways of tackling the language learning task.

Ways to present learner strategies to younger learners

Younger students may initially find that strategies are rather abstract and difficult to understand. In the presentation step, teachers model how strategies can be used for a particular task to make them as concrete as possible. By modeling their own use of learner strategies, teachers are making their thinking public and sharing it with the class. This modeling is generally done by 'thinking aloud' while working on a learning task. Often strategies in checklists are presented in brief, generalized statements describing an action such as, 'When I'm reading I like to visualize what is happening in the story'. However younger students may benefit from the teacher providing simple, concrete, personalized exemplifications such as, 'Visualizing is a learner strategy. It helps me make sense of a story. If what I visualize doesn't make sense in the story, then I know that I need to check what I just read, because I probably misread something' (Chamot in press). In this way, students can attach a name to a strategy and can understand when, why, and how it is used.

The use and limitations of think-alouds as a research tool are discussed in Chapters 5 and 7. Here the focus is on their use as a teaching tool. An example of a step-by-step approach to teacher's 'thinking aloud', geared to this level of learner (Chamot in press) follows:

[The teacher shows an overhead transparency of a reading text and says:]
I'm going to show you what I do when I read. I'm going to describe my thinking. The first thing I do is to look at the title. And I think, 'What is this story going to be about? What do I already know about this topic?'
[The teacher makes a guess about the topic and also describes some personal prior knowledge related to the topic.]
Now that I've made a prediction about this story, I'm ready to start reading.
[The teacher reads aloud, pointing to the words as she goes.] Oh, here's a word I don't know. [The teacher points to a difficult word.] What shall I do? Maybe if I read the next sentence it will give me a clue.
[The teacher reads on and uses context to make an inference about the meaning of the difficult word.]

Table 7.1 A teacher thinks aloud

After a few minutes of modeling by thinking aloud, the teacher engages the class in a discussion of the process by asking students to recall what she did first, second, etc. and why they think she did that. The teacher can then name the strategy ('Yes, I used the strategy "predicting" to figure out the topic of the story').

The teacher then asks students to provide examples of when they have used a strategy and whether it worked for them. In other words, the teacher does not assume that any particular strategy is unknown to students. Some students might not know the strategy while others may already be using it. The focus is on *naming* the strategy and discussing how it can be used for different kinds of learning tasks.

An additional way to make strategies more concrete for younger learners is to provide visual reinforcement. For example, teachers prepare strategy posters with icons to represent each strategy. Some teachers have used toy tool kits with each tool labeled with a different strategy name to provide concrete examples of 'tools for learning'.

Ways younger learners can practice LLS

Besides teacher modeling, students also need extensive practice opportunities. Learner strategies are part of procedural knowledge and thus need to be practiced as much as any other procedure or skill (Chamot in press). In the beginning stages of practice, teachers usually need to remind students to try the new strategies. However, as students become more familiar with the strategies, they themselves should gradually assume responsibility for using them.

Since a sense of self-efficacy[1] is a major component of motivation (see Graham 2004 for a review of studies) and yet younger learners have a limited linguistic repertoire, there is a particular need to build their confidence. For example, beginners can engage in activities that reveal that they are not entirely dependent on their restricted L2 resources but can draw on their prior knowledge of the topic and context. In their study of reading and listening SBI with 12–13-year-old pupils, Harris and Prescott (2005) described how students were presented with a magazine advertisement for a computer game but with only the title and pictures showing. They were asked to predict both the content and the likely words they would find in the hidden section of the page. Macaro (2001) suggests that to model communication strategies such as intonation and mime, pairs of students are provided with a dialogue but can only use one word to convey each message. The rest of the class has to guess the meaning.

Most students need multiple practice opportunities with LLS before they are able to use them independently and appropriately without teacher prompting. Strategies can be practiced with any classroom learning task, provided it poses a degree of challenge—if the task is too easy, students will not need to use strategies. Activities that involve collaboration, problem-solving, inquiry, role-playing, and hands-on experiences also lend themselves to practicing new learner strategies, especially since interaction with peers offers an additional source of scaffolding (Donato and McCormick 1994). Younger learners may require more extensive opportunities for such pair- and group-work than older learners since, however hard teachers seek to describe strategies in readily accessible terms, students may be better at explaining strategies to each other than their teachers are. Any student can learn much during 'think-alouds' from observing the strategies their partner uses but adolescents in particular may be more convinced by each other's positive opinion of the potential value of a certain strategy than the teacher's exhortations to use it. A further advantage is that, in spite of outward appearances, these adolescent students may lack confidence and the principle of 'think-pair-share' can lead to more productive whole class discussions. Initial practice with new learner strategies requires extensive support and scaffolding from the teacher. This support should be gradually faded to reminders and eventually students should be asked to choose the strategies they plan to use for a task or to identify the strategies they used after completing a task.

Ways to promote self-evaluation with younger learners

Just as students need practice in using the strategies, they also need to practice the metacognitive strategy of 'evaluation' after trying out new strategies. This provides them with an opportunity to reflect on how they applied the strategies and how successful they were in helping them complete the learning task. For example, teachers ask students to write down the strategies they used during an activity or assignment, indicate how each strategy worked, and note any personal adaptations of each strategy. They then guide a class discussion about the strategies that seemed most useful for the learning task. Many of the same activities used during consciousness-raising such as class discussion, writing learning logs, and completing checklists can be used for students to evaluate their own use of strategies (Chamot *et al.* 1999). This phase is especially important in developing students' ability to reflect on their own learning and develop their procedural knowledge.

A further potential incentive well-suited to younger learners is a 'Strategy Progress Card' with a checklist of strategies on one side and space on the other for students to record their test results over the period of time allotted for the SBI, so that they have a concrete representation of their progress. As Chamot and Rubin (1994: 773) stress, 'if strategies are presented in such a way that learners perceive immediate success, they are more willing to use them'.

Once students are familiar with new cognitive and socio-affective strategies and have had opportunities to practice them, they generally find that certain strategies work better for them than others for specific tasks. Students differ in their approaches to learning and can be expected to have strong preferences in the types of strategies they like to use. At this point they should be encouraged to develop their own personal repertoire of effective cognitive and socio-affective learner strategies which work for specific kinds of tasks. Students should not be forced to use one strategy or another, but rather encouraged to build their repertoire so as to increase their tools for learning.

Ways to promote strategy transfer in younger learners

LLS research has shown that students often do not automatically transfer the strategies they learn in one context to a different situation (O'Malley and Chamot 1990; Davidson and Sternberg 1998). Typically they will restrict a learner strategy to the specific context in which that strategy was first learnt, though students who have developed effective strategies in their L1 are more likely to transfer them to similar tasks in the L2 (García, Jiménez, and Pearson 1998). Teachers assist in strategy transfer in two ways: first by developing students' metacognition through explicit strategy instruction and, second, by discussing with students how they might apply a strategy in a different context. For example, in relation to access to academic language, the teacher might ask students to transfer the strategy that he/she taught them to a content subject class and then report back on its effectiveness in that class. Other approaches are to have students teach the strategies they are learning to a friend or sibling and then evaluate how effective they were in explaining and modeling the strategies to others. One class decided to develop a class book on learner strategy tips that would be passed on to students in the teacher's next class the following year. By showing students how to apply learner strategies in new contexts, teachers can help them develop skilled use of strategies with different types of language and academic content tasks and the knowledge base to use them effectively.

As Cohen, Weaver, and Li (1998: 113) suggest, transfer can be encouraged not only across L2 task and text types but also across L1 and L2. They highlight the value of explicit instruction in facilitating transfer across languages, arguing against Kellerman's (1991) assertion that learners automatically transfer communication strategies from their L1:

> some or many of the L1 strategies will eventually transfer on their own but explicit training may hasten the process along, as well as teaching some communicative behaviour that is not learnt automatically.

Wenden's (1999) review of related studies indicated the key role played by metacognitive knowledge in facilitating such transfer.

To encourage them to transfer 'guessing from the context' across languages adolescent students in one foreign language classroom in England where the SBI was designed to foster transfer were given examples of complex terms associated with particular curriculum areas ('alliteration', 'particle', 'infrastructure') and then encouraged to discuss how they worked out the meaning (for example, guessing from context or prior knowledge of the subject area). They also explored roots of words common to English and French (*cent, corp, dent*) and how these carried clues to meaning. Harris and Grenfell (2004) describe in more detail how the exploration of cross-disciplinary connections between English and L2 can illuminate ways in which secondary school learners in the UK context might understand and then take more effective control of their own language learning.

Issues in SBI for younger learners

Three issues that can become potential stumbling blocks in SBI for younger learners are the use of the L2 for SBI, the effect of multiple strategies combined with difficult texts, and insufficiently developed metacognition.

Harris and Snow (2004) and Macaro (2001) discuss whether, for younger learners, the declarative knowledge involved in SBI is best filtered through L1. They argue that reflecting on and verbalizing their own internal thought processes already presents students with a sufficient challenge and that the priority is to fully engage in L1 discussions both with the teacher and in pairs. A judicious mix of L1 and L2 can be used, however, in the instructional materials.

While the existing literature suggests a broad sequence of general steps to be followed, tensions may arise, particularly with younger learners, in establishing progression in SBI over a prolonged period of time. These relate to the choice of texts and tasks, the integration of the steps into the scheme of work, and sustaining student motivation. Chamot *et al.* (1999: 99) warn:

> If the task is too easy, students will not need strategies to succeed; they may therefore see strategies as a waste of time. However, if the task is too difficult students may not be able to succeed even when they do use appropriate strategies.

As Oxford, Cho, Leung, and Kim's (2004) study suggests, an additional consideration is the adaptation of both task and text according to the learners' proficiency levels.

While the use of authentic materials enables students to perceive the immediate relevance of the reading strategies presented, and offers opportunities to teach strategies not apparent in contrived textbook texts, the combination of difficult authentic texts and a wide number of new strategies can place too heavy a burden on students' mental processing capabilities (Harris and Prescott 2005). An alternative approach entails a gradual progression starting with practicing a cluster of related strategies[2] that the teacher identifies as related through a brief initial activity and then proceeding with the usual lesson. A textbook passage then recycles the strategy clusters at the end of several weeks. Finally, once the students are comfortable with the use of the cluster of strategies within familiar contexts, extended group-work encourages them to move from supported practice in the use of a limited number of strategies to deploying the full range independently and from reading textbook texts to tackling authentic material.

All SBI models suggest that students should plan what strategies to use for a task, monitor comprehension and production while the task is in progress, and upon task completion evaluate how well a strategy has worked and actively transfer strategies to new tasks. That is, the models (explicitly or implicitly) advocate the development of learners' metacognitive strategies along with cognitive strategy instruction. However, it is generally acknowledged that metacognitive understanding is a developmental process and that younger children are not as fully aware of their own thinking and learning processes as are adolescents and adults (Hacker 1998). This poses a potential stumbling block in SBI for children, who have not yet developed full metacognitive abilities. While the L2 research on SBI with young children is sparse, there is some evidence of considerable variation in their ability to report on their own thinking and problem-solving with reading and writing tasks in the target language (Chamot 1999). In Chamot's (1999) LLS study of children in foreign language immersion classrooms, some children as young as six could describe their own thinking processes, but for most, this ability developed gradually over the six years of the study.

Facilitating effective use of strategy knowledge in adult, university, and self-access centers

The learning context

This section considers ways to facilitate effective use of strategy knowledge for adults who are learning a language in a variety of settings and with a variety of motivations. What is perhaps most critical to note about these settings is that possibly more than with classes of school age children, within any one class of adults, learners' goals can be quite different. This difference can affect learner motivation and willingness to do more than the minimum to enhance learning. On the other hand, improving learning can often enhance motivation.

Variation in these settings include:

1 how much experience with language learning the student has had. This can range from people who have a strong academic background and extensive language learning experience to those who may have never studied a language or are not even literate;
2 what the consequences of not meeting a required language course are; for example from having to repeat a course to more pressing outcomes for adults who need a language for work and therefore may not get a cherished assignment or raise; and
3 whether the facilitator is a teacher or a counselor (as in a self-access center).

In the first case, unlike younger learners, those who have had considerable language learning experience have most likely acquired substantial strategic knowledge. However, they may need help with focusing on a few specific learning problems. Or, if the type of language they are learning is quite different (for example, one with a different script), they may need to acquire additional strategic knowledge to deal with new kinds of learning. If the learner has not had a successful language learning experience or if they do not have much experience with learning a language (despite the fact that they do well in other subjects), they will more than likely need to gain a great deal of knowledge about strategies and their own learning styles as well as learn how to manage the entire learning process.

The second case is related to the learners' goals and will directly affect motivation. (See Chapter 3.) When the goal is pedagogical, there can be considerable variation among learners. Many who take a *required* course are not very motivated and this can directly affect their receptiveness to efforts to facilitate their learning. On the other hand, students who are achievement oriented and want to earn a passing grade, will be more open to such efforts. Those adults for whom learning is clearly related to personal or life goals, especially related to career, are likely to be the most motivated and more open to learning about learning.

In the third case, the teacher has the opportunity to consider ways of providing the knowledge and skill of effective use of strategy knowledge to the whole group while at the same time making sure that individual learners gain what they need from the attention to process. In a self-access center however, while counselors can provide just the right amount of attention to address a learner's needs, they may also be constrained in the amount of time they can give an individual learner. The teacher or counselor needs to bear these considerations in mind when helping learners to use their strategic knowledge and needs to ascertain (a) how much knowledge the learner has, (b) how to help learners identify goals that will serve to motivate their learning, and (c) how to make sure that individual needs are being addressed and that the learning is useful to them.

Ways to raise older learner's awareness of LLS

Just as with younger learners, awareness of LLS and how well they work for a particular task and for a learner's particular goal is central to the successful use of cognitive and affective strategies. The use of 'think-alouds' has already been discussed in the first section. In addition to think-alouds, of particular relevance for raising adult learners' awareness are questionnaires, focus groups, 'ask a question', journals, and reading about the topic. Each of these teaching strategies is first defined below and then a chart (Table 7.2) is provided describing advantages and disadvantages of using them to raise awareness.

Questionnaires Although these can be used with younger learners, care has to be taken to ensure the wording is accessible. In selecting a questionnaire, it is helpful to note that the closer the questionnaire is to the actual skill and tasks the learner needs to accomplish, the more useful it will be to the learner because it focuses on actual tasks. For example, the Survey of Reading Strategies (SORS) (Sheorey and Mokhtari 2001; Mokhtari and Sheorey 2002) is specifically designed to help learners become better readers and raise their awareness of reading strategies.

Focus groups In this activity, learners focus on a particular skill (for example, listening) and spell out the range of goals they might have (follow instructions, understand a soap opera, make some friends). Then students are divided into focus groups, with each focus group working on a specific goal and considering what *problems* they might have achieving this goal and what *solutions* they might use to address the problem.

Ask a question This is a very simple technique to draw attention to strategy usage. When a learner gets an acceptable response the teacher asks the learner to report how he/she came up with that answer. In this way, learners share the process and make it available to others.

Journals With their highly developed metacognitive skills, older learners can use journals as a way of promoting awareness of strategies, especially if they are done in a focused manner. Rubin (2003: 12) provides an example of the kind of questions to promote effective reflection. Such questions include:

'What problems do/did you have in class or with your homework? How did you deal with these problems? How well did these solutions work for you?'.

Reading about the learning process There are several volumes written for learners that describe the learning process which adult learners can be encouraged to read in their own time. These can help tackle possible student resistance by promoting the idea that learners can take charge of their learning and consider which strategies work best for them and for their particular problems (Brown 1991; Rubin and Thompson 1994; Paige, Cohen, Kappler, Chi, and Lassegard 2002).

Technique	Advantages	Disadvantages
1 Questionnaires	Material is ready to go; does not take a lot of time	Hard to make clear how important it is for a strategy to be related to task, goal, and the learner's particular problem
2 Focus groups	Can be directly related to goal and to learners' perceived problems; allows teacher to show how a strategy is directly related to a specific task	Takes class time; teacher needs to be quite familiar with a range of strategies in order to debrief discussions
3 Ask a question	Can be used at any time	Learners may need prompting to access their strategies
4 Journals	Very individualized; helpful for consciousness raising, for helping learners consider alternatives	If used with a beginning class or individual, language of the journal is a consideration
5 Reading about process	Very individualized, learners can read in detail as they need to. Can be done outside class	Language level usually not appropriate for beginners, except where translated (see references)

Table 7.2 Advantages and disadvantages of awareness raising techniques

Ways to present and practice strategies

The adult learning context has both advantages and disadvantages. On the one hand the diversity of adult learners' goals and knowledge poses a particular challenge, and requires the development of a high level of learner self-management. On the other hand, the teacher can draw on adults learners' greater ability to articulate their thought processes and to work independently. In addition, self-access centers can provide more opportunities for individualized support than classes of younger children.

If teachers are trying to build strategy knowledge of cognitive or affective strategies, the instruction should always be in context, that is, it should be directly related to something a learner is having a problem with. Learners need to recognize where they have a pattern of errors and when they are ready to work on a problem. If strategies are presented in the kind of context in which learners have a need to know or are feeling overwhelmed by material, then the help offered will be more readily accepted. There are several ways to bring learners to the recognition that they might need help and that it might be useful to focus on the learning process. The think-aloud, focused journal writing, and focus groups with a particular skill and particular function, can help learners begin to identify their individual patterns of problems and provide the opportunity for them to consider which ones they want to work on. Another way to help learners recognize their need for help is to consider problems after getting back an exam or quiz. It is at this time perhaps that learners are most aware of their need.

Since use of strategies varies by learner, by task, and by goal, presentation of strategies is in terms of possible usefulness rather than recommendation. There is no 'right' or 'wrong' strategy but rather one that works for the particular learner for the particular task and goal. The Aymara memory exercise (Cohen 1990; also in Paige *et al.* 2002) offers learners the opportunity to consider which kinds of mnemonics work best for them.

Some teachers find it useful in teaching a particular strategy or even set of strategies to follow the sequence described above for younger learners (modeling, describing the modeling, naming the strategy, providing examples of when they might have used a strategy, and considering when it might be useful). However, it may be less productive for experienced adult learners if several learners in a class already know those strategies or use others that are more effective for them.

There are several think-aloud type activities used in presenting strategies which, although they can be used with younger learners, may be easier to use with adults. One is the 'think-aloud hot seat'. Teachers invite someone who seems to really grasp the notion of an effective strategy to model for his/her peers, so that they can see someone in their own class engaged in effective strategy use. Within this context, students often reveal strategies that teachers had not thought of.

The think-aloud protocol can also be implemented for one-on-one conferences with a learner. A teacher can learn a great deal about a learner by inviting him/her to do a language learning task while he/she watches. Then the teacher invites the student to talk about the strategies that he/she used while performing the task. This often helps learners who are struggling to overcome challenges to learning because they become aware of what they are doing and because the teacher makes suggestions to try out strategies to address their problems.

Teachers/counselors also help learners practice strategies, when they run into difficulty doing an activity, by reminding them of ones that have already met. Using a 'just in time' approach is very powerful because it meets a learner's immediate need and is not done in the abstract.[3]

Ways to promote self-evaluation of strategy use

It is critical that learners develop their own repertoire of strategy knowledge, gaining an understanding of their own learning style, which strategies work best for them, and how to connect strategies to the task and goals they may have. Insights into what has worked for them in the past help them do so, and there are a range of ways to support them in developing the ability to self-evaluate. One technique involves encouraging learners to set goals in advance for a particular task, identify which strategies might work for them, determine their criteria for success, and then notice after completing the task how well those strategies worked.

Kato (2000) used the following technique in helping her students of Japanese manage their learning. She asked them on a day-by-day basis to set the number of words they wanted to learn, to select one or more strategies to use to learn them, and then to determine whether they had done so. If they failed, they were asked to reconsider their goals (i.e. number of words learnt), and the success of their strategies. It is worth noting that in order to consider success, learners' goals need to be very specific (not just number of words, but what 'learning a word' means; see Nation (2001) for an outline of ways of knowing a word) and they need to know how to check their success, independent of feedback from the teacher.

Without an awareness of whether a strategy works for them, the learner is unlikely to see the benefit of using it so this phase of instruction is critical.

Issues in SBI for older learners

One issue, true of many ESL or other second language contexts, is that learners in a class may have many different native languages so that there is no common L1 in which to carry out the instruction. At the same time, learners may have limited target language abilities. A creative solution is to pair more advanced learners in higher level courses with those with more limited target language skills. More advanced learners can carry out some of the awareness work in the native language and then write it up as they would for a research report. In this way, they do three things at the same time: they raise the awareness of the beginning learners, they learn about the learning process and how to do research, and they learn how to write a research report. This approach was successfully used by Sharon McKay (personal communication) with a group of advanced, college-bound learners. The lower level learners were pleased to talk about their learning processes and exclaimed that 'no one had ever asked them'. The more advanced learners gained both in knowledge about the learning process but also about how to collect data and write it up.

Research into SBI

Research on the intervention or teaching of language learner strategies has been undertaken with the aim of exploring the extent to which it enables students to become more effective language learners. Issues have been raised, however, about the reliability and robustness of some of the studies (McDonough 1999). A recent review of strategy instruction in language learning identified a relatively small number of intervention studies that were truly experimental in design (Hassan, Macaro, Mason, Nye, Smith, and Vanderplank 2005), that is, studies in which the effectiveness of strategy instruction with a group of language students was measured against a comparable group of students who either received a different type of treatment or no treatment at all. Moreover, of the 38 studies meeting the established criteria, only 11 were of younger, school-aged students, while 27 were of older learners. In general, Hassan *et al.* concluded that training language students to use learner strategies was effective in the short-term, but there was no evidence of whether its effects persisted over time. This review also differentiated between the effects of learner strategy instruction in different language modalities, finding weak evidence for effectiveness of strategy training for listening, speaking, and vocabulary acquisition, but strong evidence supporting the teaching of learner strategies for reading and writing in a second or foreign language. A full discussion of many of these studies can be found in Part Two of this book.

A smaller-scale review of intervention studies also found gaps in the research that should be addressed in future studies (Chamot 2005a). It called for additional and rigorous intervention studies with a variety of language students, including children in foreign language immersion and non-immersion programs, school-aged students in bilingual and second language programs, older students with differing educational levels in their native language, and students in different learning contexts around the world. In addition, it called for research on the development of language teacher expertise for integrating learner strategies into their classrooms, including teacher characteristics such as teaching approach, attitude, and teacher beliefs. Suggestions for teacher education are discussed in the next section of this chapter.

An essential requirement for the accurate and reliable reporting of SBI is a careful description of the research and instructional methodology used, including details on what strategies were taught, how they were taught, the level of explicitness of the instruction, types of activities students were engaged in to practice the strategies, how the use of strategies was evaluated, the length of time the SBI took, and most importantly, whether the instruction included metacognitive awareness raising. Learner strategy instruction also needs to be assessed for its effects on language proficiency, not just on student self-report of strategy use.

An important direction in future LLS research is to examine whether any such improvement in performance coincides with changes in strategy deployment and in attitudes. A further avenue is the investigation of the longitudinal effects of strategy instruction. Once students have been taught to use learner strategies to facilitate their second language acquisition, do they continue using the strategies (or continue to develop their use of more sophisticated strategies) over time? Do they need periodic reminders of the strategies and 'refresher' courses?

Allied to the longitudinal issue is the transferability of learner strategies to new tasks. Research in first language contexts has shown that strategy transfer is often difficult, but that explicit instruction and the development of metacognitive awareness promote strategy transfer. There is limited research on transfer of strategies in second language acquisition, but new work in this area promises to provide insights that can help teachers teach for transfer (see Harris 2004).

Further directions for possible research are related to the distinction between younger and older learners drawn in this chapter. Cross study comparison of the impact of strategy instruction is rendered problematic by differences in learning settings, the periods of time over which it is undertaken and the nature of the SBI itself. Few studies indicate how the choice of skill areas and strategies has been tailored to meet learners' age, stage, and proficiency level. Although Macaro (2001: 267) provides a brief overview of a possible SBI programme from Beginner through Intermediate to Advanced level, a number of issues related to progression bear further exploration. They might include:

1 The benefits and limitations of focusing on the strategies involved in one skill area as opposed to highlighting the overarching metacognitive strategies in any task the learner faces. Of the 38 studies selected by Hassan *et al.* (2005), 24 were in cognitive training, eight were in metacognitive training and the remainder in mixed strategy training. On the one hand, concentrating on one skill area may be less time consuming and more manageable for the teacher. But it is likely to reduce the learners' ability to perceive the potential for transfer. As O'Malley and Chamot (1990) conclude, the optimum way of grouping strategies to minimize potential learner confusion is an aspect of SBI that awaits further investigation.

2 The choice of skill area on the basis of the age and proficiency level of the learner. Harris *et al.* (2001) argue that vocabulary memorization strategies may be a suitable starting point for beginners and this is also implied in Macaro's (2001) overview. There appears however to be both a lack of discussion as to the possible criteria for the selection of a skill area and a lack of rigorously evaluated programs, where each skill area is taught to the same group of learners over a prolonged period.

3 The selection of strategies within the particular skill area according to the age and proficiency level of the learner. While strategies drawing on sophisticated grammatical knowledge are clearly more suitable for advanced learners, other strategies are less readily categorized.

4 The relationship between the age, proficiency, and motivation level of the learners to the optimum number of strategies to be taught over the course of the SBI and even the number to be presented in any one lesson.

Perhaps the most striking characteristic of strategic learners is that they are able to manage their own learning effectively. That is, they not only understand their own learning strengths and weaknesses, but are able to act on this knowledge to plan, monitor, and evaluate their language learning. Research is needed that can measure this ability to self-manage language learning and examine its relationship to a range of factors such as attainment, personality, and attitude.

Teacher concerns and teacher education

A number of researchers have worked closely with teachers to guide them in incorporating SBI into their language classes. Even with close collaboration, there have been differences in the degree to which teachers have been able to successfully implement learner strategy instruction (Rubin, Quinn, and Enos 1988; O'Malley and Chamot 1990; Grenfell and Harris 1999; Macaro 2001; Chamot and Keatley 2003). Factors that may explain why some teachers experience difficulty in implementing learner strategy instruction include curriculum constraints, teaching style, comfort with current style, teacher beliefs, and lack of knowledge and skill in promoting strategies (Vieira 2003).

The curriculum may determine how much time teachers are willing to spend on SBI. Curricula with detailed standards and mandated assessments of these standards can make the teacher feel that there is no time to spare for 'extras' such as teaching strategies. In addition, some curricula effectively dictate the types of tasks undertaken in the language classroom. Tasks differ depending on whether the context is a second language or foreign language setting and whether the curricular goal is for learners to acquire social language or academic language or both (Cummins 2000; Cohen 2003; Chamot 2004; Oxford, Cho, Leung, and Kim 2004).

Teachers who prefer a transmission style of teaching may tell students to use strategies without investigating student preferences and prior knowledge about strategies. In this type of language classroom, strategies become one more thing that students must memorize rather than take an active and personal approach to learning.

Learners and parents of younger learners may also be more comfortable with the transmission style. Teachers report facing some resistance to strategy intervention both from students and parents. This is often based on their expectations of the teacher role and their beliefs about the learning process. As has been seen, it can be helpful to have learners read about the learning process to raise their awareness of the importance of being more active, or to hear how more successful learners manage their learning.

A further concern reported is the difficulty of providing individual support and advice when working with large classes (50 students or more). This calls for teachers to be highly creative in finding ways to promote the development of effective strategy use by putting learners into smaller groups or by using peer feedback.

In order to overcome these constraints and effectively promote the use of strategies, teachers themselves need to gain a great deal of knowledge and skill. Yet, how to teach strategies is not usually a topic studied in professional preparation programs for second language teachers. The major focus in such programs is on pedagogical techniques, lesson planning, and classroom management. They may study second language acquisition processes but this theoretical knowledge may not be translated into specific practices for helping students become better language learners. Teachers usually become interested in learner strategies either through self-study, exposure in a professional development workshop, or collaboration on a LLS research project.

Most researchers (for example, see Harris *et al.* 2001) agree that, in order to support teachers in effective SBI, an active, experiential approach is necessary. This enables teachers to discover their own strategies, consider new ones, learn how to model and teach them, have many opportunities to practice and evaluate these teaching approaches, and plan how they will integrate strategy-based instruction into the curriculum. As such, the process is similar to ones their learners should experience through the four SBI steps highlighted earlier in the chapter. In addition, just as learners need to self-reflect on how well they are learning and how well they are managing the learning process, so too teachers need to be clear about how well they are facilitating learners' ability to manage their learning. Anderson (2005) argues that in order to have metacognitively aware learners, we must have metacognitively aware teachers. A specific example of a checklist for reflection for language teachers is given below (Table 7.3). A more general education one can be found in Costa and Kallick (2004).

Wenden 1995, Chamot *et al.* 1999, and Rubin 2001 and 2005 suggest that it is critical throughout for teachers to engage in the overall process of planning, taking into consideration the task, the learner's goal and purpose, and encouraging them to establish a time frame. This will involve task analysis: for example considering the task classification and task demands. The process can then be further fine-tuned as learners become aware of how to enhance learning by monitoring, evaluating and considering the reasons for their success or failure, and considering what changes they need to make to improve their learning process. To deploy strategies successfully, learners must use the strategies in a contextualized manner using their knowledge about tasks, skills, and background information in selecting strategies. They need to have well developed procedures of planning, monitoring, evaluating, and problem-solving, and to be flexible and adaptable so that when they encounter difficulties, they can come up with alternative solutions (Rubin 2005). For a teacher to be able to bring all this together, he/she needs a great deal of knowledge and skill.

1 What were your goals?	
2 What were your evaluation criteria to know you have reached your goal?	
3 What teaching strategies will you use to accomplish your goal(s)?	
4 How much time will you need to accomplish your goal(s)?	
5 What problems arose while presenting the strategic knowledge?	
6 Identify any problem sources (your goals, your teaching strategies, your emotions, amount of time for presentation)	
7 Identify all problem solutions (adjust goal(s), teaching strategies, pace, your emotions, amount of time)	
8 Type of revisions you will make next time you teach strategic knowledge	

Table 7.3 Evaluating your success in teaching learner strategies

Conclusion

This chapter has provided an overview of current practice in SBI, highlighted issues for a SBI research agenda and discussed the implications for teacher education. It has suggested that although SBI is tailored to different settings, there are common underlying principles:

1 Strategy intervention should be directly related to problems that learners are seeking to solve. This means that unless learners recognize that they have a problem and have the motivation to solve that problem, providing them with more strategic knowledge will not be well received.
2 Strategic intervention should lead to immediate and recognizable success. Since we know that motivation is critical in learning (Pintrich and Schunk 1996; Dörnyei 2005), and that feeling competent (self-efficacy) is a major component of motivation, learners should themselves directly feel that the knowledge given through strategy intervention is immediately and directly useful to them.
3 Since there is a great range of variation in learning, much as it might be simpler for the teacher and/or counselor, there is no such thing as 'one size fits all'. Teachers need to become more aware of the sources of variation (individual, group, cultural, and developmental)[4] and need to develop skills

and knowledge to facilitate the learning process given this kaleidoscopic diversity.

4 Strategy intervention should include sufficient scaffolding, modeling, practice, and development of self-assessment. Providing just the right amount of scaffolding is more an art though some have suggested a sequence for evaluating the development of such knowledge (Sinclair 1999).

5 The amount of time it takes to develop a learner's ability to manage his/her own learning can vary tremendously. Some factors which can affect this are: a learner's beliefs about the teacher and learner roles, the teacher's skill in integrating strategy intervention with course material, and student disposition toward an already developed skill in learner self-management.

For many teachers, the element of time in promoting strategies can be an issue. Yet, the evidence discussed in this chapter and in Part Two of the book suggests that if effectively done:

1 It increases ability to manage cognitive and affective strategies.
2 It increases learner motivation.
3 It increases performance.
4 It provides learners with the knowledge and skills to continue learning on their own. As Nunan (1996: 41) recommends, 'language classrooms should have a dual focus, not only teaching language content but also on developing learning processes as well'.

From the teacher's or counselor's perspective, promoting learner self-management provides a never-ending kaleidoscope of information and sharing so that, not only does the student gain knowledge and skills, but the teacher is also learning new ways to help students resolve their learning problems and be more effective learners.

Notes

1 Self-efficacy refers to a feeling of competence, that the learner knows how to accomplish the task. For a discussion of self-efficacy in general education, see Bandura (1995).

2 An example of the cluster would be: identifying cognates then using context to work out whether they are *faux amis* or false cognates.

3 There are several sources for forms to use to promote this 'just in time' approach. See for example, the following: Willing (1989), Chamot (1999), and Riley and Harsch (2006).

4 Strage (1998) provides data showing that different kinds of parenting can affect a learner's willingness to become more independent.

Reviewing thirty years of empirical LLS research

An introduction to systematic reviewing

ERNESTO MACARO

and ANDREW D. COHEN

Systematic reviewing is a practice which is now widespread in the natural sciences (especially in the field of medical research) and one which is also gaining a foothold in the social sciences. It was adopted in Part Two of this book in preference to 'narrative reviews' (or 'traditional reviews') of the research literature as 'systematicity' offers a number of advantages. These are summarized below. Space does not allow the reporting of the full systematic review process for each chapter but interested readers can access these useful details in Appendices 8.1–12.1 on www.oup.com/elt/teacher/lls, as well as tabular overviews of studies reviewed in each chapter.

First and foremost, systematic reviewing aims to provide a comprehensive picture of the research available in a particular field. Reviewers are not content with describing research they have already read or have at hand. Rather their task is to search as thoroughly as possible all the relevant available electronic and paper databases in order to ensure that no useful study goes unnoticed. Thus, each review team undertook extensive electronic and hand-searching. Then, very importantly, the search procedure is made transparent to the reader so that s/he may replicate and compare the search at a later date. This transparency extends to the 'search terms' used. As an example, for the chapter on writing strategies, the search terms were: 'composing', 'writing', 'second language', 'foreign language', 'processes', 'strategies', the combinations thus being: 'second/foreign language composing/writing strategies/processes'. The reader can judge the appropriateness and comprehensibility of these search terms against the review questions.

Another approach to ensure comprehensibility is to identify extensive reviews already undertaken. Thus the authors of Chapter 12 on vocabulary strategies consulted the 2000 entries from I. S. P. Nation's website and bibliographies, whilst the authors of Chapter 11 on writing strategies were fortunate in the availability of previous syntheses including their own.

Of course the comprehensive nature of the review process is limited by the resources available. The authors of the chapter on listening were fortunate in having secured funding and were thus able to obtain virtually all the doctoral dissertations identified by their electronic search—a costly exercise. Another limitation is the languages that the reviewers had available. For example, not all reviewers were able to review papers written in German as was possible in the chapter on reading strategies.

A second advantage of systematic reviews over traditional reviews is their quest for reliability. At every stage of the review process measures are taken to ensure objectivity. After avoiding the bias of the search process, reviewers must also guard against bias in selecting the studies that answer the review questions, by having clear and theoretically driven inclusion criteria. They also guard against the bias inherent in assessing the quality of each study—its validity, reliability, and generalizability—and its relevance to the review questions. In the chapter on speaking, for example, the two authors independently reviewed studies and the summaries written, and then these were checked by the other author. Where disagreements as to quality or interpretation occurred, the study was re-examined. Finally systematic reviewers guard against possible bias when synthesizing the research evidence reviewed. In the chapter on listening, for example, each review section was independently summarized by two of the authors with a third monitoring the synthesis of the two summaries. Disagreements about conclusions were ironed out before a final version was arrived at. The same procedure was adopted for the overall conclusion.

We would argue that systematicity in reviewing research evidence is a first step towards 'good science'. Moreover, it provides future researchers, practitioners, and policy makers with more secure theoretical and empirical foundations for their beliefs and activities. We are thus more confident in offering our readers the findings of these reviews on strategy research.

8

A review of listening strategies: focus on sources of knowledge and on success

ERNESTO MACARO, SUZANNE GRAHAM, and ROBERT VANDERPLANK

Introduction

In this chapter we adopt a systematic approach to reviewing the research literature on second language listening strategies. For a detailed account of how this review process was carried out the reader is invited to go to Appendix 8.1 (www.oup.com/elt/teacher/lls). The studies reviewed are divided into four sections covering approaches to strategy elicitation, the relationship between strategy use and listening success, prior knowledge as a processing strategy, and studies seeking to improve students' strategy use. Our conclusions are that the relationship between successful listening and strategy use needs to be explored more rigorously, that prior knowledge can easily be misused, and that, whilst there is a considerable body of literature exploring listening strategy use, the literature related to strategy instruction is more sparse, although there is an emerging research agenda. We identify a number of theoretical and methodological problems in the literature which future research will need to overcome.

The importance of listening to foreign language teaching and learning has been reflected in a 30-year shift towards interaction-based acquisition. Listening and speaking have accrued much greater prominence as the vehicles through which language learning takes place, especially in instructed environments claiming to be 'communicative' in nature. A great deal of research has therefore been carried out on interactional studies to see if, indeed, interaction leads both to comprehension and to learning. (See Chapter 10 for a review of interaction strategies.) By contrast, unidirectional listening comprehension (where the hearer is unable to interact with the speaker, as in the case of a recorded text) appeared to us, when we embarked on this review, to be under-researched.

Previous narrative literature reviews of listening comprehension (for example, Rubin 1994; Berne 2004; Vandergrift 2004) have identified emerging research themes. For example there has been considerable interest in the interaction of top-down processes involving the use of schemata (the complex mental representations and knowledge of the world that any individual has construed at any moment in time) and bottom-up processes (the decoding of individual words and phrases). Each of these processes subsumes a number of cognitive and metacognitive strategies and these have been a focus of investigation. There has also been an interest in text-types (including such variables as speech-rate) and task-types (including those which focus on inference rather than factual information). A third theme of research has been to investigate the efficacy of pre-listening activities in order to stimulate the student's schemata so that they can bring this to the act of listening to an L2 text. The authors of the above reviews conclude their accounts by suggesting the following areas for further research: the balance between top-down and bottom-up processes, the relationship between proficiency level and strategy use, and the kinds of strategy interventions that might result in more successful listening. Above all they call for more research on 'learning to listen'.

Review findings

We have divided the chapter into four sections. These are:

1 ways in which listening strategies used by students have been elicited;
2 studies which have examined the relationship between strategy use and other variables;
3 studies which have looked at prior knowledge as a processing strategy; and
4 studies which have looked at the effects of strategy instruction on listening performance.

Ways in which listening strategies used have been elicited

Think-aloud protocols have been the preferred method of eliciting from learners their strategy use when listening. In relation to this technique, authors have investigated their usefulness as a data elicitation tool. (See Chapter 5 for a full discussion.) O'Malley, Chamot, and Küpper (1989) used think-aloud protocols to determine whether it was possible to distinguish the phases in listening comprehension as identified by the theoretical literature (Anderson 1985)—that is, a perceptual phase, a parsing phase, and a utilization phase—and concluded that it was. Both Murphy (1985) with audio, and Long (1991) with video, investigated the extent to which participants were capable of articulating their listening strategies via think-aloud, and concluded that they were.

A number of different techniques have been used within the general think-aloud method, and one of these relates to who it is (the participant or the researcher) that stops the tape being listened to and at what point, this being the moment the participant begins verbalizing his/her thoughts. One approach taken was to encourage participants to self-select the moments at which they wished to verbalize (Murphy 1985; Laviosa 2000). Another was to ask participants to nod or raise a finger when they were aware of thinking about what they had heard, but not to describe this until they had finished listening (Bacon 1992a). On the other hand, Vandergrift (1997b, 2003) chose 'natural discourse boundaries' at which to stop the tape for thinking aloud, as did Peters (1999).

The study on which Goh's interrelated articles (1998, 1999, 2002) are based used three different elicitation methods: diaries over an eight-week period; retrospective verbal reports, conducted mainly in L2; and group interviews, where beliefs about listening and strategy use were elicited.

Not all studies report whether participants were trained in the think-aloud technique. Pre-training was carried out by Peters (1999), Vandergrift (1997b, 2003), and Young (1996). We are not aware of studies which specifically avoided pre-training.

A final issue has been whether to focus on listening problems (Goh 2000; Laviosa 2000) and see what strategies were deployed, or whether to try to elicit all strategies being deployed regardless of problems encountered.

Some limitations have been reported by investigators with regard to think-aloud protocols during listening:

a only conscious strategies can be reported;
b verbalization needs to take place as soon as possible after the event to limit forgetting (particularly problematic when listening);
c the phase of the task will influence the type of strategy reported as will the difficulty of the task;
d researcher 'prompting' may affect elicitation; and
e triangulation methods (such as combining think-aloud with retrospective interviews) might provide more reliable data.

Summary

Although the predominant elicitation technique has been the think-aloud protocol, there has been a variety of experimentation with regard to the moment at which to ask participants to self-report, and what they should report on. There is, we would argue, an unconvincing reporting of possible limitations by some of the authors reviewed. Yet, of all the language skills, listening, it would seem to us, is the most difficult from which to obtain a true picture of the cognitive and metacognitive strategies being used by participants. The problems associated with stopping a highly recursive process such as listening and asking participants to articulate their thoughts does raise validity questions. Training participants to think-aloud may have its problems as well as its merits in that it may be artificially channeling their thought processes. The fact that two tape recorders have to be used (one for listening to the text, the other for recording both the verbalizing and the precise moment in the text when the verbalizing takes place) adds to the problem of reliability during the analysis process.

Strategy use and its relationship with other variables

Researchers have investigated a number of relationships among variables which might interact with strategy use.

Strategy use and successful listening comprehension

The relationship between variables that has received most attention is that between strategy use and successful listening comprehension. This is not surprising as strategy use and successful performance is one of the main claims made by strategy theorists. (See Chapter 1.) Such research is often described as investigating 'successful listeners' versus 'unsuccessful listeners'. Successful listening, however, has been measured in a number of different ways. For example, in the O'Malley *et al.* (1989) study, participants were simply designated as successful or otherwise by their teachers; in Young (1996), the students self-rated listening proficiency; in Vandergrift (1997b, 1998a, 1998b) success was assessed qualitatively by the researcher via the analysis of the participants' verbal protocols; in Vogely (1995), Osada (2001), and Chien and Wei (1998) comprehension was assessed via free recall tasks; in Laviosa (2000) and Vandergrift (2003) by a multiple-choice task; in Goh (1998) via a national listening test; in Murphy (1985) by two different listening tests and a reading test; and in Peters (1999) via a whole range of tests including multiple choice. This variety of outcome measures makes it difficult to compare and assess the overall impact of strategy use on listening success because each test is likely to be measuring different aspects of the skill. The problem, however, goes beyond assessing comprehension success. We therefore examine theoretical issues behind this research area before examining the results.

We would argue that there are a number of factors impeding a putative claim for a correlation between strategy use and listening success. Firstly, there is little consensus on the unit of analysis as far as strategy measurement is concerned. (See Chapters 1 and 2.) Secondly the notion of 'the more strategies the better' has now generally been rejected. (See, for example, Chapter 6.) Both these factors call into question the use of statistical strength of correlation to examine the relationship between the two variables. Even if the two variables could be measured with high levels of validity, this would not provide us with any information with regard to direction of causality. In order to demonstrate causality one needs to measure other aspects of learner competence in order to ensure that the choice of listening strategies is not influenced, as Laviosa (2000: 134) argues, by the general proficiency level in the target language. If strategy use is the 'value added' component in skill-related L2 processing, then, researchers need to control *at the very least* for linguistic knowledge (vocabulary and grammatical knowledge).

Once we have established that a correlation between strategy use and listening success cannot be a sufficient explanation of what is involved in L2 listening, we need to ask three different research questions when considering a listening strategies research agenda. The first question is: does *unequal* linguistic knowledge result in different listening strategies being deployed? Here strategies are the dependent variable and linguistic knowledge is the independent variable. The second question should be: is there evidence of different strategies being deployed among participants who have *equal* linguistic knowledge? In this case, listening success is the dependent variable and strategy use is the independent variable. The third research question is: are there cases of students with lower linguistic knowledge who are *so strategic* in their listening that their lack of linguistic knowledge is compensated for by their strategy use, leading to comprehension that is as good as (or better than) that of students with higher linguistic knowledge? With this third research question, listening success is the dependent variable, but we now have two independent variables: linguistic knowledge and strategy use. Although these three research questions can be answered within the same study, they should be examined separately and to answer each of them, there must be some kind of measure of linguistic knowledge. We will now use this theoretical framework to examine studies which have related strategy use to listening success.

In the O'Malley *et al.* (1989) study the students were of unequal 'general proficiency' by which, we assume, they also had unequal linguistic knowledge. Here unsuccessful listeners were reported as using different strategies from successful listeners. The latter appeared to segment the text into larger chunks and linked 'concatenated' segments of text together rather than focusing on individual words. 'Selective attention' (a strategy in the perception phase), 'elaboration', and 'inferencing' (strategies in the utilization phase) were also the mark of the successful listener, as was 'self-monitoring'. The importance of 'elaboration', 'inferencing', and 'self-monitoring' suggested a predominance of top-down strategy use for effective listening, as well as the metacognition involved in being selective in one's attention to the incoming text.

Unequal 'general proficiencies' were also used by Young (1996, 1997[1]) when investigating the listening strategy use of university-level Chinese ESL students in Hong Kong. Unlike O'Malley *et al.* (1989), however, she found that listening ability was not linked to strategy use, neither in terms of frequency of use nor in terms of strategy repertoires. General L2 achievement levels had a greater effect on the repertoire of strategies used.

We would want to signal at this point the problematic nature of using 'general proficiency' as a controlling variable in exploring the relationship between strategy use and listening success. 'Proficiency' is a term applied to the four language skills, usually aggregated, and is a measure of success in those skills regardless of chronological age and of the number of years that a language has been studied. Consequently, not only may it be masking other variables (for example, level of psychological maturity and language learning experience) but also *includes* listening proficiency by up to 25 per cent.

Nevertheless proficiency of some kind is the measure that has repeatedly been used. A series of results around one major study investigating strategy use and successful listening have been reported by Larry Vandergrift. In these studies (1997b, 1998a, 1998b), Vandergrift controlled for variation in proficiency via an Oral Proficiency Interview and, as a result, students were classified from 'Novice I' to 'Intermediate III' proficiency. He found differences in strategy use by general proficiency. In the 1998a paper, he reports that novice-level students relied more heavily on prior knowledge in order to compensate for large chunks of unfamiliar input. Intermediate-level students, because of their larger linguistic base, relied less on schematic knowledge, because they were not being overwhelmed by the stream of speech. In his 1997b paper, what distinguished intermediate from novice students was the comprehension monitoring of the former (a metacognitive strategy) and the extensive use of 'translation', 'transfer', and 'repetition' strategies by the novices (all bottom-up surface processing strategies).

In Vandergrift's 2003 study, 36 grade 7 'core French' students were classified as 'more skilled' or 'less skilled' in listening via a multiple choice listening test. Although the length of exposure to instruction ranged from three to six years, general language proficiency was partially controlled by the ACTFL[2] level they had reached (described as 'about Novice Level II', Vandergrift 2003: 483). In the quantitative analysis, Vandergrift again found that more successful listeners used significantly more 'comprehension monitoring' and metacognitive strategies in general. They were also more likely to question their 'elaborations' of what they thought they understood. Less successful listeners used more 'translating'.[3] Vandergrift concluded that these findings contribute to 'an emerging model of a skilled listener' (2003: 463) who is in 'control of the listening process' (2003: 485). However, Vandergrift also found strategic differences among students of roughly equal general proficiency, for example two Novice I listeners.

Vandergrift (1998a) concluded that successful listening comprehension necessitates overcoming cognitive constraints in working memory by being strategic. What listeners select for processing becomes crucial, and listeners need to 'focus on semantic cues that can be encoded in memory quickly, resist the compulsion to translate, and chunk larger units of meaning into propositions' (Vandergrift 1998a: 391). The problem, however, is in separating strategy-related success from perception/vocabulary-related success, because, as the data provided suggest, the more successful Novice I listener actually appeared to hear (or recognize) more words on which to base an inference than the less successful listener. Similarly in the qualitative analysis of his 2003 study, it appears that Nina, 'the more skilled' listener, is able to construct more meaning from what she hears simply because she recognizes the key word *gagnante* (Vandergrift 2003: 479) whereas Rose, the less skilled listener, does not.

Vandergrift is one of the few authors to recognize that limited linguistic knowledge may be the underlying reason for differences in strategy use: 'because of their limited linguistic knowledge, they recognize very few words' (1997b: 400) and 'their limited linguistic base forces them to rely more on cognates as a basis for inferencing' (1997b: 399). On the other hand he appears to argue that limited linguistic knowledge can be overcome by extra-linguistic contextual clues and other strategies to 'instantiate a schema' (Vandergrift 1998a: 391). However, it is unclear to us how some of these strategies can be deployed by listeners who are struggling to perceive and recognize anything from what they hear, let alone the key words of what is being said.

Differences in strategy use by listening success have also been reported by Goh (1998) where 16 students were selected from a group of 80 to form two groups, higher and lower listening ability. She too found that lower ability listeners failed to use certain strategies that higher ability listeners did use successfully, as follows:

- 'contextualization': placing a key word in a familiar context to understand it, or relating an item to something from an earlier part of the passage
- 'real-time assessment of input': assessing how important a word or phrase is to the understanding of the passage
- 'comprehension evaluation': determining the accuracy and completeness of comprehension.

This last strategy differs from 'comprehension monitoring' (see above) in that while 'comprehension monitoring' takes place almost at the same time as listening, 'comprehension evaluation' seems to take place after listening and when some kind of interpretation has been made. As with Vandergrift, Goh reported (1998) that higher ability listeners used a greater number of strategies, particularly metacognitive ones. An additional finding seemed to be their ability, or willingness, to keep on listening and not be distracted by unfamiliar words.

Thus, results so far do indeed point to a successful listener using different strategies from an unsuccessful one. But do they provide evidence for a skilled versus unskilled listener? It depends what one means by 'skilled'. If there is a suggestion that 'skilled' involves compensating for lack of linguistic knowledge by being strategic, then the answer is that we do *not* yet have that evidence. One of the reasons that an unsuccessful listener may be overusing the 'translating', or underusing the 'comprehension evaluation' strategies is precisely because they have 'an inadequate linguistic base' (Vandergrift 2003: 480). In other words, successful listeners do indeed use very different strategies from unsuccessful ones. But success may be explained as much by greater linguistic knowledge as by anything else.

One of the few studies to use lexical and vocabulary knowledge as controls for examining different listening comprehension success was by Chien and Wei (1998). The researchers found significant differences in strategy use, both in terms of quantity and type, in relation to degree of listening success. However, there was also some evidence that 'students at the same level of grammar and vocabulary did not necessarily perform as well in their listening comprehension' (Chien and Wei 1998: 74) and the authors attributed this to strategies such as 'listening out for single words', 'translating into L1', and 'relying on vocabulary lists'. Unfortunately, however, this avenue was not explored in any great depth in their paper and the methodology was not sufficiently detailed to explain why participants had vocabulary lists to look at in a recall protocol.

Other studies have neither controlled for linguistic knowledge nor for general proficiency. For example, Murphy (1985), Hwang (2003), and Osada (2001) all based their conclusions about differences between groups of learners on the basis of *listening* proficiency. Murphy reported more strategies being used by the higher listening proficiency group. Hwang concluded that more proficient listeners used more 'selective attention', 'prediction', and 'contextualization' whereas the less proficient listeners were too creative in their application of prior knowledge (i.e. they misused it). Osada claimed that less successful listeners were not able to activate top-down strategies simply because they were too preoccupied with extracting local information from the text. Yet, because in these studies there was no control for vocabulary, grammar knowledge, or any other kind of relevant skill, it is impossible to tell whether this difference in strategy use was due to a linguistic deficiency, lack of awareness of strategies, or the inappropriate use of strategies.

Peters (1999) found no difference in the number of strategies used between successful and less successful listeners, but a difference lay in the degree of successful use. More successful listeners appeared to understand *how to use* cognitive and metacognitive strategies, using them in a more varied way. However, as we do not know the extent to which these young beginners had differing general language proficiency, nor the percentage of words they recognized, we cannot be certain that it was not the latter variable which, in the successful listeners, may have facilitated metacognition by freeing up working memory capacity. That this may be the case is indicated by the fact that Peters reports greater use of metacognition as the school year progressed. The less able listeners used guessing a great deal in the early part of the year but then largely abandoned it as their linguistic knowledge improved.

Strategy use and group differences

Less attention has been given to group differences as variables interacting with strategy use. One of these is gender. Bacon's (1992b) study found statistical differences between male and female listeners among university students of Spanish. Females appeared to use 'comprehension monitoring' more frequently as well as more consistently across different texts. Males were more likely to translate parts of what they were listening to into L1. However, these differences in strategy use did not appear to have a significant effect on levels of comprehension. Similarly, Vandergrift (1997b) found few and insignificant differences in strategy use by males and females and on their impact on listening success. For a more general overview of the impact of gender on strategic behavior, see Chapter 4 of this volume.

Other, even less investigated variables are the relationship of cultural background and learning preferences. Braxton (1999) found that cultural background and preferred learning styles did influence the listening strategies of ESL university students. Memorization, participation, religion, and body language were perceived cultural variables which seemed to influence the strategies used. Two learning styles, visual and auditory, were preferred and these two learning styles seemed to influence the students' listening behaviors.

Strategy use, awareness, and attitudes

Another exploration of the relationship between variables has been between learner awareness of strategies, deployment of strategies, and learner beliefs about listening. Vogely (1995) investigated university students' perceptions of what makes a good listener and compared this to the strategies they reported using. She found that the following were all reported as being characteristics of a good listener: understanding gist, using background knowledge, vocabulary knowledge, word recognition, continuing listening when problems occurred, and using the next segment to understand the previous one. However, Vogely noticed a discrepancy between what the students believed and the strategies that they actually used.

Other studies have investigated learners' strategic reactions to particular types of listening texts. For example, Kim (1999) identified Korean listeners' dispositions towards authentic input and students' listening strategies in relation to authentic material. Among the strategies reportedly used were 'concentrating', 'pre-reading of a task', 'catching the first word in a sentence', and 'focusing on interrogatives'. The author found that, as well as level of listening proficiency, the students' dispositions to authentic material were related to whether they were able to deploy certain strategies.

Summary

The majority of studies describing listening strategies have focused on whether more successful listeners can be differentiated from less successful ones by their strategy use. It is difficult to compare the findings of the different studies because factors such as age and proficiency level of the learners varied from study to study, as did the methods used to determine more and less successful listeners. Furthermore, listening is performed either with the possibility of re-listening or without that possibility, both in pedagogical and naturalistic listening situations, and it would be wrong to assume that the strategies are the same for both types of task. Yet, many of the studies examined used 'interrupted listening' to elicit strategies, but 'uninterrupted listening' to test listening proficiency, before going on to explore the link between strategy use and listening success.

A related problem is that most studies have focused on students of unequal general proficiency where greater vocabulary and grammar knowledge might result in faster and more automatic lexical recognition and processing, thus freeing up working memory capacity to deal with comprehension problems. In other words, whilst we are given an insight by the research into how less successful listeners process text, we do not know *why* they do so. Of our three research questions above, only the first one has been dealt with and the evidence is that students who experience greater listening success do use different strategies. However, in order to demonstrate the main claim of listening strategy research, namely, that orchestrating one's strategies *causes* listening success, we need to study samples of students who are matched much more carefully according to their linguistic knowledge. Indeed, we may have to go beyond this and match students for their perception ability, their ability and level of automaticity in distinguishing known and unknown lexical items in a speech stream, and their ability to hold differing lengths of utterances in working memory.

In spite of these methodological problems across the studies, researchers have identified certain strategies which are common to more proficient listeners. Some of these are cognitive strategies, such as listening to chunks of language rather than focusing on individual words, and avoiding direct translation. More important, however, seems to be the employment of meta-cognitive strategies, especially those involving comprehension monitoring. These seem necessary for the successful orchestration of a range of strategies. The importance of metacognition also emerges in the small number of studies investigating learners' beliefs about listening. These indicate that learners are able to articulate their beliefs about the factors that influence listening. However, recognizing the importance of certain strategies does not guarantee their use.

The fact that we can identify problems with the research methodology does not necessarily mean that we should dismiss the conclusions reached by these studies. Rather they should be treated with more caution than is sometimes expressed. The layers of evidence regarding the importance of metacognition are clearly showing through. The importance of metacognitive knowledge in L2 listening parallels the importance attributed to it in the literature on educational psychology.

We now turn to the relative importance of top-down and bottom-up processes, focusing on prior knowledge of the topic or context in particular. In doing so, what we are in fact exploring is the relative importance of two different sources of knowledge that the listener has at his/her disposal: linguistic knowledge and non-linguistic knowledge.

Using prior knowledge as a strategy

Researchers have investigated the role of prior knowledge in listening from a wide variety of perspectives: the pitfalls of deploying prior knowledge as a largely compensatory strategy; prior knowledge and text/task type; prior knowledge and the balance of so-called 'top-down' and 'bottom-up' processing; different uses according to general proficiency or listening ability level; and the use of advance organizers.

An unreliable strategy

A great deal of interest has centered on whether the deployment of prior knowledge of the topic is effective or ineffective in overcoming vocabulary and syntax comprehension difficulties. This interest derives from a theoretical notion, in both psychology and applied linguistics, that the most efficient comprehension is one where the listener uses the least amount of information from the text to achieve the maximum amount of meaning (Conrad 1989).

An influential study which exposed the complexity of the issue was carried out by O'Malley *et al.* (1989). In their terms, prior knowledge can be divided into 'world knowledge' which is generally shared, and 'personal knowledge', which is generally restricted. Prior knowledge was used positively by students in their study to assist comprehension and to assist in recall after listening. Students used prior knowledge to 'self-question' about the material they were listening to rather than abandoning the text, as ineffective listeners often did. Effective listeners used prior knowledge to create some meaning from the text even if the meaning proved to be inaccurate. There were also instances where use of prior knowledge might be successful at one point in recalling the text and unsuccessful at another point. In this respect, it was found that where elaborations based on prior knowledge were inaccurate, they might emerge as wrong inferences later, when being asked to recall. In other words, prior knowledge can be 'superimposed' on a listening task unsuccessfully.

In Bacon's (1992a) study of the strategies used by Spanish learners to deal with authentic input, only 50 per cent of subjects were able to make connections between prior knowledge and the input, and it was not clear what led to their ability to do so. The dangers of distraction through deployment of prior knowledge were highlighted by Dobson (2001) in a study of students' strategies when listening to the website of *France 2* TV. It was found that students' prior knowledge of current events hindered comprehension by leading listeners to lose their train of thought.

Focusing on the familiar and the unfamiliar

While the above studies focused on strategies generally and not specifically on the role of prior knowledge, other studies have put this issue at the heart of their research questions and have obtained broadly similar findings. In the study by Markham and Latham (1987), groups were created on the basis of self-reported religious beliefs—specifically students from a Christian background, students from a Muslim background, and students with no specific religious background. In a study by Long (1990), students listened to two texts which were deemed to contain different levels of prior knowledge. Participants in both studies understood more if they had prior knowledge of the topic but also resorted at times to 'wild guessing' or distorting the information on the basis of prior knowledge. In addition, when listening to the topic familiar text, no significant differences were found when subjects were asked to respond to specific items. This suggests a strong effect for prior knowledge when listeners are free to respond to a text as they wish, but less effect when they are guided by specific tasks in their responses.

Clearer evidence on the role of prior knowledge in familiar and unfamiliar texts was found by Young (1996, 1997). With familiar passages, all participants were able to use the 'elaboration' strategy to help them activate their personal experience and connect the information to the content of the text. However, less successful listeners tended to over-extend their use of prior knowledge and had difficulty in making connections. When listening to an unfamiliar passage, more successful listeners tended to rely on their more profound linguistic knowledge and used metacognitive strategies to plan their listening process, and to evaluate comprehension, while the less successful listeners concentrated on word level and used 'repetition', 'summarization', and 'translation' to understand the text.

In order to explore the interaction between the application of prior knowledge (as a strategy) and the listener's prior knowledge of the topic, Bonk (2000) attempted to control for the second of these variables. University students listened to four texts of varying lexical difficulty about fictitious tribal customs in Africa, a topic they could not have prior knowledge of. Although a few subjects were able to achieve reasonable comprehension with a lexical knowledge of less than 75 per cent, most others needed almost 100 per cent lexical knowledge in order to achieve comprehension. In contrast, in a study of American university students by Jones and Plass (2002), the findings were far from conclusive. The study was designed to determine how their knowledge of the vocabulary related to familiar topics in the texts they would hear. All students were found to have low prior knowledge of the topic vocabulary but it was unclear whether they were familiar with the content of the topic and, therefore, the interaction could not be explored.

Processes involving prior knowledge at different levels of proficiency

An early study looking at the balance of processes involved in listening was by Vanderplank (1988). He sought to investigate the extent to which native and non-native speakers of English 'follow' the text (being able to repeat aloud or sub-vocally or see it in the mind's eye) or 'understand' (integrate it into their existing knowledge). Vanderplank argued that the distinction is roughly equivalent to top-down/bottom-up processing. Vanderplank found that native speakers were able to switch from 'understanding' dominant, to 'following' dominant, to 'balanced' between the two, whereas non-natives were much less flexible and 'following' was more dominant. Listeners could sometimes *understand* the meaning of the discourse when the content was simple, even though they might not follow it very well (i.e. they were able to deploy prior knowledge). For other texts, they might follow the language but get lost in the argument or the amount of information (i.e. they were unable to deploy prior knowledge).

An indirect interest in prior knowledge can be detected in Conrad's (1989) study as to whether listeners of different general proficiency levels differed in their processing strategies when listening to text which had been 'time-compressed' at three different speeds—i.e. accelerated to the point where it became impossible to process all of the verbal message, thus forcing listeners to rely on prior knowledge to a greater or lesser extent. Conrad reported significant differences among the three groups in terms of obtaining information from what they heard. Native speakers' superior knowledge of the language led them to selectively omit certain items of the syntax which were redundant to meaning and then relied on their prior knowledge. Non-natives tended to use strategies which relied on inferring (presumably through prior knowledge deployment) from first and last position words, thus not necessarily key words.

Whether listening proficiency level changes the way prior knowledge is deployed was also investigated by Jensen and Hansen (1995) in their study of students listening to university lectures. The prior knowledge effect was inconsistent: there was statistical significance on only five of the 11 lectures. Prior knowledge only accounted for 3–9 per cent of the variance in lecture comprehension performance whereas the listening proficiency variable accounted for between 25 per cent and 52 per cent of the variance.

Matching prior knowledge to text and task

Chiang and Dunkel (1992) explored the importance of prior knowledge and the relative importance of passage-dependent and passage-independent test items in listening to lectures among 360 Chinese ESL students of high and low listening proficiency. For both levels of proficiency, prior knowledge had a significant impact on subjects' recall of information contained in the *passage-independent* test items. Subjects' performance on *passage dependent* items, however, did not differ significantly whether the familiar or unfamiliar topic was presented. In other words, prior knowledge was only effective in aiding comprehension when the information in the passage actually *matched* the listener's guess of what the passage might contain.

The effects of trying to match prior knowledge to information in texts and test items were extensively explored by Tsui and Fullilove (1998) in a key piece of research which compared mean scores on different types of test items used in listening comprehension examinations. The data set used seven years of exam papers examining 20,000 students on responses to 177 questions. Results consistently showed that (correct) items of *non-matching schema type* (i.e. harder, since they could not be directly matched using prior knowledge) yielded the higher mean criterion scores (i.e. were chosen by the most successful students). This effect of non-matching schema type items was found both among 'global questions' and 'local questions'. In other words it was the ability to verify one's own predictions (arrived at through prior knowledge) against later in-text information (arrived at through decoding skills) which was the mark of the successful listener. The authors conclude that the findings highlight the need for a pedagogy which encourages a balance between top-down and bottom-up processing.

This interest between 'global' and 'local' information was then pursued by Osada (2001), who investigated Japanese EFL students' responses to global and local level questions at three relatively low levels of proficiency. Global questions proved to be more difficult than local questions. However, as the level of proficiency decreased so the difference between the number of correct global and local questions decreased.

More recently, Field (2004) attempted to tease out how listeners deal with top-down and bottom-up information in apparent conflict. Forty-eight EFL students with a wide variety of L1s took part in a series of experiments designed to test the extent to which listeners are inclined to place their trust in top-down rather than bottom-up information. The key finding was that in over 40 per cent of cases a target word was substituted for another, usually more frequent, word even where that word did not fit the context semantically. Field suggested that the findings provide evidence of top-down expectations (non-linguistic knowledge) overruling the evidence of the listeners' ears (linguistic knowledge), but only when the sentential context is highly constraining. Field also argued that, in terms of top-down/bottom-up processing, when a salient word is unfamiliar, learners do not consistently adopt a strategy of visualizing the orthographic form of the word and then infer its meaning from context. Instead, they frequently choose to match what they hear with a known word which is approximately similar. The findings, and Field's conclusions from them, illustrate well the highly variable nature of the strategies used in listening, particularly at a relatively low level of skill.

Activating prior knowledge as an advance organizer

A number of researchers have been interested in whether pre-listening activities such as the stimulation of prior knowledge through so-called 'advance organizers' may help with listening comprehension. This practice can be viewed as an attempt to see whether a strategy involving the use of prior knowledge can be activated by the teacher and whether this activation is successful.

The type of advance organizer instruction has varied considerably. For example, Teichert (1996) provided, in advance of the listening task, illustrations of what the text was about, brainstorming vocabulary and cultural background, and general questions about the topic; similarly, Ruhe (1996) presented students with a mind map of the topic they would hear. On the other hand, Herron, Cole, York, and Linden (1998) presented the students with either declaratives (statements about the content of the video to be viewed) or interrogatives (questions about the content to be listened to), and Chung (1999) provided listeners with alternatives: advance organizers, captions in the L2, and a combination of both. All four studies found an advantage for the advance organizer condition over the non-advance organizer condition. Whilst the type of advance organizer did not appear to make a difference, the effect was enhanced if it was combined with other strategy stimulating activities, as in the Chung study. We interpret the strategies stimulated in this last study as 'prediction' through advance organizers, 'visualization' via captions, and combining 'monitoring of predictions with visualization'. Although this strategic behavior is not explored in the study, it may be a future direction for researchers in the field.

A different approach to the activation of prior knowledge was explored by Kawai (2000) by including words related to the listener's L1 culture and measuring whether they contributed to better motivation to work on listening tasks, increased use of listening strategies, and better comprehension. There were no statistical differences in comprehension between groups which had used texts containing either Japanese words and concepts or American/Western words and concepts, although both groups improved. No statistically significant gains were found for either group in terms of motivation or attitudes to English. Home culture concepts did not increase strategy use.

Summary

The influence of top-down strategies, in which prior knowledge is employed to make sense of a spoken text, is a complex one. While several studies argue that the application of prior knowledge while listening aids comprehension, even these studies suggest that it can also hinder it. From the findings of the studies reported, it appears that for prior knowledge effects to guarantee success, certain criteria need to be met:

a the information contained in a text needs to be congruent with the listener's prior knowledge of the topic of the text;
b learners' lexical knowledge needs to exceed a 'threshold' level; and
c learners need to know how to make effective use of prior knowledge by deploying it flexibly and in combination with linguistic information contained in the input.

This last point seems to be especially important; it seems to relate to one of the conclusions reached in the last section, concerning key differences between more and less successful listeners. The more successful listeners are able to employ prior knowledge flexibly, in appropriate situations, and to an appropriate degree, and can combine it with other strategies, that reduce the risk of prior knowledge leading to wild guessing behavior. However, further research needs to confirm that better listeners, in the end, are not simply those with superior linguistic knowledge who are able to draw on a greater range of linguistic resources—phonological, syntactical, or morphological—and are thus able to use prior knowledge more flexibly. The more interesting question then, it seems to us, would be how successful listeners compensate for lack of linguistic knowledge by flexible prior knowledge use.

An additional problem is that the definition of prior knowledge is not sufficiently comprehensive to explain how schemata interact with the incoming text. For example, we do not know what types of prior knowledge (global, specific event, personal involvement) are most relied on and whether the type affects the listening processes significantly. We do not have sufficient knowledge of how knowledge of the topic interacts with topic-specific lexical knowledge in the L2.

From the perspective of top-down and bottom-up strategies in listening, the findings of the studies indicate that while any straightforward dichotomy may appear on the surface to be too crude and simplistic, given the complexity of listening processes, it does have value. This may be not only in operational and analytical terms but also in terms of what learners perceive their own psycholinguistic processes to be. Listeners adjust their focus of listening according to their prior or linguistic knowledge, the perceived difficulty of the listening, their level of skill, the task or purpose in listening, and their ability to deploy specific strategies.

The studies of advance organizers show positive findings. They appear to make comprehension easier by stimulating the prior knowledge of the topic before listening begins. The type of advance organizer which is most efficient is not clear but, as with pictures and graphics, any stimulus which activates schemata in long-term memory and which matches the general content of the text is likely to be helpful. What is, however, unclear is how presenting listeners with advance organizers helps with listening comprehension skills in the long term, in situations where the advance organizer is not available or not provided by the teacher. One hypothesis would be that advance organizers make a text more accessible, thereby increasing the amount of comprehensible input available for learners and freeing up processing capacity in order to deploy certain under-used strategies. However, we have little evidence as yet to support this hypothesis, and we have insufficient evidence of learners being able to *independently* deploy advance organizer-type strategies.

Training students to use strategies effectively

The potential benefits of predicting the likely content of a passage and listening out for certain linguistic items (as outlined above in the discussion of advance organizers), have been explored in many studies investigating the effects of listening strategy instruction. One of the earliest, by O'Malley, Chamot, Stewner-Manzanares, Russo, and Küpper (1985b), concentrated on three strategies: 'selective attention', 'note-taking', and 'co-operation'. Seventy-five intermediate ESL learners were randomly assigned to one of three teaching groups: a 'metacognitive' group who received instruction in all three strategies, a 'cognitive' group who were instructed in note-taking and co-operation only, and a control group who received no strategy instruction. The strategy instruction took place for 50 minutes a day over eight days. Pre-tests, post-tests, and interim measures were given to all three groups in the form of videotapes and multiple-choice questions. The results of the intervention were mixed, with differences between the means for the groups at post-testing approaching but not reaching significance.

The strategy of 'predicting', together with 'inferencing' and 'integrating new material', appears in another early intervention study (Henner-Stanchina

1986/1987). The instruction was given to ESL/EFL learners and results were presented as extracts from a questionnaire completed by learners at the end of the training, indicating that they responded favorably to it. Some of these strategies were taken up again by McGruddy (1995), who studied the impact of strategy instruction in 'predicting', 'selective attention', and 'inferring'. Instruction took place over 14 weeks. Both the experimental group (N = 10) and the two comparison groups (N = 10 and 12) were pre- and post-tested using both a standardized and a researcher-designed test, and strategy-use questionnaires were administered to triangulate test scores. Significant differences (in favor of the intervention group) were found only in the non-standardized listening test with increases only in the 'selective attention' strategy.

A wider range of strategies, both metacognitive and cognitive, was included in an intervention study by Thompson and Rubin (1996), with third-year Russian learners in an American university against a comparison group. The instruction lasted an academic year. The metacognitive strategies included were: 'planning', 'defining goals', 'monitoring', and 'evaluating'. Cognitive strategies included 'predicting content', 'listening to familiar words and cognates', 'listening for redundancy', 'listening to tone of voice and intonation', and 'resourcing' (for example, jotting down phrases to see what they mean). The researchers found that the intervention students (N = 24) made significant gains over the comparison students (N = 12) in the video test, but gains were less positive on an audio test, possibly because it differed from the instructional mode, which was mainly by video.

Positive findings were also reported by Seo (2000) who investigated the efficacy of cognitive and metacognitive strategy instruction with ten university-level learners of Japanese in Australia over 19 weeks. Three strategies were selected for the instruction: 'identifying key terms', 'elaboration', and 'inferencing'. The intervention group performance overtook that of the control group in the two final tests in a series of eight, which were conducted from the outset each week. However, learners appeared to benefit more in their use of bottom-up strategies, with strategies such as 'inference' and 'elaboration' appearing less sensitive to intervention.

Socio-affective strategies ('questioning for clarification', 'co-operation') featured alongside metacognitive strategies ('directed attention', 'selective attention', 'self-evaluation') and cognitive strategies ('note-taking', 'inferencing', 'summarizing') in the instruction implemented by Ozeki (2000) involving 25 female EFL first-year college students in Japan, against a comparison group of 20. The intervention does not appear to have been successful. There was no significant difference between the experimental and control groups' listening scores at post-test. Questionnaire data suggested that at post-test the control group made more use of cognitive and socio-affective strategies than the intervention group, though the intervention group reported use of more metacognitive strategies.

Metacognitive strategies were the main focus of a study by Kohler (2002), although the training was not exclusively aimed at listening skills. Seventy 'lower achieving' learners of Spanish received instruction in: 'determining their task-related goals', 'identifying what strategies they might use', 'assessing how well the strategies were working', and 'selecting alternative strategies'. Listening comprehension significantly increased along with vocabulary knowledge when compared to a non-intervention group. There does not, however, appear to have been a pre-test. The intervention group reported a clear increase in the perceived *value* of strategy use.

Summary

Relatively few studies have been conducted into the effects of strategy instruction for listening comprehension and none of the studies reviewed showed an unequivocal benefit for students receiving instruction against a comparison group. Most studies, however, apart from Ozeki (2000), report at least partial improvement in learners' listening.

As the studies provided instruction over different periods of time, with learners of different proficiency levels, it is difficult to draw clear conclusions about what the key elements of successful strategy instruction might be. However, the two interventions that appear to have been the most successful, Thompson and Rubin (1996) and Kohler (2002), focused more sharply on metacognitive strategy development, including strategy evaluation (both studies) and comprehension monitoring (Thomson and Rubin 1996 only). The previous sections of this chapter suggest that this last strategy is vital for effective comprehension.

The lack of clarity in the literature regarding how listening strategy instruction can be most effectively implemented may be related to some of the problems identified in previous sections. Studies describing strategy use and the relationship between variables have so far provided an incomplete picture of what is going on in this very complex area. We concur with Vandergrift's (2004: 18) conclusions that 'we need to continue to investigate the relative contribution of top-down and bottom-up processes at different proficiency levels for different tasks'. We would reiterate the need to arrive at a much clearer definition of proficiency level, as related to the skill of listening, before proceeding to observe its interaction with strategy deployment.

Limitations of the studies in this review

A number of limitations have been identified both by the authors of the studies in this review and by us, the authors of the review itself.

1 Levels of linguistic knowledge or other potentially useful measures have almost never been determined in order to control for possible confounding effects and, therefore, a causal relationship between strategy use and listening success is unconvincing. Rarely do authors make clear in their exploration of relationships which are the dependent variables and which

are the independent ones in the way that we have formulated them in this chapter. Instead, tentative and possibly unjustified correlations between strategy use and listening success are made. In some studies listening success is actually measured by strategy use, rendering the argument completely circular.

2 Levels of prior knowledge have often been assumed rather than measured, making it difficult to judge the extent of its effectiveness as a strategy. Additionally, potential interest in the text being listened to has not been measured.

3 The selection of samples for intervention groups in strategy instruction has lacked sufficient rigor to be totally convincing and the degree of generalizability is left to the reader to guess at. Rarely are we told how the sample reflects the population via the sampling frame and the way that groups are allocated to intervention and comparison is lacking in detail. Differential attrition between groups used in controlled interventions is not reported on. Some studies lack baseline tests, and rely on comparisons based on either teacher or student self-estimates of proficiency.

4 Problems associated with strategy elicitation are still unresolved. Perhaps in listening more than in other skills, strategy elicitation via think-aloud may influence the actual strategies elicited. After all, a think-aloud forces the subject to break up the texts where listening to a radio broadcast, for example, just would not allow this. Use of recall protocols to measure listening comprehension, where working memory capacity may be a variable, may favor the reporting of top-down processes in some participants and reporting of single-word translation strategies by others. In some studies, participants were 'instructed' to listen in a particular way, perhaps forcing the adoption of certain strategies over others, yet were tested for proficiency in a different way.

5 The analyses of descriptive studies of strategy use are open to different interpretations and inter-rater reliability procedures were not always described.

6 It is sometimes unclear whether the strategy classification is hierarchical or not (for example, is Laviosa's (2002) 'contextual inferring' superordinate to 'using background knowledge'?). In general we found the strategies reported not sufficiently 'fine-grained', or not sufficiently exemplified.

7 The reliability of the testing instruments has not always been reported. The extent to which the test type matched the experimental group's experience of learning was rarely explored.

8 We disagreed with some of the conclusions drawn in the studies in the light of the findings reported. A typical example was the assumption in some studies' conclusions that making listening easier (for example, via advance organizers) facilitates the development of the skill of listening. This assumption is unproven. It may be that making listening easier will in the long run improve the skill of listening by facilitating access, but we do

not know how facilitating access develops strategy use and how this leads to better performance.

Two studies, one quantitative, one qualitative, were chosen by the review team as exemplifying particularly good research and reporting procedures.

The Tsui and Fullilove (1998) study was judged to be of high trustworthiness for the following reasons. The study used a very large sample. The authors report that the reliability of the examination had been established, and that individual items could be relied upon to discriminate well between candidates of different proficiency levels. They outline the measures taken to ensure the reliability of their procedures for coding items as either global or local questions on the one hand, and either matching or non-matching items on the other. The study by Young (1996) was also rated highly. Although this study uses what appears to be a convenience sample (N = 20) of volunteers, it adopts a grounded approach in terms of strategy identification. Procedures are then refined and the main study is carried out with attention to issues of both reliability and validity. Young outlines measures taken to improve reliability and validity, such as pilot testing think-aloud procedures to assess the impact on real-time listening, careful think-aloud training, improving inter-coder reliability, and triangulation of think-aloud procedures with student feedback and questionnaires. There is also triangulation through discussions with participants and through checking self-ratings with achievement scores.

Conclusions

The research reviewed in this chapter has concerned itself with carrying out extensive documentation of the cognitive and metacognitive strategies available to listeners. Some has focused on how strategy use relates to listening success, some on the balance between sources of knowledge or between top-down and bottom-up processes, and some on whether students can be encouraged to use strategies better.

Strategy research has provided fairly conclusive evidence that successful listeners use different strategies and in different combinations to less-successful listeners. There is mounting evidence that within those strategy combinations metacognition plays an important part. What research has not provided an answer to is why more effective listeners are able to employ strategies flexibly and in appropriate combinations. In other words, how have they reached that state of affairs? It may be that greater linguistic knowledge *allows* them to do so more easily. Future research which clearly describes the relationship between its variables and the hypotheses it is trying to test is urgently needed to answer these remaining questions.

Strategy-related research has identified prior knowledge of what is being listened to as an important top-down strategy available to the listener. Although most studies recognize pitfalls in its use, the overwhelming impression one obtains from some conclusions is that top-down processes are what distinguish good listeners from poor ones. Other studies contradict this and point much more forcefully to its misuse as being something to which poor listeners are prone. In a number of studies the reader is left with an impression of an unchallenged assumption that top-down processes are what teachers should be advocating in preference to bottom-up processes. We believe the evidence does not support this assumption. On the other hand, those studies which refer more cautiously to a combination of top-down and bottom-up processes as being effective do not provide sufficient detail of how these combinations are to be deployed against specific listening tasks. Further research is needed to identify *why* some listeners misuse prior knowledge. The answer to this question may lie in pursuing with much greater determination how prior knowledge interacts with general lexical knowledge, with topic-specific lexical knowledge, as well as with perception, learning experience, and level of maturity. For example, we need research which compares the strategies which learners deploy, together with the sources of linguistic knowledge they draw on.

Given that listening comprehension can be measured via quite distinct task types, future strategy elicitation needs to be carried out using both interrupted and uninterrupted listening approaches with the same participants in order to ascertain the extent to which their strategy combinations differ in response to the different task requirements.

Strategy instruction in the skill of listening is still very much in its infancy. Very few studies have explicitly tested clear and different models of such instruction. Few studies tell us much about what it is that specifically might improve the skill of listening. Where there are positive results, the causal link between training in specific strategies and greater success at listening is not sufficiently exposed. We urgently need more intervention studies that identify more clearly what kind of strategy instruction works with what kinds of learner.

Acknowledgements

We are very much indebted to Larry Vandergrift and Joan Rubin for the valuable advice given on earlier drafts of this chapter.

Notes

1 1997 published at http://www.cuhk.edu.hk/ajelt/vol7/art3.htm.
2 Novice level of proficiency of the American Council of Teachers of Foreign Language.
3 Described by the author as 'rendering ideas from one language in another in a relatively verbatim manner' (Vandergrift 2003: 406).

9

A review of reading strategies: focus on the impact of first language

LYNN ERLER and CLAUDIA FINKBEINER

Introduction

This chapter presents an overview of empirical research published since the 1970s on strategies for second and foreign language (L2)[1] reading comprehension. A detailed account of the systematic procedure by which this review was carried out can be found in Appendix 9.1 (www.oup.com/elt/teacher/lls). We begin the chapter with a brief conceptualization of the processes involved in reading. We note that research findings are still not conclusive as to whether these processes are, on the whole, universal or language specific. Some might assume that reading processes are the same, regardless of whether the written form of the L2 appears alphabetically such as English, as a syllabary language such as Arabic, or logographically, for instance Chinese. However, these assumptions may be wrong. We believe that it is important, in a review of reading strategies, to consider the processes involved in reading comprehension because these can be initiated, accompanied, or followed by strategies. These strategies are chosen and activated to facilitate and evaluate comprehension.

We review studies which illustrate: (1) variables associated with reading comprehension; (2) the interaction of the L1, the L2, readers and reading strategies; and, (3) research into reading strategy instruction. To conclude this review we propose future avenues for reading strategies research.

Reading processes and reading strategies

The main challenge for any study about reading lies in the fact that L2 'reading' cannot easily be defined. A complete model of reading has yet to be devised. Such a model ought to show what is brought to, made use of, and what happens during reading, at what levels of processing, and for what purpose(s). It has taken many years of research to arrive at some understanding of what successful first language (L1) reading consists of and these understandings have begun to filter into conceptualizations of L2 reading over the last 30 years (Bernhardt 2000; Grabe and Stoller 2002). We will now take a brief look at models of reading which have influenced the conceptualizations of strategies for L2 reading comprehension.

Two early models of reading labelled 'top-down' (Goodman 1967) and 'bottom-up' (Smith 1978/1986) emerged from reading research in English as a first language (EL1) and influenced the conceptualization of L2 reading into what was thought to be two fundamentally different approaches to text. Top-down processes were characterized as higher-level processes, such as discerning meaning at whole text-level and using schemata or background knowledge to support comprehension. Bottom-up processes included so-called lower-level processes, such as identifying words and basing comprehension on meanings at word or phrase level. These two metaphors described two different processing directions during reading: from the reader to the text, and from the text to the reader. These two directions have been linked to levels of reading proficiency as shown in the studies below.

In the late 1970s and in the 1980s, a model of reading as the *interaction* of both top-down and bottom-up processing emerged from the field of cognitive psychology. (See, for example, Rumelhart 1977; Stanovich 1980.) L1 reading comprehension was further conceptualized by Van Dijk and Kintsch (1983) as happening concurrently on several levels: (a) the word level, (b) the level of propositions, (c) the level of local coherence, (d) the level of the macrostructure of the text, and (e) the level of superstructure including the context of the reading event. In addition, Van Dijk and Kintsch (1983) contributed to the field of L1 reading by inserting the notion of 'strategies' into their text comprehension model. Researchers in the L2 reading research community have acknowledged the interactivity of reading processes (for example, Carrell 1985; Carrell, Devine, and Eskey 1988; Urquhart and Weir 1998; Bernhardt 2000; Grabe and Stoller 2002). This has led to a conceptualization by some of a continuum rather than a dichotomy, one that takes into account different combinations of strategies involved in top-down and bottom-up processing depending on the different learner and context variables. (See Finkbeiner 2001, 2005.)

Since the 1990s reading comprehension has been seen increasingly to be the result of complex interactions between text, setting, reader, reader background, reading strategies, the L1 and the L2, and reader decision making. Nevertheless the dichotomous labels of 'top-down' and 'bottom-up' for reading processing and associated strategy use have continued to be useful for conceptualizing reading research. (See, for example, Brantmeier's 2002 review.)

Another issue in the L2 reading strategy literature is the often unclear definition of the strategies construct as argued in previous publications (R. Ellis 1994: 592) and as presented in Chapter 1 of this volume. Taxonomies of reading *strategies* (for example, Grabe and Stoller 2002) for reading in both L1 and L2 have overlapped with lists of reading *skills* particularly in teacher guidance books (for example, Grellet 1981; Nuttall 2005) and reading *activities* (for example, Pressley and Afflerbach 1995). Reading strategies have been theorized in relation to levels of reading processes and to reading skills as consciously chosen actions that activate effective processing (for example, Van Dijk and Kintsch 1983; McDonough 1995). In this chapter we conceptualize strategies as intentional actions chosen to facilitate reading at any level of processing.

Review findings

Despite the fact that there was a vast range of research foci, during the final stage of our search and selection process, we were able to identify the main areas which demonstrated the development of researchers' thinking and findings in the field since the 1970s.

We identified three main areas of focus and finally selected, read, and summarized 46 empirical studies which we believe represent these areas. These were:

1 strategy types and their relationship with reading proficiency;
2 L1 and L2 reading strategies involving both linguistic and non-linguistic factors; and
3 reading strategy instruction.

Focus on types of reading strategies and on their relationship with reading proficiency

In a seminal descriptive study of reading strategies, Hosenfeld (1976) published findings from an exploratory research project with 14-year-old learners of French. The purpose of her published report was twofold: first, to describe ways that teachers could gain insight into learners' strategic interactions with the written L2 using think-aloud self-reports based on an unstructured interview format; and second, it was to report on the strategies that the learners were using. As a result of her research Hosenfeld conceptualized reading strategies as being on two levels: one for 'main meaning' and the other focusing at 'word level'.

In a later publication, Hosenfeld (1977) went further. She described a coding system which she had developed to analyze self-report protocols to discover the reading strategies of successful and unsuccessful L2 students of French, Spanish, and German. She equated 'successful' with high proficiency in the L2 which was determined by using a standardized reading test (MLA-Co-operative Test of Reading Proficiency). The 20 highest scorers and 20 low scorers reported using different strategies during their efforts to comprehend a text. Successful FL readers used primarily 'main meaning' strategies:

1 they kept the meaning and context in mind;
2 they read or translated in broad phrases;

3 they either skipped unknown words or inferred their meanings from the surrounding text;
4 if after several attempts they had failed to establish a meaning for an unknown word, they then ignored it;
5 they looked up words as a last resort 'when more efficient strategies [had] failed' and if they did look up a word, did so correctly; and
6 they were usually 'successful in following through with a proposed solution to [a reading comprehension] problem' (p. 121).

The less successful readers lost track of main meaning. They:

1 read or translated in short phrases;
2 lost the meanings of words, phrases, or sentences soon after they had 'decoded' what their meaning was; and
3 seldom skipped words, viewing all words 'as "equal" in terms of their contributing to total phrase meaning' (p. 120).

Hosenfeld (1977) acknowledged that her lists of strategies were not exhaustive and urged more research using think-aloud and retrospective verbal self-report methods to find out which strategies students were using as a preliminary step toward teaching less successful students to adopt more effective reading strategies. Hosenfeld's (1976, 1977) work set out methods and raised issues that were developed in empirical research projects over the next decades: think-aloud and retrospective self-reports from which reading strategies could be coded; taxonomies of strategies; the metaphoric banding of strategies into higher-level strategies and lower-level strategies often linked with relative success in reading comprehension; using proficiency tests to divide participants into more and less successful groupings; the role of reading tasks in the choice of strategies employed; and, proposing that more effective strategy use could be taught to learners.

A number of researchers attempted to classify strategies and strategy users following on from the early work of Hosenfeld. For example Block (1986) studied generally non-proficient students of English as a foreign language (EFL) and observed that, among them, there were more and less successful readers. Using think-aloud protocols to elicit reading strategies, Block found that the more successful readers used more 'general' strategies which included the ability to integrate their understandings from the text with information which they discerned about the text structure. Similarly Carrell (1985) found, from a strategies questionnaire with adult learners, that low-proficiency readers used more text-based strategies. Although Sarig (1987) also found a link between bottom-up or 'local' strategy use and less successful reading comprehension, this link did not extend to what she called 'global' strategies. In her investigation of ten older adolescent girls, Sarig (1987) used a think-aloud protocol to discover the girls' strategies while they were reading in their L1, Hebrew, and in English L2. She observed that the choice and effectiveness of strategies in terms of comprehension results were similar for both L1 and L2 and she proposed that strategies were apparently transferred by her readers from L1 to L2. However, 'global' strategies led to both successful and unsuccessful reading in both languages. Another key contribution to the strategies research field was Sarig's (1987) suggestion that there were many possible, co-occurring variables during an L2 reading event which were due to individual differences and which influenced the choice and combinations of strategies. In other words, strategy types could not be linked in a simple fashion to proficiency in L2 reading or to individual readers.

While many other studies have been conducted since Hosenfeld's (1977) study, linking specific strategies with reading comprehension success (for example, Knight, Padrón, and Waxman 1985), by the end of the 1980s, research was already widening its scope to consider other variables which might be interacting with strategy choice and use. The two basic categories of reading strategies were again identified by Parry (1991, 1993) in her case study research but what was particularly noteworthy about Parry's interpretation of her findings was that she proposed that her individual reader's preference for one or the other type of strategy was driven by cultural and L1 backgrounds. On the other hand Abraham and Vann (1987) found that personality type appeared to be a stronger explanatory reason for a reader's predilection for 'top-down' or 'bottom-up' reading strategies. Thus we can see that research findings were breaking away from a strict association of L2 reading proficiency with 'top-down' or 'bottom-up' strategies.

A more complex, interactive conceptualization of strategies linked to reading processing was proposed by Anderson (1991). He elicited strategies university students were using during two reading tasks: text reading and test taking. He divided the students into three different levels of reading proficiency and detected a total of 47 strategies that he allocated to five distinct categories which he labelled: 'supervising', 'support', 'paraphrase', 'coherence', and 'test-taking' (Anderson 1991). Both top-down (general/holistic) and bottom-up (analytic) strategies appeared within each of the five categories. Other key findings by Anderson (1991) were that his better readers used *more* but not different strategies than did the less successful readers. Moreover, successful readers were more skilled at monitoring the success of strategies. There was not a distinct set of strategies which contributed to successful reading but rather the better readers chose, combined, applied, and monitored strategies more effectively.

The actions involved in monitoring strategy use, taken by Anderson's (1991) readers, have been labelled 'metacognitive' strategies (for example, O'Malley and Chamot 1990). The importance of metacognitive strategies was examined with a special focus on text structure by Carrell (1989, 1992). Carrell studied 45 university students with respect to their L2 reading ability and their judgments (or metacognitive awareness) about various reading strategies. She measured the quantity and quality of idea units recalled by the students after having read two texts. She found that subjects who used the text structure to organize the presentation of their recall achieved better results; they recalled more main ideas and major topics. Carrell proposed that to improve L2 reading comprehension, students should be instructed in the use of metacognitive strategies. Extrapolating from their review of strategies literature, Carrell, Gajdusek, and Wise (1998) posited that metacognitive strategies for monitoring comprehension, and for perceiving and addressing reading problems could be deemed the most valuable strategies for developing reading comprehension.

In sum, by the end of the 1990s the complexities of reading and the types of strategy use were beginning to be addressed in the research literature, influenced by interactive conceptualizations of reading in L1 and L2. Although the broad-brush picture continued to show 'top-down' and 'bottom-up' dichotomies in strategy lists, closer research of the strategies used revealed a less dichotomous delineation and consequent link to successful and unsuccessful L2 reading. Rather, successful comprehension was associated with metacognitive strategies which involved the monitoring of cognitive strategies, *including* 'bottom-up' strategies. There was a growing interest in reader-centered variables, during reading events, which might influence the strategic approach adopted, such as readers' linguistic backgrounds, including their proficiency in their L1. There was, moreover, growing speculation about the impact of readers' non-linguistic characteristics on reading strategy choice, such as affective, attitudinal, and cultural variables (for example, Parry 1993; Finkbeiner 2005, 2006b). These will be examined in the sections which follow.

Focus on L1 and L2 reading strategies

In 1991 a special edition of the *AILA Review* entitled 'Reading in two languages' appeared, edited by Jan Hulstijn, in which a general call was made by the authors for a greater understanding of the components involved in L2 reading. From their reviews of the literature, the authors argued that further research was needed into the cross-linguistic and intra-individual variables in order to understand the interactions of multilingual reading events.

Prior to the *AILA Review* (1991) there had already been an ongoing discussion regarding the role of L1 reading proficiency and the strategies used in L2 reading. An early broaching of the topic had been made by Alderson (1984) in an often-cited question: is foreign language reading a reading problem or a language problem? That is, is an L2 reading problem caused by lack of L1 literacy or by a deficient knowledge of the L2?

Thus, the review question that guided our choice of literature for this section was: what is the impact of the L1 on strategy use at various levels of L2 reading processing? The research literature that addresses this question is vast and complex. We therefore selected studies that investigated: (a) the possible transfer of L1 strategies to L2 reading strategies, (b) the actual use of the L1 as a strategy in L2 reading, and (c) the role of the setting in strategy choice and use.

L1 to L2 reading strategy transfer

A very important question is whether there is a particular threshold level in L2 proficiency that has to be achieved before L1 reading strategies can be transferred to L2 reading tasks. For example, Clarke (1980) researched adult Spanish readers of English (L2) and proposed that there existed an L2 language proficiency threshold below which the L2 reader was 'short-circuited' from transferring effective L1 reading strategies to L2 reading. Hudson (1982), however, proposed that the threshold of L2 proficiency alone did not explain whether L2 readers were able to employ effective L1 reading strategies in L2.

In support of this view, Kern (1989) argued that if an L2 language threshold existed, it was relative to and affected by numerous individual learner variables. Hardin (2001: 417) went further by claiming that 'the level of second language proficiency played a less prominent role in second-language strategic reading than did the level of strategy use in L1'. However, Schoonen, Hulstijn, and Bossers (1998: 72) reported that, from their findings, '[t]he limited FL knowledge "short-circuits" the transfer of [metacognitive] reading skills to the FL [reading]'. As well as the threshold issue addressed here, this quotation again shows the confusion of terminology: in this case metacognitive reading strategies are referred to as skills.

Alderson (2000) theorized that the more demanding the reading task, the higher the L2 linguistic threshold would have to be for the effective application of knowledge stemming from the L1 background. Macaro (2001) found that the very limited L2 knowledge of an adolescent learner resulted in the (in this instance, inappropriate) use of the strategy, known from L1, of applying world knowledge in an attempt to achieve comprehension of a text. The L2 knowledge threshold was very low in this case. It can be argued that the attempt to employ schema knowledge was a compensatory strategy for inadequate L2 knowledge and not a true transfer of an L1 strategy.

The issue of threshold and the transfer of L1 knowledge has, therefore, not been solved in the literature but rather the issues have widened and deepened to include many variables. We look more closely at studies which have dealt with some of these issues.

L1 impact on L2 reading strategy use: the role of orthography

If reading is, at base, a pattern recognition process which accumulates information from many sources (Massaro and Cohen 1994), then a reader's strategies for L1 word identification may affect how that reader deals with L2 words. Two aspects of the way that a word is written have been investigated as having a possible impact on L2 word-reading strategies. The first aspect pertains to differences between the representational units of the L1 and the L2, that is, what the signs on the page represent. The representational units of alphabetic, syllabary, and logographic languages stand for phonemes, syllables, or words/morphemes, respectively.

Differences in representational units in languages have been shown to require different strategies for word-level reading comprehension. Koda (1990) asked university students, with Arabic, Spanish, and Japanese L1s, to read an English text that contained Sanskrit symbols in place of selected words. She found that the Sanskrit symbols significantly impeded the Arabic and Spanish readers' reading times and text comprehension compared to the reading times and text comprehension of the Japanese readers. When faced with the unknown Sanskrit word, readers whose L1 representations were alphabetic or syllabary could not use their L1-based strategy of decoding from graphemes to phonemes to support their reading comprehension. The Japanese could transfer their attention away from phonology, as they did with their L1 orthography, to achieve relatively faster reading rates and greater comprehension.

The second aspect of orthography which can cause interference in strategy use is the relative transparency of a language, that is, how regular or 'matched' is the system of spellings corresponding to the sounds of words. For example Frost, Katz, and Bentin (1987) conducted a series of experiments with 48 Hebrew, 48 English, and 48 Serbo-Croatian university students reading their L1 in their native countries. They found that word reading in these various languages required different word-reading strategies depending on the transparency of the language. Relative opaqueness (Hebrew and English) required more direct lexical access whereas the more transparent language (Serbo-Croatian) involved phonological recoding.

There has, therefore, been considerable interest in the strategies required for the phonological processing of the written L2 by readers with different first languages. In a further example Holm and Dodd (1996) compared the word and non-word reading performance of 40 university students from The People's Republic of China, Hong Kong, Vietnam, and Australia. The tasks required strategies for the phonological processing of English. The students from Hong Kong had no phonological strategies from their L1 (which required none) and were limited by their whole-word L1 strategies when trying to segment English phonemes, thus resulting in longer reading times. The researchers found that the Chinese group who used pinyin, an alphabetic form of Chinese not used in Hong Kong, achieved higher scores on the tests because they knew how to segment words.

In a completely different setting with much younger subjects, Durgunoğlu, Nagy, and Hancin-Bhatt (1993) found a positive cross-language strategy transfer at pre-word level and word levels with 31 Spanish-speaking primary school beginner readers of English (L2). The better the respondent's L1 phonological awareness and word recognition skills, the more successful were his or her results in L2 word reading. The researchers argue that this was partly due to the high number of cognates in the two languages (see also Nagy, Garcia, Durgunoğlu, and Hancin-Bhatt 1993, for the same study in greater detail). Working with early adolescents, Erler (2004) reported that when the learners lacked viable knowledge of the spelling-sound system of

French (L2), they used the strategy of employing the spelling-sound system of their L1 English, to pronounce French words. This strategy sometimes helped to access the meaning of aurally stored words, but it could also impede word access and text comprehension.

It is clear, therefore, that an interest in writing systems has generated a considerable body of research that has examined the impact of the L1 on L2 reading strategy use at the level of orthography. However, surprisingly, we found hardly any studies examining its impact at the syntax level.

One of the few studies to take up the syntax issue was reported by Stevenson, Schoonen, and de Glopper (2003) who investigated 300 students aged 13–16 in Dutch schools. Among other research questions, the researchers wondered whether these students employed the same kinds of reading strategies in Dutch L1 as in English L2. The researchers found that students spent more time and processing energy both on the word and syntax aspects of the L2 than they did for texts in their L1, due presumably to the limits of their L2 knowledge. The students did not compensate for any difficulties at the L2 word level by using more top-down strategies to aid in comprehension by trying to construct a global idea of the L2 text as Macaro's (2001) student had tried unsuccessfully to do. Stevenson *et al.* (2003) speculate that this was because their L2 readers were under no time pressure to complete the reading event, and therefore did not resort to more global strategies in lieu of concentrating on text-based processing.

The issue of a possible impact of L1 strategies on L2 strategies leads us logically to the role that bi-literacy might play in L2 reading comprehension.

L1 impact on L2 reading strategy use: focus on bi-literacy

The effect of bi-literacy on reading strategy use and reading comprehension has been investigated by several authors (for example, Padrón, Knight, and Waxman 1986; Carrell 1989). In a detailed description of their research project Jiménez *et al.* (1996) report on the strategies of eight successful and three less successful Latina/o readers of English compared to the strategies employed by three successful monolingual readers of English. All participants were aged 12 and 13; 'success' was determined by teachers' judgments, by participants' self-assessments, and by standardized reading scores in English. The authors found that the better readers in their L1, regardless of whether it was Spanish or English, used similar reading strategies to gain comprehension during reading, in L1 and L2. The successful EL1 readers had more and deeper vocabulary knowledge in English than did the EL2 readers, which was to be expected. Successful L2 readers, on the other hand, made use of specific strategies across languages which included looking for and evaluating cognates, evaluating comprehension on the premise that reading must make sense, and re-reading and questioning. These better L2 readers had what Jiménez *et al.* (1996) labelled a 'unitary view of language'. They were aware of the similarities and the differences between the two languages and made use of that knowledge in employing strategies for reading comprehension in their

L2. Less successful L2 readers paid more attention to getting the task done than to comprehension. They monitored problems but they did not employ strategies to solve them. They did not acknowledge that what was useful for reading in one language could be transferred to reading in the other. Although the findings in this study have some interest value for future research, we would like to raise a note of caution with regard to the findings because of the limitations in the research design, which examined three different groups in one setting with very small samples.

The same issue of transfer was researched with a larger sample of even younger children. Fifty 9–10-year-old Spanish L1 students were observed for the ways they used reading strategies for L1 reading and whether they could transfer those strategies to EL2 reading tasks (Hardin 2001). Think-aloud data and interview questions were used with the children in both languages. As a result of their findings the researchers proposed a cross-linguistic, L1/L2 reading strategies taxonomy which included:

1 thinking in the language of the text to ensure concept development;
2 translating, mostly from the stronger to the weaker language;
3 transferring prior knowledge learned in the other language; and
4 using cognates to access the meaning of individual words.

They also found that more able readers had a greater focus on meaning-making in both languages, thus echoing the findings of Jiménez *et al.* (1996). Students from all proficiency groups transferred comprehension problem-solving strategies from Spanish L1 to English L2 reading. Second language proficiency was a less important predictor of reading success than the level of strategy use in the L1. Hardin (2001) concluded that strategic reading behaviors in L1 predicted strategic behaviors in L2 reading. Both Hardin (2001) and Jiménez *et al.* (1996) noted the educational (and political) consequences of their findings, namely that, at least for younger bilinguals, in order to enhance L2 reading achievement, L1 literacy and strategy use should be improved, rather than ignored (as normally happened in the classroom).

L1 impact on L2 reading strategy use: focus on 'translation'

We conclude the discussion on L1 impact on L2 reading strategy use with a short focus on 'translation'. The strategy of mental translation from L2 into L1 to support reading comprehension emerged from a study by Chamot and Küpper (1989). This idea was taken up by a number of researchers. For example, Kern (1994) found that one reason for using the strategy of translating parts of an L2 text to the L1 was to relieve pressure on readers' working memory as they worked out portions of L2 text. The L1 helped hold comprehended meaning and maintain concentration while hypothesis testing as to possible meaning was being carried out on other parts of the text. In addition, translation supported the reader's sense that what was comprehended was correct. In other words, the L1 was used to reduce the cognitive load during L2 reading comprehension.

Among several L1-based strategies identified in a study by Upton and Lee-Thompson (2001) with Japanese and Chinese EFL learners, translation emerged as a strategy in six different forms, that is, it was used in six situations involving difficulties with reading comprehension:

1 to translate a word directly from L2 to L1;
2 to infer the meaning of an L2 word;
3 to hypothesize the meaning of larger chunks of text;
4 to confirm comprehension of larger chunks of text;
5 to predict text structure and content; and
6 to monitor text characteristics and the reader's own reading behavior.

The authors grouped the participants by their English L2 proficiency and, using think-aloud protocols and retrospective interviews, found that more proficient L2 readers made more effective use of L1 particularly for 'metalinguistic functions: making observations about the text or their reading behavior, or choosing to take some action based on the text or the reading demand' (p. 487). The least proficient employed L1 more often for direct translation but less effectively at a metacognitive level. Referring back to the topic of threshold level, Upton and Lee-Thompson (2001) proposed that there may be a threshold of L2 proficiency where thought in L1 becomes less efficient than simply reading the L2 text using automatic and proficient L2 reading skills. Furthermore, the authors detected a possible contribution of the L1 cultures, which may have affected the amount of comprehension evaluation which students engaged in. Upton and Lee-Thompson (2001: 491) suggested that this monitoring role of the L1 supported a sociocultural view of language as a tool for thought in that 'the L1 would quite naturally serve as a tool to help students think about and make sense ... of L2 texts'. In this respect the role of the reader's cultural background was one of the variables which required further research.

This point brings us to the next research focus which is on variables involved in strategy use other than linguistic factors. These include cultural background, motivation, and interest which are beginning to receive increasing attention in foreign and second language strategy research, possibly as a result of the fact that major research studies (OECD 2006) have highlighted the relevance of those factors for both immigrant and native students.

Reading strategies and non-linguistic variables

The interplay between strategies and culture, as well as between strategies, motivation, and interest was considered in the field of foreign language reading as far back as Rubin's *TESOL Quarterly* paper in 1975, but it did not develop initially into a specific research focus. Recently, however, Bernhardt (2005) hypothesized that these variables might explain up to 50 per cent of the variance of L2 reading success. Foreign language acquisition does not only happen 'in the head' but also 'in the world' (Atkinson 2002: 525; see also Chapter 3 this volume). The same is true for L2 reading which cannot be separated from the social, cultural, institutional, and personal practices of L2 readers (Barton and Hamilton 2000; Finkbeiner 2005, 2006a).

Reading strategies and culture

In recent years researchers have begun to address the complex interplay of culture and successful L2 reading comprehension. However, the topic is still in its infancy as we found only a few studies which focused on cultural, national, and/or ethnic influences in connection with successful reading strategies.

In an overview of early studies on the relationship between culture and reading (for example, those by Greaney and Newman 1990, Hewett 1990, Pritchard 1990a), Field (1992) described 'culture and reading' as one of six very important research areas.[2] Another meta-analysis of reading research with special reference to cultural differences and schema was conducted by Singhal (retrieved 2006). More specifically, factors of cultural differences: content/background knowledge schema, formal/textual schema, linguistic/ language schema were investigated. The survey examined the differences and similarities between L1 and L2 reading. It reviewed studies that examined cultural differences, such as content schema, cultural orientation, and background knowledge (including Carrell 1981, 1987; Johnson 1981, 1982; Steffensen and Joag-Dev 1984; Ammon 1987; Shimoda 1989; Langer, Bartolome, Vasquez, and Lucas 1990). Furthermore, it reviewed studies that took account of cultural differences and/or similarities and their links with formal and linguistic schema and text comprehension (Kaplan 1966; Bean, Potter, and Clark 1980; Carrell 1984; Stone 1985; Lindeberg 1988; Mauranen 1992; Connor 1996). Singhal's survey concluded that both L1 and L2 reading required knowledge of cultural content and of formal and linguistic schema. However, from the evidence, he argued that the major differences between L1 and L2 reading are that L2 readers who are not familiar with content schema or do not possess appropriate L2 sociocultural knowledge will have comprehension difficulties in that they cannot perceive the L2 text in a culturally authentic way.

Research has begun to link these ideas with L2 reading strategies but from very different perspectives. For example, Parry (1991, 1993) investigated readers studying in two countries of differing cultural and geographical background whilst Taillefer (2005) compared two nationalities of participants studying in the same country. Parry's (1991, 1993) university participants from Nigeria and China were investigated for differences in their English L2 reading strategies. The question as to whether such a comparison is appropriate may be questionable, however. Twenty male secondary school students in their late teens and early twenties from northern Nigeria were compared to 25 female university graduates in their twenties and thirties from a highly developed region in China participated. The Nigerian students were multilingual; this was not the case in China. Whereas the research in Nigeria was conducted in 1983–1984, the study in China was carried out ten years later in 1994–1995. Despite these methodological problems, the study does provide a perspective on reading as related to cultural practices, and how native educational and social practices influence L2 reading strategies. One of the results was that the Chinese students attended highly to detail, whereas in contrast, the Nigerian students sought comprehension in broad concepts.

In contrast to the small sample selected by Parry (1991, 1993), Taillefer (2005) studied a larger sample (N = 177) of international university students involved in ERASMUS exchanges in Europe. Taillefer did not account for cultural background but for national origin. The investigation focused on whether L2 academic reading skills and strategic approaches differed significantly between specific academic disciplines and between national groups. Despite the fact that the study was piloted and the procedures and methods were meticulously described in the paper, the sample size could be considered problematic as 177 European (study abroad) students of law and economics were compared with only 12 native French undergraduates in a pre- and post-exchange visit design. Whilst warning of the dangers of cultural stereotyping, Taillefer reports that national origin did impact both on measures of reading comprehension and measures of strategy use.

A reader's engagement with the text has also been linked to cultural background. This link has been considered in two exploratory studies with 77 high-school students aged 16 in Taiwan, Germany, and the USA (Finkbeiner 2005; in press), and two intercultural studies (N = 77) in Taiwan and the USA (Finkbeiner 2005; in press). The analyses of culture and reader response showed that reader response could not be predicted by culture alone. It also depended on an individual's text access strategies. Moreover, reader response was also influenced by personality, gender, motivation, and interest.

Reading strategies, motivation, and interest

Despite the fact that the roles of motivation and interest have been widely acknowledged in educational research, there has been a problem with the construct definition of these terms. Some researchers refer to categories of motivation such as integrative, instrumental, intrinsic, extrinsic, affective, and so on. However, we found hardly any studies that relate motivation and interest directly to reading strategies. One of the few was by Bacon and Finnemann (1990) who conducted a complex study on attitudes, motives, and the strategies of university L2 students and their dispositions to authentic oral and written input. One of their key research questions was whether learners' perceptions of general language learning (attitudes, motivation, choice of strategies) would predict learners' comprehension and reading strategy use. The value of this study is in the research design which involved pilot studies before the main study and also involved a large sample. Two pilot studies (N = 200) and a main study (N = 938) were conducted with students of Spanish. The authors report that (a) 'the most important obstacle to a sense of comprehension or satisfaction is unwillingness to confront the input' (Bacon and Finnemann 1990: 467), and (b) affective factors (for example,

instrumental motivation, non-instrumental motivation, unwillingness) functioned as predictors of global/synthetic strategies and decoding/analytic
strategies. The findings suggest an interaction effect between perceived strategy use and perceived interest and motivation. The authors concluded that
'non-instrumentally motivated learners are more likely to use global/synthetic
strategies and avoid decoding/analytic comprehension strategies when
exposed to authentic input' (p. 468).

A study which further investigated these issues was carried out by Finkbeiner
(2005). The research comprised two pilot studies, a main study in two
phases including a learner study, (N = 287) and a teacher study (N = 13). The
research methods relied on data triangulation and a combination of qualitative
and quantitative data analysis. Four main constructs were examined:
(a) reading interest; (b) reading strategies; (c) reading comprehension; and
(d) self-concept.

Major findings of the main study were: (a) strategies varied according to
text, themes, contents, context, and emotional involvement; (b) elaboration
strategies, if used, were highly developed and automated; (c) procedural
knowledge was identified as mostly subconscious routines; (d) strategies
differed in their level of consciousness; (e) there was a high correlation between
elaboration strategies and interest scales; (f) interest differed between the
subgroups, such as gender and educational tracks. (In the German secondary
school system there are three different tracks: lower track—*Hauptschule*, from
grades 5–9 or 10; middle track—*Realschule*, from grades 9–10; and higher
track—*Gymnasium*, from grades 5–12 or 13.); (g) there was a discrepancy
between teachers' view and students' view with regard to concepts such as
good, interested, and strategic reading (Finkbeiner 2003).

To verify the reading model which was developed on the basis of the major
findings on strategies and interest in the above main study, a LISREL analysis
was conducted. The analysis provided four principal insights (Finkbeiner
2005: 384–95):

1 Personal elaboration strategies functioned as a mediating variable between
interest in reading and deep-level text processing. There was no direct causal
effect of interest on deep processing, but, rather, personal elaboration was
necessary for interest to take effect.
2 A learner's ability to self-regulate his/her learning had a direct causal effect
on deep-level text processing.
3 The ability to self-regulate one's learning had a stronger effect on deep
processing for middle-track students than for high-track students.
4 Conversely, personal elaboration strategies had a stronger effect on deep
processing for high-track students than for middle-track students.

The study points to the complex nature of variables involved in L2 reading
strategy use and to the uses that can be made of advanced statistical modeling
to gain insights into the variables behind strategy use. This is why the LISREL
analysis is given prominence here; it is a form of causal modeling that goes

beyond factor analysis and regression analysis. The above study complies with Bernhardt's (2005) call for further research to create a full model of L2 reading which includes reading strategies.

To finish this review we address the question as to whether the insight gained in the studies above have been implemented in strategy based instruction (SBI) in the field of L2 reading.

Research into reading strategy instruction

Research involving L2 reading SBI has had as its goal the improvement of reading comprehension through the reader's use of more effective strategies. This is in line with the fundamental aim of strategy research in general (see Chapter 1). However, the choice of strategies to be taught has depended on the researchers' conceptualization of which strategies would be most effective for improving participants' reading comprehension in a particular teaching and learning setting.

Reading comprehension has been measured in numerous ways making comparisons between studies difficult. Although the L2 being learnt has frequently been English, there have been a number of studies carried out with other languages. The ages of learners have been from primary school learners to adults, and the length of the instruction period has varied, although it has usually been fairly short-term. A model of L2 reading processes has rarely been included in published studies, although mention of top-down and/or bottom-up strategies has often been linked to levels of reading processing. Virtually all studies involve instruction in metacognitive strategies either directly or indirectly, if for no other reason than that the metacognitive strategy of evaluating the use of a new strategy is an integral part of strategy intervention models (Chamot 2004).

A combination of word-level and metacognitive strategies was used by Kitajima (1997) for an SBI program involving US university students of Japanese. The instruction was in identifying referents in text, which involved strategies at syntax and discourse level. The intervention and comparison groups underwent a course of four sessions per week for 15 weeks. Outcomes were measured for identifying referents and for reading comprehension. The intervention group achieved higher results on all the post-tests but not equally high in both comprehension and referent recognition. The design and results suggested that students could successfully learn to use a strategy presented in an instruction program and that improved comprehension might be achieved at the same time, although a causal link could not be shown.

In a similar attempt to develop university students' strategy use at different levels of processing, Kern (1989) organized an instruction program of strategies for word recognition, inferring meaning, and engaging in synthesis-of-meaning. He divided 53 anglophone university students of French as a foreign language into experimental and control groups. Pre- and post-tests for comprehension revealed that only the lower-ability students achieved a statistically significant gain in comprehension. Kern suggested that perhaps the middle and higher participants were already using the strategies contained in the instruction, indicating that a closer understanding of participants' strategy use was needed from the outset.

The effects of two metacognitive strategy approaches on reading comprehension were measured by Carrell, Pharis, and Liberto (1989). Two intervention groups were created of US university students with various L1s. One intervention group was taught pre-reading semantic mapping of information which was then mapped against information they gleaned from the text. The other intervention group was taught to activate their own knowledge about the text topic before reading. Key findings were that both types of intervention improved reading comprehension. Criticism levelled at this study (see Hassan *et al.* 2005) pointed to the similarity between the strategies that were instructed and the test sections. In other words, there is a possibility that what was shown to have taken place was simply repetition of what had been practiced rather than evidence of the deployment of strategies in a new context. What Carrell *et al.* (1989) did show was that metacognitive strategies could be successfully incorporated into an SBI program.

A later metacognitive SBI program was carried out by Kusiak (2001) who sought to develop the metacognitive knowledge and monitoring strategies of Polish secondary school readers of English as their L2. Kusiak (2001) wondered whether reading comprehension could be positively affected by increased metacognition and how these two variables—metacognition and comprehension—were related to L2 language competence. The instruction produced results that showed increased metacognitive awareness on the part of the participants. Their evaluation strategies improved as did their L2 reading comprehension. Particularly positive results were gained by students who had been placed in the lower-proficiency group at the beginning, based on an initial general L2 language competence test.

SBI success was detected with an intervention cohort of high-intermediate proficiency learners of French in a research project by Raymond (1993). These students were taught to identify text genre, structure, and content through linguistic text markers; that is, they were given training in a combination of text-based strategies and metacognitive strategies. At post-intervention testing, the intervention group reported greater use of these strategies than did the control group but the intervention students achieved higher comprehension results on only one of the post-intervention texts. According to Raymond (1993: 455) these findings pointed to the complex 'interaction of strategy use, text content, reader interest, background knowledge, and reader perceptions of text difficulty', all of which required further investigation before clear statements could be made about the effect of the intervention.

While it is acknowledged that there are myriad variables involved in L2 reading, there is a danger both in trying to take too many variables into account and also in inadvertently ignoring variables. This problem is particularly acute when designing and carrying out SBI research. Bimmel, van den Bergh, and Oostdam (2001) reported a strategies intervention project in which strategies for reading comprehension were taught to students both in their L1 (Dutch) and in their English L2, with the expectation that the strategies would be successfully transferred from L1 to L2 reading. The four strategies were: looking for key fragments, paying attention to structural markers in the text, creating questions about the text, and semantic mapping of the most important information in the text. The results of the intervention group of twelve 15-year-olds were compared to those of a control group of 112. Improvement was found in the intervention group's L1 reading comprehension. The results for L2 reading were, however, not ascertainable. The authors assumed that the project teachers did not explicitly teach strategies for L2 reading because they had thought that students would transfer their L1 reading strategies to the L2 context but this L1–L2 strategy transfer did not happen. In addition, the authors remarked that there were too many variables involved in the complex interactions between participants, including the teachers, to be able to track specific effects of strategy instruction on L2 reading comprehension. Although the project was otherwise well described, the untracked variables make replication of the project very difficult.

Thus, when the transfer of successful L1 SBI to an L2 setting is attempted, a number of potentially important variables need to be considered and controlled for. Similar problems appear to have been encountered by Cotterall (1993). In her study, results of an SBI program were inconclusive due to her uncritical assumption that L1 strategies could be transferred without modification into the L2 learning environment. She found that learners needed to be able to apply the targeted cognitive strategies fairly automatically during their L1 reading before they could successfully engage in, and benefit from, the related metacognitive strategies being taught for improving their L2 reading. Cotterall further evaluated that the SBI had attempted to draw active attention to too many strategies, each of which consisted of sub-strategies, which in turn needed to be unpicked and handled individually. This program complexity was exacerbated by the fact that her learners found discussions in the L2 to be inhibiting of the whole SBI process.

A complex SBI program was also carried out by Dreyer and Nel (2003) in which strategy use development was attempted with study guides, an online data management and reference program, and personal contact with tutors. Over a 13-week semester, a combination of cognitive and metacognitive strategies were taught to and practiced by 131 first-year Afrikaans and Setswanan L1 students learning English for professional purposes at a South African University. The students were divided vertically into experimental and control groups and horizontally into successful and at-risk students, based on standardized tests. Reading comprehension and reading strategy use were measured pre- and post-intervention. At the onset of the project, at-risk students apparently lacked metacognitive strategies for monitoring and evaluating their comprehension in order to deploy cognitive strategies to deal with reading problems. By the end of the programme both successful and at-risk students in the experimental group achieved significantly higher comprehension scores than did the control group. There were also changes in the choice and orchestration of strategies which intervention students used.

In summary, SBI has been carried out with a range of learners at a variety of proficiency levels in a range of contexts with a variety of languages, but results have often been less than conclusive and long-term effects not measured. Many issues surrounding strategy interventions remain, as described in Chapter 7 of this volume. These include the restrictions of the research design, text and task characteristics, possibly culturally biased research instruments, the number of participants, and participants' individual characteristics. There is, moreover, a lack of program transparency. SBI studies ought to clarify whether they are embedded in normal teaching or separate, how long the intervention program lasted, whether the outcome measures can be related to the intervention or to other factors, and whether the design included triangulation or not. This would assist in replicating the SBI project, and would contribute to generalizability of findings to larger populations.

Noting in a review article that L2 reading strategy instruction programs have usually involved only single or a few specific strategies, Grabe (2004) proposed that what was needed was the development of *strategic* L2 readers. Such readers would monitor their comprehension and the task requirements and know what, where, when, and why to instigate strategies. To achieve such a vision of independent and competent L2 readers there is need for a great deal of further research in SBI at all levels of L2 reading with many different L2 languages, readers, and settings.

Limitations of the review process

In order to present a somewhat linear story of the developments which have taken place in reading strategy research since the 1970s, much literature has not been included here. The studies presented were published in English with a few in German; studies in other languages were not consulted. Other limitations lie in context variables, such as time, staff, and money involved in this review project. Given the limited time and the number of studies available, this review had to set priorities as to the most salient issues in this field over the time span of this volume.

Limitation of studies reviewed

Virtually none of the intervention studies reviewed were easily replicable nor was it easy to assess their generalizability. Small sample sizes and non-random aspects of sampling in studies appear to prevent their generalizability to larger populations. As pointed out above, replication requires very detailed published reports of the research undertaken. Few studies triangulated their data collection to include more than one method of finding out what strategies were being used by the participants. Few intervention studies had pre- and post-test designs; none had delayed post-tests. Few classroom-based studies have described the role of the classroom teacher in relation to the research being undertaken or given more than cursory details of the settings. Despite these limitations, all the studies presented here reveal that there is a wide range of enquiry in L2 strategy research.

Summary conclusion to this review

In her review of L2 reading strategy literature, Brantmeier (2002) refers to the impossibility of comparing the many studies that have been undertaken with so many different methods, populations, languages, texts, and tasks. Given these restrictions, we have not tried to compare studies so much as to present research which has contributed in the first instance to the conceptualization of L2 reading strategy types and then the use and instruction of strategies. Viewing L2 reading as taking place on 'levels' has facilitated the conceptualization of L2 reading strategies. Since Hosenfeld's early seminal work was published over 30 years ago, researchers have attempted to identify strategy-types and have linked them to levels of learner proficiency. They have also recognized the interactivity of reading 'levels' which means that a single reader may employ many types of strategies in the course of an L2 reading event. We have attempted to demonstrate in our review how the research community has widened its perception of what L2 reading involves in terms of cognitive processing and in terms of the many variables which arise from L1 linguistic and cultural backgrounds and individual characteristics of the reader. All these aspects have been seen to impact on strategy choice and employment. To some extent we have been able to follow this conceptualization of the development of L2 reading strategy research in SBI where the objective has been improved L2 reading comprehension. Finally, we have attempted to demonstrate that over the last decades researchers have recognized ever-increasing numbers of variables as being key to readers' L2 reading strategy use and comprehension.

Future research in the field of L2 reading strategies

In recent reviews of reading strategies research, both in terms of elicitation and instruction, (for example, Brantmeier 2002; Grabe and Stoller 2002; Chamot 2004; Bernhardt 2005) authors have pointed to areas of the field which need further research. More research is needed into the cross-language factors that cause variance in the cognitive processing involved in L2 reading (Koda 2005). Cross-language factors have implications for strategy choice, use, and transfer. Although L2 reading is different from L1 reading, developments in L1 reading research will continue to appear on research agendas for L2 reading improvement. Since the 1980s, more complex, non-linear models of L1 reading have been proposed using connectionist concepts of the parallel distributed processing (PDP) of information. Virtually no research into L2 reading strategies using a PDP framework has been undertaken.

A principled, comprehensive model of L2 reading is still missing. New statistical procedures, such as path models and LISREL analyses, may contribute to such a model. Future studies will also have to address the weaknesses of construct definitions. This implies an explicit presentation of the conceptualization or model of reading comprehension which underlies the project design. Clearly, as we have argued, these procedures would strengthen our call for empirical projects to be reported rigorously and thoroughly in the published literature. This is important as informed L2 reading is a critical element for viable membership in global communities; it is an important precondition for democracy (Finkbeiner 2006a: 45).

However, terminology for and classification of reading strategies may well change as reading models develop. L2 reading is not only linked to L1 reading research but probably also to other disciplines, such as, learning psychology, sociology, anthropology, and the neurosciences. Avenues will have to be developed in L2 reading strategy research for undertaking multilayered and multidimensional research to understand L2 reading strategies and their use.

Acknowledgements

We wish to express our gratitude to the anonymous reviewers of a very early version of this chapter, all of whom provided guidance for its further development. A special thanks goes to Ernesto Macaro for his valuable help throughout.

Notes

1 We use 'L2' for both foreign and second language throughout this chapter as we make no important distinctions between the two.
2 The other five areas out of the six included schema theory, reading strategies and processes, comprehension studies, methods for teaching reading, and cognition/metacognition (Field 1992).

10

A review of oral communication strategies: focus on interactionist and psycholinguistic perspectives

YASUO NAKATANI and CHRISTINE GOH

Introduction

This chapter examines trends in second and foreign language communication strategy research by reviewing research studies from interactional and psycholinguistic perspectives. The interactional view focuses on the way learners use strategies during interaction that could help to improve negotiation of meaning and the overall effectiveness of their message. The psycholinguistic view addresses mental processes that underlie learners' language behavior when dealing with lexical and discourse problems. For our review of research within each broad conceptualization, we highlight how different researchers have described communication strategies and how the use of such strategies is examined in relation to learner and task variables. We also examine intervention studies involving strategy instruction and their pedagogical implications. We conclude with some general observations about the strengths and limitations of the reviewed studies.

Learners' speaking strategies, commonly referred to as *communication strategies* (CSs), captured the interest of scholars in the 1970s. The use of CSs was recognized as a key interlanguage process (Selinker 1972). Great importance was attached to CS research especially after Canale and Swain (1980) put forward their influential conceptual framework for teaching and testing second language (L2) communicative competence. In the last three decades, interest in CSs has engendered scholarly discussion and studies that address issues related to CS descriptions, use, and teachability. There is, however, little agreement about what CSs really are, their transferability from L1 to L2, and whether they can be learnt in the classroom. In fact, many competing taxonomies of CSs have emerged, thus making comparisons and conclusions problematic. See Dörnyei and Scott (1997) for a summary of the various definitions and taxonomies.

In spite of this diversity, many useful insights about CS use among language learners have been offered by researchers working from two major perspectives: interactional and psycholinguistic. The *interactional* view of

CS focuses on the interaction process between language learners and their interlocutors, and in particular the way in which meaning is negotiated by one or both parties (for example, Tarone 1980; Rost and Ross 1991; Williams, Inscoe, and Tasker 1997). CSs are regarded not only as problem-solving phenomena to compensate for communication disruptions, but also as devices with pragmatic discourse functions for message enhancement. The *psycholinguistic* view, on the other hand, examines learners' problem-solving behaviors arising from gaps in their lexical knowledge (for example, Bialystok 1983a; Poulisse 1990). Most researchers of a psycholinguistic orientation have narrowed the description of CSs to lexical-compensatory strategies. While this narrow focus allows researchers to concentrate on one clear aspect of learners' strategy use, a psycholinguistic perspective should, in our view, be broad enough to encompass research on other cognitive processes during speech production.

Our review of CS research is organized into two main sections according to these two key perspectives on CS. Some studies which do not fall neatly into one or the other category will be placed in the category we think is more representative of the work. In each section we first review studies which primarily aimed to identify and describe CSs. This is followed by a review of studies which explored the relationship between CS use and learners' target language (TL) proficiency and other learner and task variables. Finally, we review intervention studies which have sought to enhance the effectiveness of strategy use in oral production and have offered implications for teaching and curriculum development.

The review methodology for this chapter can be accessed on www.oup.com/elt/teacher/lls in Appendix 10.1.

Section 1 Communication strategies: the interactional view

Tarone, Cohen, and Dumas (1976) initially regarded learner's problem-solving behavior during target language (TL) communication as involving 'communication strategies' (CSs). They argued that learners had a tendency to use CSs to compensate for their lack of appropriate TL knowledge when expressing or decoding meaning of their intended utterances. Tarone further defined CSs as 'mutual attempts of two interlocutors to agree on a meaning in situations where the requisite meaning structures do not seem to be shared' (1980: 420). By focusing on interactions, Tarone regarded CSs as any attempts at avoiding communication disruptions. She also suggested the distinction between CSs which are strategies for language use and 'learning strategies' which are used for developing linguistic and sociolinguistic competence in the TL.

CSs were then included by Canale and Swain (1980) as one of the sub-competencies in their model of communicative competence. Strategic competence was the ability to use verbal and non-verbal strategies to avoid communication breakdowns that might be caused by learners' lack of appropriate TL knowledge. They noted that low-level students could benefit from learning effective CSs such as paraphrasing, using gestures, and asking questions for clarification. Canale (1983) extended the concept of CSs by presenting two types of CSs: (1) strategies to compensate for disruptions in communication problems due to speakers' insufficient TL knowledge, and (2) strategies to enhance the effectiveness of communication with interlocutors (1983: 12). The first type concerning interlocutors' problem-solving behaviors is regarded as negotiation of meaning, which has been an important object of study for some time (for example, Long 1983b; Varonis and Gass 1985; Pica 2002). However, these studies have concentrated on negotiation devices and excluded other types of CSs. Recently some researchers (for example, Clennel 1995; Williams, Inscoe, and Tasker 1997) claim that CS research should also include the second type of strategies because interlocutors have to use strategies for maintaining discourse and gaining time to think in actual communication.

Identifying communication strategies

To explore the concept of CSs, Tarone (1978) recorded interactions between a native speaker (NS) and a non-native speaker (NNS). She analyzed the transcription data and proposed the first conceptual framework for CSs that became a major influence on research in the field. Tarone presented five main categories: intra-language based, inter-language based, appeal for assistance, mime, and avoidance. Faerch and Kasper (1983a, 1983b, 1984) proposed a broader definition of CS by emphasizing planning and execution of speech production during oral communication. CSs were regarded as 'potentially conscious plans' for solving a problem in reaching a particular communicative goal. They argued that in order to solve communication problems, learners did not only have to co-operate with their interlocutors but also find a solution themselves without co-operative assistance. Their claim was based on the analysis of the PIF (Project in Foreign Language Pedagogy) corpus data at Copenhagen University. The project collected the spoken and written English of 120 Danish learners from various proficiency levels. The research by Faerch and Kasper was the first attempt to investigate CS use by utilizing corpus data in the analysis of interlanguage discourse.

CSs were categorized into achievement strategies and reduction strategies. The former enable learners to work on an alternative plan for reaching the original goal by means of whatever resources available. The latter allow learners to avoid solving a communication problem by abandoning the aim of conveying the message. Achievement strategies consist of compensatory strategies and retrieval strategies. The former include code switching, interlingual transfer, intralingual transfer, interlanguage (IL)-based strategies, co-operative strategies, and non-linguistic strategies. The latter are used when learners have difficulties in retrieving specific items. Reduction strategies consist of formal reduction strategies: using reduced systems to avoid producing non-fluent or incorrect utterances, and function reduction strategies: avoiding a specific topic or giving up sending a message.

Faerch and Kasper's studies advanced our understanding to some extent, but an issue of reliability emerged when Haastrup and Philipson (1983) produced slightly different taxonomies using the same PIF data. They selected a part of the PIF data consisting of eight samples at three schools in order to analyze how learners used CSs differently according to their school levels focusing particularly on learners' achievement strategy use. The researchers found that individual differences in using specific CSs was more significant than differences in their school levels.

Some researchers (for example, Long 1980, 1981, 1983a; Pica and Doughty 1985; Varonis and Gass 1985; Doughty and Pica 1986) investigated the learning effects of interlocutors' mutual attempts to avoid and repair impasses in their L2 conversational discourse (negotiation of meaning). Interlocutor's signals for negotiation of meaning include comprehension checks, confirmation checks, and clarification requests. Comprehension checks occur when interlocutors try to ascertain whether others have understood the preceding utterances. Interlocutors use confirmation checks to evaluate their own understanding by repeating or paraphrasing what the previous speakers has said. When interlocutors seek assistance in understanding others' preceding utterances, they make clarification requests. When NNSs indicated difficulty in understanding the meaning of an utterance, NSs repeated, reworded, or used a less complex sentence to make their message understood. Long argued that such NSs' repairing behavior created the ideal environment which could provide learners with comprehensible input.

While comprehensible input through negotiation was necessary for L2 acquisition, Swain (1985) pointed out that it was insufficient. She investigated learners' performance in immersion classrooms and found their spoken production to be less developed than their listening, reading, and writing. She argued that learners should experience meaningful interaction that could lead them to produce increasingly grammatical utterances, or what she referred to as comprehensible output. Learners' modifications of their previous utterances could be motivated by feedback from interlocutors such as clarification requests or confirmation checks. It is important therefore that learners not only receive modified input but also modify their output by manipulating their interlanguage in creative and complex ways.

Pica, Holliday, Lewis, and Morgenthaler (1989) investigated whether low-proficiency NNSs could modify their output when receiving signals from NSs. Ten Japanese ESL learners (TOEFL scores: 397–467) in the US were paired with NSs in three different tasks: a picture description information gap task, a jigsaw task, and a discussion task. The results showed that regardless of task type, NNSs modified their output most often when NSs signalled an explicit need for clarification, rather than provided a model of the utterance for confirmation.

The effect of L2 learners' interaction with other learners was explored by Pica, Lincoln-Porter, Paninos, and Linnell (1996). They studied whether NNS–NNS interaction could produce modified input toward comprehensibility, send feedback focused on form, and modify output. Two jigsaw tasks were used to compare negotiation behavior between ten NNS–NNS dyads and ten NS–NNS dyads. Participants' discourse data were coded for lexical and syntactic modification. It was found that negotiation in NNS–NNS interaction produced less quantitatively rich data compared with negotiation in NS–NNS interaction. Nevertheless, learners in NNS–NNS interactions could negotiate with each other and offer feedback to peers of considerable quality. The researchers recommended the use of peer communicative tasks in classrooms to enhance learners' use of CSs for negotiation of meaning.

Research on negotiation of meaning has deepened our understanding of CSs for interaction. One conclusion that can be drawn is that CSs for meaning negotiation can have an effect on learning because they play a facilitative role in assisting TL input, receiving feedback, offering opportunities for modifying output, and promoting learners' attention to developmentally difficult relationships of L2 form and meaning that they have not fully acquired.

In all the studies we have reviewed so far, learners' interaction was examined by the single method of analysis of transcribed data, thus excluding the possibility of interpreting learners' actual intentions in their use of certain strategies. Furthermore, most of these studies were conducted in experimental settings, not in classroom contexts, thus making it difficult to draw conclusions about the impact of negotiation on the development of TL proficiency in normal classroom situations.

Foster (1998) examined how L2 learners carried out negotiation of meaning in four classroom tasks: a grammar-based task, a dyad information gap task, a discussion task and a jigsaw task. Participants were 21 part-time intermediate-level students at a large municipal college with a wide variety of L1 backgrounds and ages. Their class met three times a week for two hours. The transcripts were coded for confirmation checks, comprehension checks, clarification requests, and modified output. She found that dyad tasks requiring exchange of information were the best for enhancing negotiations and modified output between interlocutors.

Compared with results from previous studies conducted in experimental settings, the frequency of CSs used in Foster's study was very low. She speculated that learners did not show many problems with understanding for fear of losing face. She concluded that subjects in experimental settings might have been more conscious of their language use, while subjects in classroom settings were less aware of the need to negotiate for meaning. Her claims raise the crucial question of whether learners' proficiency can be improved if strategy instruction included explicit activities which enhance learners' awareness of using strategies such as negotiation. We will return to this question when we review studies on metacognitive strategy instruction. Researchers who have highlighted the impact of negotiation on L2 development have concluded that CS has a positive effect on learning.

Williams, Inscoe, and Tasker (1997) argue that it is important to link the findings of interactional adjustment research with those of CS research. They investigated strategic behavior for maintaining discourse through conversational modification in an authentic classroom setting by video-recording NS–NNS interaction in three two-hour organic chemistry laboratory sessions. The NNSs were teaching assistants whose L1 was Mandarin. They were in their late twenties or early thirties and their TOEFL scores ranged from 597–610. NSs were American students majoring in chemistry or related subjects. This context was different from typical L2 classroom contexts. Williams and colleagues adopted common concepts for negotiation of meaning, such as confirmation checks and clarification requests, but they extended the definition of interactional adjustments to include discourse-level strategies. These were assigned to any expressions that were not immediately contingent to the preceding utterances. All three authors transcribed and coded the data together, but there was no report of inter-coder agreement. Contrary to the findings in Foster's study, they found that both NNSs and NSs used a number of strategies for negotiation. In order to improve mutual comprehension and maintain their discourse, the participants actively used CSs for conversational adjustments. The results indicated that the frequency of interlocutors' negotiations of meaning can be influenced by the nature of tasks and the roles of participants engaged in the tasks.

Nakahama, Tyler, and van Lier (2001) suggested that when examining interactional modifications, researchers should go beyond repair negotiations for the preceding utterances. They investigated the quantity and quality of interaction in three NS–NNS pairs doing an information gap task and a conversation task. The information gap task was audiotaped and the conversation task was videotaped. The researcher and participants reviewed the tapes together for the purpose of collecting retrospective interview data to validate the results of the transcription analysis. There were certain limitations regarding the amount of data, as the number of participants was small and only two NNSs could participate in the retrospective interview. Nevertheless, the study's interesting findings suggest that the definition of negotiation of meaning should be expanded to include other interactional phenomena which go beyond repair of preceding utterances. Compared with information gap interactions, conversations produced fewer instances of repair negotiation for preceding utterances. Yet, in conversations participants generated a variety of discourse strategies for discourse management, interpersonal dynamics, and topic continuity to maintain interaction and to improve mutual understanding. The results suggested that an investigation of the learning effects of TL interaction by examining negotiation strategies *exclusively* may limit the potential of such research. It is important to investigate the role of other CSs such as strategies for enhancing discourse as well.

The pragmatic function of CSs in interactive discourse was emphasized by Clennel (1995), who in following Canale (1983) adopted a definition of CSs that included strategies for enhancing communication effectiveness. The study was unique in making use of techniques of discourse analysis such as stress and pitch. Tone of speech was included to investigate learners' attempts to use CSs for overcoming communicative deficiencies. Six NS–NNS dyads conducted two tasks: an information gap task and a discussion about the language learning process. Their task performance was videotaped and transcribed. Immediately upon completion of the task, each dyad reviewed the videotape and answered the researcher's questions. This post-task interview was also videotaped and used to validate the results of the discourse analysis. CSs were categorized into three types: strategies for overcoming lexical problems, strategies for collaborative facilitation, and strategies for message-enhancement.

Summary

Many researchers have argued that negotiation has an impact on TL development and that CSs have a positive effect on learning. While many studies have been conducted into the use of CSs for negotiation and repairs in research settings, few have explored L2 learners' CS use in actual classroom contexts where learners might use CSs that are quantitatively and qualitatively different from experimental settings. More classroom studies dealing with various language learning tasks should be done to investigate L2 learners' strategies for specific kinds of communication. Some researchers adopted Canale's (1983) definition of CSs as consisting of any attempts to solve communication problems and enhance communication. They extended the scope of CS research to analyze discourse data not only for negotiation devices, but also for other strategies used in maintaining and developing discourse. All the studies reviewed so far used relatively small samples, thus making it difficult to generalize the outcomes. To increase the value of the body of research on CSs during interaction, it is necessary for these studies to be replicated with more subjects across different learning and sociocultural contexts.

Interactional CS use and target language proficiency

Compared with the psycholinguistic view of CSs, less attention has been given to the issue of how TL proficiency affects learners' strategy use in interaction. One study that investigated this was conducted by Labarca and Khanji (1986) among novice French learners. Fifty-three university students were divided into two groups: a Total Physical Response (TPR) group (N = 23) and a Strategic Instruction (SI) group (N = 30). At the end of each 12-week course, all the participants took an interview test with native French interviewers. The test performance, which lasted between 10 and 15 minutes, was videotaped and rated by ACTFL procedures. Their interaction was analyzed by making use of Tarone's typology which included message abandonment, language switch, appeal for assistance, mime, and answering full sentences. Negative correlation was found between participants' total use of CSs and their test scores. Based on these results they argued that high-proficiency learners used fewer CSs as they had better control over the activity with their acquired linguistic competence.

In order to analyze how L2 students' proficiency affect the use of CSs, Khanji (1996) used a scenario task. The task was unique in creating a simulated context in which participants should interact spontaneously in order to solve unexpected problems. Thirty-six EFL students at a university in Jordan were divided into three proficiency groups based on the results of a placement test. The data was collected from the scenario dyad test during the final examination. Each student dyad was randomly assigned from the three respective levels. The 5–10 minute interaction was audiotaped, transcribed, and then analyzed. It was found that each level group used different types of CSs. Low-level students most often resorted to repetition and message abandonment. Middle-level students tended to use mainly transliteration, semantic contiguity, and code switch. Advanced students frequently used topic shift and semantic contiguity. The results indicated that the advanced students used achievement strategies by which they could develop an alternative solution for the communicative problem they were facing. Compared to structural tasks such as information gap tasks, the scenario task generated authentic contexts in which learners could interact freely with each other in order to resolve a communication problem in various ways.

Nakatani (2006) also introduced a scenario task to identify how EFL learners' proficiency level relates to their recognition of CS use. Based on the results of exploratory factor analysis conducted on 400 Japanese students' self-reports regarding the use of CSs in communicative tasks, the Oral Communication Strategy Inventory (OCSI) was developed. The OCSI includes eight categories of strategies for coping with production problems and seven categories for coping with reception problems during interaction tasks. The reliability of the instrument was estimated by Cronbach's alpha (production part: .86, reception part: .85). The concurrent validity of the OCSI was determined by intercorrelation with the Oxford's Strategy Inventory for Language Learning (SILL) (production part: $r = .62$, reception part: $r = .57$). Sixty-two low-intermediate female students at a Japanese college completed a scenario task in which their classroom teacher played the role of a communication partner. Their task performance was videotaped and scored by two independent NS judges (inter-rater reliability: .89). According to the participants' task scores, which correlated significantly with their TOEIC test scores ($r = .72$), they were divided into higher- (N = 18), middle- (N = 18), and lower-proficiency groups (N = 26). Immediately after completing the task, students reported their strategy use by means of the OCSI. The higher-proficiency group reported more use of social-affective, fluency-maintaining, and negotiation-for-meaning strategies when they had production problems than did the other two proficiency groups. When they encountered reception problems, the group reported a greater use of strategies for reacting smoothly such as conversational shadowing for maintaining their interaction.

Summary

The number of studies dealing with the relationship between strategy use and TL proficiency remains small to date, making it difficult to make definitive statements about the relationship. It has also been difficult to attribute specific strategies exclusively to effective or high-proficiency learners. Some researchers claim that higher-proficiency learners use fewer CSs because they have enough linguistic or sociolinguistic knowledge to solve potential communicative problems. In contrast, others have argued that higher-level learners do not use reduction strategies, but still use some achievement strategies by which they can skilfully manage their interaction and avoid potential problems. One of the reasons for this discrepancy has to do with the fact that definitions of 'levels' differ across research settings. Some researchers used in-house placement tests or oral proficiency tests, while others used the length of learning experience. Clearly, we need more studies where participants' proficiency is defined by standardized scales such as TOEFL, TOEIC, IELTS, or ACTFL.

Another reason for the discrepancies in research findings may have to do the way researchers 'counted' CSs. Some studies included achievement strategies, which work to enhance TL interaction, as well as reduction strategies which could work against the maintaining of discourse. As these two types of CS are very different in nature and purpose, it may be more useful for them to be considered separately when examining the link between the frequency of CS use and proficiency levels.

Strategy instruction

One of the earliest classroom intervention studies was conducted by O'Malley, Chamot, Stewner-Manzares, Russo, and Küpper (1985b), who compared the effectiveness of different types of strategy instruction. Seventy-five high school students were divided into three groups: Group 1 (metacognitive group) received combined metacognitive, cognitive, and social/affective strategy instruction. Group 2 (cognitive group) received cognitive and social/affective strategy instruction. Group 3 (control group) had no particular strategy instruction. They used integrated tasks involving listening, speaking, and vocabulary for 50 minutes a day over eight days. The effects of these various types of strategy instruction on speaking was examined by comparing the pre- and post-test audiotaped data. They found that strategy instruction had a significant positive effect on developing speaking skills. Their results indicated the usefulness of strategy instruction which aimed at activating students' schemata in order to deliver meaningful messages in speaking tasks. However, they only dealt with ways to deliver a monologue to an audience, and so the effects of strategy instruction for conversation with others were not explored.

Unlike O'Malley and his colleagues, Dörnyei (1995) examined speaking skills in conversations. He examined the teachability of CSs by focusing on whether instruction in specific strategies could enhance the strategy use of Hungarian high school EFL learners. The experimental group was instructed in three types of oral communication strategies: (1) topic avoidance and replacement, (2) circumlocution, and (3) fillers and hesitation to remain in the conversation, for 20–40 minutes during three regular English lessons per week over a period of six weeks. Three different tasks (topic description, cartoon description, and definition formulation) were used to evaluate the effectiveness of the instruction. The focus was on self-description skills about specific items without interaction with others. The strategy instruction group showed a significant improvement in the quality and quantity of strategy use, and in their overall speech performance. In addition, students in the group showed positive attitudes towards their instruction. The study, however, excluded negotiation strategies. The question of how to integrate metacognitive strategy awareness instruction into a strategy-based program was also not directly addressed.

An intervention study by Cohen, Weaver, and Li (1998) included meta-cognitive strategy development for enhancing speaking. In their program, foreign language university students in the US were explicitly taught strategy use over a ten-week period. Experimental-group learners in three different classes—advanced intermediate French (N = 7), intermediate French (N = 11) and intermediate Norwegian (N = 14)—were instructed to use metacognitive strategies for preparing to speak, self-monitoring during speaking, and self-evaluation after having spoken. In order to evaluate students' improvement in speaking ability, the results of the pre- and post-semi-direct audiotaped speaking tests for both the experimental and control groups were analyzed. These tests consisted of three speaking tasks, namely self-description, story retelling, and city description. Students' performances were evaluated using the criteria of self-confidence, vocabulary, and grammar. They were also requested to make checklists for their use of strategies before, during, and after these tasks. These checklists were used to examine the correlation between frequency of strategy use and a rating of their task performance.

The experimental group outperformed the control group only on the city description task, implying that some resourceful students in the control group might have used strategies effectively. No significant difference was found between the two groups in the self-description and story-retelling tasks. Like other studies mentioned above, the instruction model in this study did not introduce negotiation between interlocutors as a crucial component for learning the TL. Their tests used semi-direct one-way audiotape recording and did not include interactional aspects of oral production.

The effect of strategy instruction for speaking skills on EFL proficiency were investigated by Dadour and Robbins (1996) with 102 Egyptian university students. The experimental groups consisted of a first-year group (15 males, 15 females) and a fourth-year group (15 males, 16 females). The control groups also consisted of a first-year group (15 males, 15 females) and a fourth-year group (15 males, 16 females). Explicit strategy instruction was embedded into 15 weekly three-hour sessions for pre-service English teacher development courses. In the experimental groups, instructors presented new strategies and offered students opportunities to practice the strategies and discuss their usefulness. There was little information about the instruction for control groups. At the end of the courses, the participants had an oral role-play test. They also reported their strategy use in a questionnaire. No information about the instrument was available. The experimental groups outperformed the control group in the oral test. The fourth-year experimental group scored better than the first-year experimental group. The experimental groups reported more use of strategies than the control groups. In general male students obtained better test scores than female students.

Bejarano, Levine, Olshtain, and Steiner (1997) integrated modified-interaction strategies for negotiation of meaning and social-interaction strategies for maintaining conversation flow into their CS instruction program. Thirty-four high school students in Israel were divided into an experimental group with CS instruction (N = 15) and a control group without CS instruction (N = 19). Both groups had three 60-minute lessons per week over eight weeks. The experimental group had extra instruction of strategies for interaction in small-group activities. For both pre- and post-test, each group had a discussion task with other students limited to ten minutes. These tests were videotaped and then transcribed. The experimental group significantly increased their use of modified-interaction strategies ($p < .005$) and social-interaction strategies ($p < .05$) compared with the control group. The results indicated that it was useful to design CS instruction by combining strategies for solving interaction problems and strategies for enhancing communication effectiveness. Although they did not examine direct effects on proficiency, the researchers suggested that learning to use CSs could promote TL development.

Nakatani (2005) introduced metacognitive instruction for interactional strategy development. The participants consisted of 62 female Japanese learners on a 12-week EFL course taught using a communicative approach. The strategy instruction group (N = 28) received metacognitive instruction, focusing on interactional strategy usage, while the comparison group (N = 34) received only normal communicative instruction with no explicit focus on CSs. The effects of the instruction were assessed through: pre- and post-oral communication test scores, transcription data from the tests, and retrospective protocol data for their task performance. The findings revealed that the strategy instruction group significantly improved their oral proficiency test scores, whereas improvements in the comparison group were non-significant. The results of the transcription and retrospective protocol data analysis confirmed that their success was partly due to an increased general awareness of CSs, and the use of specific interaction strategies, such as maintenance of fluency as a communication enhancer, negotiation of meaning, and issues of face-saving.

Summary

The studies conducted on strategy instruction suggest that instruction in CS use can produce positive results. This is particularly true of the studies that incorporated the use of metacognitive strategies and awareness-raising into CS instruction. Many of the learners might not have possessed extensive knowledge about how to control their use of CSs. It was therefore useful to help them notice how to plan, monitor, and evaluate their CS use to avoid potential disruptions. Although examining the increase of specific CS use is important, we need concrete evidence to reveal the direct relationship between strategy instruction and L2 development. To evaluate the effect of strategy instruction on oral proficiency development, it is essential to introduce not only a standardized general proficiency test but also an oral test.

In addition, only a few studies have used oral tests which examined interactional ability. Although semi-direct oral tests could offer important information regarding learners' performance, tests which can examine how respondents develop the discourse with their interlocutors may be more valid for the purpose we have been discussing. Some studies used learner–learner interaction for oral testing which may be useful for drawing implications for classroom tasks. However, using other students as a communicative partner in tests may introduce intervening variables that affect test results. For example, one candidate's individual characteristic or specific deficiencies could affect the performance of the other. To date, there have been few studies that have presented the validity and reliability of using student dyads for speaking tests. As there were few studies that examined the possible effect of proficiency level on the results of CS instruction, it is essential to explore this research area in future studies.

Section 2 Communication strategies: the psycholinguistic view

CS studies with a psycholinguistic orientation typically examine the ways in which learners make up for a lack in lexical knowledge when they engage in various communicative tasks, ranging from the highly structured to the more open-ended ones. Such a view of CSs is most closely associated with a group of Dutch researchers in the Nijmegen project on the use of a subset of CSs referred to as compensatory strategies. One of the ideas that distinguished the Nijmegen studies from other early studies on achievement strategies is the importance attached to examining the thought processes that underpin learners' compensatory strategies (Poulisse, Bongaerts, and Kellerman 1987).

Poulisse (1987) noted that classification of CSs had largely been product-oriented, distinguishing achievement or compensatory strategies strictly on the basis of the resources (for example, L1 or L2) used to encode the strategy.

She argued that product-based taxonomies were inadequate for practical and theoretical reasons. Instead she proposed an alternative process-oriented approach which distinguished two basic strategy types—'conceptual' (holistic and analytic strategies) and 'linguistic' (transfer and morphological creativity). The psychological plausibility of CS taxonomies of a cognitive nature was further enhanced with Bialystok's (1990) proposal of an analysis-control dichotomy and Poulisse's (1993) application of speech processing theories. More recently, the synthesis of existing Nijmegen and Bialystok's taxonomies by Kellerman and Bialystok (1997) further increased the explanatory and descriptive power of CS taxonomies.

Our review includes studies that focused on lexical problems and those that examined CS use for managing gaps in linguistic knowledge. It also includes studies that related learner variables to CS use and those that investigated the effectiveness of CS instruction on the use of compensatory strategies.

Identifying communication strategies

Bialystok (1983b) conducted one of the earliest studies based on her definition of CSs as 'all attempts to manipulate a limited linguistic system in order to promote communication'. This study involved two main groups of subjects of different ages and learning background. One group consisted of 14 adults (civil servants) and the other 16 high school students from grade 12 who were further divided into ten (regular) and six (advanced) learners. Each subject was given a picture to describe in French. The aim was to help a French-speaking interlocutor reconstruct it on a large flannel board using cut-out objects. The data were analyzed according to the source of the information on which the strategies were based: (1) the subjects' L1 or a language other than the target language, (2) the target language, or (3) non-linguistic or contextual information. Only information in 1 and 2 was used, and the distinction was made between L1-based strategies (language switch, foreignizing, and transliteration) and L2-based strategies (semantic contiguity; description: general physical properties, specific features, and interactional/functional characteristics; and word coinage). It was found that L1-based strategies were used least frequently by the Grade 12 advanced French learners.

In a study on referential communication by L2 learners, Dutch (secondary school) learners of English described a set of unconventional shapes first in Dutch and then in English (Bongaerts and Poulisse 1989). They used two types of strategy, focusing on holistic or segmental features of the shapes respectively. On the whole there was a strong preference for holistic perspectives in both Dutch and English descriptions. In more than 70 per cent of all cases of strategy use in both L1 and L2 referential communication, the subjects adopted a holistic perspective. When a holistic strategy was used, the subjects named a referent similar to or approximated the one in question (for example, 'squirrel' for 'chipmunk'). Subjects would switch to using an analytic conceptual strategy (for example, listing different features of the object in question in the L2) if they still had problems, rather than a linguistic strategy (for example, an L1 word). The researchers argued that the holistic and segmental perspectives revealed in the subjects' referential communication further underscored the importance of conceptual strategies for closing lexical gaps. They acknowledged, however, that the nature of the task might have limited the number of occasions that learners could resort to linguistic strategies. This point was noted by later researchers.

Yarmohammadi and Seif (1992) explored CS use by Persian learners of English for solving communication problems in interrelated oral and written tasks. The participants were 51 university students attending general English classes. They were at intermediate proficiency level and selected from various disciplines. First, they wrote a picture-based story in English and then in Persian. They then translated the Persian version back into English. A few days later, they narrated the story orally in English. The students' interpretation of the picture in Persian was compared to the English versions to identify problems related to lexis and other aspects of the language. The analysis revealed that the subjects used similar strategies in both oral and written tasks. Oral tasks, however, revealed further use of mime, co-operative strategies, and retrieval strategies. On the whole, the subjects used achievement strategies that drew on L1 as well as L2 resources, but there were significantly more L2-based strategies. Co-operative strategies were used sparingly (11 per cent of strategy use) and only during oral tasks, indicating that the learners did not frequently appeal for help and suggesting, as the researchers claimed, that the CSs used were 'non-interactive' in nature.

The psycholinguistic view of CSs has been mainly associated with strategies for overcoming limitations in lexical knowledge, but it is not confined to this aspect of language use. A broader conceptualization of psycholinguistic CSs was demonstrated by Dechert (1983) in a case study that examined what an L2 learner did when telling a story. The subject was a female English major of German descent who had had nine years of high school English instruction. She narrated stories based on two cartoon strips; one of them in particular had proved to be linguistically problematic for other advanced English learners. The subject demonstrated a concise knowledge of story grammar as well as the ability to use phrases that facilitated the flow and cohesion of the narrative, creating what were referred to as 'islands of reality'. These 'islands' were chunks of language that were fluent and grammatical, serving as bases for lexical search processes when planning and executing speech (p. 184). As her compensatory CSs, the subject primarily made use of paraphrase and superordinate terms in place of specific words. The subject also abandoned original plans for what to say in favor of using cognitively less demanding language. As this paper was published more than two decades ago, the researcher's hypotheses about the subject's cognitive processes was based on a linear model of processing, rather than on the interactive or connectionist views that are widely held today. Nevertheless, Dechert's study was significant in its attempts to interpret not only surface features of strategic utterances, but also the psycholinguistic processes during speech production.

Another case study that examined CSs in narrative construction was Fakhri's (1984) research on a female learner of Moroccan Arabic. The subject, an adult English speaker, had in the past studied Moroccan Arabic for two months. The data were collected in daily casual conversations with the researcher over a period of four weeks. Fakhri concluded that CS use in narratives was not random but constrained by text features. To fill in the gaps in her knowledge of Moroccan Arabic, she used five CSs: circumlocution, lexical borrowing, elicitation of vocabulary, use of formulaic expressions, and morphosyntactic innovation. Results of cross-tabulations showed that CS use was determined to a large extent by the narrative component in which each strategy occurred. In the episodic component, for example, lexical borrowing (using L1 terms) was the main CS used. Fakhri suggested that this was most likely because the subject did not want to delay her narration by circumlocutions or elicitation of vocabulary in what was typically the most detail-packed part of a narrative. In the evaluation part of the narrative, the subject often relied heavily on formulaic expressions, even when they were not appropriate, so as not to violate discourse constraints.

Summary

The identification of cognitive CSs has traditionally focused on compensatory strategies that learners used to overcome lexical problems in tasks where they described or named objects. Studies along this line have provided us with numerous insights, as well as several taxonomies into the way CSs were used. The taxonomy that is in our opinion the most influential is the distinction between conceptual and linguistic strategies by Poulisse and her colleagues in the Nijmegen Project. This taxonomy has since been modified to accommodate new data. On the whole, there were relatively few studies that focused on purely identifying the CSs used. Learner and task variables were usually examined at the same time, as was the case with Bialystok's pioneering study. The next part of the review will focus on several studies that explicitly examined these relationships.

Cognitive CS use and learner/task variables

An important learner variable examined in CS studies is L2 proficiency. One of the early studies to do this was Paribakht's (1985) research on Persian ESL learners in Canada. The subjects were asked to describe twenty single lexical items in a concept-identification task. Each subject was matched with a different native-speaker interlocutor to prevent the interlocutors from making subjective judgments about sufficiency of information for accurate identification. It was found that the use of these strategic approaches was constrained by the type of concept being communicated. Both groups of Persian ESL learners as well as their NS interlocutors used the same four communicative approaches but differed in the use of specific strategies within each approach. Although both L1- and L2-based strategies were used, there appeared to be less use of L1 strategies among higher-proficiency learners. Quantitative results showed significant differences among the three groups in their frequency of use of the four strategic approaches. Native speakers and advanced students used more strategies from the linguistic approach (for example, semantic contiguity, circumlocution, and metalinguistic clues), while the intermediate learners resorted more to contextual strategies (for example, target language idioms, transliteration, and idiomatic transfer). The researcher concluded that patterns and characteristics of CS use might have been linked to different development stages of the learners' interlanguages.

This view was also shared by Corrales and Call (1989) who examined the relationships between strategy use and the variables of TL proficiency and task types among Spanish ESL learners. One task involved answering tightly structured comprehension questions about reading passages. The other involved a simulated telephone conversation. In addition, they also examined the effect of time on strategy use by examining patterns of use at the beginning and end of a five-week period of intensive study. The researchers categorized the subjects' methods of conveying lexical meaning into process-based strategies (transfer and overgeneralizations) and task-influenced strategies (circumlocution, language switch, appeal for assistance, and avoidance). When intermediate and advanced learners were compared, no statistically significant difference was found. On the whole, it was also found that the relatively unstructured task of simulated conversation generated more transfer strategies (literal translations and foreignizing). A within-group comparison showed that the intermediate learners used more task-influenced strategies at the end of the five weeks of study than at the beginning. The difference among the advanced learners as a function of time was not as notable. The researchers concluded that the use of CSs might have peaked before declining as learners developed greater TL proficiency.

The influence of proficiency- and task-related factors was corroborated in a study by Poulisse and Schils (1989). The Dutch subjects consisted of three groups of 15 English learners of different proficiency levels. Data was elicited on their use of compensatory strategies or 'alternative speech plans' for overcoming lexical problems to achieve communication goals (p. 18). The subjects participated in three tasks: a picture naming/description task, a story-retelling task, and an interview with a native speaker. The absolute number of compensatory strategies used was inversely related to proficiency level; the least proficient learners used the most strategies and vice versa. The stronger relationship with strategy types, however, was found in the task factor. Poulisse and Schils found that holistic (conceptual) and transfer (linguistic) strategies were frequently used in story retelling and oral interview, while more analytic (conceptual) strategies were used in the picture naming/description task. Some reasons given were task demands, context, time constraints, and the presence of an interlocutor.

The relationship between TL proficiency and Chinese EFL learners' strategic competence was examined by Chen (1990), whose study showed that the frequency, type, and effectiveness of CSs varied according to the learners' proficiency level. Twelve subjects comprising high- and low-proficiency English learners explained a list of pre-selected concrete and abstract concepts to a NS listener. Two-hundred and twenty instances of CS use were classified in five categories: linguistic-based, knowledge-based, repetition, paralinguistic, and avoidance. Chen challenged the validity of some existing categories such as circumlocution and word coinage, arguing that while they appeared to be different on the surface, the underlying psychological processes were in fact similar. Low-proficiency learners used significantly more CSs than the high-proficiency learners. The researcher suggested that the learners' overall lack of use of L1-based strategies was due to the great typological distance between Chinese and English.

Some scholars have argued for a need to link CS research with wider issues of language competence. Ellis (1984) concluded that there was some evidence for evaluating L2 communicative performance through an examination of learners' CSs, most notably the use of reduction or avoidance strategies and achievement strategies such as paraphrase. In his study, two groups of young learners in Britain were asked to tell a story illustrated through three pictures. One group consisted of six L2 learners, aged 10–12, who had studied English for about a year. The second group consisted of six native speakers of the same age from the same school. Each child told the story to a teacher. The L2 learners were found to use more avoidance and paraphrase strategies, and communicated less information about the pictures. Ellis proposed that teachers assess learners' communicative performance by attending to the degree which learners avoided referring to important items of information and paraphrased information they selected to encode.

Another study that focused on young language learners also compared CS use of effective and less-effective learners. The participants in the study by Marrie and Netten (1991) were 22 French immersion learners in a third-grade class at a Canadian primary school. They were divided into proficiency groups based on the scores of the *Tourand Test Diagnostique de Lecture* and their classroom teacher's observation of their class performance. Picture description tasks were conducted with all students and their performance was tape-recorded. Three independent judges evaluated the speech samples. Three students with the highest scores and another three with the lowest were identified for further CS analysis. No transcriptions were made, but the recorded utterances were listened to at least ten times. The effective learner group used more achievement strategies than reduction strategies. The low-score group used fewer CSs, and used achievement and reduction strategies to approximately the same degree. Due to the small number of participants, no tests of statistical significance were used.

Most of the earlier studies focused on language proficiency as the main learner variable. Later studies, however, showed a shift in focus to traits such as cognitive style as a function of CS use, reflecting more recent developments in the field of L2 acquisition. Littlemore's (2001) study suggested that cognitive styles may have helped to determine her subjects' CS preferences. Eighty-two French-speaking Belgian university students specializing in English participated in a concrete picture description task adapted from a study by Poulisse (1990). To address a limitation found in the earlier study, Littlemore selected 15 different items to minimize any bias towards certain kinds of conceptual strategies. Both groups used significantly more conceptual CSs than linguistic ones. The holistic students used a significantly higher proportion of holistic conceptual strategies than their analytic counterparts. The same predicted tendencies were also confirmed among the analytic students.

Littlemore (2003) related the use of CSs to an extended model of 'synoptic' (i.e. holistic) and 'ectenic' (i.e. analytic) learning styles (Ehrman and Leaver, cited in Littlemore 2003: 332) and examined the communicative effectiveness of the various types of CSs used. Whereas synoptic learners favored comparison-based strategies, ectenic learners focused on individual features of the referent. Transcripts were shown to two native-speaker English teachers, who rated each student on ease of comprehension, stylishness of expression, and proficiency. Inter-rater agreement was .89. Strategies used by ectenic learners were found to be most communicatively effective. They apparently assumed less shared knowledge and were therefore more explicit.

Summary

TL proficiency and task types were the two most commonly examined variables for their relationship with CS use. More recently cognitive learning styles have also been examined. Many studies found an inverse relationship between frequency of CS use and proficiency level, while task type was also found to have an effect on the types of CSs used. It was suggested that in object naming/describing tasks, the types of referent might have created a bias on the type of strategies used. These tasks also appeared to have directly encouraged the use of compensatory strategies for bridging lexical gaps while others such as narrative production could be carried out with less recourse to these strategies.

Strategy instruction

Is CS instruction effective, and can learners use CSs for overcoming lexical problems without explicit teaching? Salomone and Marsal (1997) attempted to answer this question by investigating the effects of strategy instruction on circumlocution for oral French examinations. The data, however, were collected entirely through written tasks, thus severely limiting the value of the findings for CS use during speaking. Rossiter's (2003) study, on the other hand, directly investigated whether CS instruction in speaking could lead to a greater use of CSs and improved L2 oral performance. The treatment focused on strategy instruction in paraphrasing. The researcher claimed that paraphrase encompassed strategies from both analytic and holistic categories, and included techniques such as approximation, superordination, analogy, using an all-purpose word, and different ways of carrying out circumlocution. The tests consisted of picture story narratives and object descriptions. No significant between-group differences were found in the use of strategy tokens in both tasks, but the treatment group used significantly more strategy types in the object description tasks for the immediate post-test. The difference for L2 performance also did not reach statistical significance. Rossiter observed that these results could be partly attributed to task effects, as paraphrase was not entirely necessary for narrative tasks. She concluded that CS use might be transferable from L1 to L2 (as evidenced in the increase in use by both groups in the delayed post-tests) and suggested that time spent on teaching paraphrase would therefore have been better spent on other activities, especially those that promoted vocabulary acquisition.

Our search revealed few studies on the effects of CS instruction. Nevertheless, some non-intervention studies may offer possible directions for future CS instruction research. We include here two such studies that focused on the use of CS by native speakers and native-like or advanced level speakers. Jourdain (2000) compared the way six native speakers and native-like speakers of French and English used CSs. Both groups used predominantly L2-based strategies, abstained from reduction strategies, and used similar strategies for circumlocution. More importantly, all the subjects framed their message by setting the global context in which the description was about to be given. Konishi and Tarone (2004) identified syntactic constructions that native speakers used in compensatory strategies and found that syntactic patterns were not random but dependent on the types of referent. A similar kind of systematicity in relation to the types of referent was also found in the attributes (for example, function, taste, location) that the subjects focused on. Konishi and Tarone made a case for CS instruction to include opportunities for practising and acquiring specific syntactic patterns—in particular, post-modification constructions.

Summary

There have been very few studies which examined the effect of CS instruction on the use of cognitive CSs. Among those that did, the focus was mainly on circumlocution and other paraphrase strategies, and their results suggested that CS instruction might not be significant because these CSs appeared to be transferable from L1. Some future directions for strategy instruction have been suggested by studies which collected baseline data on CSs used by highly-competent speakers. They include the use of discourse strategies that set the context or provide the frame for descriptions and explanations, as well as describing grammatical features that are closely associated with various kinds of lexical problems in different tasks. This linguistic focus is thus a possible future pedagogical application.

Limitations of the studies in this review

Some limitations of individual studies have already been identified. We highlight here issues that concern the studies in general. The main issue is the divergence of expert opinion on what constitutes a CS and how CSs should be categorized. Ironically, one of the reasons for this complex problem of CS description arises from the rich authentic data on speech production, an advantage enjoyed by studies on oral production. Unfortunately, these kinds of data are often difficult to transcribe and analyze, and the problem is compounded by the absence of an established set of procedures for analyzing and coding them. One way of ensuring some consistency, at least in the interpretation of CSs, is to ensure that a sample of the data is checked by independent coders at various stages of transcription and analysis. A few of the reviewed CS studies have used this method to ensure greater reliability in their findings. Most, however, did not offer much information on the way the subjects' utterances were analyzed. In general, there were few reports of inter-coder reliability in identification and categorizations of strategies. There was also no mention of how intra-rater reliability was achieved in cases where the researchers' own expert judgments were applied. Many of the earlier studies also included few excerpts from the transcriptions of actual strategy use which would have helped readers to evaluate CSs identified.

CS research could be further improved by including some form of data triangulation. This could be partially achieved by including subjects' self-reports on their strategy use. Learners' intention in specific CS use can be investigated through oral interviews, retrospective verbal protocol, or validated self-report questionnaires. Only a few researchers have introduced multiple ways of collecting data in order to validate their investigation of strategies for speaking.

Finally, there is also the issue of inadequate cross-referencing of work in at least two related disciplines—L2 learning and bilingual acquisition—in which CSs are researched. There is a body of research on CSs of L2 (bilingual) speakers that is conducted outside the traditional second/foreign language learning contexts (for example, Malt and Sloman 2003), with little cross-referencing to work on CSs done in SLA and vice versa. Poulisse's (1993) work in an early collection of papers on bilingualism held promise for some synthesis of CS research across the two-related disciplines, but more could have been achieved in the intervening years.

Conclusion

A major issue in CS research is the presence of different definitions of strategies and categories/taxonomies for describing them. While this is a conceptual issue that could not be realistically dealt with by individual researchers, the quality of data analysis in individual studies should continue to be ensured. Another issue that future research needs to address is the accurate measurement of oral proficiency levels. Future researchers should aim to use similar sets of criteria for determining proficiency, in particular, oral proficiency. To do this, it may be useful to use standardized tests for interactional benchmarking of learner proficiency. More research is clearly needed in determining the effects of various types of CS instruction on enhancing learners' oral proficiency. It is also vital to focus on students' learning processes and natural classroom environments. Detailed information on what actually occurs in the classroom under investigation is important and should be included when reporting results as this can help readers assess the validity of the strategy instruction effects on CS use. It is useful to make videos of students' performance in classrooms and to collect ethnographic field notes. Data triangulation can be further improved by combining various procedures such as data analysis of transcriptions with examples of CSs, retrospective interviews, and a validated questionnaire on CS use. More longitudinal studies are needed to examine the effects on students' oral proficiency and CS use, as well as ascertaining whether CSs are accessible for future TL use beyond the classroom.

Oral production is the result of complex cognitive and pragmatic factors, with language proficiency and task demands playing an important but not exclusive role. With regard to the learning and use of CSs, learning experience, learning styles, metacognitive knowledge, and affective factors are all likely to play an important part. Some researchers have begun to examine these variables, but they would need to be better controlled in future experimental studies. As a future research strand, it would be desirable to investigate the interrelationships between CS use, CS instruction, and variables such as learning styles, attitude, anxiety, motivation, metacognitive knowledge, confidence, and self efficacy. Though these individual variables are thought to have a significant influence on TL performance, they have not been well integrated with CS research. By focusing on these aspects, it might be possible to draw implications for the development of classroom-based and self-directed modes of CS development.

A review of writing strategies: focus on conceptualizations and impact of first language

ROSA M. MANCHÓN, JULIO ROCA DE LARIOS, and LIZ MURPHY

Introduction

The study of writing strategies should be viewed within a wider research movement known as 'process writing', which emerged in the field of native language (L1) writing with the aim of gaining insights into the mental actions writers engage in while composing. Originally, in the 1980s, this research was purely cognitive in orientation and composition was viewed as a goal-oriented, recursive, cognitively-demanding, problem-solving task. In the words of Scardamalia and Bereiter (1986: 792):

> expert composing [is] a form of problem solving. It is a heuristic search through a space consisting of mental representations of possible text. It is, however, [...] problem solving carried on through parallel action in a number of different problem spaces, each characterized by a different kind of mental representation of possible text.

Since the mid-1990s the social dimension of the act of composing has been emphasized, thus positing that writing is a socially situated, cognitive, communicative activity, and leading to the post-process movement in writing theory, research, and pedagogy (see Kent 1999).

Following these trends in L1 writing research, scholars in the second and foreign language (L2) fields have also attempted to probe the actions (termed inter alia 'processes', 'writing behaviors', and 'strategies'; see below) writers engage in while they generate, express, and refine their ideas in a non-native language. This scientific enquiry has produced abundant research evidence on the criterial aspects of L2 composing (for recent reviews see Cumming 1998, 2001; Manchón 2001; Roca de Larios, Murphy, and Marín 2002), while the insights gained have also informed L2 writing pedagogy. (For a review, see Johns 1990; Grabe and Kaplan 1996; Manchón 1999.) Also in line with trends in the L1 literature, research into L2 writing strategies has gradually shifted from a purely cognitive approach to a more socio-cognitive orientation.

What follows is a systematic review of the empirical research on composing strategies published in English since 1980. The detailed procedures for carrying out this review can be found in Appendix 11.1 on www.oup.com/elt/teacher/lls.

The analysis is structured in three parts: (1) conceptual issues; (2) research methodology; and (3) research trends and findings. We finish the chapter with some suggestions for theory and research.

Aims of this review

The aims that have framed our enquiry revolve around three main areas:

1 *Conceptual issues* Given recent claims concerning the shaky theoretical foundation of research on learner strategies (cf. Dörnyei and Skehan 2003; Dörnyei 2005; Manchón in press; Chapter 1 this volume), one of our aims has been to analyze how the strategy construct has been conceptualized in the empirical research on composing, and to identify the frameworks informing these conceptualizations.
2 *Methodological issues* It has also been our intention to document the research designs used in the field.
3 *Research trends and findings* We attempted to summarize the main research insights regarding (1) the strategies used by L2 writers (analysis of descriptive studies), and (2) whether or not writing strategy use can be modified through instruction (analysis of interventionist studies). In both cases we have also searched for the writer-internal and writer-external variables that may influence the quantitative and/or qualitative use of writing strategies on the one hand, and the effects of strategy instruction programs on the other.

Given the general aims of this book, we approached this review with a view to offering suggestions for moving forward in L2 writing strategy theory and research.

Analysis of research 1: conceptual issues

A first glance at the abundant literature published on composing strategies makes the reader realise that, in the field of L2 writing, the term 'strategy' is frequently used but rarely defined. This is the case both of empirical research and of strategy literature in general. What is more, again in line with the study of strategies in other domains of L2 learning and use, the absence of an agreed operational definition of the strategy construct is a notable feature of this field of enquiry. (See Chapter 2 this volume.)

As pointed out by previous reviewers (cf. Manchón 1997), writing strategies have been referred to as 'writing behaviors' (Whalen 1993; Armengol-Castells

2001), 'composing behaviors' (Raimes 1987), and 'composing operations' (Armengol-Castells 2001), while other authors use the expression 'strategies and behaviors' of L2 writers (Zamel 1983; Pennington and So 1993; Matsumoto 1995). Other terms used interchangeably with strategies are 'writing techniques and procedures' (Khaldieh 2000), '(composing) processes' (cf. Skibniewski 1988; Chamot and El-Dinary 1999; Hatasa and Soeda 2000; Zainuddin and Moore 2003), 'production processes' (Whalen and Ménard 1995), 'process-related skills' (in contrast to 'language-related skills', Pennington and So 1993), and 'skills' (Ching 2002). Sasaki (2004: 529) talks about 'writing-process strategies', and Cumming, Busch, and Zhou (2002: 193) refer to 'the level of strategic operations for the activity of writing (i.e. composing processes)'.

The list of terms mentioned above corresponds to the plethora of writing actions identified as strategies in different empirical works. These include both (1) general macro writing processes—planning, writing, and revising (cf. Raimes 1985, 1987; Arndt 1987; Moragne e Silva 1989; Whalen and Ménard 1995; Sasaki and Hirose 1996; Akyel and Kamisli 1997; Hatasa and Soeda 2000; Sasaki 2000, 2002; Armengol-Castells 2001); and (2) very specific phenomena, such as 'avoidance' (Olsen 1999), 'backtracking' (Manchón, Roca de Larios, and Murphy 2000a, 2000b; Wolfersberger 2003; Wong 2005), 'evaluation' (Whalen 1993), 'evaluation of audience response' (Zainuddin and Moore 2003), 'questioning' (Wong 2005), 'reformulation' (Cumming 1989; Zimmermann 2000), 'rehearsing' (Raimes 1987), 'restructuring' (Roca de Larios 1999; Roca de Larios, Murphy, and Manchón 1999), 'rhetorical refining' (Sasaki 2000, 2002, 2004), or 'use of models' (Zhu 2003).

In an attempt to categorize this plethora of definitions and phenomena identified as strategies, Manchón (2001) recently distinguished between a *broad* and *narrow* characterization of the construct, a distinction that we shall adopt in the ensuing discussion.

The broad characterization

As depicted in Figure 11.1, a broad conceptualization of the construct has informed two important lines of research: one has taken a learner-internal perspective, whereas the other has adopted a more socio-cognitive stance. In the first case, writing strategies are explicitly or implicitly equated with how L2 writers go about composing, i.e. with any action employed in the act of producing a text. Some representative definitions of this trend are those by Whalen—'a process or operation applied to the task of writing' (1993: 607), or more recently by Khaldieh—'techniques and procedures used to perform the writing task' (2000: 522).

The socio-cognitive perspective, in contrast, has been adopted by scholars (cf. Leki 1995; Riazi 1997; Spack 1997; Cumming *et al.* 2002; Yang, Baba, and Cumming 2004) who have investigated strategies from the perspective of the actions carried out by L2 writers to respond to the demands encountered in the discourse community where they write and learn to write. Being socio-cognitive in orientation, this research accepts that 'writing is text, is composing, and is social construction' (Cumming 1998: 61).

Conceptualization	Definition	Theoretical frameworks
A *Broad conceptualization*	• *Learner-internal perspective:* any action employed in the act of composing a text	• Cognitive models of L1 writing • Research on language learning and language use strategies[1]
	• *Socio-cognitive perspective:* actions employed by L2 writers to respond to the demands encountered in the discourse community where they write and learn to write	• Socio-cognitive accounts of literacy development • Goal theories in educational psychology
B *Narrow conceptualization*	• *Learner-internal perspective:* Control mechanisms used to regulate cognitive activity (i.e the writer's problem-solving behavior while writing)	• Cognitive models of L1 writing
	• *Learner-internal perspective:* Heuristics used when the L2 writer engages in problem-solving activity	• The problem-solving paradigm in cognitive psychology

Figure 11.1 Theoretical frameworks guiding empirical research on composing strategies

The learner-internal perspective

The research guided by the broad conceptualization of strategies and taking an intra-learner perspective has been framed in two theoretical paradigms: cognitive models of L1 writing, and that emerging from research on strategies for language learning and use.

Taken together, these studies have attempted to provide holistic descriptions of L2 writers' composing behavior either (1) globally (cf. Cumming 1989; Roca de Larios 1999; Sasaki 2000, 2002; see Appendix 11.1), or (2) with reference to just one macro-writing process, be this planning (Jones and Tetroe 1987; Akyel 1994; Lally 2000), writing (Zimmermann 2000; Chenoweth and Hayes 2001), or revision (Gaskill 1986; Hall 1990; Porte 1995, 1996, 1997; Sengupta 2000; Takagaki 2003).

These studies have produced a catalogue of strategies that can be categorized at different levels of generality. At the more general level, some of the phenomena identified as writing strategies are actually what others would call macro-writing processes, i.e. planning, writing, and revision. In contrast, other taxonomic approaches organize strategies in subgroups, some of which correspond to macro-writing processes. The strategies listed in each group include (1) specific actions engaged in while planning (for example, organizing), writing (for example, rehearsing, pausing, or translating), or revising (for example, rereading, evaluating, or editing); and (2) goals set for a given macro-process or aspects of the task attended to, especially in reference to planning (for example, planning content, global planning, local planning), and writing (for example, paying attention to overall organization or to linguistic matters).

Apart from macro-writing processes, other taxonomic approaches in the literature of strategies have been used in the classification of writing strategies. Thus, the tripartite distinction among metacognitive strategies (planning, monitoring, and evaluation) guides part of Victori's (1995, 1997) and Riazi's (1997) classification. Wong (2005) groups the strategies used by her participants as metacognitive, cognitive, and affective in nature. In a similar vein, some investigations (Khaldieh 2000; Olivares-Cuhat 2002; Grainger 2005) follow Oxford's (1990a) well known taxonomic approach and thus distinguish metacognitive, cognitive, compensatory, social, and affective composing strategies. Finally, the data analysis in three studies on writing 'communication strategies' (Shaw 1991; Olsen 1999; Chimbganda 2000) follow general classifications used in the oral communication strategies research.[2]

The socio-cognitive perspective

The more socio-cognitive research trend mentioned in Figure 11.1 has been guided by socio-cognitive views of literacy development (Leki 1995; Riazi 1997; Spack 1997), as well as goal theories in educational psychology (Cumming *et al.* 2002; Yang *et al.* 2004).

As an example of the first group, Leki (1995: 240) equates strategies with the 'methods these participants used to approach and complete the writing tasks assigned'. The list of strategies identified in the data include (1) those used to conceptualize and fulfil writing tasks (clarifying and focusing strategies); (2) those that involve making use of previous knowledge and experience (relying on past writing experience, using past ESL training, taking advantage of first language and culture); (3) strategies that make the most of the social context (using current experience or feedback, looking for models, using current ESL writing training); (4) taking a stance towards teachers' demands (either accommodating or resisting them); and, finally, (5) finding ways of managing and regulating the demands (in terms of time and effort required) of their courses and assignments.

Another example of a study fully embedded in the socio-cognitive paradigm is Riazi's (1997) longitudinal study of four postgraduate Iranian students in Canada. The author concludes that achieving disciplinary literacy 'is fundamentally an interactive social-cognitive process in that production of the texts required extensive interaction between the individual's cognitive processes and social/contextual factors in different ways' (p. 105). The author emphasizes how the participants' strategic behavior was motivated by their goals, an idea that links up with the research informed by goal theories in educational psychology (Cumming *et al.* 2002; Yang *et al.* 2004). The latter adhere to the principle that 'goals integrally relate to (and may perhaps even determine) the strategic operations that people undertake in performing specific tasks' (Cumming *et al.* 2002: 193). As a result, these scholars talk about 'strategies for acting on the goals' (p. 202) and strongly and convincingly argue against decontextualized research approaches to documenting strategy use. Instead, they favor a research path in which strategies 'are analyzed in reference to the goals people have to motivate and guide their task performance as well as other essential aspects of these activity structures and the contexts in which they are embedded' (Cumming *et al.* 2002: 193). They go as far as suggesting that

> A major challenge in thinking about applications of goals to educational practices will be to avoid the kinds of decontextualized, atheoretical proclamations about learning that have arisen from studies of communication strategies in second languages [...] or inventories of strategies for learning languages (p. 204).

As an example of the categories of strategies identified in this line of research (see also Cumming 2006), in Cumming *et al* (2002) the participants' strategies were grouped under five headings: (1) seeking assistance from other people (peers, teachers, tutors, relatives, friends); (2) self-regulation (for example, outlining prior to writing, planning, editing, and revising their texts); (3) stimulation (such as playing music or talking to people); (4) use of tools (books, magazines, computers, dictionaries, and newspapers); and (5) language practice.

In short, this more socio-cognitive research trend has provided empirical evidence of the interplay between the social and cognitive dimensions involved in the development of the L2 writer's strategic competence. These studies also fit in well with the socio-cognitive orientation of the post-process writing research (see contributions in Atkinson 2003), while at the same time the research framed in educational goal theories has opened up a research avenue very much in line with the path that Dörnyei (2005) suggests future research on L2 learning and use strategies could move along to be on a more sound footing.

The narrow conceptualization

The narrow view of strategies mainly applies to the research that has investigated writing strategies from a purely cognitive, intra-learner angle, and has been informed by both cognitive theories of L1 writing and the problem-solving paradigm in cognitive psychology. In this characterization, and in contrast to the research guided by the learner-internal perspective within the broad view, writing strategies are considered to be merely a set of writing phenomena and, as such, different from macro-writing processes (i.e. planning, writing, and revising) or aspects of the task attended to (language, discourse, content, etc.). The term is restricted to two specific phenomena: control mechanisms of one's writing behavior, and problem-solving devices (cf. Cumming 1989; Cumming, Rebuffot, and Ledwell 1989; Roca de Larios 1996; Bosher 1998; Manchón *et al.* 2000a, 2000b).

Strategies as control mechanisms

As an example of the view of strategies as control mechanisms, Cumming (1989), in his study of 23 young adult Francophone Canadians studying in a university English/French bilingual program, observed two tendencies in his data. On the one hand, more expert writers deployed control strategies for goal setting and for the online management of goals. As a result, their writing behavior was a self-regulated process which, in turn, entailed more problem-solving behavior and thus greater use of problem-solving mechanisms to resolve the problems posed. In contrast, less expert writers lacked appropriate self-regulation strategies, which resulted in 'unmonitored production of writing' (p. 113) and in their display of a 'what next?' strategy guiding their writing. (See Pennington and So 1993 for similar findings.)

Strategies as problem-solving devices

In line with the characterization of writing strategies as problem-solving devices, Sasaki (2004: 541) defines a writing strategy as 'a writer's mental behavior employed to achieve a goal in the ill structured problem-solving [...] activity of writing'. Similarly, Wong (2005: 31) adopts the Flower and Hayes (1980) characterization of composing strategies as 'decisions taken to cope with the problems (both linguistic and rhetorical) posed by the writing task as perceived by the writer'. In a recent publication, Manchón, Murphy, and Roca de Larios (2005) explain the way in which the problem-solving paradigm has informed their empirical research on composing strategies. Another example of how the problem-solving paradigm has informed research in composing strategies was offered in the pioneering study by Cumming (1989) mentioned above. The analytical categories established to analyze the participants' problem-solving behavior distinguished between problem-solving behavior and problem-solving mechanisms. The latter are heuristic search strategies in Cumming's terminology, and include search processes, code-switching, and generating and assessing alternatives.

Analysis of research 2: methodological issues[3]

Most studies reviewed have focused on young adults performing writing tasks (usually involving composing) in academic settings, including both second and foreign language acquisitional contexts. The countries in which these studies were carried out were Canada and USA (almost 50 per cent), followed by Spain (12), Japan (9), China (3), Hong Kong (2), Australia (2), UK (2), Turkey (2), Botswana (1), France (1), Germany (1), Iceland (1), Israel (1), Italy (1), Malaysia (1), Netherlands (1), Norway (1), Poland (1), and Singapore (1).

Participants

Number

The number of informants ranges from one (cf. Leki 1995; McDonough and McDonough 2001; Moragne e Silva 1989; Qi 1998; Spack 1997) to 126 (Berman 1994). Generally, studies using questionnaires or analyses of written texts as their main data collection procedures involve a range from 20–126 informants (see Appendix 11.1), while small-scale studies, involving between one and 15 informants, use think-aloud, stimulated recall, observation, interviews, and self-report as data sources. (See Appendix 11.1.) In between, there are investigations which, despite the labour-intensive nature of the data collection techniques used (think-aloud, stimulated recall, self-report or semi-structured interviews), include a reasonably large number of informants—between 12 and 43. (See Appendix 11.1.) The small sample sizes in most studies constitute a limitation in L2 composing strategy research since this wealth of case studies on so few writers may have contributed rich analyses but they can hardly be said to have spawned robust generalizations for the field.

Age

The research on composing strategies has mainly studied people in their late teens, twenties, or even thirties, the vast majority of participants being university undergraduates or postgraduates. A few studies, however, have included academics (Matsumoto 1995; Sionis 1995; McDonough and McDonough 2001; Sasaki 2000, 2002), educated professionals (Levine and Reves 1998), school children (Chamot and El-Dinary 1999), and high school students (cf. Berman 1994; Olsen 1999; Sengupta 2000).

L1 and L2

Most of the participants in both second and foreign language contexts were learning English, although some studies have focused on other languages such as Arabic (Khaldieh 2000), Hebrew (Cumming *et al.*1989; Levine and Reves 1998; Schwarzer 2004), French (Whalen 1993; Whalen and Ménard 1995; Brooks-Carson and Cohen 2000; Lally 2000; Chenoweth and Hayes 2001; Cohen and Brooks-Carson 2001;), German (Chenoweth and Hayes 2001),

Spanish (Valdés, Haro, and Echevarriarza 1992; Armengol-Castells 2001; Olivares-Cuhat 2002; Woodall 2002), Greek (McDonough and McDonough 2001), and Japanese (Uzawa and Cumming 1989; Pennington and So 1993; Hatasa and Soeda 2000; Woodall 2002) .

Proficiency level

With the exceptions of Schwarzer (2004) and Wolfersberger (2003), the writers in these studies were of intermediate level or above in L2 proficiency level.

The participants' level of proficiency has been assessed in a variety of ways which include (Roca de Larios *et al.* 2002) institutional status (i.e. level of L2 proficiency required to register for a given course, cf. Zamel 1983; Arndt 1987; Valdés *et al.* 1992), teachers' impressions (Pennington and So 1993), in-house assessments (cf. Cumming 1989; Whalen and Ménard 1995; Kobayashi and Rinnert 2001), and a range of standardized tests. (See Appendix 11.1.)

Research designs and instruments

The studies under review have made use of a variety of research instruments and designs. Following Brown (1988) and Seliger and Shohamy (1989), we found (see Appendix 11.1) both cross-sectional studies (68) and longitudinal ones (14); case studies (17) and statistical studies (65), and within the latter, both survey (13) and experimental studies (52).

Regarding instruments, research reports can be classified into two groups. The first one includes those studies that have collected empirical data on writing strategies via questionnaires and interviews, two instruments which, according to Chamot and El-Dinary (1999: 321) 'provide retrospective information on students' recollection of strategies they have used for particular tasks and, often, of the frequency (sometimes, often, usually, etc.) with which they use the strategy'. As mentioned in a previous section, various studies (Khaldieh 2000; Olivares-Cuhat 2002; Grainger 2005) have used Oxford's (1990a) widely used strategy questionnaire, whereas others have developed their own questionnaires. It should also be remembered that the study by Petric and Czárl (2003) is one based on the validation of a strategy writing questionnaire. Quite often, questionnaire data have been supplemented with interview data, these interviews being conducted with all or just a sample of the participants.

The studies in the second group have delved into composing strategies by asking a group of participants to engage in actual writing, and they have two common characteristics. First, this research has made use of direct/indirect and/or simultaneous/successive elicitation procedures (Janssen, van Waes, and van den Bergh 1996) commonly employed in process-oriented writing research. Second, the use of multiple-data collection procedures is the norm, including direct observation, text analysis, process logs, and introspection techniques (two commonly used procedures being think-aloud protocols and retrospective interviews/questionnaires).

The type of writing tasks the participants were asked to perform were for the most part within the range of those that involve 'composing' (Grabe and Kaplan 1996). As exceptions, Johnson (1992) analyzed writing strategies in sentence-combining tasks, Schwarzer (2004) focused on the strategies used in dialogue journals with the teacher, and Kobayashi and Rinnert (2001) asked students to revise previously prepared texts. In a few cases researchers collected a number of course-related assignments, although most studies opted for short time-compressed compositions. In the latter case, clear differences can be observed among studies regarding the amount of time for the task, the topics and text types set, the indication of audience, and the possibility of using external aids while composing. (See Roca de Larios *et al.* 2002 for a full elaboration.)

Issues in data analysis

Five aspects concerning the validity and reliability of data analysis are worthy of comment:

1 As pointed out by Roca de Larios *et al.* (2002), most studies using concurrent or retrospective introspection techniques have not reported the criteria used to divide the resulting transcriptions of protocols into segments to which the coding categories can further be applied. (For exceptions, see Cumming 1989; Uzawa 1996; Porte 1997; Roca de Larios *et al.* 1999; Manchón *et al.* 2000a; 2005.)

2 Only about 50 per cent of the studies reviewed report inter-rater and/or intra-rater reliability coefficients. This is an important issue when it comes to protocol data, given the qualitative nature of the data and the amount of interpreting required by the researchers. (See Manchón *et al.* 2005.)

3 Not all the questionnaires used had been previously validated. Along the same lines, when analyzing protocol data, only a few studies report how the researchers counteracted the threats to validity associated with this methodology.

4 We found that regarding the operationalization of the strategy construct guiding this research, three different situations could be discerned. First, as stated in an earlier section, in some studies there is no explicit indication of which concept of strategy guided the research. Second, when the construct was operationally defined, this operationalization was strictly followed in the data analysis in some studies, whereas in others there was a total or partial mismatch between the definition of writing strategies adopted and the actual phenomena identified as instances of strategies. This, we believe, is an important methodological problem that should be avoided in future research.

5 Another problem to be avoided relates to the shortcomings associated with some approaches adopted in the categorization of strategies, especially in cases in which the data have been obtained via introspection methods. It

has been suggested that encoding must have a theoretical basis, and that the resulting coding scheme ought not to be a mere list of observed phenomena. According to Kasper (1998: 359), the coding scheme guiding the data analysis should ideally be 'a theoretically grounded model of the cognitive processes and types of information involved in the activity under study, not a mere list of strategies'. Along the same lines Manchón *et al.* (2005: 202) contend that a theoretical approach to the data analysis 'forces the researcher to look for levels of analysis and levels of generalization, so the resulting coding scheme offers a more valid and complete account of the data'. Instead of these theoretically grounded categories, far too often one comes across atheoretical, list-like catalogues of varying (in number and type) phenomena grouped under the umbrella heading of a never-defined construct, 'strategy'.

Analysis of research 3: research trends and findings

Research findings on L2 composing strategies can be conveniently grouped under four headings: (1) the strategies deployed by L2 writers; (2) variables influencing the L2 writer's selection and implementation of strategies; (3) the transfer of L1 strategies to the L2 situation; and (4) the influence of instruction and training on strategy use. Our analysis of research trends and findings will therefore be guided by these four categories.

Given the amount of data to be accounted for, the review of findings is necessarily selective and synthetic, rather than fully comprehensive and elaborated upon.

The strategies used by L2 writers

It is possible to group the studies under review into different categories according to whether they present a global picture of L2 writers' strategic repertoires or focus on specific strategies. Since we accounted for the 'global picture' in the two previous sections, we shall now focus on one very characteristic strategy deployed in L2 writing, namely, L1 use.

Use of the L1

Switching to the L1 is without any doubt one of the most characteristic features of L2 writing, if not the most. This strategy appears in various forms, serves different purposes, is influenced by different learner- and task-related variables, and is deployed by writers while planning, writing, and revising, as well as serving as a control mechanism for the writing process.

The L1 in the planning process

One of the distinctive features of L2 writing is the planning of ideas in the writer's L1 (Lay 1982; Jones and Tetroe 1987; Cumming 1989; Friedlander 1990; Whalen and Ménard 1995; Sasaki and Hirose 1996; Hu

2003;Wolfersberger 2003). Researchers have concluded that L1 use for planning ideas is an asset in L2 composing, both for topics related to L1 culture (Lay 1982; Friedlander 1990) and for topics which are not L1 culturally bound (Lally 2000). Resorting to the L1 in these cases leads to longer and more detailed plans and drafts, as well as better essays in terms of ideas, organization and details.

The L1 in the writing process

During the process of formulation, i.e. when writers are actually trying to put their ideas down on paper in a syntactic form, the L1 is used for three main purposes: generating text, tackling linguistic and stylistic problems, and organizing and structuring texts.

Different studies (Jones and Tetroe 1987; Uzawa and Cumming 1989; Kobayashi and Rinnert 1992; Whalen and Ménard 1995; Qi 1998; Cohen and Brooks-Carson 2001; Wang and Wen 2002; Woodall 2002; Wolfersberger 2003) have reported language switching for *text generation purposes*, although there is still much debate about the possible beneficial or detrimental effects of this use of the mother tongue in relation to both the writing process and the resulting written product.

Regarding the *process* dimension, Whalen and Ménard (1995) have found that this strategy imposes an extra burden on writers as the very act of translating may add to linguistic problems, and lead to an overload in short-term memory capacity, or may even slow down the writing process (a suggestion that also finds support in Cohen and Brooks-Carson 2001) or block the idea generation process. Consequently, writers may have to back-translate into their L1 in order to generate further text. However, this detrimental effect has only been reported for inexperienced writers. Expert writers are also said to translate local plans from the L1 into the L2, though less frequently than novice writers (Whalen and Ménard 1995; Sasaki and Hirose 1996). With these expert writers, using the L1 has been found to be an aid.

Regarding the *product* dimension, Kobayashi and Rinnert (1992) reported beneficial effects of L1 use: the texts generated through the mother tongue rather than directly into the L2 were judged to be better on content, organization and—perhaps more surprisingly—style/language use, which in this study refers to richness of vocabulary and variety of sentence structure. However, Cohen and Brooks-Carson (2001) challenged these results because, in their data, direct writing in the L2 (French) led to compositions that were rated better than those produced via translation on four categories: sense of the language (i.e. how French they sounded), organizational structure, clarity of points, and smoothness of connectors. This would seem to contrast with Kobayashi and Rinnert's (1992) results on the points of 'organization' and 'sense of the language/language use'. In spite of these discrepancies on essay *ratings* with respect to which language of generation benefits the writer most for each category, the informants' answers to questionnaires in both studies corroborated the beneficial influence of the mother tongue on three aspects of the writing process in particular: vocabulary, the number of ideas generated, and being able to think through one's ideas more clearly.

Resorting to the native language can also serve *linguistic and stylistic purposes*, especially in relation to lexical problems (for example, Jones and Tetroe 1987; Cumming 1990; Qi 1998; Wang 2003). A consensus view among researchers is that this L1 use is part of the strategic repertoire of skilled writers only and also that, in contrast to the debate on the effects of generating text via the L1, the use of the L1 for these purposes is an asset in L2 writing. In addition, it has also been reported that the L1 is deployed for two further linguistic purposes: in lexical search processes (Cumming 1989; Smith 1994), and in the assessment of lexical and syntactic language choices. This assessment via the L1 is further support for the idea that L2 writers use 'standards of mother tongue knowledge as a reliable test of linguistic validity' (Cumming 1990: 495) and that by doing this they 'proceed from the cognitive principle of assessing unfamiliar knowledge against elements of existing knowledge' (Cumming 1990: 495). Since Cumming drew attention to this cross-linguistic phenomenon, other studies have provided further empirical evidence of this activity (Qi 1998; Wang 2003; Wolfersberger 2003).

The mother tongue has also been found to help in the process of *organizing information and structuring texts* (Jones and Tetroe 1987; Lay 1988; Uzawa and Cumming 1989; Cohen and Brooks-Carson 2001; Wang and Wen 2002; Woodall 2002; Wang 2003). The explanation behind this particular use may be that students do not have the required meta-language to be able to talk/think about these issues in the second language and so are forced to fall back on their native language, perhaps in an attempt to 'keep up the standards'.

The L1 in the revision process

Regarding the macro-process of revision, some studies (for example, Manchón, Roca de Larios, and Murphy 1998, 2000a, 2000b; Manchón and Roca de Larios 2005) have drawn attention to the fact that writers go back over what they have written or the assignment itself, back-translating into their L1 in order to check or improve on any of the following: the solutions they have worked out to problems related to the task requirements, the appropriateness of the ideas in the global plan, the match between the original plan and its actual implementation, or the solutions given to problems that crop up during formulation.

Evaluation is also a fundamental part of the revising process (as well as feeding into the other macro-processes and monitoring, see below) and frequent references have been found to the fact that it can take place in the mother tongue (for example, Wang 2003, Wolfersberger 2003).

The L1 in the monitoring process

In the Flower and Hayes (1980) model of L1 composing, the three macro-processes of planning, transcription (for which we prefer the term 'formulation') and revision are controlled by a monitor function. In many L2 composing studies the L1 has been found to be used strategically for this monitoring or controlling function in the writing process (for example, Jones and Tetroe 1987; Wang and Wen 2002; Woodall 2002). Moreover, it seems that this use of the L1 for monitoring does not necessarily decline with increasing L2 proficiency, as text generation does. This may link up both with factors uncovered in studies of bilingualism, where it appears that the two languages of a bilingual individual can be used to play different social roles (see, for example, Grosjean 1982) and also with Vygotskyan notions of private speech, 'a mental tool for difficult non-automated tasks' (Woodall 2002: 24). Several studies have remarked on the way that writers seem to carry on an inner dialogue (for example, Lay 1988) where they are asking and answering their own questions as if they were split into two personae: writer and reader/critic. Evaluation and monitoring would then seem to be a major part of the reader/critic's role and by using the mother tongue—as opposed to the language of the written text—for these purposes, the writer may be able to switch between these two roles more easily.

Summary for L1 use

The picture that emerges, then, is one in which the mother tongue is used as a compensatory strategy in the early stages of learning in order to deal with the multiple simultaneous problems that arise for low-proficiency students in producing text in an L2. One can imagine that for students at this early stage the process might begin with almost everything in the mother tongue except the emerging text, particularly in FL situations. The L1 allows the learner to think, access ideas, then access words, albeit slowly, then evaluate those words by back-translating to judge appropriateness. As proficiency develops, the writer must obtain greater control over language, and thereby fluency is increased. But although fluent text production starts to develop gradually, multiple problems still crop up to break up the process. Many of these problems will be lexical ones, and the L1 can help with framing the problem and accessing meanings and forms stored in memory as well as with the assessment of the forms accessed, part of the monitoring process. As fluency increases and the generation process becomes more automatic, more mental capacity is freed to attend to higher levels of processing—planning, organization, solving rhetorical, and discourse problems—which may continue to take place in the mother tongue because of the deeper processing involved, particularly if the task presents high cognitive demands. This might explain why, even at high levels of proficiency, some writers continue to use the mother tongue for such activities as task conceptualization, planning ideas and organization, monitoring the writing process, or evaluating the task. However, this use of the L1 may be mitigated by such social factors as one's conception of what good writing should be, one's identity, one's prior training, etc., as we shall shortly see.

The variables that influence strategy use

Given the socio-cognitive nature of the act of writing, both writer-internal and writer-external variables have been found to influence the use of writing strategies. What is more, a mutual interplay of variables in strategy deployment seems to be the norm. Another important research finding is the notable individual variation observed in the choice and implementation of writing strategies.

Writer-internal variables

In an earlier section we mentioned an emergent line of research that tries to see the relationship between writers' goals and their deployment of strategies. Still, the two writer-internal variables most widely studied are the writer's *L2 proficiency* (cf. Cumming 1989; Whalen 1993; Whalen and Ménard 1995; Sasaki and Hirose 1996; Sasaki 2000, 2004), and his/her degree of *writing competence* or expertise, with important differences reported between skilled and unskilled writers (cf. Raimes 1985, 1987; Cumming 1989; Whalen and Ménard 1995). These two factors seem to influence the quantitative and qualitative use of strategies, as well as the effect that a given strategy may have. (See Roca de Larios *et al.* 2002 for a review of empirical research on writer-internal variables.)

The writer's deployment of strategies has also been reported to be mediated by *previous L1/L2 literacy and educational experience* (cf. Jones and Tetroe 1987; Cumming 1989; Porte 1995; Sasaki and Hirose 1996; Akyel and Kamisli 1997; Bosher 1998; Sasaki 2000, 2004; Zainuddin and Moore 2003). In this respect, the actual context in which this literacy experience has taken place seems to play an important role. For instance, with regard to language switching, Cohen and Brooks-Carson (2001) found that their participants (an intermediate group of Spanish-English bilinguals studying French in an American university) reported thinking or translating mentally into English rather than Spanish while composing in French. This was unexpected given the proximity between Spanish and French. The authors attributed this finding to the fact that American foreign language textbooks use English as the language for explanations. Moreover, these bilinguals were used to functioning in an English language university. Indeed, it is the 'language medium' associated with staying abroad, that has featured in recent studies on foreign language writing (Shaw 1991; Zainuddin and Moore 2003; Sasaki 2004). Sasaki (2004), for instance, reports a differential use of the strategy of translation between one group of Japanese EFL university learners who spent some time in the United States and another who did not, the former relying significantly more on English than the latter.

Closely related to the learner's previous writing experience is another factor influencing strategy use, namely, the *writer's mental model of writing* (Cumming 1989; Devine, Railey, and Boshoff 1993; Victori 1999; Sengupta 2000), which constitutes a whole set of conceptions and beliefs that underlie and guide writing performance. In this respect, notable differences have been observed between more and less competent (or skilled) L2 writers. Skilled writers' mental models seem to be more multi-dimensional and thus they are prepared to take risks in the construction of complex sentences (Khaldieh 2000), emphasize the importance of fluency and clarity (Kasper 1997), and have a broader conception of what writing entails. Less skilled writers, in contrast, appear to be guided by a mono-dimensional mental model of writing and thus tend to see writing mainly as a grammatically-driven juxtaposition of sentences (Victori 1995; Kasper 1997) rather than the construction of a whole discourse (Zamel 1983).

Part of the beliefs writers hold relate to the perception of the usefulness of strategies, which seems to depend on what we may call the learner's 'appropriation' of strategies over time. Chamot and O'Malley (1994a) claimed that 'an important requirement for viewing oneself as a successful learner is self-control over strategy use' (p. 383), an idea also emphasized by Whalen (1993) when she states that 'a writing strategy necessarily becomes more powerful and consequential when the writer becomes conscious of how he manipulates and applies the strategy to a specific writing task' (p. 607). Similarly, the participant in Spack's (1997) study enlarged her strategic repertoire, but also became adept at matching strategies to text demands, a finding also present in Leki's (1995) study, in which the participants 'displayed the flexibility needed to shift among strategies as needed' (p. 241). Sometimes this appropriation of strategies entails 'taking a stance towards teacher's demand', a strategy used by Leki's participants and also recently documented by Sasaki (2004). The latter is a study in which the participants reported going back to using more local planning after being taught to use more global planning because they were aware that the 'quality' of their local planning had improved over the years. This finding is interpreted by Sasaki as a sign that these writers learnt to 'loosen that strict rule' (p. 566) of spending time planning before starting to write.

Writer-external variables

Two main writer-external variables have been found to mediate the writer's deployment of strategies:

1 *task-related factors* including both task types and differences resulting from varying experimental intervention (Cumming 1989; Hall 1991; Johnson 1992; Koda 1993; Porte 1995, 1996; Broekkamp and van den Bergh 1996; Qi 1998; Chimbganda 2000; Manchón *et al.* 2000a, 2000b; Ellis and Yuan 2004); and

2 *topic-related factors* (cf. Raimes 1985; Friedlander 1990) with topic familiarity being an important variable (cf. Gaskill 1986; Friedlander 1990; Manchón *et al.* 2000a).

Regarding task-related factors, *more and less cognitively demanding tasks* seem to influence strategy use. Thus, argumentative tasks have been found to trigger more decisions involving simultaneous thinking about gist and language than letter writing (Cumming 1989), and backtracking behavior was found to differ in narrative and argumentative tasks (Manchón *et al.* 2000a).

Another task-related factor that appears to mediate strategy use is *time*. For example, in Sasaki (2004) the amount of local or global planning used was influenced by the time available: less time meant more local planning. Similarly, the use of translation was affected by time considerations, according to the same informants. Although the L1 may be beneficial for generating content, translating may be less efficacious if time is limited, as extra time is required later to translate the generated content into the L2. This might explain the apparently contradictory findings on the benefits of L1 use reported by Kobayashi and Rinnert (1992) and Cohen and Brooks-Carson (2001): in the first study the participants were allowed twice as much time in the translating mode as in the direct writing mode, with positive effects reported for the former (see above). In Cohen and Brooks-Carson (2001), however, the participants in the direct and translating modes were given equal amounts of time to carry out the writing task, and in this case (interestingly) direct writing was found to be better. Porte (1995, 1996), analyzing how his EFL writers' revision behavior was mediated by time, suggested that encouraging deeper and widespread revision is not a matter of allowing more or less composing time on a single occasion but rather of being able to create a distance between writers and their texts 'by judicious distribution of time across a number of sessions' (Porte 1996: 115).

The transfer of strategies across languages

The research evidence shows that the qualitative use of strategies transfers across languages (Arndt 1987; Jones and Tetroe 1987; Cumming 1989; Cumming *et al.* 1989; Pennington and So 1993; Whalen 1993; Hirose and Sasaki 1994; Smith 1994; Matsumoto 1995; Hatasa and Soeda 2000; Takagaki 2003), whereas L1 and L2 writing vary regarding quantitative use of strategies (Jones and Tetroe 1987; Whalen and Ménard 1995; Armengol-Castells 2001; Takagaki 2003).

The quantitative differences can be explained by considering the labour-intense nature of L2 writing, especially regarding the text-generating process, which has been found to be the one that consumes most writing time (Roca de Larios, Marín, and Murphy 2001; Wang and Wen 2002) and that entails most problem-solving behavior. This process has also been found to be notoriously less fluent in L2 writing, which entails twice as much problem solving as L1 writing (Roca *et al.* 2001). As a result, from a textual point of view for instance, there seems to be a decrease in the number of goals generated in the L2 (Skibniewski 1988) as L2 writers tend to concentrate their attention on the morpho-syntactic and lexical levels at the expense of the rhetorical and textual dimensions of the composition process (Whalen and Ménard 1995).

It also seems that the number of ideas planned that are actually incorporated into the text tends to be lower in the L2 task in spite of their qualitative similarities across languages.

It follows from this that one important research finding is that the transfer of strategies seems to be mediated by the writer's proficiency—but see Cumming 1989. Other variables mediating the transfer of skills are related to the writer's goals and purposes as well as to task-related factors. Of special interest in this context is the study by Uzawa and Cumming (1989), in which the participants approached the L2 task in the form of a dilemma or as a kind of 'mental dialectic' which involved either keeping up the standard of their mother tongue writing by means of rehearsing, organizing information in the L1, etc., or else lowering the standard by reducing the amount of information to be covered, downgrading the syntax and the vocabulary or avoiding audience concerns. Valdés *et al.* (1992) provided support for this view when they claimed that the transfer of L1 organization skills shown by their writers (American university students of Spanish as a FL) would probably not have been so automatic if a different type of task, demanding more cultural authenticity, had been set. In that case, Valdés *et al.* speculated, the students would have had to 'restructure' the voice and style acquired in their L1 to accommodate it to the new demands of the L2, which would have involved much more than a simple transfer of writing skills.

Finally, it is worth emphasizing the important role that resorting to the L1 plays in the writer's attempt to maintain L1 standards in L2 writing. As an example, it has been found that second language writers are able to maintain their L1 planning levels in the second language in spite of L2 proficiency limitations by planning in the mother tongue (cf. Jones and Tetroe 1987; Uzawa and Cumming 1989).

Collectively considered, research findings indicate that writing strategies transfer across languages, although their frequency of use may differ from the L1 to the L2, and that this transfer is mediated by both writer-internal factors (for example, proficiency and one's own goals) as well as by writer-external factors (for example, task type).

The influence of instruction on strategy use

This is an under-researched area representing less than ten per cent of the studies in our corpus, although scattered observations on the issue can be found in the discussion sections of different research reports.

Those studies that have investigated the issue are both descriptive studies that report how the participants' past writing instruction has shaped their deployment of strategies (cf. Kobayashi and Rinnert 2001; Sasaki 2004), and interventionist studies that have experimentally measured the effects of strategy training, either generally (Sasaki 2000) or with reference to a specific macro-process, be it revision (Sengupta 2000), writing (Cresswell 2000), or planning and revision (Ching 2002). In the last three cases, the strategies that were the focus of the training include metacognitive strategies—monitoring (Cresswell 2000) and self-regulation (Ching 2002)—and specific text-related strategies, i.e. how to make a text more reader-friendly (Sengupta 2000). The actual implementation of the strategy training program was explicit and integrated, in all cases including a metacognitive component and gradually diminishing the scaffolding provided in the first stages.

The measurement of the success of the training was operationalized as the effect it had on the participants' mental model of writing (Cresswell 2000; Sengupta 2000; Ching 2002), their use of strategies (Sasaki 2000, 2002) and other learner-internal factors (such as the writers' self-determination or attribution, Ching 2002), as well as on the quality of the essays produced before and after treatment (Sengupta 2000). The research evidence indicates a positive influence of instruction on how students approach writing tasks (as a result of their mental models becoming more multi-dimensional) and how confident and autonomous they become. In addition, instruction and training influences the quality of the essays produced. Interestingly, in the only longitudinal study that has looked at the role of instruction over time (Sasaki 2004), it became evident that for the effect of instruction to be long-lasting, writing practice is crucial. In her longitudinal study of a group of university students, Sasaki (2004) found that the effects of the process instruction that the participants received in their first year at university were neutralized by the subsequent lack of writing practice.

The positive effects of these strategy instruction programmes may be attributed to the way they were put into practice. In her review of the issue in the strategy research at large, Manchón (in press) isolated three variables that have been deemed to be crucial: (1) the teacher's own training as a good predictor of success; (2) the duration of the programme (longer programmes— at least between ten and 15 weeks—seem to produce better outcomes than shorter ones); and (3) the inclusion of a metacognitive component. The three interventionist studies under review fulfil the last two requirements. In addition, Cresswell was the teacher-researcher in his study (Cresswell 2000) and Sengupta (2000) provided scaffolding to the teacher implementing the strategy instruction in her own study.

Conclusions

The general picture that emerges from the research reviewed is that enquiry into composing strategies has been informed by a variety of theoretical frameworks; this has resulted in a plethora of conceptualizations and taxonomies of writing strategies, as well as in a diversity of empirical approaches to operationalize and investigate the phenomenon. In line with general strategy research, the strategy construct in its application to writing has been defined in a variety of ways that range from a broad conceptualization that equates strategies with any action applied to the act of writing, to views in which strategies are just a set of writing actions, and thus differentiated from other aspects of the process of composing. Following trends in both SLA research as well as in the writing literature, there has been a gradual expansion of the theoretical frameworks guiding empirical enquiry, as well as a shift from purely cognitive approaches to understanding the L2 writer's strategic behavior, to more socio-cognitive accounts that emphasize that cognitive processes and strategies are historically and situationally constructed.

Collectively, the rich body of knowledge accumulated over the years has contributed to advancing our understanding of the characteristic features of the L2 writer's strategic behavior. Research findings point in three main directions: (1) L2 writers implement a wide range of general and specific strategic actions in their attempt to learn to write and to express themselves in writing in an L2; (2) given the socio-cognitive dimensions of composing, the L2 writer's strategic behavior is dependent on both learner-internal and learner-external variables; and (3) the writer's strategic behavior is mediated by the instruction received and can be modified through strategy instruction, although this finding needs further empirical validation. The effect of instruction appears to come about as a result of a more encompassing effect of strategy instruction, namely, that of changing the writer's mental model towards a more multidimensional one. Among the strategies used by L2 writers, the use of the L1 has emerged as an important problem-solving resource used purposefully by L2 writers in order to understand the assignment they are given, plan content and organization, generate and re-scan text, struggle to find a way to express intended meaning, evaluate and refine their lexical and syntactic choices, and monitor the writing process. Furthermore, these uses of the L1 have turned out to be some of the most striking L2 writing-specific phenomena.

At a more general level, the research insights obtained have contributed to the theorizing on perennial issues in the field of second language acquisition and use, such as the long-standing enquiry into the nature of the phenomenon of transfer of knowledge and skills, and the debate as to whether or not strategy instruction makes a difference, although the research concerning the latter is sparse and it would therefore be premature to form conclusive generalizations from it.

The lack of research on strategy instruction is not the only area in which there is scope for further research. In fact, while acknowledging that one merit of this research is the effort made to triangulate qualitative and quantitative data by using a combination of different elicitation procedures, it is our view that in order to move forward in theory and research, certain theoretical and methodological refinements would be welcome. First, future researchers ought to take a stance regarding which theoretical framework is going to inform their enquiry and exploit it fully. The main suggestion here would be to avoid engaging in research that simply leads to the establishment of atheoretical and decontextualised taxonomies of strategies, an endeavor of limited value for the development of the field.

Second, we feel it is necessary to overcome certain limitations of previous research in terms of designs and data analysis. Regarding the former, one problem of existing research relates to subject populations, mainly composed of young adults in academic settings whose proficiency in the language is above an intermediate level, which casts doubt on the generalizability of findings. The existing studies should thus be extended to younger and less-proficient writers, as these populations represent a large percentage of L2 learners who are learning and performing writing. A further methodological issue is that the majority of the studies reviewed are cross-sectional, an issue that again limits the contribution of this research given that, as pointed out by McDonough (1999), 'work on strategies is hampered by the lack of a coherent theory of how strategies [...] are selected, invented and discarded in favor of better ones' (p. 14).

Regarding data analysis, we mentioned above that future research must necessarily overcome certain shortcomings related to issues of validity, reliability, and categorization in the data analysis, as well as to the necessary decisions that one must take regarding the operationalization of the strategy construct guiding the research, and the strict application of this operationalization when trying to make sense of the data.

In short, the last 25 years have produced an abundant body of knowledge on the writing strategies deployed by L2 learners of many different language backgrounds (encompassing L1/L2 combinations of related and more distant languages) learning to write in second and foreign language contexts. This is a good starting point from which to move forward in theory and research, although the success of this advance will depend on whether future research follows the path initiated by those researchers in the field who have engaged in theoretically-grounded and methodologically-principled enquiry into composing strategies.

Acknowledgements

This chapter is part of a research programme financed by the Spanish Ministry of Education and Science, Research Grant SEJ2005-04266. We should like to express our gratitude to Andrew Cohen, Alister Cumming, Ilona Leki, Steve McDonough, Alicia Martínez, Pilar Safont, and Larry Vandergrift for their generosity in making available to us a number of studies included in this review. We should also like to thank the two anonymous reviewers and the Editors for their careful reading of our text and their constructive criticism. Further thanks must also go to Zoltan Dörnyei who was kind enough to read and offer some thoughts on the original manuscript.

Notes

1 Not a theoretical framework as such.
2 Sionis (1995), in contrast, is also a study of Communication Strategies in writing but it uses a totally different framework to classify the strategies

used by the participants in the study (two groups of French academics wishing to publish internationally).

3 See Roca de Larios *et al.* (2002) for a full discussion of many of the methodological issues covered in this section.

A review of vocabulary learning strategies: focus on language proficiency and learner voice

MARTHA NYIKOS and MAY FAN

Introduction

In this review we consider the lexical dimension of language learning, reporting on studies which describe strategies through which L2 learners discover the meaning of unknown words, and integrate and consolidate newly acquired vocabulary. This chapter examines vocabulary learning strategies (VLS) with particular focus on learner voice, that is, how learners report their own perceptions regarding their actual use of VLS.

This chapter presents:

1 our review methodology of VLS research approaches which elicit learner voice;
2 factors that effect VLS use, including proficiency, individual variation, and learning environment;
3 decontextualized VLS: memorization strategies, repetition, association, and keyword;
4 contextualized vocabulary inferencing strategies;
5 dictionary and electronic look-up strategies;
6 strategy instruction studies;
7 future research on strategy instruction; and
8 conclusions and pedagogical implications.

Vocabulary has a crucial role in both the receptive and productive skills associated with effective communication. From early calls for vocabulary-focused research (Richards 1976; Meara 1980) to more recent re-examinations (de Bot 1992; Laufer and Nation 1995; Paribakht and Wesche 1997), the last 30 years can generally be divided into two periods. In the years preceding the 1990s, SLA research was centered on syntactic issues as well as productive skills related to communicative competence and proficiency, thereby shifting focus away from discrete-point vocabulary learning (Segler, Pain, and Sorace 2002). Indeed, traditionally instructional emphasis has been on grammar with vocabulary learning being left to the learners' own devices (Oxford and Scarcella 1994).

Since 1990, there has been increasing scholarly recognition of the central importance of vocabulary (Nation 1990; Huckin, Haynes, and Coady 1993; Coady and Huckin 1997; Schmitt and McCarthy 1997). In order to master vocabulary, students must learn multiple word meanings and connotations, derived forms, spellings, pronunciations, proper grammatical uses, and collocations, well enough to have almost instantaneous oral and written word recognition and production abilities (Nation 1990). The fact that the academic and interpersonal vocabulary needs of learners outpace their ability to learn and effectively integrate newly acquired vocabulary, has prompted research into how VLS can assist learners (Kojic-Sabo and Lightbown 1999; Hunt and Beglar 2005; Folse 2006). Learners themselves have consistently identified a dearth of vocabulary as the primary factor holding them back from attaining their larger linguistic goals at a satisfactory rate (Yorio 1971; Richards 1976; Keller 1978; Ludwig 1984; Crow 1986; Nunan 1988; Gass 1990; Knight 1994; Gan, Humphreys, and Hamp-Lyons 2004).

For a detailed account of how the review process was carried out the reader is invited to go to Appendix 12.1 on www.oup.com/elt/teacher/lls.

Research approaches to vocabulary learning strategies

Historically, VLS research has been firmly rooted in cognitive and psycholinguistic research paradigms concerned with issues of (1) time and memory, (2) linguistic properties, and (3) text type.

Issues of time and memory

These studies include:

a the optimal time needed to commit words, which are often sequenced in a given order, to memory (Dempster 1987; Laufer and Osimo 1991; DeGroot and Keijzer 2000; Waring and Takaki 2003); and

b associative memory–effects of rote repetition compared to various meaningful associations, especially the keyword mnemonic and imagery (Raugh and Atkinson 1975; Paivio and Desrochers 1981; Cohen 1987; Nyikos 1990; Ellis and Beaton 1993; Hogben and Lawson 1994). Reviews of this area are found in Gu (2003b), Sagarra and Alba (2006), and DeGroot and Van Hell (2005).

Issues of linguistic properties

Some studies have focused on linguistic and especially grammatical properties of vocabulary including familiarity with word structure (morphology, affixation), word frequency, collocations, and pragmatic usage (Ludwig 1984; Kern 1989; Holmes and Ramos 1993; Laufer 1997; Nation 2001; Schmitt 2000; Barcroft 2002; Morin 2003).

Issues of text type

Other studies have dealt with issues associated with text type, including genre, graded readers (texts using controlled vocabulary), and varying levels of contextual cues (word, sentence, and discourse analysis) (Kern 1989; Mondria and Wit-de Boer 1991; Knight 1994; Horst, Cobb, and Meara 1998; Laufer 2003; Waring and Takaki 2003; Horst 2005).

The role of learner voice

Notably, SLA's interest in incidental vocabulary acquisition generally fails to account for learner strategies *per se*, focusing instead on input processing, lexical intake/uptake of form and meaning through inferencing, and incidental word learning in context. These SLA studies (such as Rott 2000; Pulido 2004; Horst 2005), while eschewing learner strategy research, none the less succeed in addressing VLS obliquely through attention to actions learners engage in while processing vocabulary in isolation or in texts. As a researcher who has considered the learner's voice in vocabulary learning through VLS, Gu (2003b) highlights the sociocultural nature of language and communication in specific contexts, presenting an organizational schema drawing upon the works of Williams and Burden (1997), Flavell (1979), Brown, Bransford, Ferrara, and Campione (1983), Wenden (1987), and Cohen (2001). He seeks to account for the complex of variables which enter into the choice and effectiveness of VLS in various environments, with four essential variables of person, task, context, and strategies.

Many of the studies we reviewed stopped short of asking the crucial question following an experimental task: did the students exclusively use the strategy under study, or did they also, or only, employ strategies already familiar to them? Without asking respondents whether and to what extent they applied VLS, or had the conceptual grasp of the targeted strategy to apply it to the task, its use can only be inferred by the investigator. Such researcher-based inferences may be incorrect (Ott, Blake, and Butler 1976; Hall, Wilson, and Patterson 1981; Cohen 1987) due to students not following directions or applying themselves to the task (Wesche and Paribakht 2000).

Through learner voice we gain first-hand insight into learners' perspectives regarding: (a) actual use, (b) preferences for types of VLS and their practical utility, and (c) varying combinations of VLS. In this VLS review, the most productive questions and research methodologies sought to determine: (1) learners' own evaluations of their learning environments, assigned tasks, resource materials, and learning pressures and (2) how these impacted their choices and willingness (volition) to use VLS.

Obtaining learner voice

In the VLS studies described below, elicitation of learners' voice came from four methodological approaches: questionnaire, interview, self-report (via diary/checklist/learning log/written description), and think-aloud. In the case of think-aloud, because the protocols themselves simultaneously integrate student voice with the VLS data, the researcher can validate the use and process of the strategies applied.

Although think-aloud was used in many studies, post-treatment checks for validity through follow up interviews and questionnaires were used in relatively few of the reviewed studies. (See Appendix 12.)

Of the above methods, concurrent think-aloud is the only real-time measure of student voice and thus, administered properly, the most likely to catch inconsistencies, anomalies, false starts, contradictory actions, and task-incompatible VLS use, all of which may be difficult for learners to later recall. (See Chapter 5.) Another limitation of the think-aloud method is that its use may change 'spontaneous' LLS behavior or divide a subjects' attention, though it can simultaneously positively raise metacognitive awareness, promoting thoughtful and systematic VLS use. A general limitation is that learners are unable to fully verbalize their often partially subconscious and automatic VLS use or may provide inaccurate rationales for their behavior in an effort to please the researcher (Cohen 1987; Ahmed 1989; Wesche and Paribakht 2000). On the lower end of the learner voice continuum are studies utilizing questionnaires which ask learners to respond to broad decontextualized statements about their general VLS use. The validity of such survey studies would be improved if learners were asked to perform specific vocabulary learning tasks coupled with these questionnaires.

Classification of VLS

Classification of VLS has achieved only mild consensus to date. Building on basic distinctions between receptive and productive knowledge (Schmitt 2000), researchers have identified and classified various patterns or con-figurations of VLS. Ahmed (1989) classified the 38 strategies his Sudanese learners used into five macro-strategies of memorization, practice, dictionary use, note-taking, and group-work; while Gu and Johnson (1996) organized 91 VLS strategies in their study of Chinese students into two major categories: metacognitive and cognitive. Notably, Schmitt (1997, 2000) recognized the overlap of cognitive, metacognitive, memory and social func-tions in 58 VLS in his adaptation of Oxford's (1990a) more general SILL classifications and added determination of meaning strategies under his overarching distinctions between discovery strategies (strategies for learning what an unknown word means) and consolidation strategies (strategies for both learning word meaning and integrating it into the vocabulary). These VLS classifications combine the broader psycholinguistic categories of direct (memory/cognitive/compensation) and indirect (metacognitive/social/affect-ive) found in Oxford (1990a) and O'Malley and Chamot (1990).

One reason researchers often overlap categories is that they frequently utilize *a priori* conceptual constructs from cognitive and social psychology to classify strategies, rather than specifically relying on emerging patterns of how learners deploy VLS. Promising research approaches include a grounded theory approach (which starts with patterns in data and creates a theory based on those findings) or through the application of statistical tools such as cluster analysis (Ahmed 1989; Gu and Johnson 1996; Kojic-Sabo and Lightbown 1999) and factor analysis (Nyikos and Oxford 1993; Stoffer 1995).

The resulting lack of uniformity in terminology among researchers has made it difficult to compare even the most rigorous research findings across studies. An exhaustive and mutually exclusive typology of VLS coupled with standardized valid measures of proficiency and vocabulary learning would permit more exact analysis and comparison of future research findings. The more clearly and unambiguously that researchers can define VLS, as well as word knowledge levels (breadth and depth) before and after instruction, the more valid and reliable future research comparisons can be.

Factors influencing VLS use

Our review identified four main factors which influence VLS use, revealing systematic patterns which will be examined in this section: (1) proficiency level of the learner, (2) individual variation and gender, (3) strategy use development, and (4) learning environment (classroom-restricted FL versus social context-embedded ESL settings).

Proficient versus less proficient vocabulary learners

Researchers have analyzed VLS using the dichotomy of successful versus less successful students in order to better characterize the VLS that lead to success on tasks described in the reviewed studies. In an early study, Hosenfeld (1977) found that good readers read at the phrase level (see Chapter 9), keeping the meaning of the passage in mind while skipping unessential words and guessing from context rather than using the glossary. By contrast, her poor readers read word-by-word often losing the meaning of sentences, rarely skipped words and used the glossary as the primary VLS rather than guessing from context. By using daily written records and oral interviews of 72 ESL and FL students, Sanaoui (1995) noted that the successful students took a structured approach which entailed disciplined, independent study characterized by self-devised learning tasks. Successful students actively monitored and reviewed the vocabulary words they were learning, using spare time while jogging, driving, or waiting to practice newly learnt words, either alone or with others. Unsuccessful learners followed unstructured approaches, i.e. they were less systematic, motivated, pro-active, or disciplined (doing little or no work which was not required by the course and spent hardly any time reviewing vocabulary).

Success measures consisting of vocabulary tests and a proficiency test were applied by Kojic-Sabo and Lightbown (1999) when adapting Sanaoui's

(1992) questionnaire with 47 ESL and 43 EFL students. They ascertained that more frequent and elaborate strategy use, including practicing vocabulary outside of the classroom, was associated with higher levels of vocabulary learning and overall English proficiency, whereas lack of self-reported effort was linked to poor performance. Using a think-aloud protocol, direct observation, and a structured interview to collect data and scholastic records to determine learning success, Ahmed (1989) found that the good learners were distinguished from the unsuccessful ones by their frequent use of the 'practice' strategy category, including using new words in real and imagined contexts, asking for tests, asking for assistance, using written sources to verify knowledge, and self-testing. On the other hand, two groups of less successful learners 'showed little awareness of what they could learn about new words, and they did not show any interest in learning words in context. Each new word was learnt as if it had no relationship with any previously learnt words' (p. 9). In general they used fewer strategies, and used other less elaborate clusters of strategies than more successful students, indicating that learners' VLS repertoire can be inadequate or even counterproductive.

A study relating VLS to language proficiency used success on the national English proficiency test and a vocabulary test as a benchmark (Gu and Johnson 1996). The researchers collected VLS data by questionnaire from 850 Chinese university students and found that 'self-initiative' and 'selective attention' the two metacognitive strategies under study, were positive predictors of general proficiency. The strategies which correlated positively with both general proficiency and vocabulary scores included 'contextual guessing, skilled use of dictionaries, note-taking, paying attention to word formation, contextual encoding and activation of newly learnt words' (p. 643). Similarly, Fan (2003) used a VLS questionnaire and a simultaneous vocabulary test in her study with 1,067 Hong Kong ESL students who were newly admitted to the universities. More proficient students reported planning their vocabulary learning both inside and outside class and used both guessing strategies in concert with their knowledge of grammar and morphology and, dictionary strategies, including consulting English definitions, pronunciation, derived forms, and appropriate usage of the new words. Our review found that more proficient students have requisite knowledge needed to effectively apply a greater range of strategies than their less proficient peers.

Individual variation and gender differences

Although there is general agreement regarding the VLS of good vocabulary learners, there is marked individual variation in strategy use even among proficient learners. Ahmed's (1989) cluster analysis clearly showed three distinct groupings of successful students using different combinations of strategies to achieve success, further strengthening the argument for increased attention to individual variation among similar learners sharing similar characteristics, including gender. For example, Gu (2005) reported that the female participants significantly outperformed their male counterparts in both vocabulary size and general proficiency. Experimental evidence in Nyikos (1987) showed that men significantly outperformed women when using a visual and color association strategy for vocabulary learning, whereas women found simple color coding significantly more useful as a retrieval strategy when learning German vocabulary. Notably, female participants in Catalan's (2003) study exhibited a greater range of VLS use, including formal rule-related strategies, input elicitation (social elicitation strategies), planning and rehearsal strategies, and consolidation strategies than males. Grace (2000) compared males' strategic preference for translations to females' use of guessing from context when learning new vocabulary in CALL. Although the postulated differences were not significant, she provides a useful roadmap for future research in this area.

The evidence thus suggests that successful language learners should not be characterized by their uniform use of a certain set of VLS. Indeed, it is the implementation of varied combinations of VLS which may enable very different students to be equally successful in a given task or situation (Gu 2003b). Even among the four most successful students out of the 15 learners of Italian studied by Lawson and Hogben (1996), at least one student made extensive use of contextual clues, note-taking, and mnemonic strategies, while at least one other made almost no use of these strategies. Gu (1994) characterized good learners as being flexible and metacognitively aware in evaluating their own strategy use, pointing to a possible key distinguishing factor among better VLS users namely, their ability to use metacognitive strategies in tandem with multiple task-appropriate sub-strategies. This finding has strong implications for strategy instruction and general pedagogical applications. This may also be the reason why the few VLS instructional studies we found (see below) focused primarily on metacognitive strategies. The instructional section of this paper will consider the degree to which studies find that these metacognitive, organizational, and self monitoring strategies can be productively taught to learners of all proficiency levels.

Strategy development and proficiency

Few studies have investigated the change in strategy use over time and with increasing proficiency. However, Schmitt (1997) did compare three different age groups (junior high school grades 7–9; high school grades 10–12; university students and adults). Results based on the self-report of the students indicated that the focus on written repetition, word spelling, word lists, textbook vocabulary activities, and flash cards decreased as these Japanese learners reached higher proficiency levels. On the other hand, the use of bilingual dictionaries, guessing from context, imaging word meanings, asking teachers for paraphrase or synonym, skipping new words, analysis of parts of speech, and connecting words to personal experience, all increased as the learners became more proficient.

A developmental trend in VLS use from novice to more advanced learners was also noted by Harley and Hart (2000) in their comparison of a 9th-grade extended and an 11th-grade early immersion French class. Ninth-grade students found it very helpful to do list learning by rote with English translation, which was not considered as helpful by the grade 11 immersion students who, with their greater proficiency, were able to successfully adopt more rewarding L1-like strategies which were analogous to those used in higher level L1 vocabulary acquisition. Increased oral recognition skills of the 11th graders enabled them to consider hearing a new word in spoken English context to be more helpful than reading it in context. By contrast, the 9th graders who needed more processing time found reading new words in context to be more helpful than new words in oral context. Regardless of stage of development, research results indicate that successful learners tend to present a profile of greater metacognitive decision-making to select more appropriate, task-compatible strategies to achieve similar results as more advanced students, a pattern also noted in many other VLS studies.

Learning environment: classroom-restricted FL versus socially-embedded ESL

Differences in findings of VLS use in SL and FL settings suggest a relationship between learning environment and strategy use that reflects the communicative demands and learning opportunities of these radically different environments (see Chapter 4). Kojic-Sabo and Lightbown (1999) noted that ESL learners have both access to, as well as a preference for, extra-curricular English language activities as sources of vocabulary learning and reported significantly greater efforts to acquire and practice new lexical items than the EFL group which used review strategies significantly more. The EFL students attempted to compensate for their linguistically poor environments by reviewing readings, words, and notes—both alone and with friends—whereas ESL learners reported reviewing new words by using them in their daily conversations.

This pattern holds true even for Chinese EFL and other FL students who share a cultural and educational tradition favoring rote memorization (Gu and Johnson 1996 and Gu 1994, 2003a, 2005). Chinese EFL learners in China and Chinese ESL learners in formerly British Hong Kong reported a preference for authentic communicatively based L2 learning—also seen in other studies contrasting EFL and ESL populations (Kojic-Sabo and Lightbown 1999). Hong Kong ESL students reported using the newly learnt words in English speaking environments, including guessing strategies rather than the word lists and memorization strategies found among Chinese EFL learners (Fan 2003). Students' tendency to favor authentic communicative activities to book learning is also born out by Leeke and Shaw's (2000) finding that two thirds of learners discontinued vocabulary list learning as they entered an L2 environment and increased their L2 reading and proficiency. Vocabulary list learning became marginalized and was used only for words that were difficult and needed to be rapidly added to their active vocabularies.

Having examined the factors which generally effect strategy use by individual students, the following three major sections will focus on VLS, as they have been studied and applied to (a) decontextualized, (b) contextualized, and (c) dictionary use. The research in these three areas is anchored in key theories of memory and retention.

Decontextualized VLS

A large proportion of the reviewed research falls into the decontextualized vocabulary category: memorization, repetition, and associative strategies as well as the keyword mnemonic. Traditionally, instructional studies focus on teaching vocabulary in isolation without the benefit of one of the following theory-based approaches.

Memorization strategies

Most studies on rote memorization or simple repetition were carried out before the 1970s and were guided by cognitive psychology, which was more interested in issues of memory capacity, time constraints, cognitive load, and memory decay rather than the search for how VLS might contribute to communicative competence (Gu 2005). These studies rarely alluded to learner strategies used by the subjects. Associative memory, one of the theories of information processing, utilizes strategies of elaboration (for example, imagery, colors) verses shrinkage or reduction (for example, graphic organizers) for effective verbal retention and retrieval. (See Bransford 1979; Cohen 1987; Nyikos 1987, 1990 for reviews.) Additionally, Paivio (1971) proposed dual coding of words interacting with images for meaningful information retrieval (Paivio and Desrochers 1981).

One of the most influential theories supporting associative memory is focused on the depth of processing hypothesis (Craik and Lockhart 1972; Craik and Tulving 1975) which states that activities requiring a deeper cognitive involvement promote learning. The theory posits that simple rote repetition should be less conducive to learning than more complex strategies involving analysis, individually chosen associations to events and images, and construction of mnemonic devices such as the keyword method (Cohen 1987). Recently, Folse (2006) provided counter-evidence, challenging the depth-of-processing hypothesis on both theoretical and practical grounds, noting that vocabulary learning in these studies had time-on-task as a confounding variable. By controlling this factor, he found that supposedly shallow fill-in-the-blank exercises featuring multiple retrievals of target words led to significantly better retention than equal time spent by students processing vocabulary into original sentences.

Repetition strategies

Researchers using different methodologies have found that untrained learners starting to study a new FL spontaneously and overwhelmingly use some form of silent or written repetition of the target word and its meaning but make relatively little use of mnemonic VLS unless trained to do so (Cohen and Aphek 1981; Tinkham 1993; Hogben and Lawson 1994; Sanaoui 1995; Gu and Johnson 1996; Lawson and Hogben 1996). The predominant use of repetition can be seen in Nassaji's (2003) reading study of 21 intermediate adult ESL learners who used 'repeating' as the major strategy (63 per cent) compared to other strategies such as analogy (8.5 per cent), verifying (9.7 per cent), monitoring (7.2 per cent), self-inquiry (7.2 per cent), and analysis (5.5 per cent).

Repetition can be a highly efficient and rapid VLS with empirical studies showing that lists of 100 or more L2–L1 word pairs can be studied and remembered within a short time and, if properly followed by spaced recall and repetition at longer intervals, can be integrated into long-term memory (Schmitt 2000). Indeed, some learners have a preference for repetition and this is seen with many Asian learners whose 'ability to memorize and the preference for memorization are dependent upon [their] cultural background' (Gu 2003b). For example, in Schmitt's (1997) survey of 600 Japanese EFL learners of English, 'verbal repetition' and 'written repetition' were the top two strategies reported to be used by the learners for consolidating (i.e. learning) meaning. Repeating aloud has generally been found to be more effective than silent repetition in terms of vocabulary retention (for example, Kelly 1992; Hill 1994; Gu and Johnson 1996).

However, repetition alone is often used by students for whom additional strategies would be more effective. For example, using think-aloud protocols, Lawson and Hogben (1996) found that repetition strategies were the most frequently used although elaboration strategies were more effective than repetition. Fan's (2003) survey study found that among the 18 strategies identified as used significantly more often by proficient vocabulary users, none were repetition strategies. In contrast, one of the two strategies found to be used significantly more often by the low scoring groups was repetition.

Associative strategies

Associative memory principles have guided the few studies on use of elaboration to connect words to meanings. Cohen and Aphek (1981) identified different types of associations used to memorize Hebrew words including associating a word or part of it to: (1) English words with similar sounds and/ or meanings, (2) another Hebrew word according to structure, (3) a letter, and (4) a frequently seen street sign or a mental image of the word's referent. In a follow-up study published in 1980, Cohen and Aphek instructed 26 similar learners of Hebrew to generate associations of their own. Words which were learnt through association were more successfully retained one month later than words for which associations were not used. A relatively high correlation was found between general second-language proficiency and performance on recall based on association. A relationship was also found between language aptitude and the ability to form associations, confirming the earlier findings in Ott, Butler, Blake, and Ball (1973). Another study instructed students of German to associate three colors with grammatical gender to aid retrieval of article-noun lexical units and their meanings. Nyikos (1990) established that students remembered word meanings significantly better using color coding and color plus picture associations than in the picture-only condition.

The keyword method

One of the most frequently researched associative mnemonics during the past 30 years has been the keyword strategy (Atkinson 1975; Atkinson and Raugh 1975). This is an imagery mnemonic in which the sound of the target word is associated with an L1 word (acoustic link or keyword) and a visual image of the L1 word linked to the meaning of the L2 word (visual link). Thus, Spanish *pato* (meaning duck) is provided as a picture of a duck sitting in a pot (since 'pot' in English, as the native language, sounds like Spanish *pato*, thus giving the acoustic link, or keyword). The keyword mnemonic assumes that the target word will be retrieved more quickly and effectively as a unit or chunk via multiple visual and acoustic links. Because this strategy requires analysis of the word and extra creative effort to invent personally meaningful links, the depth of processing theory predicts that it is more conducive to learning (Cohen and Aphek 1981; Schmidt 1990, 1992; Laufer and Shmueli 1997). Although results of keyword studies are overwhelmingly positive, van Hell and Mahn (1997) reported that they achieved poor results with supplied keywords, possibly because supplied keywords are less effective than self-generated ones. According to the depth of processing theory, neither cognitive processing nor time spent on task provided deep processing when the words were supplied by the researchers.

The past three decades have witnessed the publication of numerous intervention studies supporting the effectiveness of the keyword method. For general reviews see Cohen (1987) and Hulstijn (1997). For comparison of the keyword method with other semantic methods, see Brown and Perry (1991), Hogben and Lawson (1994), Sagarra and Alba (2006). For the role of context, see Moore and Surber (1992) and Mondria (2003). For comparisons with rote rehearsal, see Wang and Thomas (1992), Wang, Thomas, and Ouellette (1992), van Hell and Mahn (1997). Next we examine some keyword studies in detail.

Avila and Sadoski (1996) found that those trained in the keyword method had superior comprehension and recall a week later compared to the control group which mainly used rote repetition. Although students might find the keyword method useful, it is generally considered by learners to be time-consuming and sometimes frustratingly difficult to create images, causing many to switch from the imaging portion of the keyword to a more semantic approach (Brown and Perry 1991). Research concludes that the keyword method works better the closer the L2 is related to the L1, that is where there is greater similarity in both pronunciation (acoustic similarity) and writing systems, enabling greater fit between target words and available L1 words to map them to. Furthermore, the more readily imaginable the word is (for example, concrete noun rather than abstract concept), the more readily the keyword strategy can be applied. These factors were stronger for productive vocabulary acquisition in the L2 than for receptive understanding of vocabulary (Ellis and Beaton 1993).

The utility of the keyword method also decreases if the L2 is unrelated to the L1. For example, Asian learners learning English find it difficult to utilize acoustic links and so do not favor the keyword method. Fan (2003) found that the keyword technique was reported to be seldom used and considered least useful by Chinese students among the examined 60 VLS, supporting survey results of O'Malley, Chamot, Stewner-Manzanares, Russo, and Küpper (1985) among Asian students and reports of Japanese students by Schmitt (1997, 2000). Nor was the keyword technique identified as one of the 18 strategies used by the students most proficient in vocabulary in Fan's (2003) study, supporting Gu and Johnson's (1996) finding that use of mnemonic devices by Chinese students was, in fact, a negative predictor of language proficiency. Future research could investigate the applicability, utility, and relative efficiency of the keyword mnemonic for students with varying L1, target FL, and proficiency levels.

Contextualized vocabulary inferencing strategies

Most contextualized vocabulary inferencing strategies are covered in the reading comprehension literature (see Chapter 9) and hence the discussion here is brief. (See Appendix 12 for studies on: reading with hypermedia annotations (Chun and Plass 1996); extensive reading (Horst 2005); computerized glosses (Hulstijn 1993); with explicit strategy instruction (Kern 1989); and with graded reader (Waring and Takaki 2003).)

Vocabulary acquired by inferring meanings from contextualized readings appears to be more meaningful and better remembered than decontextualized rote memorization due to:

1 the subconscious, natural acquisition of vocabulary as posited by Krashen (1989);
2 more distributed recognition, recall, and practice through repeated exposure to frequently used words (Nation 1990); and
3 multiple textual examples of new words with their proper grammatical use in their varied meanings in a broad semantic field with collocations and connotations (Oxford and Scarcella 1994; Lewis 2002). This provides a

natural way to learn prepositions and copula verbs which are learnt, even in L1, not as abstract entities, but as parts of meaningful phrases.

In its relative efficiency as a VLS, such inferred meanings tend to be better remembered than given meanings or decontextualized rote memorization (Hulstijn, Hollander, and Greidanus 1996), although as Nation (2001) indicates, such gains are relatively small compared to intentional vocabulary learning. Oxford and Scarcella (1994) argue that teaching contextualized or at least partially contextualized vocabulary (where words are associated with semantically similar or analogous words, images, or actions) is clearly superior to decontextualized approaches, which divorce words from meaningful context. The most efficient incidental vocabulary learning through reading seems to occur when incidental learning is coupled with intentional VLS. This occurs when contextualized strategies are induced through exercises which utilize the new vocabulary and make its meaning concrete and hence more readily memorable (Paribakht and Wesche 1997; Hunt and Beglar 2005; Folse 2006).

Dictionary and electronic look-up strategies

Dictionary use is essential in language learning and popular among L2 learners (Ahmed 1989; Gu and Johnson 1996; Li 1997; Schmitt 2000; Segler, Pain, and Sorace 2002; Fan 2003). However, looking up words using a dictionary is a complex skill which few learners truly master (Miller and Gildea 1985). Learners must judiciously select those words worth looking up, correctly utilize the dictionary to find the words, distill from the definition the relevant and worthwhile information, and then select the correct definition to complete the sentence, while considering the contextual and grammatical clues of the text (Scholfield 1982, 1999; Hartmann and James 1998). This requires that the learner be sufficiently proficient to understand the content of the entry and understand dictionary terminology and conventions to efficiently obtain the information (Tono 1991). However, many learners do not have the requisite knowledge and dictionary skills. For example, they may read and use only the first definition of an unknown polysemous word, such as the Japanese learners of English in Tono's (1984) study when doing a translation task, the Hebrew students in Neubach and Cohen's (1988) study while reading, or the students in Nuccorini's (1994) study when translating English into Italian.

Limited dictionary use

Most learners make limited use of their dictionaries. With immersion students, Harley and Hart (2000) found that both the 9th-grade and 11th-grade French students reported using the dictionary for finding word meanings and spellings, but only a small minority used the dictionary for proper usage of the word in context, and of these only a few of the more proficient students used the dictionary for pronunciation. By contrast, the overwhelming majority of older students who were the subjects of Fan's study (2000) reported that they used the dictionary to find the meaning of words, but also used the contextual meaning, the Chinese equivalent, or the English definition. However, here too, the least often looked-up information included collocations, pronunciation, frequency, and appropriateness, even though this information was perceived as useful. Moreover, the more students looked up the Chinese equivalents of words, the more they tended to ignore other kinds of dictionary information, including English definitions.

Problems of dictionary use in L2 comprehension and writing

To the best of our knowledge, little research has been conducted on the strategies used by learners when consulting a dictionary for the purpose of vocabulary growth. Indeed, what motivates learners to use the dictionary is when they need to understand the meaning of unknown words or find the appropriate word to express themselves especially when there are no time constraints in reading or writing. Accordingly, most research on dictionary use has focused on these two aspects.

Many researchers have looked at dictionary use and reading comprehension (for example, Bensoussan, Sim, and Weiss 1984; Neubach and Cohen 1988; Hulstijn 1993; Knight 1994; Atkins and Varantola 1997). Using verbal report and interview data, Neubach and Cohen (1988), reported that university students of various proficiency levels had problems understanding the correct part of speech and the definitions when using monolingual and bilingual dictionaries. Atkins and Varantola (1997) found in case studies that less able dictionary users often could not find the word or were frustrated by not being able to determine which of the alternative meanings given in the dictionary entry was the correct one, wasting too much time looking up every unknown word. By contrast, in Gu's (2003a) case study, one good learner concentrated on looking up commonly used words and phrases focusing on their proper usage in context. Using think-aloud protocols, Thumb (2004) used stimulated follow-up interviews and observation, noting that successful look-ups depend not only on the strategy used but also on the appropriateness of its use. However, using the correct look-up strategy for a given word still did not assure that the correct meaning of the word would be found and comprehended.

Problems in look-up strategies while writing were also noted (for example, Ard 1982; Nesi and Meara 1994; Nuccorini 1994; Atkins and Varantola 1997; Harvey and Yuill 1997). The adult non-native English speakers in Nesi and Meara's (1994) study were found to employ the 'kidrule' strategy, initially noted among L1 children (Mitchell 1983; Miller and Gildea 1985). That is to say, they used only part of the definition to substitute the target word for the selected word segment, thus producing ill-formed sentences. Computer analysis found that 56 per cent of all sentences written after consulting a definition were unacceptable and nearly a quarter of the errors were a result of the 'kidrule' strategy. Learners confused words that looked or sounded similar, failed to apply grammatical and lexical information, or rejected dictionary entry information which did not match their preconceived notions of what words meant. Harvey and Yuill (1997) had 211 EFL students use flowcharts to investigate why learners used dictionaries during essay writing. The following reasons were found for dictionary use: (1) to find the correct spelling (24 per cent), (2) to check on a meaning (18 per cent), (3) to look up the register (nine per cent), (4) collocations (eight per cent), or (5) inflected forms of the words (six per cent). Although students had problems with the length of the entry, they found the example sentences useful in getting information on meaning, grammar, and register but made little use of the grammatical coding scheme in the dictionary.

E-dictionary

Students using an e-dictionary as a macro-VLS do not seem to have any advantage over conventional dictionary users in either positive comprehension or incidental (vocabulary) learning other than speed, and hence efficiency. De Ridder (2002) confirmed the earlier findings of Roby (1991, 1999) and Aust, Kelley, and Roby (1993) by reporting that readers were significantly more willing to consult the gloss when reading a text with highlighted hyperlinks, noting that increased look-ups did not slow down their reading rate. Although L2 readers were more likely to look up words whose meaning could not be easily inferred from the context and which seemed crucial to understanding the text, neither comprehension nor incidentally learnt vocabulary increased (Hulstijn 1993). Similarly, Chun and Plass (1996) and Laufer and Hill (2000) found no significant relationship between the frequency of look-up and vocabulary retention. However, Chun and Plass (1996) noted that if pictures and definitions were provided by glosses, incidental learning with multimedia annotations yielded 25 per cent accuracy on production tests and 77 per cent on recognition tests. Similarly, Jones and Plass (2002) found that 'the students remembered word translation and recalled the passage better when they had selected both written and pictorial annotations while listening rather than one of these types or no annotations' (p. 546). But these studies did not ask learners how they decided to access and use the annotations, leaving us to speculate regarding how their choice to access translates into deliberate strategic behavior.

Proficiency and successful dictionary use

Successful and unsuccessful look-up macro-strategies may be related to the language proficiency of students (Neubach and Cohen 1988; Fan 2003; Thumb 2004). For example, Neubach and Cohen (1988) observed that high-proficiency students analyzed the word and sentence before looking it up and tended to find the correct grammatical form and definition for that particular context while less proficient students generally did not. In addition, lower proficiency students had problems with other words in the definition and generally did not find the dictionary useful. Gu's (1994) case study of two Chinese learners found that the more proficient student looked up fewer words because he was highly selective when choosing which words to look up and used the ancillary information such as pronunciation, examples, and usage more frequently than the less proficient student, and preferred to use a variety of contextual cues in order to guess the meaning of a problem word before looking it up. Similarly, the Hong Kong students in Fan's (2003) study considered the immediate use of newly learnt English words in authentic communication superior to a look-up strategy. Not all proficient learners used the dictionary with the same rationale, success, or regularity. For example, Neubach and Cohen (1988) reported that some students used the dictionary less, simply because it was too time-consuming relative to the benefit they felt they derived.

Learner voice and dictionary strategies

The reviewed studies on dictionary use provide insight into the broad macro-strategies of 'dictionary use' or 'gloss look-up' but do not provide insight into learner-specific VLS clusters. We have little insight into these micro-VLS (i.e. specific strategies utilizing the macro-strategy of dictionary look-up) due to the studies' limited use of student voice. Nevertheless, even without learner voice, the superiority of student performance when learners use glosses or the dictionary as a tool is clear. However, the micro- or sub-strategies deployed within that macro-strategy and complementary strategies such as repetition, substitution, and rereading remain unknown unless learner voice is elicited. More evidence is needed to show whether learners use the sub-strategies flexibly and in task-appropriate ways. Moreover, we need evidence of decision-making processes demonstrating volition in making VLS choices. Evidence from less successful VLS learners shows that many choose to try to remember a word only if they think it is important and ignore the rest. Furthermore, dictionary VLS may only be as effective as the consolidation strategies with which they are teamed. VLS research has not begun to scratch the surface of complementary or support strategy chains or clusters which function as learning catalysts, enabling a VLS combination to be much more effective than when strategies are used on their own.

Strategy instruction studies

Research in VLS ranges from experimental (controlled) studies concentrating on one variable to more student-oriented studies which tend to be more descriptive, involving teaching and geared toward eliciting student voice.

This chapter does not consider the teaching of VLS based on classroom experience. (For reviews, see Lewis 1993, 1997, 2000; Oxford and Scarcella 1994; Nation 2001; Segler, Pain, and Sorace 2002; Thornbury 2002; Hasbún 2005.) It restricts itself rather to studies of learners of the target FL or SL using student voice. In the studies reviewed, we note that the degree to which strategies were instructed can be categorized by (1) explicitness of instruction, (2) length of time of instruction, and (3) provision of practice during the study. Later we discuss three forms of intervention found.

Explicitness of instruction

The strategy instruction studies in this review (also see Chapter 7) can be located on a continuum with the low end representing only general discussion of VLS to the high end with actual demonstrations and practice. Some strategy instruction is limited to a general discussion advocating that learners choose their own VLS. These assume that learner- or task-compatible VLS will emerge during the learning process. (See Cohen and Aphek 1980; Gallo-Crail and Zerwekh 2002.)

More explicit than the general discussion is task-induced instruction, referred to by Oxford, Crookall, Cohen, Lavine, Nyikos, and Sutter (1990) as covert and by Chamot and O'Malley (1994a) as embedded. This assumes that specific vocabulary-focused tasks will give rise to task-appropriate VLS—that doing vocabulary embedded reading exercises, for example, will automatically translate into skillful, metacognitive approaches to building VLS. On the high end of the continuum of instructional explicitness is the modeling or explaining referred to by Oxford *et al.* (1990) as overt and by Chamot and O'Malley (1994a) as direct instruction. Here concrete VLS examples are explained step-by-step perhaps demonstrating with simultaneous think-aloud and/or discussing metacognitive VLS that monitor and guide learners, as seen in Fraser (1999).

Length of instructional time

These levels of explicitness in strategy instruction vary and depend on length of time during which they are carried out. Most studies agree that both vocabulary learning and strategies used tend to increase in effectiveness with time and spaced repetition, especially among less proficient learners (Schmitt 2000; Wesche and Paribakht 2000).

Provision of practice during the study

The amount of classroom practice provided with a VLS can range from (a) none or briefly trying it out without feedback to (b) trying out and discussing the VLS, taking what is understood in principle and learning how to apply it first hand, and finally to (c) sustained practice using the VLS to make it routine and transferable to varying situations.

The probability that a VLS can be taught successfully increases (a) the more the instruction is explicit, lengthy, and provides for practice with feedback, and (b) the more conscious the steps that students take to internalize and adopt the VLS. Even if students adopt a provided VLS as a strategy of last resort, as is often the case with the keyword mnemonic, they may switch to it when a preferred VLS proves inadequate. Results indicate that VLS instruction has some long-term positive effect even if it only raises consciousness of a person's own VLS. Instruction varies in its degrees of explicitness, length, and type of practice and also in the form (content) of the instruction in terms of metacognitive, applied specific VLS, or task-induced VLS to which we turn next.

Our review found three distinctive forms of intervention represented in VLS strategy instructional studies: (1) raising learners' metacognitive awareness, (2) teacher-led VLS instruction, usually accompanied by metacognitive instruction (Kern 1989; Holmes and Ramos 1993), and (3) task-induced VLS studies (student finds or activates own VLS based on skills and procedures required to complete assignment). Most actual studies span these categories. For example, Rasekh and Ranjbary (2003) and Zaki and Ellis (1999) cover both 1 and 3 and Fraser (1999) addresses all three categories. These categories overlap in the illustrative studies reviewed below.

Metacognitive awareness studies

Several studies have found that metacognitive instruction has a significant positive effect on vocabulary acquisition. Hosenfeld's (1984) study which aimed at improving reading comprehension through teaching metacognitive strategies, indirectly succeeded in increasing vocabulary learning and retention. Zaki and Ellis (1999) demonstrated metacognitive strategies and self-questioning techniques and then had students practice in four 50-minute sessions. This instruction resulted in significantly higher comprehension and incidental vocabulary acquisition than the control group. Similarly, Rasekh and Ranjbary (2003) instructed 53 Iranian students on metacognitive strategies such as self-evaluation and self-questioning for dealing with unknown words in context. Learning logs and ongoing checklists kept by students reported their strategy applications and were further buttressed by debriefing discussions and open-ended questionnaires in which students expressed their opinions about the usefulness of particular strategies. The ten weeks of instruction based on the Cognitive Academic Language Learning Approach (CALLA) of Chamot and O'Malley (1994b) included the five steps of preparation, presentation, practice, evaluation, and expansion of VLS instruction. The test group demonstrated significantly greater vocabulary gains than the control group.

Similarly positive results were found by Fraser (1999) who provided high- and low-proficiency students with metacognitive strategy instruction for the duration of a course in which she gave instruction on a range of lexical processing strategies (ignore, consult dictionary, infer) consisting of an explicit presentation of the strategies, guided practice (teacher to student modeling and outside class practice) coupled with discussion of the trial application to bring about strategy adoption. Extended vocabulary practice activities applied to reading were coupled with periodic review. Through reading alone, 28 per cent of vocabulary was retained. When participants consulted dictionaries 30 per cent was retained, when they inferred meaning 31 per cent was retained, and when they used the two strategies together their recall increased to 50 per cent.

Teacher-led VLS studies

A second group of studies have focused on specific VLS as opposed to the more generally applicable metacognitive strategies covered above. In two experimental studies, university students were taught morphological patterns. Kern (1989) explicitly taught morphology including cognates, prefixes, suffixes, and orthographic cues. Follow-up exercises in determining word meaning based on such cues were assigned for homework. Findings indicated that strategy instruction had a positive but statistically non-significant effect on subjects' ability to infer the meanings of unfamiliar words from context, with some evidence that low ability readers derived greater benefit from the treatment than did middle and high ability readers. This may indicate that less proficient students would benefit most from VLS training (Kern 1989; Brown and Perry 1991).

Further supporting evidence for the effectiveness of specific VLS training with cognates comes from Holmes and Ramos (1993) who instructed 15 postgraduate students to monitor their initial guesses of cognate meanings while reading. Students practiced identifying cognates and were encouraged to check on their initial inferences through discussion with their peers, hence encouraging social strategies. Almost all cognates were recognized successfully, and few misrecognitions could be found when comparing the reading text with summaries written by students.

Task-induced VLS studies

The final group of studies examined task-induced instruction which relies on learners' discovery of appropriate VLS during assigned exercises under conducive conditions. According to Donato and McCormick (1994), strategies are the 'byproduct' of socioculturally inclusive teaching methods and tasks. Laufer and many SLA researchers hypothesize that it is the nature of the materials and task, not the strategic approach taken by the vocabulary learner that brings about effective learning. To a lesser extent, the research that utilizes and capitalizes on the availability of learning resources such as graded texts, annotations, glosses, and electronic dictionaries posits that these tools may trigger or induce VLS that would otherwise not have come into being.

Two studies which attempted to determine the relative effectiveness of metacognitive instruction coupled with strategy-inducing practice exercises compared to task-induced strategy instruction alone were done by Paribakht and Wesche (1997) and Wesche and Paribakht (2000) using think-aloud methodology. In the first study, the experimental group was instructed in five metacognitive strategies and had to complete vocabulary activities which required them to use selective attention, recognition, manipulation, interpretation, and production while the control group received no instruction and was only required to answer comprehension questions after the readings. The experimental group was able to use many words productively while the control group's new vocabulary knowledge remained at the recognition level. In the second study, Wesche and Paribakht (2000) omitted the strategy instruction and ascertained that readings and associated vocabulary activities alone were sufficient to induce appropriate strategy use and improve vocabulary retention. It would be valuable for studies to examine which VLS can be effectively task-induced and which need explicit instruction.

Future research on strategy instruction

Future research should address several current shortcomings in many of the reviewed studies including problems with methodology, validity, reliability, and the need for studies on underserved populations and topics. During our present review, we repeatedly noted studies which did not sufficiently account for the variety of learning preferences of participants, their characteristics, proficiency levels, learning environments or settings, nature of tasks and materials studied, vocabulary knowledge level of participants before and after instruction, nature and length of instruction and how these variables were measured. For example, future VLS studies should distinguish levels of word knowledge (between word recognition, comprehension, and communicatively competent production). Moreover, previous intervention studies lacked learner voice and did not provide equal instructional time. As a result of these limitations, it might be possible to attribute differences in results between experimental and control groups to greater focus on the task rather than to the utilization of the instructed strategy.

Another major problem is that our current knowledge of VLS development is based on the learning and VLS preferences of students at different proficiencies rather than longitudinal studies of individuals. In the reviewed studies, results seem to indicate that learners have shifting preferences for vocabulary learning strategies depending on environment and increasing proficiency. Kojic-Sabo and Lightbown (1999) found that students in an L2 environment preferred using the resources of that environment such as seeking out and talking to native speakers in the L2. Such shifts in VLS and learning preferences must be documented through longitudinal studies tracking specific individuals through changing environments (FL, ESP, and EAP in classroom context, and L2 in the second language environment) that demand different types of vocabulary learning and use. Researchers such as Gu (2003b) and Fan (2003) found that the language and the communicative opportunities in the L2 environment tend to be taken advantage of by learners, thereby shifting VLS away from book learning and rote memorization. In the FL environment, VLS tend to shift to L1 vocabulary acquisition strategies, acquiring vocabulary from written or spoken context rather than through repetition, association, or mnemonic devices. Students prefer learning texts and exercises which are relevant to their academic, professional, or daily communicative needs, and prefer to consult informants, glosses, or bilingual dictionaries rather than traditional dictionaries. Each of these learner preferences is linked to evidence that indicates that more proficient students tend to use these strategies. Further research is needed to determine if and at what proficiency level these are indeed preferred VLS.

The same methodological difficulty involved in conducting longitudinal studies also explains the lack of research on listening and writing. Most of the studies on VLS have focused on the comprehension of vocabulary (passive or receptive knowledge), while the production of vocabulary (acquisition and integration of newly learnt words into active vocabulary) has been relatively neglected. Studies have stressed memorization strategies and the inferencing strategies relative to how learners use text types and exercises, and how they use semantically based strategies in the learning and actual use of vocabulary. Vocabulary acquisition and consolidation have been too often considered solitary activities, whereas the role of social strategies and group-work has been relatively neglected. Listening for spoken vocabulary in oral text presents confounding challenges as seen in Vandergrift's (2006) study with ESL students who found that the need to understand the message overwhelmed their ability to concentrate on the targeted vocabulary. This problem is not great enough to exclude incidental vocabulary learning during listening to graded texts or oral communication with more proficient learners (Kelly 1992; Jones and Plass 2002; Vidal 2003).

The relative lack of methodological models for research also explains the paucity of attention to VLS during multitasking, or integrated VLS such as note-taking. Methodologies need to be worked out for effectively examining VLS used during multitasking and distributed practice where vocabulary learning is combined with physical activities during rehearsal and consolidation. With younger generations growing increasingly adept at multitasking and electronic access, researchers should investigate when and how students practice vocabulary. Computer tracking of multitasking, including vocabulary look-up behavior is an obvious, unobtrusive means of obtaining large volumes of readily analyzable data. Attention should also be given to how learners integrate note-taking and underlining/highlighting strategies into their VLS repertoire during reading or listening to assist with other VLS such as morphological or semantically based strategies in the learning and using of vocabulary.

Crucially, there is a need to broaden research beyond the traditional intermediate and advanced level university students and include younger and underserved language learners as well as those with learning disabilities to see how VLS can assist them. If we consider the various populations of language learners of different ages, cultures, and environments, then the vast majority of them have been largely overlooked by researchers.

The two strands of (a) controlled intervention (which tends to focus not on students but on the way materials and contexts drive VLS application), and (b) pedagogical or teaching-based studies (which tend to address instructional activates that promote VLS use) need to come together to create more innovative research designs which vary one factor between two groups receiving otherwise identical VLS instruction and also use learner voice to increase validity. Future research would be more productive if greater collaboration could occur among SLA, other fields of applied linguistics, language education, and learners themselves to create a richer, more accurate, and pedagogically useful understanding of VLS.

Learner voice must play a stronger complementary role in theoretical, methodological, experimental, conceptual, and catagorizational works reviewed. We can learn much from our SLA research base but more from learners of all ages and stages who, in collaborative dialogue with researchers and teachers can help us better understand the nature and strategic approaches to vocabulary learning, retention, and use. It is a vital reality check for researchers to maintain continuous feedback and to document their subjects' perceptions without which it is easy to stray into speculation and conjecture having more to do with researcher's postulations than the learner's reality. Learner voice is also the avenue to insight into the individual learner's cognitive processes, beliefs, perceptions, priorities, and values. We are in the infancy of using learner voice and discovering the learner strategy clusters which are most effective for various learning tasks.

Conclusions and pedagogical implications

Various researchers have tackled the VLS pedagogical application question, including Laufer and Shmueli (1997), Kost, Foss, and Lenzini (1999), Morin and Goebel (2001), Kitajima (2001), Harley and Hart (2000), Marefat (2003), Ma (2004), and Nation (2005). Scholars have increasingly realized that mastery of vocabulary is a complex multidimensional task in which students greatly benefit from the instruction of VLS (Oxford and Scarcella 1994). Since much vocabulary learning must by necessity be done individually, it is all the more imperative that we scrutinize the research findings for productive VLS-supported teaching. The Latin saying *repetitio est mater studiorum* is supported in this research review. Spaced repetition of vocabulary, occurring either through multiple exposures during reading or listening (serving as a type of repetition) or through explicit teaching, must additionally receive overt learner attention through simultaneous or follow-up vocabulary tasks supported by strategy instruction (Laufer 2003; Folse 2006). In the same vein as repetition, multiple exposures to new vocabulary words coupled with production via repetition in fill-in-the-blank or computer-assisted language learning exercises are a more efficient and effective means of learning vocabulary than spending the same amount of time on the presumably deeper processing exercises such as using the new words in original sentences (Folse 2006). While Laufer (2003) specifies that particular exercise types promote vocabulary learning, Folse underscores the need for focused simultaneous or subsequent attention-related strategies in learning vocabulary.

The evidence in this review indicates that instruction in metacognitive self-regulatory strategies allows students to better monitor their use of guessing, inferencing, repetition, and focused attention strategies, significantly improving general student performance and vocabulary acquisition. Such VLS instruction especially benefits weaker, less proficient learners and is most effective when integrated into the teaching of the entire course. Effectiveness at all proficiency levels is further improved if exercises are provided to apply the taught strategies and practice time is provided in class.

Pedagogically, the main lessons of research are: (1) that integration of VLS into instruction appears to be more effective than non-integration, (2) that significantly better vocabulary performance is possible with VLS instruction, and (3) that combination of metacognitive and specific VLS seems to work better than either in isolation. In combination with our other research findings, this indicates that instructors should (1) order the teaching of VLS according to the level of skill and ability of students to use those VLS, (2) demonstrate the VLS through modeling, (3) reinforce the VLS with in-class practice sessions providing opportunities for clarification, and (4) motivate students with genuinely communicative, relevant, and interesting material. In short, VLS instruction should be integrated throughout a course as a crucial pedagogical component in course materials which are sensitive to the learner's needs.

Acknowledgements

The first author is deeply grateful for the steadfast assistance of graduate students, Snea Thinsan and Deahyeon Nam, who spent countless hours on the Internet retrieving references and organizing data. Additionally, we would like to thank the reviewers and editors for their supportive feedback and guidance.

Conclusions
LLS and the future: resolving the issues

ANDREW D. COHEN
and ERNESTO MACARO

LLS and the future

The purpose of this volume was to bring together some of the world's leading experts on language learner strategies and to have them work collaboratively to 'push the envelope' on just what language learner strategies are and where the field is in relation to them. There was method in our madness in that, instead of just talking about how international scholars need to collaborate, we felt it imperative to demonstrate what we actually meant by this.

In our Editors' Introduction, therefore, we made claims as to the innovative nature of this edited volume. These claims were based on two fundamental re-conceptualizations of what an edited book might offer the reader:

1 It should provide a reappraisal of what it is to be a part of and contribute to a community of intellectual inquiry.
2 It should promote the view that the body of knowledge and understanding that such a community produces is best served by introspection and auto-critique rather than by a parochial protectionism of its outputs and values.

It is under these two broad conceptualizations that this concluding chapter seeks to examine whether the issues, posited both by non-participant critics to the field of language learner strategies *and* by its self-reflecting participants, have been resolved. Where they have not been resolved we try to summarize the possible ways forward—in effect proposing a future research agenda.

LLS as a community of research practice

What should a community of researchers working in the LLS field look like and what should be its operating principles?

One of the anonymous reviewers to our proposal for this book argued that authors working in the LLS field belonged to 'a strategies club'. We would respectfully disagree. Whilst it is true that a dozen or so authors have featured prominently in the 30 years of research literature on LLS, and some have often worked together, there have been many more authors, publishing in books and journals of all kinds, that have been less central to the theoretical and empirical developments but who have made no less of a contribution. Both parts of this book, but particularly Part Two, attest to the wealth of research that can be broadly grouped under the LLS umbrella. Many of these researchers have been doctoral students who were drawn to the research area by the importance of its aspirations and the practical nature of its application in their own contexts, not by a desire to belong to a club.

So, is this relationship between a more central community and a broader one beneficial? We believe that it is, whilst remaining fully cognizant of the problems that the relationship poses. On the one hand the loose-knit relationship favors investigations into the huge diversity of L2 learning environments. On the other, it is an amorphous body often incapable of building its empirical efforts on the basis of a single theoretical framework. As Manchón, Roca de Larios, and Murphy argue in Chapter 11, and not working towards a common agenda on the basis of a common conceptualization of the unit of analysis, as elaborated on by Grenfell and Macaro in Chapter 1. The gap between the theoretical principles discussed in Chapters 3 and 5, and the trustworthiness of some of the empirical evidence reviewed in Part Two of this book, bears witness to this problem. Yet to try to subdue the enthusiasm of a broader community of enquiry would be to starve the LLS field of the vitality and diversity that many authors in this book argue that it needs.

Let us pursue this argument further. It is not merely a question of 'not subduing' the enthusiasm of a wider community, but also one of not fearing to go beyond the immediate boundaries of the research area. For example, to nurture this fear would lead us to deny the importance of connecting a psycholinguistic framework with a sociocultural one, an aspiration that is alluded to in many parts of this book but particularly in Chapters 3, 4, 5, and 11. Moreover, as we have seen from Oxford and Lee (Chapter 6), there is a yawning gap in the LLS literature with regard to morpho-syntax related strategy use. The authors of that chapter clearly benefited from making links with research in implicit and explicit learning, and with notions of saliency; their exploration of research on inferencing in reading and their discussion of depth of processing of vocabulary has led to proposals for fruitful avenues for research, something they have in common with Nyikos and Fan. Similarly, there are many avenues to pursue in the association between meaning negotiation research and oral communication strategies. As Nakatani and Goh discovered, meaning negotiation studies have observed strategic behavior but rarely have they elicited and compared the cognitive and metacognitive strategies that learners deploy while negotiating meaning. Lastly, Oxford and Schramm have proposed radical rethinking of research into language aptitude by arguing for a dynamic conceptualization of aptitude based on the possibility of strategic development.

All these expeditions outside the field of LLS raise the issue of closer collaboration within the community of SLA researchers. This is not an easy undertaking. We, as Editors, have understood that many of the chapters in this volume were a challenge for the co-authors to write together since the task sometimes forced them to stretch beyond their comfort zone, given both conceptual and spatial divides between some of the participants in this project. Yet, it is precisely this going beyond familiar boundaries that has produced the more challenging ideas.

So, have we now identified the extent of the LLS research community? That is to say, an inner core of regular contributors, an outer core of strategy related investigators, and then links made between LLS researchers and those in other domains? We believe not. A pivotal contribution to this book is the one by Rubin, Chamot, Harris, and Anderson, which deals with interventions in LLS. In that chapter, the authors quite rightly remind us of the need to place teachers and learners at the center of a research community whose interest is strategic behavior in language learning. It is, after all, a major claim of LLS research (see Grenfell and Macaro, Chapter 1) that it is able to span the divide between theory and practice. It is teachers in consultation with their learners who will make the decision to dedicate valuable time to strategy instruction. Teachers, we are reminded, are those best placed to convince their students that LLS can solve their language learning problems. Indeed, our experience in teacher education also suggests that it is experienced teachers who are most capable of convincing novice practitioners of the value of learning to learn as well as the value of teaching the language.

The relationship between researchers and practitioners needs to be strengthened. This is not something new. It has been a leitmotif of many of the more enlightened SLA researchers for decades. There are two possible reasons why the relationship has not always flourished. The first is that action research appears to have been frowned upon by some members of the applied linguistics research community. Yet, paradoxically, many have also argued for increasing contextualization of studies. White, Schramm, and Chamot, in this volume, have quite rightly called for action research to be re-evaluated in the light of past deficiencies and this must be so if we are to meet the methodological challenges the authors delineate.

The second reason is that the way that research findings in the past have been 'handed down' by researchers and policy makers (or 'absorbed' by practitioners) has not always led to improved learning. Such findings have become unchallenged assumptions as Macaro, Graham, and Vanderplank conclude in the case of top-down processes in listening comprehension (Chapter 8), and Manchón, Roca de Larios, and Murphy (Chapter 11) conclude with regard to the role of first language in L2 composition. Many of these assumptions, some of us would argue, could have been avoided with greater rigor and restraint applied both to the conclusions drawn by authors of individual studies and the reviews of research presented by others periodically. In that sense, the approach adopted throughout the chapters of

Part Two of this book, one of systematic reviewing, is an approach aimed at minimizing the single reviewer bias. In that sense, Part Two has contributed to attempting to serve better the wider LLS community.

In sum, the community of LLS researchers and practitioners has been subject to the same centripetal and centrifugal forces experienced by any loose-knit community—on the one hand trying to strive for coherence and continuity, and on the other wishing to encourage inclusion and diversity. However, perhaps the time has now arrived when certain principles need to be established and parameters drawn with regard to LLS research and practice. These principles and parameters (if the reader will excuse the allusion) pertain to the central dilemmas that have bedeviled researchers in the field and opened the door to external criticism—the construct of a strategy itself, and its relationship with successful learning. It is to these dilemmas that we now turn.

The unit of analysis and its relationship to learning success

There are three fundamental issues that many authors in this book have sought to grapple with, both for themselves and in response to critiques of the field made by others.

The first is what is the unit of analysis in LLS research? What is, in effect, a strategy? That this question is still being asked after more than 30 years may come as a surprise to you. But the fact is that constructs such as aptitude, motivation, and proficiency have all undergone or are undergoing major reappraisals. And with regard to the construct of 'strategy', as Cohen first documents in Chapter 2 and Manchón, Roca de Larios, and Murphy confirm in Chapter 11, there is a split in the LLS community between those who see a strategy in large terms, as general patterns of behavior combining mental, physical, and social activity, and those who see it in small and specific terms, purely as cognitive and metacognitive behavior. The former appear to justify the macro approach for reasons of expediency related to educational practice, because of relationships within sociocultural contexts, and because of the danger of fragmentation. The latter justify their micro approach by arguing that small strategies form part of clusters or combinations and that the whole becomes greater than the sum of the parts through the role of metacognition—that it is metacognition which orchestrates the parts and makes the combination effective.

There is general agreement that 'strategies' are environment-dependent (Chapters 3, 4, 5, 10, 11) and/or task dependent (Chapters 8, 10). There is also general agreement that future research should base itself on task-specific situations or have skill-specific concerns. (See many of the chapters in Part Two and also below for further discussion.) Where the two camps appear to differ is that the macro approach regards the 'large strategy' as intrinsically and qualitatively shaped by the environment or the task; the micro approach regards the 'small strategies' as essentially the same 'tools' that we have available in any environment or task, but that learners deploy them differently to task or environmental demands, due to background characteristics, lack of awareness, lack of experience, or lack of effort. It is possible that this split could be resolved in the future by adopting a 'small strategy within a larger framework' conceptualization, as Macaro (2006) has recently proposed. Here strategies are conceived as occurring in working memory, are described (but not defined) through their action, goals, and situations at *the lowest practical level*, but are then related to a broader framework of 'strategic plans', 'second language processes', and 'second language skills'.

If the above conceptualization is not adopted, and the two approaches remain irreconcilable, then it is at the very least incumbent on future researchers to state quite clearly, in their accounts, which theoretical interpretation of the unit of analysis they are adopting. Moreover, if new names to strategies are to be coined, there should be a clear statement as to why there is a need for this (as Manchón, Roca de Larios, and Murphy argue in Chapter 11)—and why the plethora of taxonomies should be increased.

The second fundamental issue is how we should be dealing with our unit of analysis. For too long it would appear that the field of language learner strategies has relied largely on 'frequency of reported strategy use' as its benchmark for determining whether strategies are used and even to intuit as to how they are used. We now know that we must collect more data on the *quality* of strategy use. We need to better understand a variety of strategy-related issues such as:

1 the nature of the strategy retrieval process (for example, ease or difficulty in remembering and retrieving the strategy from the learner's strategy repertoire);
2 the role that the teacher may play in learners' strategy use (for example, what 'providing the right amount of scaffolding' actually means);
3 the role that strategy instruction may play in learners' strategy use (for example, the extent to which given learners perceive it as relevant to the tasks at hand);
4 what learners know about how to use the strategies for the given task;
5 the influence of the particular speech community (or community of practice) on the nature of the learners' metacognitive, cognitive, affective, and social strategy use;
6 the actual way in which learners use metacognitive, cognitive, affective, and social strategies on the task at hand (according to individual, group, cultural, and developmental differences);
7 the results from using these strategies individually on that task;
8 the results from using strategies in a chain (for example, in looking up a word in a dictionary or summarizing a text) or in a cluster (for example, using both metacognitive, cognitive, affective, and social strategies to break into an L2 conversation between two acquaintances);
9 the relationship between the particular way the strategies are used by given learners and their success at given language tasks;

10 the relationship between the use of the strategies and the style preferences of the learner.

A real advantage of doing this kind of close-order analysis of strategies in use is that it can help to clarify the extent to which particular strategies, strategy chains, and strategy clusters have a mental component, a goal, an action, a metacognitive component, and a potential use that leads to learning. Such research will also help to clarify the advantages and disadvantages of fine-tuning our strategy descriptions.

The third fundamental issue is a strategy's (or combination of strategies') relationship with 'achievement', 'success', 'expertise', and 'proficiency'. And there we have the problem in nutshell! As the authors of Chapters 1, 8, 10, and 11 argue, researchers have been remarkably unclear about what they mean by these four terms. It would be helpful, in future, if LLS researchers limited themselves to the standard definition of 'proficiency' which is the level an individual has achieved in one or more language skills (and specifying *which* skills), against a recognized set of criteria, regardless of age, exposure to the language, and teaching environment. If they want to use the term 'success' then this, we recommend, should be against a specific task—'some learners were more successful at this task than others'. 'Expertise' then, might more usefully be a measure of the type of learner being studied, particularly in relation to the uses they put their first language to. For example, academic postgraduates would have more expertise at writing in their first language than students who are skilled mechanics but studying an L2 for the purpose of traveling or living abroad. 'Achievement' should be, in our view, a measure of success, not against set criteria, but against that of peers—i.e. the variation in *rate of progress* that one would expect among a group of learners after *equal* exposure to the L2 in the same learning environment.

Once these measures become standard in the literature, there will be a need to control for confounding variables when exploring the relationship between strategy use and proficiency in a skill, or strategy use and success at a task, or strategy use and the expertise of the participant, or strategy use and rate of progress.

Controlling for these variables will help us more clearly to isolate the key independent variable(s)' impact on the dependent variable(s). The most obvious confounding variable is the level of linguistic knowledge (as Macaro, Graham, and Vanderplank argue in Chapter 8) which may be having a huge impact on strategic behavior. But there are others: the first language of the learners in reading and writing (see Chapter 9 by Erler and Finkbeiner, and Chapter 11 by Manchón, Roca de Larios, and Murphy), or initial levels of motivation (Chapter 3 by Oxford and Schramm). Only by researchers controlling for confounding variables, and by using more sophisticated methods of analysis (see Chapters 5 and 9) can we move beyond evidence of correlation between strategy use and success (or proficiency, or achievement) towards a causal representation. That causal representation may be unidirectional. For example: whether effective strategy use leads to success at a task regardless of variability in linguistic knowledge; whether lower linguistic knowledge excludes the possibility of certain strategies being deployed. Or, it may be that we discover that the causal representation is bidirectional, that it is impossible to straighten the chain of causation—that it is in fact circular. In any event, LLS research must move towards establishing causation rather than remaining at the level of correlation. A number of examples of this hopeful trend have been documented in this book (for example, that of Erler and Finkbeiner) by using emerging and more sophisticated statistical procedures.

In order to unpack the above constructs we have to refine further our research methods for strategy elicitation (as argued in Chapters 5 and 10). It is the consensus of the authors in this book (as reported by Cohen in Chapter 2) that strategies are, *at least at some point*, conscious, and therefore accessible. However, it is generally agreed that accessing them poses a number of challenges. It is also generally agreed that all the trends in LLS research point to elicitation via task-based scenarios. In such scenarios a number of measures of validity and reliability need to be explored further as different task-types can lead to the elicitation of different strategic behaviors.

White, Schramm, and Chamot have come out in favor of 'training' respondents to verbalize rather than not training them, using prompts rather than not using them, and giving respondents the choice of language in which to report their strategic behavior rather than imposing a single language. Yet the authors themselves (as others do—see Macaro, Graham, and Vanderplank) acknowledge that there are disadvantages to each of these methodological decisions—but believe that, on balance, orientation in how to provide verbal report, prompting, and allowing choice of language are the more valid research techniques. We would argue, as indeed they do, that further methodological research is needed to reassure us that this is the correct path.

The same authors also warn of the dangers of mis-analyzing transcripts because the transcripts themselves have not been prepared in a sufficiently fine-grained manner. Hopefully, researchers will take heed of White, Schramm, and Chamot's (Chapter 5) critical analysis of elicitation and transcription issues in the use of verbal report and will accept their invitation to engage in (a) careful orientation, practice, and prompting, (b) multiple language use, and especially (c) the integration of think-alouds into an authentic action context. Their chapter also raises the issue of how our research paradigms may need to shift in order to conduct strategy research in relatively new contexts such as that of online learning and of heritage language use. This is linked to the notion of institutional or situational or cultural differences as described by Takeuchi, Griffiths, and Coyle in Chapter 4. Contextualizing the analysis of a transcript is essential when one thinks of the number of cultural differences which might impact on the nature of the think-aloud discourse. To this end, LLS researchers need once again to look to other domains, within applied linguistics, for guidance and rigor (in this case conversation or discourse analysis).

We also know that there are numerous other concerns regarding data collection of this sort. For example, to what extent will the learner's report of strategy use vary according to the task? To what extent might this report vary on the same task from moment to moment? This is an even more taxing issue since it calls into question the reliability of the measure.

An agenda for further research

Having established future goals for conceptual, theoretical, and methodological rigor, the LLS research community can turn to the areas where more research is needed in terms of strategies for language learning and for language use.

Clearly Part Two of this book has established an imbalance of research effort among the four language skills. Despite the authors' criticism with regard to quality of research, Chapter 11 documents a huge array of studies on writing processes. Similarly Erler and Finkbeiner, in Chapter 9, had to impose very stringent exclusion criteria in order to make the task of reviewing studies on reading strategies practicable, such is the volume of literature available. Yet, both sets of authors call for more specific research. In writing (as indeed many other aspects of SLA, including vocabulary, see Nyikos and Fan's Chapter 12) there is a need to look at the progress that beginner and particularly younger learners make in the composing process. In reading there is a need to look at cross-language factors that may impact on L2 reading success or proficiency. It is probably no coincidence that the two literacy skills have generated their own specific journals but, to our knowledge, speaking and listening have not. In speaking, Nakatani and Goh conclude in Chapter 10 that the number of studies dealing with the relationship between strategy use and oral proficiency remains small and clearly here there is an important research agenda.

Many of the authors in Part Two call for much more research into the effectiveness of interventions with a specific focus on which are the best types of intervention programs, or which are the most important strategies to focus on. Indeed, most authors in Part Two recognize that there is still a need to provide convincing evidence that strategy instruction should be an essential component of L2 learning curricula. It is strange that after nearly three decades of working with a concept of communicative competence that includes 'strategic competence' (see Grenfell and Macaro, Chapter 1), the essential requirement of strategy instruction should still be in doubt. We need to remove those doubts, and to reaffirm that, in L2, communicative competence arises from (relatively limited) linguistic knowledge plus the ability to deploy that knowledge in sociocultural contexts. To reaffirm this position, we need more and different intervention studies. Particularly, authors of Part Two have identified a dearth of longitudinal studies which map the changes in strategic behavior over time. They have also called for clearer and more detailed reporting of interventions, so that these can be replicated not only by other researchers but by teachers themselves.

Part Two has also demonstrated, as alluded to above, that there exists an almost total absence of research on the acquisition of the L2 rule system and the part that strategic behavior plays in this. This is so much the case that while we had originally intended to put Chapter 6 in Part Two as a systematic review of research on grammar strategies, we were unable to do so. We are baffled by the lack of research in this area. It is possible that the need has been partly met by studies in writing where the focus has been on editing strategies and studies on monitoring strategies in speaking where, in both, some element of explicit knowledge of the rule system would come into play. We would argue, however, that this area of research merits investigation in its own right in a way similar to the acquisition of vocabulary, as demonstrated by Nyikos and Fan in Chapter 12.

To summarize our conclusions about resolving the issues and proposing a future research agenda for language learner strategies:

1 The LLS research community should remain an inclusive one, encouraging both central and peripheral players in the research effort.
2 The community should explore links with other research areas and other theoretical frameworks in order to foster greater understanding and arrive at more informed synthesis.
3 The community should hold on to its valuable principle of serving a wider community of teachers and learners and, indeed, should strive to involve these in the research effort wherever possible.
4 In order for unsubstantiated pendulum swings in teaching methods not to occur, the community should encourage the practice of systematic reviewing of research evidence.
5 It is unlikely that complete consensus will ever be reached on the unit of analysis (a strategy) even though we should continue to strive for such a consensus and towards a definitive model of a strategy within a cognitive framework. In the absence of a consensus, researchers should state clearly the theoretical framework on which they are basing their research and why there might be a need to use different terminology rather than building on established terminology.
6 The trend towards task-based research (with task interpreted in its broadest sense) should be encouraged as it appears to be a more fruitful trend than a more general-learning approach.
7 Researchers should clearly identify their dependent and independent variables, particularly making clear what their measures of success, achievement, experience, or proficiency are. We recommend, in any case, that these are used as separate terms. Only in this way can we gain insights not only into *what* learners do but into *why* they do it.

8 We have come a long way in establishing principles for strategy elicitation in (mainly) qualitative research. However, there is still work to be done in validating these principles. Greater rigor should also be applied to the analysis stage. We have also come some way in establishing skill-specific questionnaires and these should be continually scrutinized for validity in different contexts.

9 More research is needed particularly in listening, in speaking, and in the acquisition of the L2 rule system. However, some further research in specific areas of reading and writing is also needed.

10 Given that the fundamental mission of strategy research is to improve the learning of all our learners, there is still much work to be done on strategy instruction in order to prove to learners, teachers, and the wider SLA research community that such an undertaking in the classroom is worthwhile.

The ultimate goal of any language instruction program is not only to teach the L2 for the moment, but to instill within the learner a sense of what it is like to be a lifelong language learner. We are increasingly living in a global world where communicative skills, in more than one language, can be not just an added bonus but rather a true necessity. Hence, having our language learners more skilled at using their strategy repertoire—whether at the elementary, secondary, tertiary, or graduate level—can ideally have both a short-term and a long-term impact. While the potential role that enhanced language learner strategies can have in this endeavor is great, it remains to be seen how effective the field is in harnessing that potential.

There are lots of ways to conclude a book. Probably the most valuable one for the language learner strategy field is to issue a call to action. If we have accomplished something by this book's endeavor, it has been to call attention to where we have been, to take stock of where we are, and to give suggested directions for where the field needs to go. We would envision this book more as an opening than as a point of closure and we invite our readers to join in this effort.

Notes on authors

Neil J. Anderson is a Professor of Linguistics and English Language in the TESOL program at Brigham Young University in Provo, Utah, USA. He is the Coordinator at the English Language Center. His interests include language learning strategies, particularly as they relate to teaching second language reading.

Anna Uhl Chamot is Professor of Secondary Education and Faculty Advisor for English as a Second Language and Foreign Language Education in the Department of Teacher Preparation and Special Education at the George Washington University. She is also Co-Director of the National Capital Language Resource Center (NCLRC). Her research interests are in language learning strategies, content-based second language instruction, and literacy development in adolescent English language learners.

Andrew D. Cohen, Professor of Applied Linguistics and Chair of the MA in ESL Program and Director of the Undergraduate ESL Minor at the University of Minnesota, has been strategizing about foreign language learning from his first (Latin) to his eleventh (Japanese). He has published four books on language learner strategies, as well as volumes on bilingual education and language assessment, along with numerous research articles on language teaching, language learning, language testing, and research methods.

Do Coyle is Associate Professor in Education and Director of the Visual LearningLab. She has published widely in the field of content and language integrated learning, particularly in technology-enhanced settings. Her work on strategic classrooms as communities of practice, using advanced videoconferencing links, focuses on the interrelationship between social interaction, mediation, and the development of learner strategies.

Lynn Erler researches reading in a foreign language within the context of secondary schools in the UK. Her specific interests lie in the cognitive processing required to overcome and/or make best use of the L1 when accessing meaning during L2 reading.

May Fan is an Associate Professor in the Department of English in the Hong Kong Polytechnic University, teaching both BA and MA programs. Her research interest is related to vocabulary, learning strategies, legal English as well as the use of collocational knowledge by L2 learners.

Claudia Finkbeiner is a Professor in the English Department, School of Modern Languages, at the University of Kassel, Germany. Her field is applied linguistics with a strong emphasis on foreign language research and teaching English as a foreign, second, or other language. Her research and teaching concentrate on learning strategies, motivation, and interest in reading, literacy, intercultural education, holistic learning, multiple intelligence activities, co-operative learning, content-based language learning, and computer-assisted language learning.

Christine Goh is Associate Professor in the Department of English Language and Literature, National Institute of Education, Nanyang Technological University, Singapore. Her main interests are listening and speaking proficiency and development, the role of metacognition in L2 learning and discourse intonation of L2 speakers.

Suzanne Graham, formerly a teacher of French and German in English secondary schools, has worked in the field of language teacher education since 1994. She is Senior Lecturer in Language and Education at the University of Reading, where she leads the initial teacher education program for modern foreign languages. She also contributes to Masters and doctoral programs. She has a range of research publications in the field of learner strategies in the UK context.

Michael Grenfell is Professor in the School of Education at the University of Southampton. He teaches on courses in applied linguistics, teacher education, and the philosophy of education. He has researched and published extensively on communicative language teaching and language learner strategies, including *Modern Languages and Learning Strategies* (with V. Harris), and *Modern Languages Across the Curriculum.*

Carol Griffiths has been a teacher for many years and has specialized as a teacher and manager of English for speakers of other languages (ESOL) for more than ten years. She currently works for Beijing Sports University in China. She is working on an edited book which explores the multiple characteristics of good language learners.

Peter Yongqi Gu is Senior Lecturer at Victoria University, Wellington, New Zealand, where he teaches language testing and assessment. He has extensive teaching and teacher training experience in Beijing Normal University (China), Hong Kong Institute of Education (Hong Kong), Lingnan University (Hong Kong), and the National Institute of Education (Singapore). His academic interests include second language acquisition, computer-assisted language learning, teacher training, and language planning.

Vee Harris is Senior Lecturer at Goldsmiths College where she heads up the Modern Languages Initial Teacher Education Program. Her particular interest in learning strategies research is exploring strategy instruction with younger learners and the focus of her current funded project is strategy instruction with pupils in the 12–13 age range.

Kyoung Rang Lee is a doctoral candidate at the University of Maryland. She is interested in individual differences in teaching and learning English, including L2 grammar strategies. Currently, she is exploring how to teach and assess reading strategies, using various methods, including color-coding which is an innovative tool for reading strategy instruction and assessment.

Ernesto Macaro is Professor of Applied Linguistics (Second Language Acquisition) in the Department of Educational Studies at the University of Oxford. He co-ordinates the MSc in Applied Linguistics and Second Language Acquisition. He also teaches on the Modern Languages Teacher Education Program. His research focuses on second language learning strategies and on the interaction between teachers and learners in second language classrooms.

Rosa M. Manchón is Senior Lecturer in Applied Linguistics. She teaches undergraduate courses in second language acquisition and teaching, as well as postgraduate courses in research methodology and linguistic and socio-cognitive aspects of second language learning and use. Her research interests and publications focus on the socio-cognitive dimension of second language acquisition, with a special interest in second language writing.

Liz Murphy is a lecturer in the Department of Filología Inglesa at the University of Murcia in Spain, where she has taught a wide range of undergraduate courses including applied linguistics, language teaching, and general and academic writing English courses. Her main research interest involves the use of the L1 in second language composition processes.

Yasuo Nakatani obtained his PhD from the University of Birmingham and is an associate professor in the School of Management at Tokyo University of Science. He was a visiting scholar in the Department of Educational Studies of the University of Oxford in 2002. His research interests include learning strategy, second language acquisition, L2 teacher education, and business communication.

Martha Nyikos is Professor of Language Education at Indiana University. She directs the Foreign and Second Language Education program area, which preparers teachers and curriculum co-ordinators internationally. On the editorial board of the *Modern Language Journal*, her research includes socio-cognitive approaches to strategies-based language learning, models for professional teacher development, teacher resistance to change, and strategies for family native language maintenance in the diaspora.

Rebecca L. Oxford has investigated strategies for two decades and authored widely-used strategy questionnaires. She is Distinguished Scholar-Teacher and Professor at the University of Maryland. She has published books on motivation, strategies, and methods and spearheaded the strategies-enhanced 'Tapestry Program' for ESL and EFL students. Recent research is on reading strategies, grammar strategies, and technology strategies for 'millennial learners'.

Julio Roca de Larios is Associate Professor of Education at the University of Murcia (Spain). He currently teaches English phonetics and foreign language teaching processes. His current research interests include L1 and L2 composition processes and the uses of reflection in teaching.

Joan Rubin pioneered research on the 'good language learner' over 30 years ago. More recently she has developed a model of 'learner self-management' integrating procedures and knowledge. She has conducted two major research projects on promoting listening comprehension and one on promoting task analysis. Among her books are *How to be a More Successful Language Learner* and *A Guide for the Teaching of Listening Comprehension*.

Karen Schramm currently conducts second language research at the University of Münster in Germany. Her project focuses on young learners' communication strategies and scaffolding during second language story-telling. She has published on foreign language reading strategies, second language literacy, and strategy research methodology.

Osamu Takeuchi is Professor of Applied Linguistics in the Graduate School/ Institute of Foreign Language Education and Research, Kansai University, Osaka, Japan. He directs MA and PhD programs in language teaching. His research interests include language learner strategies and motivational strategies in the Japanese EFL context.

Robert Vanderplank is Director of Oxford University Language Centre and a Fellow of Kellogg College, Oxford. He teaches courses and supervises students within the program of Applied Linguistics and Second Language Acquisition at Oxford University Department of Educational Studies. His current research interests are second language attrition and learner autonomy.

Cynthia White is Professor in Linguistics and Second Language Teaching, Massey University, New Zealand. She has research interests in language learner strategies, learner beliefs, and online learning environments. Her books include *Language Learning in Distance Education* and a co-edited book entitled *Languages and Distance Education: Evolution and Change*.

References

Abraham, R. and **R. Vann.** 1987. 'Strategies of two language learners: A case study' in Wenden, A. and J. Rubin (eds.): *Learner Strategies: Implications for the Second Language Teacher and Researcher*. Englewood Cliffs, NJ: Prentice Hall.

Afflerbach, P. 2000. 'Verbal reports and protocol analysis' in Kamil, M. L., B. Mosenthal, D. Pearson, and R. Barr (eds.): *Handbook of Reading Research* (Vol. III). Mahwah, NJ: Erlbaum.

Afflerbach, P. and **P. Johnston.** 1984. 'Research methodology on the use of verbal reports in reading research'. *Journal of Reading Behavior* 16/4: 307–22.

Aguado, K. 2004. 'Introspektive Verfahren in der empirischen Fremdsprachenerwerbsforschung. Methodisch-methodologische Überlegungen' [Introspective procedures in empirical research on foreign language acquisition. Reflections on methods and methodology]. *Fremdsprachen und Hochschule* 71: 24–38.

Ahmed, M. O. 1989. 'Vocabulary learning strategies' in Meara, P. (ed.): *Beyond Words*. London: British Association for Applied Linguistics/Centre for Information on Language Teaching and Research.

Akyel, A. 1994. 'First language use in EFL writing: Planning in Turkish vs. planning in English'. *International Journal of Applied Linguistics* 4/2: 169–76.

Akyel, A. and **S. Kamisli.** 1997. 'Composing in first and second languages: Possible effects of EFL writing instruction' in Pogner, K. (ed.): *Writing: Text and Interaction. Odense Working Papers in Language and Communication* 11: 69–105.

Alderson, J. C. 1984. 'Reading in a foreign language: A reading problem or a language problem?' in Alderson, J. C. and H. H. Urquhart (eds.): *Reading in a Foreign Language*. Harlow: Longman.

Alderson, J. C. 2000. *Assessing Reading*. Cambridge: Cambridge University Press.

Allan, D. 1995. *Oxford Placement Test*. Oxford: Oxford University Press.

Allport, D. A. 1985. 'Distributed memory, modular subsystems and dysphasia' in Newman, S. and R. Epstein (eds.): *Current Perspectives in Dysphasia*. Edinburgh: Churchill Livingstone.

Allwright, D. 2003. 'Exploratory practice: Rethinking practitioner research in language teaching'. *Language Teaching Research* 7/2: 113–41.

Allwright, D. 2005. 'Developing principles for practitioner research: The case of exploratory practice'. *Modern Language Journal* 89/3: 353–66.

Alvermann, D. and **S. Phelps.** 1983. 'Elementary readers' strategic activity in processing story-length material' in Niles, J. (ed.): *Searches for Reading, Language Processing and Instruction: Thirty-Second Yearbook of the National reading Conference*. Rochester, NY: National Reading Conference.

Ammon, M. S. 1987. 'Patterns of performance among bilingual children who score low in reading' in Goldman, S. R. and H. T. Trueba (eds.): *Becoming Literate in English as a Second Language*. Norwood, NJ: Ablex.

Anderson, J. R. 1983. *The Architecture of Cognition*. Cambridge, MA: Harvard University Press.

Anderson, J. R. 1985. *Cognitive Psychology and its Implications*. (2nd ed.). New York: Freeman.

Anderson, N. J. 1989. Reading Comprehension Tests versus Academic Reading: What are Second Language Readers Doing? Unpublished doctoral thesis, University of Texas, Austin, TX, USA.

Anderson, N. J. 1991. 'Individual differences in strategy use in second language reading and testing'. *Modern Language Journal* 75/4: 460–72.

Anderson, N. J. 1992. 'A preliminary investigation into the relationships between reading comprehension and language learning strategies, personality type and language aptitude'. Paper presented at the annual Second Language Reading Colloquium, Teachers of English to Speakers of Other Languages, Vancouver, British Columbia, Canada.

Anderson, N. J. 2002. 'The role of metacognition in second/foreign language teaching and learning'. *ERIC Digest* www.cal.org/resources/digest/digest_pdfs/0110_Anderson.pdf.

Anderson, N. J. 2005. 'L2 strategy research' in Hinkel, E. (ed.): *Handbook in Second Language Teaching and Learning*. Mahwah, NJ: Erlbaum.

Anderson, N. J. Forthcoming. 'Metacognition and Good Language Learners' in Griffiths, C. (ed.): *Lessons From Good Language Learners*. Cambridge: Cambridge University Press.

Anderson, N. J. and L. Vandergrift. 1996. 'Increasing metacognitive awareness in the L2 classroom by using think-aloud protocols and other verbal report formats' in Oxford, R. L. (ed.): *Language Learning Strategies Around the World: Cross-Cultural Perspectives*. Manoa: University of Hawai'i Press.

Anton, M. 1999. 'The discourse of a learner-centred classroom: Sociocultural perspectives on teacher-learner interaction in the second language classroom'. *Modern Language Journal* 83/3: 303–18.

Ard, J. 1982. 'The use of bilingual dictionaries by EFL students while writing'. *ITL: Review of Applied Linguistics* 58: 1–27.

Armengol-Castells, L. 2001. 'Text-generating strategies of three multilingual writers: A protocol-based study'. *Language Awareness* 10/2–3: 91–106.

Arndt, V. 1987. 'Six writers in search of texts: A protocol-based study of L1 and L2 writing'. *ELT Journal* 41/4: 257–67.

Atkins, T. B. and K. Varantola. 1997. 'Monitoring dictionary use'. *International Journal of Lexicography* 10/1: 1–45.

Atkins, T. B. and K. Varantola. 1998. 'Language learners using dictionaries: The final report on the EURALEX/AILA research report on dictionary use' in Atkins, T.B. (ed.): *Using Dictionaries: Studies of Dictionary Use by Language Learners and Translators*. Lexicographic series maior 88. Tübingen: Niemeyer.

Atkinson, D. 2002. 'Toward a sociocognitive approach to second language acquisition'. *Modern Language Journal* 86/4: 525–45.

Atkinson, D. (ed.). 2003. 'L2 writing in the post-process era'. *Journal of Second Language Writing* 12/1: 3–15.

Atkinson, R. C. 1975. 'Mnemotechnics in second-language learning'. *American Psychologist* 30/8: 821–28.

Atkinson, R. C. and M. Raugh. 1975. 'An application of the mnemonic keyword method to acquisition of a Russian vocabulary'. *Journal of Experimental Psychology: Human Learning and Memory* 104/2: 126–33.

Aust, R., M. J. Kelley, and W. B. Roby. 1993. 'The use of hyper-reference and conventional dictionaries'. *Educational Technology Research and Development* 41/4: 63–73.

Austin, J. L. 1955/1999. *How To Do Things With Words* (2nd ed.). Oxford: Oxford University Press.

Avila, E. and M. Sadoski. 1996. 'Exploring new applications of the keyword method to acquire English vocabulary'. *Language Learning* 46/3: 379–95.

Bachman, L. F. 1990. *Fundamental Considerations in Language Testing*. Oxford: Oxford University Press.

Bacon, S. M. 1992a. 'Phases of listening to authentic input in Spanish: A descriptive study'. *Foreign Language Annals* 25/4: 317–34.

Bacon, S. M. 1992b. 'The relationship between gender, comprehension, processing strategies, and cognitive and affective response in foreign language listening'. *Modern Language Journal* 76/2: 160–77.

Bacon, S. M. and M. D. Finnemann. 1990. 'A study of the attitudes, motives, and strategies of university foreign language students and their dispositions to authentic oral and written input'. *Modern Language Journal* 74/4: 459–73.

Bakhtin, M. 1984. *Problems of Dostoevsky's Poetics* in Emerson, C. (ed. and trans.). Minneapolis: University of Minnesota Press.

Bakhtin, M. 1986. *Speech Genres and Other Late Essays*. McGee, V. W. (trans.). Austin, TX: University of Texas Press.

Bakhtin, M. 1998. 'Discourse in the novel' in Rivkin, J. and M. Ryan (eds.): *Literary Theory: An Anthology*. Oxford: Blackwell.

Bandura, A. 1986. *Social Foundations of Thought and Action*. Englewood Cliffs, NJ: Prentice Hall.

Bandura, A. 1995. *Self-efficacy in Changing Societies*. Cambridge: Cambridge University Press.

Bandura, A. 1997. *Self-Efficacy: The Exercise of Control*. New York: W. H. Freeman.

Barcroft, J. 2002. 'Semantic and structural elaboration in L2 lexical acquisition'. *Language Learning* 52/2: 323–63.

Barton, D. and M. Hamilton. 2000. 'Literacy practices' in Barton, D., M. Hamilton, and R. Ivanic (eds.): *Situated Literacies: Reading and Writing in Context*. London: Routledge.

Baur, R. S. 1979 'Die Interiorisationstheorie Gal'perins und ihre Anwendung auf den Fremdsprachenunterricht' [Gal'perin's interiorization theory and its application to foreign language teaching]. *Linguistische Berichte* 61: 68–87.

Baur, R. S. and J. Rehbein. 1979. 'Lerntheorie und Lernwirklichkeit. Zur Aneignung des deutschen Artikels bei türkischen Schülern: ein Versuch mit der Gal'perinschen Konzeption' [Learning theory and learning reality. About the acquisition of the German article by Turkish students: an approach with Gal'perin's ideas]. *Osnabrücker Beiträge zur Sprachtheorie* 10: 70–104.

Bean, T. W., T. C. Potter, and C. Clark. 1980. 'Selected semantic features of ESL materials and their effect on bilingual students' comprehension' in Kamil, M. and A. Moe (eds.): *Perspectives on Reading Research and Instruction*. Twenty-ninth yearbook of the National Reading Conference. Washington, DC: National Reading Conference.

Becker-Mrotzek, M., K. Ehlich, R. Glas, and C. Tebel. 1989. 'Transkription von Sprachdaten mit Computer-Hilfe: HIAT-DOS' [Computer-aided transcription of linguistic data: HIAT-DOS]. *UNI-Report* 9: 22–4.

Bedell, D. A. and R. Oxford. 1996. 'Cross-cultural comparisons of language learning strategies in the People's Republic of China and other countries' in Oxford, R. L. (ed.): *Language Learning Strategies Around the World: Cross-Cultural Perspectives*. Manoa: University of Hawai'i Press.

Bejarano, Y., T. Levine, E. Olshtain, and J. Steiner. 1997. 'The skill use of interaction strategies: Creating a framework for improved small-group communication interaction in the language classroom'. *System* 25/2: 203–13.

Bensoussan, M., D. Sim, and R. Weiss. 1984. 'The effect of dictionary usage on EFL test performance compared with student and teacher attitudes and expectations'. *Reading in a Foreign Language* 2/2: 262–76.

Berk, L. E. and A. Winsler. 1995. *Scaffolding Children's Learning: Vygotsky and Early Childhood Education*. Washington, DC: National Association for the Young Children.

Berman, R. 1994. 'Learner's transfer of writing skills between languages'. *TESL Canada Journal* 12/1: 29–46.

Berne, J. E. 2004. 'Listening comprehension strategies: A review of the literature'. *Foreign Language Annals* 37/4: 521–33.

Bernhardt, E. 2000. 'Second-language reading as a case study of reading scholarship in the 20th century' in Kamil, M. L., P. B. Mosenthal, P. D. Pearson, and R. Barr (eds.): *Handbook of Reading Research* (Vol. III). Mahwah, NJ: Erlbaum.

Bernhardt, E. 2005. 'Progress and procrastination in second language reading'. *Annual Review of Applied Linguistics* 25: 133–50.

Beyer, S. 2005. 'Introspektive Verfahren im fremdsprachlichen Unterricht' [Introspective procedures in foreign language teaching]. *Deutsch als Fremdsprache* 42/1: 18–22.

Bialystok, E. 1983a. 'Some factors in the selection and implementation of communication strategies' in Færch, C. and G. Kasper (eds.): *Strategies in Interlanguage Communication*. London: Longman.

Bialystok, E. 1983b. 'Inferencing: Testing the "hypothesis-testing" hypothesis' in Seliger, H. W. and M. H. Long (eds.): *Classroom Oriented Research in Second Language Acquisition*. Rowley, MA: Newbury House.

Bialystok, E. 1990. *Communication Strategies*. Oxford: Basil Blackwell.

Bialystok, E. 2001. *Bilingualism in Development: Language, Literacy, and Cognition*. Cambridge: Cambridge University Press.

Bialystok, E. and M. Fröhlich. 1978. 'Variables of classroom achievement in second language learning'. *Modern Language Journal* 62/7: 327–35.

Bimmel, P. E., H. van den Bergh, and R. J. Oostdam. 2001. 'Effects of strategy training on reading comprehension in first and foreign language'. *European Journal of Psychology of Education* 16/4: 509–29.

Birdsong, D. 1999. *Second Language Acquisition and the Critical Period Hypothesis*. Mahwah, NJ: Erlbaum.

Block, E. L. 1986. 'The comprehension strategies of second language readers'. *TESOL Quarterly* 20/3: 463–94.

Block, E. L. 1992. 'See how they read: Comprehension monitoring of L1 and L2 readers'. *TESOL Quarterly* 26/2: 104–28.

Boekaerts, M., P. R. Pintrich, and M. Zeidner (eds.). 2000. *Handbook of Self-Regulation*. San Diego, CA: Academic Press.

Bongaerts, T. and N. Poulisse. 1989. 'Communication strategies in L1 and L2: Same or different?' *Applied Linguistics* 10/3: 253–68.

Bonk, W. J. 2000. 'Second language lexical knowledge and listening comprehension'. *International Journal of Listening* 14: 14–31.

Bosher, S. 1998. 'The composing processes of three Southeast Asian writers at the post-secondary level: An exploratory study'. *Journal of Second Language Writing* 7/2: 205–41.

Bransford, J. D. 1979. *Human Cognition: Learning, Understanding and Remembering*. Belmont, CA: Wadsworth.

Brantmeier, C. 2002. 'Second language reading strategy research at the secondary and university levels: Variations, disparities, and generalizability'. *The Reading Matrix* 2/3: 1–14.

Bråten, I. and H. I. Strømsø. 2003. 'A longitudinal think-aloud study of spontaneous strategic processing during the reading of multiple expository texts'. *Reading and Writing: An Interdisciplinary Journal* 16: 195–218.

Braxton, M. A. 1999. Adult ESL Language Learning Strategies: Case Studies of Preferred Learning Styles and Perceived Cultural Influences in Academic Listening Tasks. Unpublished doctoral thesis, Ohio State University, Columbus, OH, USA.

Breen, M. 1985. 'The social context of language learning—A neglected situation?' *Studies in Second Language Acquisition* 7/2: 135–58.

Breen, M. 2001a. 'Postscript: New directions for research on learner contributions' in Breen, M. (ed.): *Learner Contributions to Language Learning*. Harlow/New York: Longman.

Breen, M. 2001b. (ed.) *Learner Contributions to Language Learning: New Directions in Research*. Harlow/New York: Longman.

Broekkamp, H. and H. van den Bergh. 1996. 'Attention strategies in revising a foreign language text' in Rijlaarsdam, G., H. van den Bergh, and M. Couzijn (eds.): *Theories, Models and Methodology in Writing Research*. Amsterdam: University of Amsterdam Press.

Brooks-Carson, A. W. and A. D. Cohen. 2000. 'Direct vs. translated writing: Strategies for bilingual writers' in Swierzbin, B., F. Morris, M. E. Anderson, C. A. Klee, and E. Tarone (eds.): *Social and Cognitive Factors in Second Language Acquisition*. Somerville, MA: Cascadilla Press.

Brown, A. L. 1984. 'Metakognition, Handlungskontrolle, Selbststeuerung und andere, noch geheimnisvollere Mechanismen' [Metacognition, action control, self-regulation, and other even more secret mechanisms] in Weinert, F. E. and R. H. Kluwe (eds.): *Metakognition, Motivation und Lernen*. Stuttgart, Germany: Kohlhammer.

Brown, A. L., J. D. Bransford, R. A. Ferrara, and J. C. Campione. 1983. 'Learning, remembering, and understanding' in Mussen, P. H. (ed.): *Handbook of Child Psychology: Vol. 3. Cognitive Development*. New York: JohnWiley and Sons.

Brown, H. D. 1991. *Breaking the Language Barrier: Creating Your Own Path to Success*. Yarmouth, ME: Intercultural Press.

Brown, H. D. 1994. *Teaching by Principles: An Interactive Approach to Language Pedagogy*. Englewood Cliffs, NJ: Prentice Hall.

Brown, J. D. 1988. *Understanding Research in Second Language Learning. A Teacher's Guide to Statistics and Research Design*. Cambridge: Cambridge University Press.

Brown, J. D. 2004. 'Research methods for applied linguistics: Scope, characteristics, and standards' in Davies, A. and C. Elder (eds.): *The Handbook of Applied Linguistics*. Oxford: Blackwell.

Brown, J. D. 2005. 'A second turn in the research paradigm debate'. Retrieved May 30, 2006 from http://iltaonline.com/newsletter/01-2005may.

Brown, J. S., A. Collins, and P. Duguid. 1989. 'Situated cognition and the culture of learning'. *Educational Researcher* 18/1: 32–42.

Brown, T. S. and F. Perry. 1991. 'A comparison of three learning strategies for ESL vocabulary acquisition'. *TESOL Quarterly* 25/4: 655–70.

Bruen. J. 2001. 'Strategies for success: Profiling the effective learner of German'. *Foreign Language Annals* 34/3: 216–25.

Burns, A. 1999. *Collaborative Action Research for English Language Teachers*. Cambridge: Cambridge University Press.

Cain, J., M. Weber-Olsen, and R. Smith. 1987. 'Acquisition strategies in a first and second language: are they the same?' *Journal of Child Language* 14/2: 333–52.

Canagarajah, S. 2003. *Resisting Linguistic Imperialism in English Teaching*. Oxford: Oxford University Press.

Canagarajah, S. 2006. 'TESOL at forty: What are the issues?' *TESOL Quarterly* 40/1: 9–34.

Canale, M. 1983. 'On some dimensions of language proficiency' in Oller, J. W. Jr. (ed.): *Issues in Language Testing Research*. Rowley, MA: Newbury House.

Canale, M. and M. Swain. 1980. 'Theoretical bases of communicative approaches to language teaching and testing'. *Applied Linguistics* 1/1: 1–47.

Carrell, P. L. 1981. 'Culture-specific schemata in L2 comprehension' in Orem, R. and J. Haskell (eds.): *Selected Papers from the Ninth Illinois TESOL/BE Annual Convention, First Midwest TESOL Conference*. Chicago: Illinois TESOL/BE.

Carrell, P. L. 1984. 'The effects of rhetorical organization on ESL readers'. *TESOL Quarterly* 18/3: 441–69.

Carrell, P. L. 1985. 'Facilitating ESL reading by teaching text structure'. *TESOL Quarterly* 19/4: 727–52.

Carrell, P. L. 1987. 'Content and formal schemata in ESL reading'. *TESOL Quarterly* 21/3: 461–81.

Carrell, P. L. 1989. 'Metacognitive awareness and second language reading'. *Modern Language Journal* 73/2: 121–34.

Carrell, P. L. 1992. 'Awareness of text structure: Effects on recall'. *Language Learning* 42/1: 1–20.

Carrell, P. L., J. Devine, and D. Eskey (eds.). 1988. *Interactive Approaches to Second Language Reading*. Cambridge: Cambridge University Press.

Carrell, P. L., L. Gajdusek, and T. Wise. 1998. 'Metacognition and EFL/ESL reading'. *Instructional Science* 26/1–2: 97–112.

Carrell, P. L., B. Pharis, and J. Liberto. 1989. 'Metacognitive strategy training for ESL reading'. *TESOL Quarterly* 23/4: 647–78.

Carroll J. and S. Sapon. 1959. *The Modern Language Aptitude Test*. San Antonio, TX: The Psychological Corporation.

Catalán, R. M. J. 2003. 'Sex differences in L2 vocabulary learning strategies'. *International Journal of Applied Linguistics* 13/1: 54–77.

Chamot, A. U. 1999. 'Reading and writing processes: Learning strategies in immersion classrooms' in Kassen, M. A. (ed.): *Language Learners of Tomorrow: Process and Promise*. Lincolnwood, IL: National Textbook.

Chamot, A. U. 2004. 'Issues in language learning strategy research and teaching'. *Electronic Journal of Foreign Language Teaching* 1/1: 12–25.

Chamot, A. U. 2005a. 'Language learning strategy instruction: Current issues and research'. *Annual Review of Applied Linguistics* 25: 112–30.

Chamot, A. U. 2005b. 'The cognitive academic language learning approach (CALLA): An update' in Richard-Amato, P.A. and M. A. Snow (eds.): *Academic Success for English Language Learners: Strategies for K-12 Mainstream Teachers*. White Plains, NY: Longman.

Chamot, A. U. In press. *The CALLA Handbook: Implementing the Cognitive Academic Language Learning Approach*. (2nd ed.). White Plains, NY: Longman.

Chamot, A. U., S. Barnhardt, P. El-Dinary, and J. Robbins. 1996. 'Methods for teaching learning strategies in the foreign language classroom' in Oxford, R. L. (ed.): *Language Learning Strategies Around the World: Cross-Cultural Perspectives*. Manoa: University of Hawai'i Press.

Chamot, A. U., S. Barnhardt, P. B. El-Dinary, and J. Robbins. 1999. *The Learning Strategies Handbook*. White Plains, NY: Longman.

Chamot, A. U. and P. B. El-Dinary. 1999. 'Children's learning strategies in language immersion classrooms'. *Modern Language Journal* 83/3: 319–38.

Chamot, A. U. and C. W. Keatley. 2003. 'Learning strategies of adolescent low-literacy Hispanic ESL students'. Paper presented at the 2003 Annual Meeting of the American Educational Research Association, New Orleans, LA.

Chamot, A. U., C. Keatley, S. Barnhardt, B. El-Dinary, K. Nagano, and C. Newman. 1996. *Learning Strategies in Elementary Language Immersion Programs*. Final report submitted to Center for International Education, US Department of Education. ERIC.

Chamot, A. U., C. Keatley, A. Mazur, K. Anstrom, X. Marquez, and M. Adonis. 2000. *Literacy Development in Adolescent English Language Learners*. Final report submitted to Office of Educational Research and Improvement, US Department of Education.

Chamot, A. U. and L. Küpper. 1989. 'Learning strategies in foreign language instruction'. *Foreign Language Annals* 22/1: 13–24.

Chamot, A. U. and J. M. O'Malley. 1987. 'The Cognitive Academic Language Learning Approach: A bridge to the mainstream'. *TESOL Quarterly* 21/2: 227–49.

Chamot, A. U. and J. M. O'Malley. 1994a. 'Language learner and learning strategies' in Ellis, N. C.(ed.): *Implicit and Explicit Learning of Languages*. London: Academic Press.

Chamot, A. U. and J. M. O'Malley. 1994b. *The CALLA Handbook: Implementing the Cognitive Academic Language Learning Approach*. White Plains, NY: Longman.

Chamot, A. U. and J. M. O'Malley. 1996. 'Implementing the Cognitive Academic Language Learning Approach' in Oxford, R. L. (ed.): *Language Learning Strategies Around the World: Cross-Cultural Perspectives*. Manoa: University of Hawai'i Press.

Chamot, A. U. and J. Rubin. 1994. 'Comments on Janie Rees-Miller's "A critical appraisal of learner training: Theoretical bases and teaching implications"'. *TESOL Quarterly* 28/4: 771–76.

Chen, S. Q. 1990. 'A study of communication strategies in interlanguage production by Chinese EFL learners'. *Language Learning* 49/2: 155–87.

Chenoweth, N. and J. Hayes. 2001. 'Fluency in writing: Generating text in L1 and L2'. *Written Communication* 18/1: 80–98.

Chesterfield, R. and K. B. Chesterfield. 1985. 'Natural order in children's second language learning strategies'. *Applied Linguistics* 6/1: 45–59.

Chi, M. T. H. 1984. 'Bereichspezifisches Wissen und Metakognition' [Domain-specific knowledge and metacognition] in Weinert, F. E. and R. H. Kluwe (eds.): *Metakognition, Motivation und Lernen.* Stuttgart, Germany: Kohlhammer.

Chi, M. T. H., N. de Leeuw, M.-H. Chiu, and C. LaVancher. 1994. 'Eliciting self-explanations improves understanding'. *Cognitive Science* 18: 439–77.

Chiang, C. S. and P. Dunkel. 1992. 'The effect of speech modification, prior knowledge and listening proficiency on EFL lecture learning'. *TESOL Quarterly* 26/2: 345–74.

Chien, C. and L. Wei. 1998. 'The strategy use in listening comprehension for EFL learners in Taiwan'. *RELC Journal* 29/1: 66–91.

CHILDES. Child language exchange system (n.d.). http://childes.psy.cmu.edu.

Chimbganda, A. B. 2000. 'Communication strategies used in the writing of answers in biology by ESL first year science students of the University of Botswana'. *English for Specific Purposes* 19/4: 305–29.

Ching, L. C. 2002. 'Strategy and self-regulation instruction as contributors to improving students' cognitive model in an ESL program'. *English for Specific Purposes* 21/3: 261–89.

Chun, D. M. and J. L. Plass. 1996. 'Effects of multimedia annotations on vocabulary acquisition'. *Modern Language Journal* 80/2: 183–98.

Chung, J. M. 1999. 'The effects of using video texts supported with advance organizers and captions on Chinese college students' listening comprehension: an empirical study'. *Foreign Language Annals* 32/3: 295–307.

Clahsen, H. 1985. 'Profiling second language development: A procedure for assessing L2 proficiency' in Hyltenstam, K. and M. Pienemann (eds.): *Modelling and Assessing Second Language Acquisition.* Clevedon: Multilingual Matters.

Clarke, M. A. 1980. 'The short circuit hypothesis of ESL reading—or when language competence interferes with reading performance'. *Modern Language Journal* 64/2: 203–9.

Clennel, C. 1995. 'Communication strategies of adult ESL learners: A discourse perspective'. *Prospect* 10/3: 4–20.

Coady, J. and T. Huckin. 1997. *Second Language Vocabulary Acquisition: A Rationale for Pedagogy.* Cambridge: Cambridge University Press.

Cohen, A. D. 1987. 'The use of verbal and imagery mnemonics in second-language vocabulary learning'. *Studies in Second Language Acquisition* 9/1: 43–62.

Cohen, A. D. 1990. *Language Learning: Insights for Learners, Teachers, and Researchers.* New York: Newbury House/Harper Collins.

Cohen, A. D. 1998. *Strategies in Learning and Using a Second Language.* London: Longman.

Cohen, A. D. 2003. 'The learner's side of foreign language learning: Where do style, strategies, and tasks meet?' *International Review of Applied Linguistics* 41/4: 279–91.

Cohen, A. D. and E. Aphek. 1980. 'Retention of second-language vocabulary over time: Investigating the role of mnemonic associations'. *System* 8/3: 221–35.

Cohen, A. D. and E. Aphek. 1981. 'Easifying second language learning'. *Studies in Second Language Acquisition* 3/2: 221–35.

Cohen, A. D. and A. Brooks-Carson. 2001. 'Research on direct vs. translated writing processes: Implications for assessment'. *Modern Language Journal* 85/2: 169–88.

Cohen, A. D. and C. Hosenfeld. 1981. 'Some uses of mentalistic data in second language research'. *Language Learning* 31/2: 285–314.

Cohen, A. D. and R. L. Oxford. 2001. *Learning Style Survey for Young Learners*. Minneapolis, MN: Center for Advanced Research on Language Acquisition, University of Minnesota.

Cohen, A. D. and R. L. Oxford. 2002. *Young Learners Language Strategy Use Survey*. Minneapolis, MN: Center for Advanced Research on Language Acquisition, University of Minnesota.

Cohen, A. D., R. L. Oxford, and J. C. Chi. (2003) *Language Strategy Use Inventory*. http://www.carla.umn.edu/maxsa/documents/langstratuse–inventory.pdf.

Cohen, A. D., R. M. Paige, R. L. Shively, H. Emert, and J. Hoff. 2005. *Maximizing study abroad through language and culture strategies: Research on students, study abroad program professionals, and language instructors*. Final Report to the International Research and Studies Program, Office of International Education, DOE. Minneapolis, MN: Center for Advanced Research on Language Acquisition, University of Minnesota. http://www.carla.umn.edu/maxsa/documents/MAXSAResearchReport_000.pdf

Cohen, A. D. and K. Scott. 1996. 'A synthesis of approaches to assessing language learning strategies' in Oxford, R. L. (ed.): *Language Learning Strategies Around the World: Cross-Cultural Perspectives*. Manoa: University of Hawai'i Press.

Cohen, A. D. and S. J. Weaver. 2006. *'Styles and Strategies-Based Instruction: A Teachers' Guide*. Minneapolis, MN: Centre for Advanced Research on Language Acquisition, University of Minnesota.

Cohen, A. D., S. J. Weaver, and T. Y. Li. 1998. 'The impact of strategies-based instruction on speaking a foreign language' in Cohen, A. D.: *Strategies in Learning and Using a Second Language*. London: Longman.

Connor, U. 1996. *Contrastive Rhetoric: Cross-Cultural Aspects of Second Language Writing*. Cambridge: Cambridge University Press.

Conrad, L. 1989. 'The effects of time-compressed speech on native and EFL listening comprehension'. *Studies in Second Language Acquisition* 11/1: 1–16.

Corno, L. 2001. 'Volitional aspects of self-regulated learning' in Zimmerman, B. J. and D. Schunk (eds.): *Self-Regulated Learning and Academic Achievement*. Mahwah, NJ: Erlbaum.

Corrales, O. and M. E. Call. 1989. 'At a loss for words: The use of communication strategies to convey lexical meaning'. *Foreign Language Annals* 22/3: 227–40.

Costa, A. L. and B. Kallick. 2004. *Assessment Strategies for Self-Directed Learners*. Thousand Oaks, CA: Corwin Press.

Cotterall, S. 1993. 'Reading strategy training in second language contexts: Some caveats'. *Australian Review of Applied Linguistics* 16/1: 71–82.

Coyle, D. 1999. Adolescent Voices Speak Out: The Interplay between Linguistic and Strategic Competence in Classrooms where Modern Languages are Used. Unpublished doctoral thesis, University of Nottingham, UK.

Craik, F. I. M. and R. S. Lockhart. 1972. 'Levels of processing: A framework for memory research'. *Journal of Verbal Learning and Verbal Behavior* 11/6: 671–84.

Craik, F. I. M. and E. Tulving. 1975. 'Depth of processing and retention of words in episodic memory'. *Journal of Experimental Psychology: General* 104/3: 268–94.

Cresswell, A. 2000. 'Self-monitoring in student writing: Developing learner responsibility'. *ELT Journal* 54/3: 235–44.

Creswell, J. W. 1994. *Research Design: Qualitative and Quantitative Approaches*. Thousand Oaks, CA: Sage.

Creswell, J. W. 2002. *Research Design: Qualitative, Quantitative, and Mixed Methods Approaches*. (2nd ed.). Thousand Oaks, CA: Sage.

Crow, J. T. 1986. 'Receptive vocabulary acquisition for reading comprehension'. *Modern Language Journal* 70/3: 242–50.

Cumming, A. 1989. 'Writing expertise and second language proficiency'. *Language Learning* 39/1: 81–141.

Cumming, A. 1990. 'Metalinguistic and ideational thinking in second language composing'. *Written Communication* 7/4: 482–511.

Cumming, A. 1998. 'Theoretical perspectives on writing'. *Annual Review of Applied Linguistics* 18: 61–78.

Cumming, A. 2001. 'Learning to write in a second language: Two decades of research'. *International Journal of English Studies* 1: 1–23.

Cumming, A. (ed.). 2006. *Goals for ESL Writing Improvement in ESL and University Courses*. Amsterdam: John Benjamins.

Cumming, A., M. Busch, and A. Zhou. 2002. 'Investigating learners' goals in the context of adult second-language writing' in Ransdell, S. and M. Barbier (eds.): *New Directions for Research for L2 Writing*. Dordrecht, Netherlands: Kluwer.

Cumming, A., J. Rebuffot, and M. Ledwell. 1989. 'Reading and summarizing challenging texts in first and second languages'. *Reading and Writing: An Interdisciplinary Journal* 2: 201–19.

Cummins, J. 2000. *Language, Power, and Pedagogy: Bilingual Children in the Crossfire*. Clevedon: Multilingual Matters.

Cummins, J. 2005. 'Using IT to create a zone of proximal development for academic language learning' in Davison, C. (ed.): *Information and Innovation in Language Education*. Hong Kong: Hong Kong University Press.

Dadour, E. S. and J. Robbins. 1996. 'University-level studies using strategy instruction to improve speaking ability in Egypt and Japan' in Oxford, R. L. (ed.): *Language Learning Strategies Around the World: Cross-Cultural Perspectives*. Manoa: University of Hawai'i Press.

Davidson, J. E. and R. J. Sternberg. 1998. 'Smart problem solving: How metacognition helps' in Hacker, D. J., J. Dunlosky, and A. C. Graesser (eds.): *Metacognition in Educational Theory and Practice*. Mahwah, NJ: Lawrence Erlbaum.

de Bot, K. 1992. 'A bilingual production model: Levelt's speaking model adapted'. *Applied Linguistics* 13/1: 3–24.

de Guerrero, M. C. M. and O. S. Villamil. 1994. 'Social-cognitive dimensions of interaction in L2 peer revision'. *Modern Language Journal* 78/4: 484–96.

De Ridder, I. 2002. 'Visible or invisible links: Does the highlighting of hyperlinks affect incidental vocabulary learning, text comprehension, and the reading process?' *Language Learning and Technology* 6/1: 123–46.

Dechert, H. W. 1983. 'How a story is done in a second language' in Færch, C. and G. Kasper (eds.): *Strategies in Interlanguage Communication*. London: Longman.

Dechert, H. W. 1987. 'Analysing language processing through verbal protocols' in Færch, C. and G. Kasper (eds.): *Introspection in Second Language Research*. Clevedon: Multilingual Matters.

Deffner, G. 1984. *Lautes Denken—Untersuchung zur Qualität eines Datenerhebungsverfahrens* [Thinking aloud—Studies on the quality of a data collection method]. Frankfurt am Main, Germany: Lang.

Deffner, G. 1987. 'Lautes Denken als Methode der Datenerhebung. Qualität und Anwendungsmöglichkeiten' [Think-aloud as a method of data collection. Quality and application range] in Börsch, S. (ed.): *Die Rolle der Psychologie in der Sprachlehrforschung*. Tübingen, Germany: Narr.

Deffner, G. 1988. 'Concurrent thinking aloud: An online tool for studying representations used in text understanding'. *Text* 8/4: 351–67.

DeGroot, A. M. B. and R. Keijzer. 2000. 'What is hard to learn is easy to forget: The role of word concreteness, cognate status, and word frequency in foreign-language vocabulary learning and forgetting'. *Language Learning* 50/1: 1–56.

DeGroot, A. M. B. and J. G. Van Hell. 2005. 'The learning of foreign language vocabulary' in Kroll, J. F. and A. M. DeGroot (eds.): *Handbook of Bilingualism: Psycholinguistic Approaches*. Oxford: Oxford University Press.

DeKeyser, R. 1995. 'Implicit and explicit learning of L2 grammar: A pilot study'. *TESOL Quarterly* 28/1: 188–94.

DeKeyser, R. 2003. 'Implicit and explicit learning' in Doughty, C. J. and M. H. Long (eds.): *Handbook of Second Language Acquisition*. Oxford: Blackwell.

Dempster, F. N. 1987. 'Effects of variable encoding and spaced presentations on vocabulary learning'. *Journal of Educational Psychology* 79/2: 162–70.

Devine, J. 1987. 'General language competence and adult second language reading' in Devine, J., L. Carrell, and D. E. Eskey (eds.): *Research in Reading in English as a Second Language*. Washington, DC: TESOL.

Devine, J., K. Railey, and P. Boshoff. 1993. 'The implications of cognitive models in L1 and L2 writing'. *Journal of Second Language Writing* 2/3: 203–25.

Dobson, J. E. 2001. *Self-Regulated Listening of French Language Students in a Web Environment*. Unpublished doctoral thesis, Catholic University of America, Washington, DC, USA.

Dominowski, R. L. 1998. 'Verbalization and problem solving' in Hacker, D. J., J. Dunlosky, and A. C. Graesser (eds.): *Metacognition in Educational Theory and Practice*. Mahwah, NJ: Erlbaum.

Donato, R. and D. McCormick. 1994. 'A sociocultural perspective on language learning strategies: The role of mediation'. *Modern Language Journal* 78/4: 453–64.

Dörnyei, Z. 1995. 'On the teachability of communication strategies'. *TESOL Quarterly* 29/1: 55–85.

Dörnyei, Z. 2001. *Motivational Strategies in the Language Classroom*. Cambridge: Cambridge University Press.

Dörnyei, Z. 2005. *The Psychology of the Language Learner: Individual Differences in Second Language Acquisition*. Mahwah, NJ: Erlbaum.

Dörnyei, Z. and K. Csizér. 2002. 'Some dynamics of language attitude and motivation: Results of a longitudinal nationwide survey'. *Applied Linguistics* 23/4: 421–62.

Dörnyei, Z. and M. L. Scott. 1997. 'Communication strategies in a second language: Definitions and taxonomies'. *Language Learning* 47/1: 173–210.

Dörnyei, Z. and P. Skehan. 2003. 'Individual differences in second language learning' in Doughty, C. J., and M. H. Long (eds.): *The Handbook of Second Language Acquisition*. Oxford: Blackwell.

Doughty, C. J. 2003. 'Instructed SLA' in Doughty, C. J. and M. H. Long (eds.): *Handbook of Second Language Acquisition*. Oxford: Blackwell.

Doughty, C. J. and T. Pica. 1986. 'Information gap tasks: Do they facilitate second language acquisition?' *TESOL Quarterly* 20/2: 305–25.

Doughty, C. J. and J. Williams. 1998. 'Pedagogical choices in focus on form' in Doughty, C. J. and J. Williams (eds.): *Focus on Form in Classroom Second Language Acquisition*. Cambridge: Cambridge University Press.

Dreyer, C. and C. Nel. 2003. 'Teaching reading strategies and reading comprehension within a technology-enhanced learning environment'. *System* 31/3: 349–65.

Dreyer, C. and R. L. Oxford. 1996. 'Learning strategies and other predictors of ESL proficiency among Afrikaans speakers in South Africa' in Oxford, R. L. (ed.): *Language Learning Strategies Around the World: Cross-Cultural Perspectives*. Manoa: University of Hawai'i Press.

Dulay, H., M. Burt, and S. Krashen. 1982. *Language Two*. New York: Oxford University Press.

Durgunoğlu, A. Y., W. E. Nagy, and J. Hancin-Bhatt. 1993. 'Acquiring literacy in English and Spanish in the United States' in Durgunoğlu, A. Y. and L. Verhoeven (eds.): *Literacy Development in a Multilingual Context: Cross-Cultural Perspectives*. Mahwah, NJ: Erlbaum.

Ehlich, K. 1991. 'Funktional-pragmatische Kommunikationsanalyse—Ziele und Verfahren' [Functional-pragmatic communication analysis—Goals and methods] in Flader, D. (ed.): *Verbale Interaktion. Studien zur Empirie und Methodologie der Pragmatik*. Stuttgart, Germany: Metzler.

Ehlich, K. 1993. 'HIAT: A transcription system for discourse data' in Edwards, J. A. and M. D. Lampert (eds.): *Talking Data: Transcription and Coding in Discourse Research*. Hillsdale, NJ: Erlbaum.

Ehlich, K. and J. Rehbein. 1976. 'Halbinterpretative Arbeitstranskriptionen (HIAT)' [Half-interpretive work transcriptions (HIAT)]. *Linguistische Berichte* 45: 21–41.

Ehlich, K. and J. Rehbein. 1979a. 'Sprachliche Handlungsmuster' [Linguistic action patterns] in Soeffner, H-G. (ed.): *Interpretative Verfahren in den Sozial- und Geisteswissenschaften*. Stuttgart, Germany: Metzler.

Ehlich, K. and J. Rehbein. 1979b. 'Erweiterte halbinterpretative Arbeitstranskriptionen (HIAT 2): Intonation' [Extended half-interpretive work transcriptions (HIAT 2)]. *Linguistische Berichte* 59: 51–75.

Ehlich, K. and J. Rehbein. 1981a. 'Die Wiedergabe intonatorischer, nonverbaler und aktionaler Phänomene im Verfahren HIAT' [The representation of intonatory, non-verbal, and actional phenomena in the HIAT system] in Lange-Seidl, A. (ed.): *Zeichenkonstitution* (Vol. 2). Berlin/New York: de Gruyter.

Ehlich, K. and J. Rehbein. 1981b. 'Zur Notierung nonverbaler Kommunikation für diskursanalytische Zwecke. Erweiterte halbinterpretative Arbeitstranskriptionen (HIAT 2)' [About the transcription of non-verbal communication for discourse-analytic purposes. Extended half-interpretive work transcriptions (HIAT 2)] in Winkler, P. (ed.): *Methoden der Analyse von Face-to-Face-Situationen*. Stuttgart, Germany: Metzler.

Ehlich, K. and J. Rehbein. 1986. *Muster und Institution. Untersuchungen zur schulischen Kommunikation* [Pattern and institution. Studies in school communication]. Tübingen, Germany: Narr.

Ehrman, M. and R. L. Oxford. 1989. 'Effects of sex differences, career choice, and psychological type on adult language learning strategies'. *Modern Language Journal* 73/1: 1–13.

Ehrman, M. and R. L. Oxford. 1990. 'Adult language learning styles and strategies in an intensive training setting'. *Modern Language Journal* 74/3: 311–27.

Ehrman, M. and R. L. Oxford. 1995. 'Cognition plus: Correlates of adult language proficiency'. *Modern Language Journal* 79/1: 67–89.

Ellis, G. and B. Sinclair. 1989. *Learning to Learn English*. Cambridge: Cambridge University Press.

Ellis, N. C. 1994. 'Implicit and explicit language learning: An overview' in Ellis, N. C. (ed.): *Implicit and Explicit Learning of Languages*. San Diego, CA: Academic Press.

Ellis, N. C. 1995. 'Consciousness in second language acquisition: A review of field studies and laboratory experiments'. *Language Awareness* 4/3: 123–46.

Ellis, N. C. and A. Beaton. 1993. 'Psycholinguistic determinants of foreign language vocabulary learning'. *Language Learning* 43/4: 559–617.

Ellis, R. 1984. 'Communication strategies and the evaluation of communicative performance'. *ELT Journal* 38/1: 39–44.

Ellis, R. 1986. *Understanding Second Language Acquisition*. Oxford: Oxford University Press.

Ellis, R. 1994. *The Study of Second Language Acquisition*. Oxford: Oxford University Press.

Ellis, R. 1999. *Learning a Second Language through Interaction*. Amsterdam: John Benjamins.

Ellis, R. 2002a. 'The place of grammar instruction in the second/foreign language curriculum' in Hinkel, E. and S. Fotos (eds.): *New Perspectives on Grammar Teaching in Second Language Classrooms*. Mahwah, NJ: Erlbaum.

Ellis, R. 2002b. 'Methodological options in grammar teaching materials' in Hinkel, E. and S. Fotos (eds.): *New Perspectives on Grammar Teaching in Second Language Classrooms*. Mahwah, NJ: Erlbaum.

Ellis, R. 2003. *Task-Based Language Learning and Teaching*. Oxford: Oxford University Press.

Ellis, R. 2006. 'Current issues in the teaching of grammar: An SLA perspective'. *TESOL Quarterly* 40/1: 83–108.

Ellis, R. and F. Yuan. 2004. 'The effects of planning on fluency, complexity, and accuracy in second language narrative writing'. *Studies in Second Language Acquisition* 26/1: 59–84.

Ericsson, K. A. 1988. 'Concurrent verbal reports on text comprehension: A review.' *Text*: 8/4 295–325.

Ericsson, K. A. and H. A. Simon. 1980. 'Verbal reports as data'. *Psychological Review* 87/3: 215–51.

Ericsson, K. A. and H. A. Simon. 1984/1993. *Protocol Analysis: Verbal Reports as Data* (Revised edition). Cambridge, MA: MIT Press.

Ericsson, K. A. and H. A. Simon. 1987. 'Verbal reports on thinking' in Færch, C. and G. Kasper (eds.): *Introspection in Second Language Research*. Clevedon: Multilingual Matters.

Erler, L. 2004. 'Near-beginner learners of French are reading at a disability level'. *Francophonie* 18:85–92.

Eskey, D. E. 1988. 'Holding in the bottom: An interactive approach to the language problems of second language readers' in Carrell, P. L., J. Devine, and D. E. Eskey (eds.): *Interactive Approaches to Second Language Reading*. Cambridge: Cambridge University Press.

EXMARaLDA (n.d.). http://www1.uni-hamburg.de/exmaralda/index-en.html

Færch, C. and G. Kasper (eds.). 1983a. *Strategies in Interlanguage Communication*. London: Longman.

Færch, C. and G. Kasper. 1983b. 'On identifying communication strategies in interlanguage production' in Færch, C. and G. Kasper (eds.): *Strategies in Interlanguage Communication*. London: Longman.

Færch, C. and G. Kasper. 1983c. 'Plans and strategies in foreign language communication' in Færch, C. and G. Kasper (eds.): *Strategies in Interlanguage Communication*. London: Longman.

Færch, C. and G. Kasper. 1984. 'Two ways of defining communication strategies'. *Language Learning* 34/1: 45–63

Færch, C. and G. Kasper. 1987. 'From product to process—Introspective methods in second language research' in Færch, C. and G. Kasper (eds.): *Introspection in Second Language Research*. Clevedon: Multilingual Matters.

Fakhri, A. 1984. 'The use of communicative strategies in narrative discourse: A case study of a learner of Moroccan Arabic as a second language'. *Language Learning* 34/1: 15–37.

Fan, M. Y. 2000. 'The dictionary look-up behavior of Hong Kong students: A large-scale survey'. *Educational Journal* 28/1: 123–38.

Fan, M. Y. 2003. 'Frequency of use, perceived usefulness, and actual usefulness of second language vocabulary strategies: A study of Hong Kong learners'. *Modern Language Journal* 87/2: 222–41.

Feuerstein, R., P. S. Klein, and A. J. Tannenbaum. 1991. *Mediated Learning Experience: Theoretical, Psychological, and Learning Implications*. London: Freund.

Feuerstein, R., Y. Rand, and M. Hoffman. 1979. *Dynamic Assessment of the Retarded Performer*. Baltimore, MD: University Park Press.

Feuerstein, R., Y. Rand, M. Hoffman, and R. Miller. 1980. *Instrumental Enrichment*. Glenview, IL: Scott Foresman.

Field, J. 2004. 'An insight into listeners' problems: Too much bottom-up or too much top-down?' *System* 32/3: 363–77.

Field, M. L. 1992. 'Reading research: A guide to classroom practices and teaching tools'. Paper presented at 26th Annual TESOL Meeting, Vancouver, BC, Canada, March 3–7, 1992. ERIC.

Finkbeiner, C. 2001. 'Zur Erforschung attitudinaler und affektiver Faktoren beim Lehren und Lernen fremder Sprachen' in Finkbeiner, C. and G. W. Schnaitmann (eds.): *Lehren und Lernen im Kontext empirischer Forschung und Fachdidaktik*. Donauwörth, Germany: Auer.

Finkbeiner, C. 2005. *Interessen und Strategien beim fremdsprachlichen Lesen. Wie Schülerinnen und Schüler englische Texte lesen und verstehen* [Interests and strategies in foreign language reading. How students read and understand English texts]. Tübingen, Germany: Narr.

Finkbeiner, C. 2006a. 'EFL and ESL knowledgeable reading: A critical element for viable membership in global communities'. *Babylonia* 3–4: 45–9.

Finkbeiner, C. 2006b. 'Constructing third space. The principles of reciprocity and cooperation' in Ruggiano Schmidt, P. and C. Finkbeiner (eds.): *The ABCs of Cultural Understanding and Communication: National and International Adaptations*. Greenwich, CT: Information Age Publishing.

Finkbeiner, C. In press. 'Culture and good language learners' in Griffiths, C. (ed.): *Lessons from the Good Language Learner*. Cambridge: Cambridge University Press.

Firth, A. and J. Wagner. 1997. 'On discourse, communication, and fundamental concepts in SLA research'. *Modern Language Journal* 81/3: 285–300.

Fischer, P. M. and H. Mandl. 1981. 'Selbstdiagnostische und selbstregulative Aspekte der Verarbeitung von Studientexten: Eine kritische Übersicht über Ansätze zur Förderung und Beeinflussung von Lernstrategien' [Self-diagnostic and self-regulative aspects of reading for studying: A critical overview over models of fostering and influencing learning strategies] in Mandl, H. (ed.): *Zur Psychologie der Textverarbeitung. Ansätze, Befunde, Probleme.* München, Germany: Urban und Schwarzenberg.

Flavell, J. H. 1971. 'First discussant's comments: What is memory development the development of?' *Human Development* 14/4: 272–78.

Flavell, J. H. 1978. 'Metacognitive development' in Scandura, J. M. and C. J. Brainerd (eds.): *Structural/Process Theories of Complex Human Behavior*. Alphen a.d. Rijn, Netherlands: Sijthoff and Noordhoff.

Flavell, J. H. 1979. 'Metacognition and metacognitive monitoring: A new area of cognitive-developmental inquiry'. *American Psychologist* 34/10: 906–11.

Flavell, J. H. 1984. 'Annahmen zum Begriff Metakognition sowie zur Entwicklung von Metakognition' [Assumptions about the term metacognition and about the development of metacognition] in Weinert, F. E. and R. H. Kluwe (eds.): *Metakognition, Motivation und Lernen.* Stuttgart, Germany: Kohlhammer.

Flavell, J. H. 1992. 'Metacognition and cognitive monitoring: A new area of cognitive-developmental inquiry' in Nelson, T. O. (ed.): *Metacognition: Core Readings*. Boston: Allyn and Bacon.

Flower, L. S. and J. R. Hayes. 1980. 'The dynamics of composing: Making plans and juggling constraints' in Steinberg, L. G. and E. Steinberg (eds.): *Cognitive Processes in Writing: An Interdisciplinary Approach*. Hillsdale, NJ: Erlbaum.

Folse, K. 2006. 'Effect of type of written exercise on L2 vocabulary retention'. *TESOL Quarterly* 40/2: 273–93.

Foster, P. 1998. 'A classroom perspective on the negotiation of meaning'. *Applied Linguistics* 19/1: 1–23.

Fraser, C. 1999. 'Lexical processing strategy use and vocabulary learning through reading'. *Studies in Second Language Acquisition* 21/2: 225–41.

Friedlander, A. 1990. 'Composing in English: Effects of a first language on writing in English as a second language' in Kroll, B. (ed.): *Second Language Writing: Research Insights for the Classroom*. Cambridge: Cambridge University Press.

Frost, R., L. Katz, and S. Bentin. 1987. 'Strategies for visual word recognition and orthographical depth: A multilingual comparison'. *Journal of Experimental Psychology: Human Perception and Performance* 13/1: 104–15.

Gallo-Crail, R. and R. Zerwekh. 2002. 'Language learning and the Internet: Student strategies in vocabulary acquisition' in Spreen, C. A. (ed.): *New Technologies and Language Learning: Cases in the Less Commonly Taught Languages* (Technical Report #25, pp. 55–79). Honolulu: SLTCC, University of Hawai'i.

Gal'perin, P. J. 1976/1980. *Zu Grundfragen der Psychologie* [Basic questions of psychology]. *Studien zur kritischen Psychologie* 16. Berlin, East Germany: Volk und Wissen.

Gan, Z., G. Humphreys, and L. Hamp-Lyons. 2004. 'Understanding successful and unsuccessful EFL students in Chinese universities'. *Modern Language Journal* 88/3: 229–44.

Gao, X. 2003. 'Changes in Chinese students' learner strategy use after arrival in the UK: A qualitative inquiry' in Palfreyman, D. and R. Smith (eds.): *Learner Autonomy Across Cultures. Language Education Perspectives*. Basingstoke: Palgrave Macmillan.

Gao, X. 2006. 'Understanding changes in Chinese students' uses of learning strategies in China and Britain: A socio-cultural re-interpretation'. *System* 34/1: 55–67.

García, G. A., R. T. Jiménez, and P. D. Pearson. 1998. 'Metacognition, childhood bilingualism, and reading' in Hacker, D. J., J. Dunlosky, and A. C. Graesser (eds.): *Metacognition in Educational Theory and Practice*. Mahwah, NJ: Erlbaum.

Garner, R. 1988. 'Verbal-report data on cognitive and metacognitive strategies' in Weinstein, C. E., E. T. Goetz, and P. A. Alexander (eds.): *Learning and Study Strategies: Issues in Assessment, Instruction and Evaluation*. San Diego, CA: Academic Press.

Gaskill, W. H. 1986. Revising in Spanish and English as a Second Language: A Process-oriented Study of Composition. Unpublished doctoral thesis, University of California, Los Angeles, CA, USA.

Gass, S. M. 1990. 'Second language vocabulary acquisition'. *Annual Review of Applied Linguistics* 9: 92–106.

Gillette, B. 1994. 'The role of learner goals in L2 success' in Lantolf, J. and G. Appel (eds.): *Vygotskyian Approaches to Second Language Research*. Norwood, NJ: Ablex Publishing.

Goh, C. C. M. 1998. 'How ESL learners with different listening abilities use comprehension strategies and tactics'. *Language Teaching Research* 2/2: 124–47.

Goh, C. C. M. 1999. 'How much do learners know about the factors that influence their listening comprehension?' *Hong Kong Journal of Applied Linguistics* 4/1: 17–41.

Goh, C. C. M. 2000. 'A cognitive perspective on language learners' listening comprehension problems'. *System* 28/1: 55–75.

Goh, C. C. M. 2002. 'Exploring listening comprehension tactics and their interaction patterns'. *System* 30/2: 185–206.

Goodman, K. S. 1967. 'Reading: A psycholinguistic guessing game'. *Journal of the Reading Specialist* 6/1: 126–35.

Grabe, W. 2004. 'Research on teaching reading'. *Annual Review of Applied Linguistics* 24: 44–69.

Grabe, W. and R. Kaplan. 1996. *Theory and Practice of Writing*. New York: Longman.

Grabe, W. and F. L. Stoller. 2002. *Teaching and Researching Reading*. Harlow: Longman.

Grace, C. A. 2000. 'Gender differences: Vocabulary retention and access to translations for beginning language learner'. *Modern Language Journal* 84/2: 214–24.

Graham, S. 1997. *Effective Language Teaching*. Clevedon: Multilingual Matters.

Graham, S. 2004. 'Giving up on modern foreign languages? Students' perceptions of learning French'. *Modern Languages Journal* 88/2: 171–91.

Graham, S. and K. R. Harris. 1996. 'Self-regulation and strategy instruction for students who find writing and learning challenging' in Levy, C. M. and S. Ransdell (eds.): *The Science of Writing: Theories, Methods, Individual Differences, and Applications*. Mahwah, NJ: Erlbaum.

Graham, S. and K. R. Harris. 2003. 'Students with learning disabilities and the process of writing: A meta-analysis of SRSD studies' in Swanson, L., K. R. Harris, and S. Graham (eds.): *Handbook of Research on Learning Disabilities*. New York: Guildford.

Grainger, P. R. 1997. 'Language-learning strategies for learners of Japanese: Investigating ethnicity'. *Foreign Language Annals* 30/3: 378–85.

Grainger, P. R. 2005. 'Second language learning strategies and Japanese: Does orthography make a difference?' *System* 33/2: 327–39.

Greaney, V. and S. B. Newman. 1990. 'The functions of reading: A cross-cultural perspective'. *Reading Research Quarterly* 25/3: 172–95.

Green, J. M. and R. L. Oxford. 1995. 'A closer look at learning strategies, L2 proficiency, and gender'. *TESOL Quarterly* 29/2: 261–97.

Grellet, F. 1981. *Developing Reading Skills: A Practical Guide to Reading Comprehension Exercises*. Cambridge: Cambridge University Press.

Grenfell, M. and V. Harris. 1999. *Modern Languages and Learning Strategies: In Theory and Practice*. London: Routledge.

Grießhaber, W. 1992. 'SyncWRITER' in Dette K. and P. J. Pahl (eds.): *Multimedia, Vernetzung und Software für die Lehre. Das Computer-Investitions-Programm (CIP) in der Nutzanwendung*. Berlin: Springer.

Grießhaber, W. 2005. 'Sprachstandsdiagnose im kindlichen Zweitspracherwerb: Funktional-pragmatische Fundierung der Profilanalyse' [Assessing language levels in child second language acquisition: A functional-pragmatic foundation of profile analysis]. *Arbeiten zur Mehrsprachigkeit*. http://spzwww.uni-muenster.de/~griesha/dpc/index.html. Accessed January 10, 2006.

Grießhaber, W., B. Özel, and J. Rehbein. 1996. 'Aspekte von Arbeits- und Denksprache türkischer Schüler' [Aspects of working and thinking language of Turkish students]. *Unterrichtswissenschaft* 24/1: 3–20.

Grießhaber, W. and E. Walter. 1993. 'Mit syncWRITER verschriften. Programm überträgt traditionelle Verfahren auf den Computer' [Transcribing with syncWRITER. Software performs traditional procedures on the computer]. *Uni HH Forschung* 28: 53–6.

Griffiths, C. 2003a. 'Patterns of language learning strategy use'. *System* 31/3: 367–83.

Griffiths, C. 2003b. Language Learning Strategy Use and Proficiency. PhD dissertation, University of Auckland. ProQuest Dissertation services. http://wwwlib.umi.com/dissertations/fullcit/3094436.

Grigorenko, E., R. Sternberg, and M. E. Ehrman. 2000. 'A theory-based approach to the measurement of foreign language learning ability: The *CANAL-F* theory and test'. *Modern Language Journal* 84/3: 390–405.

Grosjean, F. 1982. *Life with Two Languages*. Cambridge, MA: Harvard University Press

Grotjahn, R. 1987. 'On the methodological basis of introspective methods' in Færch, C. and G. Kasper (eds.): *Introspection in Second Language Research*. Clevedon: Multilingual Matters.

Gu, P. Y. 1994. 'Vocabulary learning strategies of good and poor Chinese EFL learners'. Paper presented at the Annual Meeting of the Teachers of English of other languages. (ED370411)

Gu, P. Y. 2002. 'Gender, academic major and vocabulary learning of Chinese EFL learners'. *RELC Journal* 33/1: 35–55.

Gu, P. Y. 2003a. 'Fine Brush and freehand: The vocabulary-learning art of two successful Chinese EFL learners'. *TESOL Quarterly* 37/1: 73–104.

Gu, P. Y. 2003b. 'Vocabulary learning in a second language: Person, task, context and strategies'. *TESL-EJ* 7/2. Retrieved September 30, 2005 from http://www-writing.berkeley.edu/TESL-EJ/ej26/a4.html.

Gu, P. Y. 2005. *Vocabulary learning strategies in the Chinese EFL context*. Singapore: Marshall Cavendish International Private Limited

Gu, P. Y., G. Hu, and L. J. Zhang. 2005a. 'Investigating language learner strategies among lower primary school pupils in Singapore'. *Language and Education* 19/4: 281–303.

Gu, P. Y., G. Hu, and L. J. Zhang. 2005b. 'Think-aloud as a Research Tool for Young Learners: Elicitation, Coding and Analysis'. Paper presented at the 14th World Congress of Applied Linguistics (AILA 2005), July 24–29, Madison, Wisconsin.

Gu, P. Y., G. Hu, and L. J. Zhang. Forthcoming. 'Coding and analyzing think-aloud protocols: Listening strategies of primary school pupils in Singapore'. Unpublished manuscript.

Gu, P. Y. and R. K. Johnson. 1996. 'Vocabulary learning strategies and learning outcomes'. *Language Learning* 46/4: 643–679.

Guba, E. G. and **Y. S. Lincoln.** 1994. 'Competing paradigms in qualitative research' in Denzin, N. K. and Y. S. Lincoln (eds.): *Handbook of Qualitative Research*. Thousand Oaks, CA: Sage.

Gunning, P., R. L. Oxford, and **E. Gatbonton.** Forthcoming. 'The ESL learning strategies of Québecois Francophone children'.

Haastrup, K. and **R. Philipson.** 1983. 'Achievement strategies in learner/native speaker interaction' in Færch, C. and G. Kasper (eds.): *Strategies in Interlanguage Communication*. London: Longman.

Hacker, D. J. 1998. 'Definitions and empirical foundations' in Hacker, D. J., J. Dunlosky, and A. C. Graesser (eds.): *Metacognition in Educational Theory and Practice*. Mahwah, NJ: Erlbaum.

Halbach, A. 2000. 'Finding out about students' learning strategies by looking at their diaries: A case study'. *System* 28/1: 85–96.

Hall, C. 1990. 'Managing the complexities of revision across languages'. *TESOL Quarterly* 24/1: 245–266.

Hall, E. 1991. 'Variations in composing behaviours of academic ESL writers in test and non-test situations'. *TESL Canada Journal* 8/2: 9–33.

Hall, J. W., K. P. Wilson, and **R. J. Patterson.** 1981. 'Mnemotechnics: Some limitations of the mnemonic keyword method for the study of foreign language vocabulary'. *Journal of Educational Psychology* 73/3: 345–57.

Hancock, Z. 2002. 'Heritage Spanish speakers' language learning strategies'. *CAL Digest*, EDO-FL-02-06.

Hardin, V. B. 2001. 'Transfer and variation in cognitive reading strategies of Latino fourth-grade students in a late-exit bilingual program'. *Bilingual Research Journal* 25/4: 417–39.

Harley, B. 1986. *Age in Second Language Acquisition*. San Diego, CA: College Hill Press.

Harley, B. and **D. Hart.** 2000. 'Vocabulary learning in the content-oriented second-language classroom: Student perceptions and proficiency'. *Language Awareness* 9/2: 78–96.

Harris, V. 2003. 'Adapting classroom-based strategy instruction to a distance learning context'. *TESL-EJ Special Issue: Strategy Research and Training* 7/2: 1–16. http://www-writing. berkeley.edu/TESL-EJ/ej26/a1.html.

Harris, V. 2004. 'Language learning strategies: A case for cross-curricular collaboration'. Paper presented at the American Educational Research Association (AERA) annual conference: San Diego, CA. April 12–16.

Harris, V., A. Gaspar, B. Jones, H. Ingvadottir, I. Palos, R. Neuburg, and **I. Schindler.** 2001. *Helping Learners Learn: Exploring Strategy Instruction in Language Classrooms Across Europe*. Graz, Austria: European Centre for Modern Languages.

Harris, V. and **M. Grenfell.** 2004. 'Language-learning strategies: A case for cross-curricular collaboration'. *Language Awareness*, 13/2: 116–30.

Harris, V. and **J. Prescott.** 2005. 'Learning strategy instruction: In theory and in practice'. *Scottish Languages Review* 11. http://www.scilt.stir.ac.uk.

Harris, V. and **D. Snow.** 2004. *Doing it for Themselves: Focus on Learning Strategies and Vocabulary Building*. ClassicPathfinder 4. London: CILT.

Hartmann, R. K. K. and **G. James.** 1998. *Dictionary of Lexicography*. London, New York: Routledge.

Harvey, K. and **D. Yuill.** 1997. 'A study of the use of a monolingual pedagogical dictionary by learners of English engaged in writing'. *Applied Linguistics* 18/3: 253–278.

Hasbún, L. 1987. Comparison of Language Learning Strategies Employed by Good Versus Poor Language Learners. Unpublished masters thesis, Indiana University, USA.

Hasbún, L. 2005. 'The effect of explicit vocabulary teaching on vocabulary acquisition and attitudes toward reading'. *Revista Electronica Actualidades Investigativas en Educacion* 5/2: 1–21.

Hashim, R. A. and **S. A. S. Sahil.** 1994. 'Examining learners' language learning strategies'. *RELC Journal* 25/1: 1–20.

Hassan X., E. Macaro, D. Mason, G. Nye, P. Smith, and **R. Vanderplank.** 2005. 'Strategy training in language learning—a systematic review of available research' in Research Evidence in Education Library. London: EPPI-Centre, Social Science Research Unit, Institute of Education, University of London. http://eppi.ioe.ac.uk/EPPIWeb/home.aspx?page=/reel/review_groups/mfl/review_one.htm.

Hatasa, Y. and **E. Soeda.** 2000. 'Writing strategies revisited: A case of non-cognate L2 writers' in Swierzbin, B., F. Morris, M. E. Anderson, C. A. Klee, and E. Tarone (eds.): *Social and Cognitive Factors in Second Language Acquisition.* Somerville, MA: Cascadilla Press.

Hayes, N. A. and **D. E. Broadbent.** 1988. 'Two modes of learning for interactive tasks'. *Cognition* 28/3: 249–76.

Haynes, M. 1984. 'Patterns and perils of guessing in a foreign language' in Hanscombe, J., R. A. Orem, and B. P. Taylor (eds.): *On TESOL '83.* Washington, DC: TESOL.

Hedgcock, J. and **N. Lefkowitz.** 1992. 'Collaborative oral/aural revision in foreign language writing instruction'. *Journal of Second Language Writing* 1/3: 255–76.

Heine, L. 2005. 'Lautes Denken als Forschungsinstrument in der Fremdsprachenforschung' [Thinking-aloud as research instrument in foreign language research]. *Zeitschrift für Fremdsprachenforschung* 16/2: 163–85.

Heine, L. and **K. Schramm.** 2007. 'Lautes Denken in der Fremdsprachenforschung. Eine Handreichung für die empirische Praxis' [Think-alouds in foreign language research. A practical guide for empirical studies] in Vollmer, H. J. (ed.): *Synergieeffekte in der Fremdsprachenforschung. Empirische Zugänge, Probleme, Ergebnisse.* Frankfurt am Main, Germany: Lang.

Henner-Stanchina, C. 1986/1987. 'Autonomy as metacognitive awareness: Suggestions for training self-monitoring of listening comprehension'. *Mélanges Pédagogiques* 17: 69–84.

Herron, C., P. Cole, H. York, and **P. Linden.** 1998. 'A comparison study of student retention of foreign language video: Declarative versus interrogative advance organizer'. *Modern Language Journal* 82/2: 237–47.

Hewett, N. 1990. 'Reading, cognitive style, and culture: A look at some relationships in second-language acquisition' in Labarca, A. and L. Bailey (eds.): *Issues in L2: Theory as Practice/Practice as Theory* (Delaware Symposium 9). Norwood, NJ: Ablex.

Hill, M. 1994. 'A word in your ear: To what extent does hearing a new word help learners to remember it?' in Bird, N., P. Falvery, A. B. M. Tsui, D. M. Allison, and A. McNeill (eds.): *In Language and Learning.* Hong Kong: Hong Kong Education Department.

Hinkel, E. and **S. Fotos.** 2002. 'From theory to practice: A teacher's view' in Hinkel, E. and S. Fotos (eds.): *New Perspectives on Grammar Teaching in Second Language Classrooms.* Mahwah, NJ: Erlbaum.

Hirose, K. and **M. Sasaki.** 1994. 'Explanatory variables for Japanese students' expository writing in English: An exploratory study'. *Journal of Second Language Writing* 3/3: 203–29.

Hogben, D. and **J. M. Lawson.** 1994. 'Keyword and multiple elaboration strategies for vocabulary acquisition in foreign language learning'. *Contemporary Educational Psychology* 19/3: 367–76.

Holliday, A. 2003. 'Social autonomy: Addressing the dangers of culturism in TESOL' in Palfreyman, D. and R. Smith (eds.): *Learner Autonomy across Cultures.* London: Palgrave Macmillan.

Holm, A. and **B. Dodd.** 1996. 'The effect of first written language on the acquisition of English literacy'. *Cognition* 59/2: 119–47.

Holmes, J. and **R. G. Ramos.** 1993. 'False friends and reckless guessers: Observing cognate recognition strategies' in Huckin, T., M. Haynes, and J. Coady (eds.): *Second Language Reading and Vocabulary Learning.* Norwood, NJ: Ablex.

Horst, M. 2005. 'Learning L2 vocabulary through extensive reading: A measurement study'. *Canadian Modern Language Review* 61/3: 355–82.

Horst, M., T. Cobb, and **P. Meara.** 1998. 'Beyond a clockwork orange: Acquiring second language vocabulary through reading'. *Reading in a Foreign Language* 11/2: 207–23.

Hosenfeld, C. 1976. 'Learning about learning – discovering our students' strategies'. *Foreign Language Annals* 9/2:117–29.

Hosenfeld, C. 1977. 'A preliminary investigation of the reading strategies of successful and non-successful second language learners'. *System* 5/2: 110–213.

Hosenfeld, C. 1984. 'Case studies of ninth grade readers' in Alderson, J. C. and A. H. Urquhart (eds.): *Reading in a Foreign Language*. London: Longman.

Howe, R. B. K. 1991. 'Introspection: A reassessment'. *New Ideas in Psychology* 9/1: 23–44.

Hsiao, T.-Y. and R. L. Oxford. 2002. 'Comparing theories of language learning strategies: A confirmatory factor analysis'. *Modern Language Journal* 86/3: 368–83. http://www.cup.cam.ac.uk/assets/elt/nation/alphabeticalbibliography.doc

Hu, J. 2003. 'Thinking languages in L2 writing: Research findings and pedagogical implications'. *TESL Canada Journal* 21/1: 39–63.

Huber, G. L. and H. Mandl. 1982. 'Verbalisierungsmethoden zur Erfassung von Kognitionen im Handlungszusammenhang' [Verbalization methods to collect data on cognition in its action context] in Huber, G. L. and H. Mandl (eds.): *Verbale Daten. Eine Einführung in die Grundlagen und Methoden der Erhebung und Auswertung*. Weinheim, Germany: Beltz.

Huckin, T., M. Haynes, and J. Coady (eds). 1993. *Second Language Reading and Vocabulary Learning*. Norwood, NJ: Ablex.

Hudson, T. 1982. 'The effects of induced schemata on the "short-circuit" in L2 reading performance'. *Language Learning* 32/1:1–30.

Hulstijn, J. H. and J. F. Matter (eds.). 1991. *Reading in Two Languages. AILA Review* 8 Erfurt: AILA.

Hulstijn, J. H. 1993. 'When do foreign language readers look up the meaning of unfamiliar words? The influence of task and learner variables'. *Modern Language Journal* 77/2: 130–47.

Hulstijn, J. H. 1997. 'Mnemonic methods in foreign-language vocabulary learning: Theoretical considerations and pedagogical implications' in Coady, J. and T. Huckin (eds.): *Second Language Vocabulary Acquisition: A Rationale for Pedagogy*. Cambridge: Cambridge University Press.

Hulstijn, J. H. 2005. 'Theoretical and empirical issues in the study of implicit and explicit second-language learning'. *Studies in Second Language Acquisition* 27/2: 129–40.

Hulstijn, J. H., M. Hollander, and T. Greidanus. 1996. 'Incidental vocabulary learning by advanced foreign language students: The influence of marginal glosses, dictionary use, and reoccurrence of unknown words'. *Modern Language Journal* 80/3: 327–39.

Hunt, A. and D. Beglar. 2005. 'A framework for developing EFL reading vocabulary'. *Reading in a Foreign Language* 17/1. Retrieved September 30, 2005 from http://nflrc.hawaii.edu/rfl/April2005/hunt/hunt.html.

Hwang, M.-H. 2003. Listening Comprehension Problems and Strategy Use by Secondary Learners of English in Korea. Unpublished doctoral thesis, University of Essex, Colchester, UK.

Hymes, D. 1967/1972. 'On communicative competence' in Pride, J. B. and J. Holmes (eds.): *Sociolinguistics*. Harmondsworth: Penguin.

Ikeda, M. and O. Takeuchi. 2000. 'Tasks and strategy use: Empirical implications for questionnaire studies'. *JACET Bulletin* 31: 21–32.

Ikeda, M. and O. Takeuchi. 2006. 'Clarifying the differences in learning EFL reading strategies: An analysis of portfolios'. *System* 34/3: 384–98.

Janssen, D., L. van Waes, and H. van den Bergh. 1996. 'Effects of thinking aloud on writing processes' in Levy, C. M. and S. Ransdell (eds.): *The Science of Writing: Theories, Methods, Individual Differences and Applications*. Mahwah, NJ: Erlbaum.

Jensen, C. and C. Hansen. 1995. 'The effect of prior knowledge on EAP listening-test performance'. *Language Testing* 12/1: 99–119.

Jiménez, R. T., G. E. Garcia, and P. D. Pearson. 1996. 'The reading strategies of bilingual Latina/o students who are successful English readers: Opportunities and obstacles'. *Reading Research Quarterly* 31/1: 90–112.

Johns, A. 1990. 'L1 composition theories: Implications for developing theories of L2 composition' in Kroll, B. (ed.): *Second Language Writing: Research Insights for the Classroom*. Cambridge: Cambridge University Press.

Johnson, K. 1992. 'Cognitive strategies and second language writers: A reevaluation of sentence combining'. *Journal of Second Language Writing* 1/1: 61–75.

Johnson, K. 1996. *Language Teaching and Skill Learning*. Oxford: Blackwell.

Johnson, P. 1981. 'Effects on reading comprehension of language complexity and cultural background of a text'. *TESOL Quarterly* 15/2: 169–81.

Johnson, P. 1982. 'Effects on reading comprehension of building background knowledge'. *TESOL Quarterly* 16/4: 503–16.

Jones, B. F., A. S. Palinscar, D. S. Ogle, and E. G. Carr. 1987. *Strategic Teaching and Learning: Cognitive Instruction in the Content Areas*. Alexandria, VA.: Association for Supervision and Curriculum Development.

Jones, L. C. and J. L. Plass. 2002. 'Supporting listening comprehension and vocabulary acquisition in French with multimedia annotations'. *Modern Language Journal* 86/4: 546–61.

Jones, S. and J. Tetroe. 1987. 'Composing in a second language' in Matsuhashi, A. (ed): *Writing in Real Time: Modelling Production Processes*. Norwood, NJ.: Ablex.

Jones, S. and J. Tetroe. 1988. 'Composing in a second language' in Matsuhashi, A. (ed.): *Writing in Real Time: Modelling Production Processes*. Norwood, NJ: Ablex.

Jourdain, S. 2000. 'A native-like ability to circumlocute'. *Modern Language Journal* 84/2: 185–95.

Jourdenais, R. 2001. 'Cognition, instruction and protocol analysis' in Robinson, P. (ed.): *Cognition and Second Language Instruction*. Cambridge: Cambridge University Press.

Kaiser, A. and R. Kaiser. 1999. *Metakognition. Denken und Problemlösen optimieren* [Metacognition. Optimizing thinking and problem-solving]. Neuwied, Germany: Luchterhand.

Kameyama, S. 2004. *Verständnissicherndes Handeln. Zur reparativen Bearbeitung von Rezeptionsdefiziten in deutschen und japanischen Diskursen* [Comprehension-securing action. Repair of reception deficits in German and Japanese discourses]. Münster, Germany/ New York: Waxmann.

Kaplan, R. B. 1966. 'Cultural thought patterns in inter-cultural education'. *Language Learning* 16/1: 1–20.

Karmiloff-Smith, A. 1979. *A Functional Approach to Child Language*. Cambridge: Cambridge University Press.

Kasper, G. 1998. 'Analysing verbal protocols'. *TESOL Quarterly* 32/2: 358–63.

Kasper, L. F. 1997. 'Assessing the metacognitive growth of ESL student writers'. *TESL-EJ Journal* 3/1: 1–20. http://www-writing.berkeley.edu/TESL-EJ/ej09/a1.html. Accessed May 6 2006.

Kato, F. 2000. Integrating Learning Strategies, Time Management, and Anxiety-Free Learning in a Tertiary Level Course in Basic Japanese: An Intervention Study. Unpublished doctoral thesis, University of Sydney, Australia.

Kawai, Y. 2000. 'Effects of cultural contextualization in listening materials on motivation and strategy use'. *ITL Review of Applied Linguistics* 127: 101–26.

Keller, H. H. 1978. *New Perspectives on Teaching Vocabulary*. Language in education series 8. Arlington, VA: Center for Applied Linguistics.

Kellerman, E. 1991. 'Compensatory strategies in second language research: A critique, a revision and some (non-) implications for the classroom' in Phillipson, R., E. Kellerman, L. Selinker, M. Sharwood-Smith, and M. Swain (eds.): *Foreign and Second Language Pedagogy Research*. Clevedon: Multilingual Matters.

Kellerman, E. and E. Bialystok. 1997. 'On psychological plausibility in the study of communication strategies' in Kasper, G. and E. Kellerman (eds.): *Communication Strategies: Psycholinguistic and Sociolinguistic Perspectives*. London: Longman.

Kelly, P. 1992. 'Does the ear assist the eye in the long-term retention of lexis?' *IRAL* 30/2: 137–45.

Kent, T. (ed.). 1999. *Post-Process Theory: Beyond the Writing-Process Paradigm*. Carbondale: Southern Illinois University Press.

Kern, R. G. 1989. 'Second language reading strategy instruction: Its effects on comprehension and word inference ability'. *Modern Language Journal* 73/2: 135–49.

Kern, R. G. 1994. 'The role of mental translation in second language reading'. *Studies in Second Language Acquisition* 16/4: 441–61.

Khaldieh, S. A. 2000. 'Learning strategies and writing process of proficient vs. less-proficient learners of Arabic'. *Foreign Language Annals* 33/5: 522–33.

Khanji, R. 1996. 'Two perspectives in analysing communication strategies'. *IRAL* 34/2: 144–54.

Kim, D. 1999. An Exploration of Listening Comprehension Linked to Authentic Input and Language Learning Strategies in a Second Language. Unpublished doctoral thesis, University of Texas, Austin, TX.

Kitajima, R. 1997. 'Referential strategy training for second language reading comprehension of Japanese texts'. *Foreign Language Annals* 30/1: 84–97.

Kitajima, R. 2001. 'The effect of instructional conditions on students' vocabulary retention'. *Foreign Language Annals* 34/5: 470–82.

Kluwe, R. H. 1981. 'Metakognition' [Metacognition] in Michaelis, W. (ed.): *Bericht über den 32. Kongreß der Deutschen Gesellschaft für Psychologie in Zürich 1980* (Vol. 1). Göttingen, Germany: Verlag für Psychologie, Hogrefe.

Kluwe, R. H. and K. Schiebler. 1984. 'Entwicklung exekutiver Prozesse und kognitive Leistungen' [Development of executive processes and cognitive achievement] in Weinert, F. E. and R. H. Kluwe (eds.): *Metakognition, Motivation und Lernen*. Stuttgart, Germany: Kohlhammer.

Knight, S. 1994. 'Dictionary use while reading: The effects on comprehension and vocabulary acquisition for students of different verbal abilities'. *Modern Language Journal* 78/3: 285–99.

Knight, S., Y. Padrón, and H. Waxman. 1985. 'The cognitive reading strategies of ESL students'. *TESOL Quarterly* 19/4: 789–92.

Kobayashi, H. and C. Rinnert. 1992. 'Effects of first language on second language writing: Translation versus direct composition'. *Language Learning* 42/2: 183–215.

Kobayashi, H. and C. Rinnert. 2001. 'Factors relating to EFL writers' discourse level revision skills'. *International Journal of English Studies* 1/2: 71–101.

Koda, K. 1990. 'The use of L1 reading strategies in L2 reading: Effects of L1 orthographic structures on L2 phonological recoding strategies'. *Studies in Second Language Acquisition* 12/4: 393–410.

Koda, K. 1993. 'Task-induced variability in FL composing: Language-specific perspectives'. *Foreign Language Annals* 26/3: 332–46.

Koda, K. 2005. *Insights into Second Language Reading: A Cross-Linguistic Approach*. Cambridge: Cambridge University Press.

Kohler, B. D. 2002. The Effects of Metacognitive Language Learning Strategy Training on Lower-Achieving Second Language Learners. Unpublished doctoral thesis, Brigham Young University, Provo, UT, USA.

Kojic-Sabo, I. and P. M. Lightbown, 1999. 'Students' approaches to vocabulary learning and their relationship to success'. *Modern Language Journal* 83/2: 176–92.

Konishi, K. and E. Tarone. 2004. 'English Constructions used in compensatory strategies: Baseline data for communicative EFL instruction' in Boxer, D. and A. D. Cohen (eds.): *Studying Speaking to Inform Second Language Learning*. Clevedon: Multilingual Matters.

Kost, C. R., P. Foss, and J. J. Lenzini. 1999. 'Textual and pictorial glosses: Effectiveness on incidental vocabulary growth when reading in a foreign language'. *Foreign Language Annals* 32/1: 89–113.

Kozulin, A. and E. Garb. 2001 (August). 'Dynamic assessment of EFL text comprehension of at-risk students'. Paper presented at the Ninth Conference of the European Association for Research on Learning and Instruction, Fribourg, Switzerland. Retrieved June 1, 2006 from http://www.icelp.org/files/research/DynamicAssessOfESL.pdf.

Kozulin, A., B. Gindis, V. S. Ageyev, and S. M. Miller. 2003. *Vygotsky's Educational Theory in Cultural Context*. Cambridge: Cambridge University Press.

Krashen, S. 1982. *Principles and Practice in Second Language Acquisition*. Oxford: Pergammon Press.

Krashen, S. 1984. *Writing: Research, Theory and Applications*. Oxford: Pergamon Press.

Krashen, S. 1989. 'We acquire spelling by reading: Additional evidence for the input hypothesis'. *Modern Language Journal* 73/4: 440–62.

Krashen, S. 1996. *The Natural Approach: Language Acquisition in the Classroom*. Northumberland, UK: Bloodaxe.

Krings, H. 1994. 'What do we know about writing processes in L2? The state of the art'. *Odense Working Papers in Language and Communication* 6: 83–114.

Ku, P. N. 1995. Strategies Associated with Proficiency and Predictors of Strategy Choice: A Study of Language Learning Strategies of EFL Students at Three Educational Levels in Taiwan. Unpublished doctoral thesis, Indiana University, Bloomington, IN, USA.

Kumaravadivelu, B. 1993. 'The name of the task and the task of naming: Methodological aspects of task based pedagogy' in Crookes, G. and S. M. Gass (eds.): *Tasks in a Pedagogical Context*. Clevedon: Multilingual Matters.

Kusiak, M. 2001. 'The effect of metacognitive strategy training on reading comprehension and metacognitive knowledge'. *EUORSLA Yearbook*: 255–74.

Labarca, A. and R. Khanji. 1986. 'On communication strategies: Focus on interaction'. *Studies in Second Language Acquisition* 86/1: 68–79.

Lally, C. G. 2000. 'First language influences in second language composition: The effect of pre-writing'. *Foreign Language Annals* 33/4: 428–32.

Lau, R. L. and R. L. Oxford. 2003. 'Language learning strategy profiles of elementary school students in Taiwan'. *International Review of Applied Linguistics and Language Teaching* 41/4: 339–79.

Langer, J. A., L. Bartolome, O. Vasquez, and T. Lucas. 1990. 'Meaning construction in school literacy tasks: A study of bilingual students'. *American Educational Research Journal* 27/3: 427–71.

Lantolf, J. and G. Appel. (eds.). 1994. *Vygotskyan Approaches to Second Language Research*. New Jersey: Ablex Publishing.

Lantolf, J. P. and A. Pavlenko. 2001. '(S)econd (L)anguage (A)ctivity. Understanding second language learners as people' in Breen, M. (ed.): *Learner Contributions to Language Learning: New Directions in Research*. London: Longman.

Larsen-Freeman, D. 1997. 'Chaos/complexity science and second language acquisition'. *Applied Linguistics* 18/2: 141–65.

Larsen-Freeman, D. 2000. 'Second language acquisition and applied linguistics'. *Annual Review of Applied Linguistics* 20: 165–81.

Laufer, B. 1997. 'What's in a word that make it hard or easy? Intralexical factors affecting the difficulty of vocabulary acquisition' in Schmitt, N. and M. McCarthy (eds.): *Vocabulary Description, Acquisition and Pedagogy*. Cambridge: Cambridge University Press.

Laufer, B. 2003. 'Vocabulary acquisition in second language: Do learners really acquire most vocabulary by reading?: Some experimental evidence'. *Canadian Modern Language Review* 59/4: 567–87.

Laufer, B. and M. Hill. 2000. 'What lexical information do L2 learners select in a CALL dictionary and how does it affect word retention?'. *Language Learning and Technology* 3/2: 58–76.

Laufer, B. and J. H. Hulstijn. 2001. 'Incidental vocabulary acquisition in a second language: The construct of task-induced involvement'. *Applied Linguistics* 22/1: 1–26.

Laufer, B. and P. Nation. 1995. 'Vocabulary size and use: Lexical richness in L2 written production'. *Applied Linguistics* 16/3: 307–22.

Laufer, B. and H. Osimo. 1991. 'Facilitating long-term retention of vocabulary: The second–hand cloze'. *System* 19/3: 217–24.

Laufer, B. and K. Shmueli. 1997. 'Memorizing new words: Does teaching have anything to do with it?'. *RELC Journal* 28/1: 89–108.

Lave, J. and E. Wenger. 1991. *Situated Learning: Legitimate Peripheral Participation.* Cambridge: Cambridge University Press.

Laviosa, F. 2000. 'The listening comprehension processes and strategies of learners of Italian: A case study'. *Rassegna Italiana di Linguistica Applicata* 2: 129–59.

Lawson, M. and D. Hogben. 1996. 'The vocabulary-learning strategies of foreign-language students'. *Language Learning* 46/1: 101–35.

Lay, N. 1982. 'Composing processes of adult ESL learners'. *TESOL Quarterly* 16/3: 406.

Lay, N. 1988. 'The comforts of the first language in learning to write'. *Kaleidoscope* 4/1: 15–18.

Leeke, P. and P. Shaw. 2000. 'Learners' independent records of vocabulary'. *System* 28/2: 272–89.

Leki, I. 1995. 'Coping strategies of ESL students in writing tasks across the curriculum'. *TESOL Quarterly* 29/2: 235–60.

Leont'ev, A. N. 1974a/1984. Der allgemeine Tätigkeitsbegriff [The general activity concept] in Viehweger D. (ed.): *Grundfragen einer Theorie der sprachlichen Tätigkeit.* Stuttgart, Germany: Kohlhammer.

Leont'ev, A. N. 1974b/1984. 'Sprachliche Tätigkeit' [Linguistic activity] in Viehweger, D. (ed.): *Grundfragen einer Theorie der sprachlichen Tätigkeit.* Stuttgart, Germany: Kohlhammer.

Leow, R. P. and K. Morgan-Short. 2004. 'To think aloud or not to think aloud. The issue of reactivity in SLA research methodology'. *Studies in Second Language Acquisition* 26/1: 35–57.

Levine. A. and T. Reves. 1998. 'Data-collecting on reading-writing strategies: A comparison of instruments: A case study'. *TESL-EJ Journal* 3/3: 1–11. http://www-writing.berkeley. edu/TESL-EJ/ej11/a1.html.

Levine, A., T. Reves, and B. L. Leaver. 1996. 'Relationship between language learning strategies and Israeli versus Russian cultural-educational factors' in Oxford, R. L. (ed.): *Language Learning Strategies Around the World: Cross-Cultural Perspectives.* Manoa: University of Hawai'i Press.

Lewicki, P. 1986. 'Processing information about covariations that cannot be articulated'. *Journal of Experimental Psychology: Learning, Memory, and Cognition* 12/1: 135–46.

Lewis, M. 1993. *The Lexical Approach.* Hove: Language Teaching Publications.

Lewis, M. 1997. *Implementing the Lexical Approach.* Hove: Language Teaching Publications.

Lewis, M. 2002. *Teaching Collocation: Further Developments in the Lexical Approach.* Hove: Language Teaching Publications.

Li, L. 1997. 'Dictionaries and their users at a Chinese university with special reference to ESP learners'. Paper read at the International Conference on Dictionaries in Asia: Research and Pedagogic Implications, Hong Kong University of Science and Technology, March 26–29 1997.

Lidz, C. (ed.). 1987. *Dynamic Assessment.* New York: Guildford Press.

Lidz, C. and J. Elliott (eds.). 2000. *Dynamic Assessment: Prevailing Models and Applications.* Oxford: Elsevier Science.

Lincoln, Y. S. and E. G. Guba. 2000. 'Paradigmatic controversies, contraindications, and emerging confluences' in Denzin, N.K. and Y. S. Lincoln (eds.): *Handbook of Qualitative Research*. (2nd ed.). Thousand Oaks, CA: Sage.

Lindeberg, A. C. 1988. Cohension, Coherence, and Coherence Patterns in Expository and Argumentative Student Essays in EFL: An Exploratory Study. Licenciate thesis, Department of English, Abo Akademi University, Turku, Finland.

Littlemore, J. 2001. 'An empirical study of the relationship between cognitive style and the use of communicative strategy.' *Applied Linguistics* 22/2: 241–65.

Littlemore, J. 2003. 'The communicative effectiveness of different types of communication strategy'. *System* 31/3: 331–47.

LoCastro, V. 1994. 'Learning strategies and learning environments'. *TESOL Quarterly* 28/2: 409–14.

Long, D. 1990. 'What you don't know can't help you. An exploratory study of background knowledge and second language listening comprehension'. *Studies in Second Language Acquisition* 12/1: 65–80.

Long, D. 1991. *Listening Processes in Authentic Texts. Acting on Priorities: A Commitment to Excellence*. Dimension: Languages '90. Report of the Southern Conference on Language Teaching.

Long, M. H. 1980. 'Inside the "black box": Methodological issues in classroom research on language learning'. *Language Learning* 30/1: 1–42.

Long, M. H. 1981. 'Questions in foreigner talk discourse'. *Language Learning* 31/1: 135–57.

Long, M. H. 1983. 'Linguistics and conversational adjustments to non-native speakers'. *Studies in Second Language Acquisition* 5/2: 177–94.

Long, M. H. 1983. 'Native speaker non-native speaker conversation and the negotiation of comprehensible input'. *Applied Linguistics* 4/2: 126–41.

Long, M. H. 1985. 'A role for instruction in second language acquisition: Task-based language training' in Hyltenstam, K. and M. Pienemann (eds.): *Modeling and Assessing Second Language Acquisition*. Clevedon: Multilingual Matters.

Long, M. H. 1987. 'The experimental classroom'. *Annals of the American Academy of Political and Social Science* 490: 97–109.

Long, M. H. 1997. 'Focus on form in task-based language teaching'. Fourth Annual McGraw-Hill Satellite Conference. Retrieved September 2, 2005 from http://www.mhhe.com/socscience/foreignlang/conf/task1.htm.

Lovejoy, K. B. 1991. 'Cohesion and information strategies in academic writing: Analysis of passages in three disciplines'. *Linguistics and Education* 3/4: 315–43.

Ludwig, J. 1984. 'Vocabulary acquisition as a function of word characteristics'. *Canadian Modern Language Review* 40/4: 552–62.

Ma, Z. X. 2004. 'The necessity of intensifying English vocabulary teaching in the remote minority area college English teaching'. *Asian EFL Journal* 6/2. Retrieved September 30, 2005 from http://asian-efl-journal.com/june_04_mzx.php.

Macaro, E. 2001. *Learning Strategies in Foreign and Second Language Classrooms*. London: Continuum.

Macaro, E. 2006. 'Strategies for language learning and for language use: revising the theoretical framework'. *Modern Language Journal* 90/3: 320–37.

Mackey, A. and S. M. Gass. 2005. *Second Language Research: Methodology and Design*. Mahwah, NJ: Erlbaum.

Maier, P. 1992. 'Politeness strategies in business letters by native and non-native English speakers'. *English for Specific Purposes* 11/3: 189–205.

Malt, B. C. and S. A. Sloman. 2003. 'Linguistic diversity and object naming by non-native speakers of English'. *Bilingualism: Language and Cognition* April: 47–67.

Manchón, R. M. 1997. 'Learners' strategies in L2 composing'. *Communication and Cognition* 30/1–2: 91–114.

Manchón, R. M. 1999. 'La investigación sobre la escritura como proceso. Algunas implicaciones para la enseñanza de la composición en lengua extranjera' [Research on writing as process. Implications for the teaching of foreign language writing] in Salaberri, S. (ed.): *Lingüística Aplicada a la Enseñanza de Lenguas Extranjeras*. Almería: Servicio de Publicaciones de la Universidad de Almería.

Manchón, R. M. 2001. 'Trends in the conceptualization of second language composing strategies: A critical analysis'. *International Journal of English Studies* 1/2: 47–70.

Manchón, R. M. In press. 'Language learning and language use strategies. The research and its implications for instructed language learning' in Usó, E. and N. Ruiz-Madrid (eds.): *Pedagogical Reflections on Teaching and Learning Modern Languages*. Castelló, Spain: Publicacions de la Universitat Jaume I.

Manchón, R. M., L. Murphy, and J. Roca de Larios. 2005. 'Using concurrent protocols to explore L2 writing processes: Methodological issues in the collection and analysis of data' in Matsuda, P. K. and T. Silva (eds.): *Second Language Writing Research. Perspectives on the Process of Knowledge Construction*. Mahwah, NJ: Erlbaum.

Manchón, R. M. and J. Roca de Larios. 2005. 'Forms and functions of backtracking in L2 writing: A study of Spanish EFL learners at different proficiency levels'. Paper presented at the XXIII Conference of the Spanish Association of Applied Linguistics, Palma de Mallorca, Spain, March 10–12.

Manchón, R. M., J. Roca de Larios, and L. Murphy. 1998. 'Language ability, writing behaviours and the use of backward operations in L2 writing'. Paper presented at the American Association for Applied Linguistics Conference, Seattle, March 14–17.

Manchón, R. M., J. Roca de Larios, and L. Murphy. 2000a. 'An approximation to the study of backtracking in L2 writing'. *Learning and Instruction* 10/1: 13–35.

Manchón, R. M., J. Roca de Larios, and L. Murphy. 2000b. 'The strategic value of backtracking in L2 writing'. Paper presented at the American Association for Applied Linguistics 2000 Conference, Vancouver, BC, Canada, March 11–14.

Marefat, H. 2003. 'The impact of teaching direct learning strategies on the retention of vocabulary by EFL learners'. *The Reading Matrix* 3/2: 47–62.

Markham, P. and M. Latham. 1987. 'The influence of religion-specific background knowledge on the listening comprehension of adult second-language students'. *Language Learning* 37/2: 157–70.

Marrie, B. and J. E. Netten. 1991. 'Communication strategies'. *Canadian Modern Language Review* 47/3: 442–62.

Massaro, D. W. and M. M. Cohen. 1994. 'Visual, orthographic, phonological and lexical influences in reading'. *Journal of Experimental Psychology: Human Perception and Performance* 20/6: 1107–28.

Matsumoto, K. 1995. 'Research paper writing strategies of professional Japanese EFL writers'. *TESL Canada Journal* 13/1: 17–27.

Mauranen, A. 1992. 'Reference in academic rhetoric: A contrastive study of Finnish and English writing'. Conference paper at Nordic Research on Text and Discourse. ERIC.

McCaslin, M. and D. T. Hickey. 2001. 'Self-regulated learning and academic achievement: A Vygotskian view' in Zimmerman, B. J. and D. Schunk (eds.): *Self-Regulated Learning and Academic Achievement*. (2nd ed.). Mahwah, NJ: Erlbaum.

McDonough, J. and S. McDonough. 2001. 'Composing in a foreign language: An insider-outsider perspective'. *Language Awareness* 10/4: 233–47.

McDonough, S. H. 1995. *Strategy and Skill in Learning a Foreign Language*. London: Arnold.

McDonough, S. H. 1999. 'Learner strategies: State of the art article'. *Language Teaching* 32/1: 1–18.

McGruddy, R. 1995. The Effect of Listening Comprehension Strategy Training with Advanced Level ESL Students. Unpublished doctoral thesis, Georgetown University, Washington, DC, USA.

Meara, P. 1980. 'Vocabulary acquisition: A neglected aspect of language learning'. *Language Teaching and Linguistics: Abstracts* 13/4: 221–46.

McNeill, D. 1992. *Hand and Mind. What Gestures Reveal About Thought*. Chicago: University of Chicago Press.

Meskill, C. 1991. 'Language learning strategies advice: A study on the effects of on-line messaging'. *System* 19/1: 277–87.

Miller, G.A. and P. Gildea. 1985. 'How to misread a dictionary'. *AILA Bulletin* 1985: 13–26.

Minick, N. 1987. 'Implications of Vygotsky's theory for dynamic assessment' in Lidz, C. (ed.): *Dynamic Assessment*. New York: Guildford Press.

Ministry of Maori Development. 2003. *Kei Te Aku Tonu Au. Strategies for Second Language Learners of Te Reo Maori*. Te Puni Kokiri, Wellington, New Zealand. http://www.tpk.govt. nz/publications/docs/keiteakotonuau.pdf

Mishler, E. G. 1991. 'Representing discourse: The rhetoric of transcription'. *Journal of Narrative and Life History* 1/4: 255–80.

Mitchell, E. 1983. *Search-do Reading: Difficulties in Using a Dictionary*. Aberdeen: College of Education.

Mochizuki, A. 1999. 'Language learning strategies used by Japanese university students'. *RELC Journal* 30: 101–13.

Mokhtari, K. 1998–2000. Metacognitive-Awareness-of-Reading-Strategies Inventory (MARSI). Unpublished instrument, Oklahoma State University, Stillwater, OK, USA.

Mokhtari, K. and R. Sheorey. 2002. 'Measuring ESL students' awareness of reading strategies'. *Journal of Developmental Education* 25: 2–10.

Mondria, J. A. 2003. 'The effects of inferring, verifying, and memorizing on the retention of L2 word meanings: an experimental comparison of the "meaning-inferred method" and the "meaning-given method"'. *Studies in Second Language Acquisition* 25/4: 473–99.

Mondria, J. A. and M. Wit-de Boer. 1991. 'The effects of contextual richness on the guessability and the retention of words in a foreign language'. *Applied Linguistics* 12/3: 249–67.

Moore, J. C. and J. R. Surber. 1992. 'Effects of context and keyword methods on second language vocabulary acquisition'. *Contemporary Educational Psychology* 17/3: 286–92.

Moragne e Silva, M. 1989. 'A study of composition in first and second language'. *Texas Papers in Foreign Language Education* 1/2. 132–51.

Morin, R. 2003. 'Derivational morphological analysis as a strategy for vocabulary acquisition in Spanish'. *Modern Language Journal* 87/2: 200–21.

Morin, R. and J. Goebel. 2001. 'Basic vocabulary instruction: Teaching strategies or teaching words?'. *Foreign Language Annals* 34/1: 8–17.

Mullins, P. Y. 1992. Successful English Language Learning Strategies of Students Enrolled at the Faculty of Arts, Chulalongkorn University, Bangkok, Thailand. Unpublished doctoral thesis, International University, San Diego, CA, USA.

Murphy, J. M. 1985. An Investigation into the Listening Strategies of ESL College Students. Unpublished doctoral thesis, University of Columbia, USA.

Nagy, W., G. Garcia, A. Durgunoğlu, and B. Hancin-Bhatt. 1993. 'Spanish-English bilingual students' use of cognates in English reading'. *Journal of Reading Behavior* 25/3: 241–59.

Naiman, N., M. Fröhlich, H. H. Stern, and A. Todesco. 1996. *The Good Language Learner*. Clevedon: Multilingual Matters.

Nakahama, Y., A. Tyler, and L. van Lier. 2001. 'Negotiation of meaning in conversation and information gap activities: A comparative discourse analysis'. *TESOL Quarterly* 35/1: 377–405.

Nakatani, Y. 2005. 'The effects of awareness-raising training on oral communication strategy use'. *Modern Language Journal* 89/1: 76–91.

Nakatani, Y. 2006. 'Developing an oral communication strategy inventory'. *Modern Language Journal* 90/2: 151–68.

Nassaji, H. 2003. 'L2 vocabulary learning from context: Strategies, knowledge sources, and their relationship with success in L2 lexical inferencing'. *TESOL Quarterly* 37/4: 645–70.

Nation, I. S. P. 1990. *Teaching and Learning Vocabulary*. Rowley, MA: Newbury House.

Nation, I. S. P. 2000. 'Learning vocabulary in lexical sets: Dangers and guidelines'. *TESOL Journal* 9/2: 6–10.

Nation, I. S. P. 2001. *Learning Vocabulary in Another Language*. Cambridge: Cambridge University Press.

Nation, P. 2005. 'Teaching vocabulary'. *Asian EFL Journal* 7/3:47–54. Retrieved September 30, 2005 from http://asian-efl-journal.com/September_05_pn.php.

National Capital Language Resource Center. 2000a. *High school foreign language students' perceptions of language learning strategies use and self-efficacy*. Research report: http://nclrc.org/products/hsflstud.pdf.

National Capital Language Resource Center. 2000b. *Elementary immersion students' perceptions of language learning strategies use and self-efficacy*. Research report: http://nclrc.org/products/immstud.pdf.

National Capital Language Resource Center. 2003. *The elementary immersion learning strategies resource guide*. Washington, DC: National Capital Language Resource Center. http://www.nclrc.org/eils.

National Capital Language Resource Center. 2004. *Sailing the 5 Cs with Learning Strategies: A Resource Guide for Secondary Foreign Language Educators*. Washington, DC: National Capital Language Resource Center. http://www.nclrc.org/sailing/index.html.

Nattinger, J. 1988. 'Some current trends in vocabulary teaching' in Carter, R. and M. McCarthy (eds.): *Vocabulary and Language Teaching*. London: Longman.

Nesi, H. and P. Meara. 1994. 'Patterns of misinterpretation in the productive use of EFL dictionary definition'. *System* 22/1: 1–15.

Neubach, A. and A. D. Cohen. 1988. 'Processing strategies and problems encountered in the use of dictionaries'. *Journal of the Dictionary Society of North America* 10: 1–19.

Newman, I. and C. R. Benz. 1998. *Qualitative-Quantitative Research Methodology: Exploring the Interactive Continuum*. Carbondale: University of Illinois Press.

Nisbet, D. L., E. R. Tindall, and A. A. Arroyo. 2005. 'Language learning strategies and English proficiency of Chinese university students'. *Foreign Language Annals* 38/1: 100–7.

Nisbett, R. E. and T. D. Wilson. 1977. 'Telling more than we can know: Verbal reports on mental processes'. *Psychological Review* 84/3: 231–59.

Norris, J. and L. Ortega. 2000. 'Effectiveness of L2 instruction: A research synthesis and quantitative meta-analysis'. *Language Learning* 50/3: 417–528.

Norton, B. 2000a. *Identity and Language Learning: Gender, Ethnicity and Educational Change*. Harlow: Longman/Pearson Education.

Norton, B. 2000b. 'Identity, investment, and language loss' in McKay, S. and S.-L. Wong (eds.): *English Language Learners in the United States: A Resource for Teachers*. Cambridge: Cambridge University Press.

Norton, B. 2001. 'Non-participation, imagined communities, and the language classroom' in Breen, M. (ed.), *Learner contributions to language learning: New directions in research*. Harlow: Pearson Education.

Norton, B. and K. Toohey. 2001. 'Changing perspectives on good language learners'. *TESOL Quarterly* 35/2: 307–22.

Nuccorini, S. 1994. 'On dictionary misuse' in Martin, W. *et al.* (eds.): *EURALEX' 94 Proceedings*. Amsterdam: Vrije Universiteit.

Nuffield Foundation. 2000. *The Nuffield Languages Inquiry. Languages: The Next Generation*. London: The Nuffield Foundation.

Nunan, D. 1988. *The Learner-centered Curriculum*. New York: Cambridge University Press.

Nunan, D. 1992. *Research Methods in Language Learning*. New York: Cambridge University Press.

Nunan, D. 1996. 'Learner strategy training in the classroom: An action research study'. *TESOL Journal* 6/1: 35–41.

Nunan, D. 1997. 'Does learner strategy training make a difference?' *Lenguas Modernas* 24: 123–42.

Nuttall, C. 2005. *Teaching Reading Skills in a Foreign Language*. (3rd ed.). Oxford: Macmillan Heinemann.

Nyikos, M. 1987. The Effect of Color and Imagery as Mnemonic Strategies on Learning and Retention of Lexical Items in German. Unpublished doctoral thesis, Purdue University, USA.

Nyikos, M. 1989. 'Memory hooks and other mnemonic devices: A brief overview for language teachers' in Westphal, P. B. (ed.): *Meeting the call for excellence in the foreign language classroom*. New Jersey: Newbury House Publishers.

Nyikos, M. 1990. 'Sex-related differences in adult language learning: Socialization and memory factors'. *Modern Language Journal* 74/3: 273–87.

Nyikos, M. and R. L. Oxford. 1993. 'A factor analytic study of language learning strategy use: Interpretations from information-processing theory and social psychology'. *Modern Language Journal* 77/1: 11–22.

OECD. 2006. *Where Immigrant Students Succeed – A Comparative Review of Performance and Engagement in PISA 2003*. Paris: OECD Publishing.

Oh, J. 1992. 'Learning strategies used by university EFL students in Korea'. *Language Teaching* 1: 3–53

Okada, M., R. L. Oxford, and S. Abo. 1996. 'Not all alike: Motivation and learning strategies among students of Japanese and Spanish: An exploratory study' in Oxford, R. L. (ed.): *Language Learning Motivation: Pathways to the New Century*. Manoa: University of Hawai'i Press.

Oliphant, K. 1997. *Acquisition of Grammatical Gender in Italian as a Foreign Language* (Net Work #7). Honolulu: University of Hawai'i. Retrieved December 9, 2006 from http://www.lll.hawaii.edu/nflrc/NetWorks/NW7.

Olivares-Cuhat, G. 2002. 'Learning strategies and achievement in the Spanish writing classroom: A case study'. *Foreign Language Annals* 35/5: 561–70.

Olsen, S. 1999. 'Errors and compensatory strategies: A study of grammar and vocabulary in text written by Norwegian learners of English'. *System* 27/2: 191–205.

O'Malley, J. M. and A. U. Chamot. 1990. *Learning Strategies in Second Language Acquisition*. Cambridge: Cambridge University Press.

O'Malley, J. M., A. U. Chamot, and L. Küpper. 1989. 'Listening comprehension strategies in second language acquisition'. *Applied Linguistics* 10/4: 418–37.

O'Malley, J. M., A. U. Chamot, G. Stewner-Manzanares, R. P. Russo, and L. Küpper. 1985a. 'Learning strategies used by beginner and intermediate ESL students'. *Language Learning* 35/1: 21–46.

O'Malley, J. M., A. U. Chamot, G. Stewner-Manzanares, R. P. Russo, and L. Küpper. 1985b. 'Learning strategy application with students of English as a second language'. *TESOL Quarterly* 19/3: 285–96.

Osada, N. 2001. 'What strategy do less proficient learners employ in listening comprehension?: A reappraisal of bottom-up and top-down processing'. *Pan-Pacific Association of Applied Linguistics* 5/1: 73–90.

Ott, C. E., R.S. Blake, and D. C. Butler. 1976. 'Implications of mental elaboration for the acquisition of foreign language vocabulary'. *International Review of Applied Linguistics in Language Teaching* 14/1: 37–48.

Ott, C. E., D. C. Butler, R.S. Blake, and J. P. Ball. 1973. 'The effect of interactive-image elaboration on the acquisition of foreign language vocabulary'. *Language Learning* 23/2: 197–206.

Oxford, R. L. 1986. *Development and Psychometric Testing of the Strategy Inventory for Language Learning*. ARI Technical Report 728. Alexandria, VA: US Army Research Institute for Behavioral and Social Sciences.

Oxford, R. L. 1990a. *Language Learning Strategies. What every teacher should know*. Boston, MA: Heinle.

Oxford, R. L. 1990b. 'Styles, strategies, and aptitude: Important connections for language learners' in Parry, T. S. and C. W. Stansfield (eds.): *Language Aptitude Reconsidered*. Englewood Cliffs, NJ: Prentice Hall.

Oxford, R. L. 1993a. 'Instructional implications of gender differences in language learning styles and strategies'. *Applied Language Learning* 4/1–2: 65–94.

Oxford, R. L. 1993b. 'La différence continue. . . : Gender differences in second/foreign language learning styles and strategies' in Sutherland, J. (ed.): *Exploring Gender*. Englewood Cliffs, NJ: Prentice Hall.

Oxford, R. L. 1994. 'Gender differences in strategies and styles for L2 learning: What is the significance? Should we pay attention?' in Alatis, J. E. (ed.): *Theory and Practice of Strategies in Second Language Acquisition*. Washington, DC: Georgetown University Press.

Oxford, R. L. 1996a. 'Employing a questionnaire to assess the use of language learning strategies'. *Applied Language Learning* 71–2: 25–45.

Oxford, R. L. 1996b. 'When emotion meets (meta)cognition in language learning histories'. The teaching of culture and language in the second language classroom: Focus on the learner. Special issue, A. Moeller (ed.). *International Journal of Educational Research* 23/7: 581–94.

Oxford, R. L. Forthcoming. 'Task-based language teaching and learning'. *Asian EFL Journal*.

Oxford, R. L. 1999. 'Relationships between second language learning strategies and language proficiency in the context of learner autonomy and self-regulation'. *Revista Canaria de Estudios Ingleses* 38: 108–26.

Oxford, R. L. 2003. 'Toward a more systematic model of L2 learner autonomy' in Palfreyman, D. and R. C. Smith (eds.): *Learner Autonomy Across Cultures*. Basingstoke: Palgrave Macmillan.

Oxford, R. L. 2006a. *Transforming learning and teaching: Strategy instruction techniques*. Presentation at the Defense Language Institute Foreign Language Center, Monterey, CA, USA.

Oxford, R.L. 2006b. 'Task-based language learning and teaching: An overview.' *Asian EFL Journal* 8/3: Article 5. http://www.asian-efl-journal.com/Sept_06_ro.php.

Oxford, R. L. and J. A. Burry-Stock. 1995. 'Assessing the use of language learning strategies worldwide with the ESL/EFL version of the strategy inventory for language learning (SILL)'. *System* 23/1: 1–23.

Oxford, R., Y. Cho, S. Leung, and H-J. Kim. 2004. 'Effect of the presence and difficulty of task on strategy use: An exploratory study'. *International Review of Applied Linguistics* 42/1: 1–47.

Oxford, R. L. and A. D. Cohen. 1992. 'Language learning strategies: Crucial issues of concept and classification'. *Applied Language Learning* 3/1–2: 1–35.

Oxford, R. L., D. Crookall, A.Cohen, R. Lavine, M. Nyikos, and W. Sutter. 1990. 'Strategy training for language learners: Six situational case studies and a training model'. *Foreign Language Annals*, 22/3: 197–216.

Oxford, R. L. and M. E. Ehrman. 1995. 'Adults' language learning strategies in an intensive foreign language program in the United States'. *System* 23/3: 359–86.

Oxford, R. L. and J. M. Green. 1995. 'Comments on Virginia LoCastro's 'Learning strategies and learning environments. Making sense of learning strategy assessment: Towards a higher standard of research accuracy'. *TESOL Quarterly* 29/1: 166–71.

Oxford, R. L., R. Z. Lavine, G. Felkins, M. E. Hollaway, and A. Saleh. 1996. *Language learning strategies around the world: Cross-cultural perspectives*. Second Language Teaching and Curriculum Centre, University of Hawaii.

Oxford, R. L. and B. L. Leaver. 1996. 'A synthesis of strategy instruction for language learners' in Oxford, R. L. (ed.): *Language Learning Strategies Around the World: Cross-Cultural Perspectives*. Manoa: University of Hawai'i Press.

Oxford, R. L., K. R. Massey, and S. Anand. 2005. 'Transforming teacher-student style relationships: Toward a more welcoming and diverse classroom discourse' in Holten, C. and J. Frodesen (eds.): *The Power of Discourse in Language Learning and Teaching*. Boston: Heinle and Heinle.

Oxford, R. L. and M. Nyikos. 1989. 'Variables affecting choice of language learning strategies by university students'. *Modern Language Journal* 73/3: 291–300.

Oxford, R. L., M. Nyikos, and M. Ehrman. 1988. 'Vive la différence?: Reflections on sex differences in use of language learning strategies'. *Foreign Language Annals* 21: 321–29.

Oxford, R. L., Y. Y. Park-Oh, S. Ito, and M. Sumrall. 1993. 'Learning a language by satellite television: What influences student achievement?' *System* 21/1: 31–48.

Oxford, R. L. and R. Scarcella. 1994. 'Second language vocabulary learning among adults: State of the art in vocabulary instruction'. *System* 22/2: 231–43.

Oxford, R. L., S. Tomlinson, A. Barcelos, C. Harrington, R. Lavine, A. Saleh, and A. Longhini. 1998. 'Clashing metaphors about classroom teachers: Toward a systematic typology for the language teaching field'. *System* 26/1: 3–51.

Ozeki, N. 2000. Listening Strategy Instruction for Female EFL College Students in Japan. Unpublished doctoral thesis, Indiana University of Pennsylvania, Indiana, PA, USA.

Padrón, Y. N. 1985. Utilizing Cognitive Reading Strategies to Improve English Reading Comprehension of Spanish-Speaking Bilingual Students. Unpublished doctoral thesis, University of Houston, Houston, TX, USA.

Padrón, Y. N., S. L. Knight, and H. C. Waxman. 1986. 'Analyzing bilingual and monolingual students' perceptions of their reading strategies'. *Reading Teacher* 39: 430–33.

Paige, R. M., A. D. Cohen, B. Kappler, J. C. Chi, and J. P. Lassegard. 2002. *Maximizing Study Abroad*. Minneapolis, MN: Center for Advanced Research on Language Acquisition, University of Minnesota.

Paige, R. M., A. D. Cohen, and R. L. Shively. 2004. 'Assessing the impact of a strategies-based curriculum on language and culture learning abroad'. *Frontiers: The Interdisciplinary Journal of Study Abroad* 10: 253–76.

Paivio, A. and A. Desrochers. 1981. 'Mnemonic techniques and second-language learning'. *Journal of Educational Psychology* 73/6: 780–95.

Paribakht, T. S. 1985. 'Strategic competence and language proficiency'. *Applied Linguistics* 6/2: 132–46.

Paribakht, T. S. and M. Wesche. 1997. 'Vocabulary enhancement activities and reading for meaning in second language vocabulary acquisition' in Coady, J. and T. Huckin (eds.): *Second Language Vocabulary Acquisition: A Rationale for Pedagogy*. New York: Cambridge University Press.

Paris, S. G., J. P. Byrnes, and A. H. Paris. 2001. 'Constructing theories, identities, and actions of self-regulated learners' in Zimmerman, B. J. and D. Schunk (eds.): *Self-Regulated Learning and Academic Achievement*. (2nd ed.). Mahwah, NJ: Erlbaum.

Park, G. P. 1997. 'Language learning strategies and English proficiency in Korean University students'. *Foreign Language Annals* 30/2: 211–21.

Park-Oh, Y. Y. 1994. Self-Regulated Strategy Training in Second-Language Reading: Its Effects on Reading Comprehension, Strategy Use, Reading Attitudes, and Learning Styles of College ESL Students. Unpublished thesis, University of Alabama, Tuscaloosa, AL, USA.

Parry, K. 1991. 'Building a vocabulary through academic reading'. *TESOL Quarterly* 25/4: 629–53.

Parry, K. 1993. 'The social construction of reading strategies: New directions for research'. *Journal of Research in Reading* 16/2: 148–58.

Peacock, M. and B. Ho. 2003. 'Student language learning strategies across eight disciplines'. *International Journal of Applied Linguistics* 13/2: 179–200.

Pennington, M. C. and S. So. 1993. 'Comparing writing process and product across two languages: A study of 6 Singaporean university student writers'. *Journal of Second Language Writing* 2/1: 41–63.

Perruchet, P. and M. A. Amorim. 1992. 'Conscious knowledge and changes in performance in sequence learning: Evidence against dissociation'. *Journal of Experimental Psychology: Learning, Memory, and Cognition* 18: 785–800.

Peters, M. 1999. Les Stratégies de Compréhension Auditive chez des Élèves du Bain Linguistique en Français Langue Seconde. Unpublished doctoral thesis, University of Ottawa, Canada.

Petric, B. and B. Czárl. 2003. 'Validating a writing strategy questionnaire'. *System* 31/2: 187–215.

Pica, T. 2002. 'Subject-matter content: How does it assist the interactional and linguistic needs of classroom language learners?' *Modern Language Journal* 86: 1–19.

Pica, T. and C. Doughty. 1985. 'Input and interaction in the communicative language classroom: A comparison of teacher-fronted and group activities' in Gass, S. M. and C. Madden (eds.): *Input and Second Language Acquisition*. Rowley, MA: Newbury House.

Pica, T., L. Holliday, N. Lewis, and L. Morgenthaler. 1989. 'Comprehensive output as an outcome of linguistic demands on the learner'. *Studies in Second Language Acquisition* 11/1: 63–87.

Pica, T., F. Lincoln-Porter, D. Paninos, and J. Linnell. 1996. 'Language learner's interaction: How does it address the input, output, and feedback needs of L2 learners?'. *TESOL Quarterly* 30/1: 59–84.

Pienemann, M., J.-U. Keßler, and E. Roos (eds.). 2006. *Englischerwerb in der Grundschule* [The acquisition of English in elementary school]. Paderborn, Germany: Schöningh/UTB.

Pintrich, P. and D. H. Schunk. 1996. *Motivation in Education Theory, Research, and Applications*. Englewood Cliffs, NJ: Prentice Hall.

Politzer, R. L. 1983. 'An exploratory study of self-reported language learning behaviours and their relation to achievement'. *Studies in Second Language Acquisition* 6/1: 54–68.

Politzer, R. L. and M. McGroarty. 1985. 'An exploratory study of learning behaviours and their relationship to gains in linguistic and communicative competence'. *TESOL Quarterly* 19/1: 103–23.

Porte, G. 1995. Estrategias de Revisión en Expresión Escrita en Lengua Inglesa como Segunda Lengua. Unpublished doctoral thesis, University of Granada, Spain.

Porte, G. 1996. 'When writing fails: How academic context and past learning experiences shape revision'. *System* 24/1: 107–16.

Porte, G. 1988. 'Poor language learners and their strategies for dealing with new vocabulary'. *ELT Journal* 42/3: 167–72.

Porte, G. 1997. 'The etiology of poor second language writing: The influence of perceived teacher preferences on second language revision strategies'. *Journal of Second Language Writing* 6/1: 61–78.

Poulisse, N. 1987. 'Problems and solutions in the classification of compensatory strategies'. *Second Language Research* 3/2: 141–53.

Poulisse, N. 1990. *The Use of Compensatory Strategies by Dutch Learners of English*. Enschede: Sneldruk.

Poulisse, N. 1993. 'A theoretical account of lexical communication strategies' in Schreuder, r. and B. Wettens (eds.). *The Bilingual Lexicon*. Amsterdam: John Benjamins.

Poulisse, N., T. Bongaerts, and E. Kellerman. 1987. 'The use of retrospective verbal reports in the analysis of compensatory strategies' in Færch, C. and G. Kasper (eds.): *Introspection in Second Language Research*. Clevedon: Multilingual Matters.

Poulisse, N. and E. Schils. 1989. 'The Influence of task- and proficiency-related factors on the use of compensatory strategies: A quantitative analysis'. *Language Learning* 39/1: 15–48.

Pressley, M. and P. Afflerbach. 1995. *Verbal Protocols of Reading: the nature of constructively responsive reading*. Hillsdale, NJ: Erlbaum.

Pressley, M., P. B. El-Dinary, J. Gaskins, T. Schuder, J. L. Bergman, J. Alma, and R. Brown. 1992. 'Beyond direct explanation: Transactional instruction of reading comprehension strategies'. *Elementary School Journal* 92: 511–54.

Pritchard, R. 1990a. 'The effects of cultural schemata on reading processing strategies'. *Reading Research Quarterly* 25/4: 273–295.

Pritchard, R. 1990b. 'The evolution of introspective methodology and its implications for studying the reading process'. *Reading Psychology* 11/1: 1–13.

Pulido, D. 2004 'The relationship between text comprehension and second language incidental vocabulary acquisition: a matter of topic familiarity?'. *Language Learning* 54/3: 469–523.

Qi, D. S. 1998. 'An inquiry into language-switching in second language composing processes'. *Canadian Modern Language Review* 54/3: 413–35.

Raimes, A. 1985. 'What unskilled writers do as they write: A classroom study of composing.' *TESOL Quarterly* 19/2: 229–58.

Raimes, A. 1987. 'Language proficiency, writing ability, and composing strategies: A study of ESL college student writers'. *Language Learning* 37/3: 439–67.

Rasekh, Z. E. and R. Ranjbary. 2003. 'Metacognitive strategy training for vocabulary learning'. *TESL-EJ* 7/2. Retrieved September 30, 2005 from http://www-writing.berkeley. edu/TESL-EJ/ej26/a5.html.

Raugh, M. R. and R. C. Atkinson. 1975. 'A mnemonic method for learning a second-language vocabulary', *Journal of Educational Psychology* 67/1: 1–16m.

Raymond, P. M. 1993. 'The effects of structure strategy training on the recall of expository prose for university students reading French as a second language'. *Modern Language Journal* 77/4: 445–58.

Read, J. 2004. 'Research in teaching vocabulary'. *Annual Review of Applied Linguistics* 24: 146–61.

Reber, A. S. 1976. 'Implicit learning of synthetic languages: The role of instructional set'. *Journal of Experimental Psychology: Human Learning and Memory* 2: 88–94.

Redder, A. 2001. 'Aufbau und Gestaltung von Transkriptionssystemen' [Organization and development of transcription systems] in Brinker, K., G. Antos, W. Heinemann, and S. F. Sager (eds.): *Text- und Gesprächslinguistik*. [Linguistics of Text and Conversation]. *Ein internationales Handbuch zeitgenössischer Forschung*. [An International Handbook of Contemporary Research] (Vol. 2). Berlin/New York: de Gruyter.

Redder, A. 2002. 'Professionelles Transkribieren' [Transcribing professionally] in Jäger, L. and G. Stanitzek (eds.): *Transkribieren. Medien/Lektüre*. München, Germany. Fink.

Rees-Miller, J. 1993. 'A critical appraisal of learner training: Theoretical bases and teaching implications'. *TESOL Quarterly* 27/4: 679–89.

Rees-Miller, J. 1994. 'The author responds...' *TESOL Quarterly* 28/4: 776–81.

Rehbein, J. 1977. *Komplexes Handeln. Elemente zur Handlungstheorie der Sprache*. [Complex action. Elements of the action theory of language]. Stuttgart, Germany: Metzler.

Rehbein, J. 1995. 'Segmentieren' [Segmenting]. *Verbmobil Memo* 64. Hamburg, Germany: Universität Hamburg.

Rehbein, J., T. Schmidt, B. Meyer, F. Watzke, and A. Herkenrath. 2004. 'Handbuch für das computergestützte Transkribieren nach HIAT' [Manual for computer-assisted HIAT transcriptions]. Universität Hamburg, Sonderforschungsbereich 538/Mehrsprachigkeit: *Arbeiten zur Mehrsprachigkeit* [Working Papers in Multilingualism], 56. http://www1. uni-hamburg.de/exmaralda/index-en.html

Reiss, M. A. 1981. 'Helping the unsuccessful language learner'. *Modern Language Journal* 65 (Summer 1981): 121–28.

Reiss, M. A. 1985. 'The good language learner: Another look'. *Canadian Modern Language Review* 41/3: 511–523.

Rheinberg, F., R. Vollmeyer, and W. Rollett. 2000. 'Motivation and action in self-regulated learning' in Boekaerts, M., P. R. Pintrich, and M. Zeidner (eds.): *Handbook of Self-Regulation*. San Diego, CA: Academic Press.

Riazi, A. 1997. 'Acquiring disciplinary literacy: A social-cognitive analysis of text production and learning among Iranian graduate students of education'. *Journal of Second Language Writing* 6/2: 105–37.

Richards, J. 1976. 'The role of vocabulary teaching'. *TESOL Quarterly* 10/1: 77–89.

Riley, L. and K. Harsch. 1999. 'Enhancing the learning experience with strategy journals: Supporting the diverse learning styles of ESL/EFL students'. *Proceedings of the HERDSA Annual International Conference*, 1–18. http://www.herdsa.org.au/branches/vic/ Cornerstones/tocauthors.html.

Riley, L. and K. Harsch. 2006. 'Promoting self-regulated learning: Resources for teachers and researchers'. Retrieved March 27, 2006 from http://www2.hawaii.edu/~kenton/srl.

Robinson, P. 2005. 'Aptitude and second language acquisition'. *Annual Review of Applied Linguistics* 25: 46–73.

Roby, W. R. 1991. Glossed and Dictionaries in Paper and Computer Formats as Adjunct Aids to the Reading of Spanish Texts by University Students. Unpublished doctoral thesis, University of Kansas, USA.

Roby, W. R. 1999. 'What's in a Gloss?'. *Language Learning and Technology*, 2/2: 94–101. Retrieved July 31, 1999 from http://llt.msu.edu/vol2num2/pdf/commentary.pdf.

Roca de Larios, J. 1996. 'Linearization strategies in L2 writing: Some observations'. *Lenguaje y Textos* 8: 191–208.

Roca de Larios, J. 1999. Cognitive Processes in L1 and L2 Writing: A Cross-Sectional Study. Unpublished doctoral thesis, University of Murcia, Spain.

Roca de Larios, J., J. Marín, and L. Murphy. 2001. 'A temporal analysis of formulation processes in L1 and L2 writing'. *Language Learning* 51/3: 497–538.

Roca de Larios, J., L. Murphy, and R. M. Manchón. 1999. 'The use of restructuring strategies in EFL writing: A study of Spanish learners of English as a foreign language'. *Journal of Second Language Writing* 8/1: 13–44.

Roca de Larios, J., L. Murphy, and J. Marín. 2002. 'A critical examination of L2 writing process research' in Ransdell, S. and M.-L. Barbier (eds.): *New Directions for Research in L2 Writing*. Dordrecht: Kluwer Academic Publishers.

Rogoff, B. 1990. *Apprenticeship in Thinking: Cognitive Development in Social Context*. Oxford: Oxford University Press.

Rogoff, B. 1994. 'Developing understanding of the idea of the community of learners'. *Mind, Culture and Activity* 1: 209–29.

Rossiter, M. J. I. 2003. 'It's like a chicken but bigger: Effects of communication strategy in the ESL classroom'. *Canadian Modern Language Review* 60: 105–21.

Rost, M. and S. Ross. 1991. 'Learner use of strategies in interaction: Typology and teachability'. *Language Learning* 41/2: 235–73.

Rott, S. 2000. 'Relationship between the process of reading, word inferencing, and incidental word acquisition, in assigning meaning to form' in Lee, J. and A. Waldman (eds.): *Issues in Language Program Direction*. Boston, MA: Heinle and Heinle.

Rubin, J. 1975. 'What the 'Good Language Learner' can teach us'. *TESOL Quarterly* 9/1: 41–51.

Rubin, J. 1981. 'Study of cognitive processes in second language learning'. *Applied Linguistics* 11/2: 117–31.

Rubin, J. 1990. 'Improving foreign language listening comprehension' in Alatis, J. E. (ed.): *Georgetown University Round Table on Languages and Linguistics*. Washington, DC: Georgetown University Press.

Rubin, J. 1994. 'A review of second language listening comprehension research'. *Modern Language Journal* 78/2: 199–221.

Rubin, J. 2001. 'Language learner self-management'. *Journal of Asian Pacific Communication* 11/1: 25–37.

Rubin, J. 2003. 'Diary writing as a process: Simple, useful, powerful'. *Guidelines* 25/2: 10–14.

Rubin, J. 2005. 'The expert language learner: A review of good language learner studies and learner strategies' in Johnson, K. (ed.): *Expertise in Second Language Learning and Teaching*. Basingstoke: Palgrave Macmillan.

Rubin, J., J. Quinn, and J. Enos. 1988. *Improving Foreign Language Listening Comprehension*. Report to US Department of Education, International Research and Studies Program.

Rubin, J. and I. Thompson. 1994. *How to be a more successful language learner*. Boston, MA: Heinle and Heinle.

Ruhe, V. 1996. 'Graphics and listening comprehension'. *TESL Canada Journal* 14/1: 45–60.

Rumelhart, D. E. 1977. 'Toward an interactive model of reading' in Dornic, S. (ed.): *Attention and Performance VI*. Hillsdale, NJ: Erlbaum.

Sagarra, N. and M. Alba. 2006. 'The key is the keyword: L2 vocabulary learning methods with beginning learners of Spanish'. *Modern Language Journal* 90/2: 228–243.

Salaberry, R. 2001. 'Task-sequencing in L2 acquisition'. *Texas Papers in Foreign Language Education* 6/1: 101–12.

Salomone, A. M. and F. Marsal. 1997. 'How to avoid language breakdown? Circumlocution'. *Foreign Language Annals* 30: 473–84.

Sanaoui, R. 1992. Vocabulary Learning and Teaching in French as a Second Language Classrooms. Unpublished doctoral thesis, University of Toronto.

Sanaoui, R. 1995. 'Adult Learners' approach to learning vocabulary in second languages'. *Modern Language Journal* 79/1: 15–28.

Sarig, G. 1987. 'High-level reading in the first and in the foreign languages: Some comparative process data' in Devine, J., P. L. Carrell, and D. E. Eskey (eds.): *Research in Reading English as a Second Language*. Washington, DC: TESOL.

Sasaki, M. 2000. 'Toward an empirical model of EFL writing processes: An exploratory study'. *Journal of Second Language Writing* 9/3: 259–91.

Sasaki, M. 2002. 'Building an empirically-based model of EFL learners' writing processes' in Ransdell, S. and M.-L. Barbier (eds.): *New Directions for Research in L2 Writing*. Dordrecht: Kluwer Academic Publishers.

Sasaki, M. 2004. 'A multiple-data analysis of the 3.5-year development of EFL student writers'. *Language Learning* 54/3: 525–82.

Sasaki, M. and K. Hirose. 1996. 'Explanatory variables for EFL students' expository writing'. *Language Learning* 46/1: 137–74.

Scarcella, R. C. and R. L. Oxford. 1992. *The Tapestry of Language Learning: The Individual in the Communicative Classroom*. Boston: Heinle and Heinle.

Scardamalia, M. and C. Bereiter. 1986. 'Research on written composition' in Wittrock, M. (ed.): *Handbook of Research on Teaching*. London: MacMillan.

Schiefele, U., A. Krapp, K.-P. Wild, and A. Winteler. 1992. *Eine neue Version des "Fragebogens zum Studieninteresse" (FSI). Untersuchungen zur Reliabilität und Validität.* [A new version of the "Study Interest Questionnaire (SIQ)". Studies on its reliability and validity]. Munich, Germany: Universität der Bundeswehr.

Schiefele, U., A. Krapp, K.-P. Wild, and A. Winteler. 1993. 'Der "Fragebogen zum Studieninteresse" (FSI)' [The "Study Interest Questionnaire" (SIQ)]. *Diagnostica* 39/4: 335–51.

Schmidt, R. 1990. 'The role of consciousness in second language learning'. *Applied Linguistics* 11/2: 129–158.

Schmidt, R. 1992. 'Psychological mechanisms underlying second language fluency'. *Studies in Second Language Acquisition* 14/4: 357–85.

Schmidt R. 1994a. 'Deconstructing consciousness in search of useful definitions for applied linguistics'. *AILA Review* 11: 11–26.

Schmidt, R. 1994b. 'Implicit learning and the cognitive unconscious: Of artificial grammars and SLA' in Ellis, N. C. (ed.): *Implicit and Explicit Learning of Languages*. San Diego, CA: Academic Press.

Schmidt, R. 1995. 'Consciousness and foreign language learning: A tutorial on the role of attention and awareness in learning' in Schmidt, R. (ed.): *Attention and Awareness in Foreign Language Learning*. Manoa: University of Hawai'i Press.

Schmidt, R. 2001. 'Attention' in Robinson, P. (ed.): *Cognition and Second Language Instruction*. New York: Cambridge University Press.

Schmidt, R., D. Boraie, and O. Kassabgy. 1996. 'Foreign language motivation: Internal structure and external connections' in Oxford, R. L. (ed.): *Language Learning Motivation: Pathways to the New Century*. Manoa: University of Hawai'i Press.

Schmitt, N. 1997. 'Vocabulary learning strategies' in Schmitt, N. and M. McCarthy (eds.): *Vocabulary: Description, Acquisition, and Pedagogy*. Cambridge: Cambridge University Press.

Schmitt, N. 2000. *Vocabulary in Language Teaching*. Cambridge: Cambridge University Press.

Schmitt, N. and M. McCarthy. 1997. *Vocabulary: Description, Acquisition, and Pedagogy*. Cambridge: Cambridge University Press.

Schnotz, W., S.-P. Ballstaedt and H. Mandl. 1981. 'Lernen mit Texten aus handlungstheoretischer Sicht' [Learning with texts: An action-theoretical perspective] in Mandl, H. *Befunde, Probleme*. München, Germany: Urban & Schwarzenberg.

Scholfield, P. 1982. 'The role of bilingual dictionaries in ESL/EFL: A positive view'. Guidelines Regional English Language Centre 4: 84–98.

Scholfield, P. 1999. 'Dictionary use in reception'. *International Journal of Lexicography* 12/1: 13–34.

Schoonen, R., J. Hulstijn, and B. Bossers. 1998. 'Metacognitive and language-specific knowledge in native and foreign-language reading comprehension: An empirical study among Dutch students in grades 6, 8, and 10'. *Language Learning* 48/1: 71–106.

Schramm, K. 2005. 'Aktives Zuhören beim Geschichtenerzählen' [Active listening during story-telling]. *Grundschule Deutsch* 8: 20–22.

Schramm, K. 2001. *L2-Leser in Aktion. Der fremdsprachliche Leseprozeß als mentales Handeln* [L2-readers in action. The foreign language reading process as mental action]. Münster, Germany/New York: Waxmann.

Schramm, K. 2005. 'Multimedia transcription of think-aloud data on the L2 reading process'. *Papers in Applied Linguistics Münster (PALM)* 22: 1–36. http://miami.uni-muenster. de/servlets/DerivateServlet/Derivate-616/palm_inhalt.html

Schramm, K. 2006. 'Interaktion bei Grundschulerzählungen in Deutsch als Zweitsprache – Exemplarische Analysen und Exploration für ein relationales Datenbank-Design' [Scaffolding L2 story-telling in the elementary school classroom] in B. Ahrenholz, (ed.): *Kinder mit Migrationshintergrund. Spracherwerb und Fördermöglichkeiten*. Freiburg i. B., Germany: Fillibach.

Schramm, K. Forthcoming. 'Grammatikerwerb beim zweitsprachlichen Erzählen' [Grammar acquisition during second language story-telling] in K.-M. Köpcke, and A. Ziegler (eds.): *Grammatik in Universität und Schule*. Tübingen, Germany: Neimeyer.

Schwarzer, D. 2004. 'Student and teacher strategies for communicating through dialogue journals in Hebrew: A teacher research project'. *Foreign Language Annals* 37/1: 77–84.

Searle, J. R. 1969. *Speech acts. An essay in the philosophy of language*. Cambridge: Cambridge University Press.

Searle, J. R. 1979. *Expression and meaning. Studies in the theory of speech acts*. Cambridge: Cambridge University Press.

Segler, T., H. Pain, and A. Sorace. 2002. 'Second Language Vocabulary Acquisition and Learning Strategies in ICALL Environments'. *Computer Assisted Language Learning* 15/4: 409–14.

Seliger, H. W. 1983. 'The language learner as linguist: Of metaphors and realities'. *Applied Linguistics* 4/3: 179–91.

Seliger, H. W. and E. Shohamy. 1989. *Second Language Research Methods*. Oxford: Oxford University Press.

Selinker, L. 1972. 'Interlanguage'. *International Review of Applied Linguistics* 10: 209–31.

Selting, M., P. Auer, B. Barden, J. Bergmann, E. Couper-Kuhlen, S. Günthner, C. Meier, U. Quasthoff, P. Schlobinski, and S. Uhrmann. 1998. 'Gesprächsanalytisches Transkriptionssystem (GAT)' [Conversation-analytical transcription system (GAT)]. *Linguistische Berichte* 173: 91–122. http://www.fbls.uni-hannover.de/sdls/schlobi/schrift/GAT/gat.pdf.

Sengupta, S. 2000. 'An investigation into the effects of revision strategy instruction on L2 secondary school learners'. *System* 28/1: 97–113.

Seo, K. 2000. Intervening in Tertiary Students' Strategic Listening in Japanese as a Foreign Language. Unpublished doctoral thesis, Griffith University, Australia.

Shaw, P. 1991. 'Science research students composing processes'. *English for Specific Purposes* 10/3: 189–206.

Sheorey, R. and K. Mokhtari. 2001. 'Differences in the metacognitive awareness of reading strategies among native and non-native readers'. *System* 29/4: 431–49.

Shimoda, T. 1989. 'The Effects of interesting examples and topic familiarity on text comprehension, attention, and reading speed'. *Journal of Experimental Education* 61/2: 93–103.

Sinclair, B. 1999. 'Wrestling with a Jelly: The evaluation of learner autonomy' in Morrison, B. (ed.): *Experiments and Evaluation in Self-Access Language Learning*. Selected Papers from the 2nd HASALD conference September 5, 1998. Hong Kong: HASALD.

Singhal, M. 1998. 'A comparison of L1 and L2 reading: Cultural differences and schema'. *Internet TESL Journal* 4/10. http://iteslj.org/Articles/Singhal-ReadingL1L2.html. Accessed January 28, 2006.

Singleton, D. 1989. *Language Acquisition: The Age Factor*. Clevedon: Multilingual Matters.

Sionis, C. 1995. 'Communication strategies in the writing of scientific research articles by non-native users of English'. *English for Specific Purposes* 14/2: 99–113.

Skehan, P. 1989. *Individual Differences in Second-Language Learning*. London: Arnold.

Skehan, P. 2002. 'Theorizing and updating aptitude' in Robinson, P. (ed.): *Individual Differences and Instructed Language Learning*. Amsterdam: John Benjamins.

Skibniewski, L. 1988. 'The writing processes of advanced foreign language learners in their native and foreign languages: Evidence from thinking-aloud and behavior protocols'. *Studia Anglica Posnaniensia* 21: 177–86.

Smith, F. 1978/1986. *Reading*. Cambridge: Cambridge University Press.

Smith, N., T. McEnery, and R. Ivanic. 1998. 'Issues in transribing a corpus of children's handwritten projects'. *Literary and Linguistic Computing* 13/4: 217–24.

Smith, V. 1994. *Thinking in a foreign language: An investigation into essay writing and translation by L2 learners*. Tübingen: Narr.

Spack, R. 1997. 'The acquisition of academic literacy in a second language: A longitudinal case study'. *Written Communication* 14/1: 3–62.

Sparks, R. and L. Ganshow. 1993. 'Searching for the cognitive locus of foreign language learning difficulties: Linking first and second language learning'. *Modern Language Journal* 77/3: 289–302.

Stanovich, K. E. 1980. 'Toward an interactive-compensatory model of individual differences in the development of reading fluency'. *Reading Research Quarterly* 16/1: 32–65.

Steffensen, M. S. and C. Joag-Dev. 1984. 'Cultural knowledge and reading' in Alderson, J. C. and A. H. Urquhart (eds.): *Reading in a Foreign Language*. New York: Longman.

Stern, H. H. 1975. 'What can we learn from the good language learner?'. *Canadian Modern Language Review* 31: 304–318.

Sternberg, R. J. 2002. 'The theory of successful intelligence and its implications for language-aptitude testing' in Robinson, P. (ed.): *Individual Differences and Instructed Language Learning*. Mahwah, NJ: Erlbaum.

Stevens, F. 1984. *Strategies for Second Language Acquisition*. Montréal: Eden Press.

Stevenson, M., R. Schoonen, and K. de Glopper. 2003. 'Inhibition or compensation? A multi-dimensional comparison of reading processes in Dutch and English'. *Language Learning* 53/4:765–815.

Stevick, E. W. 1990. 'Research on what? Some terminology'. *Modern Language Journal* 74/2: 143–53.

Stiefenhöfer, H. 1986. *Lesen als Handlung. Didaktisch-methodische Uberlegungen und unterrichtspraktische Versuche zur fremdsprachlichen Lesefähigkeit.* [Reading as action. Teaching reflections and action research on foreign language reading ability]. Weinheim, Germany/Basel, Switzerland: Beltz.

Stoffer, I. 1995. University Foreign Language Students' Choice of Vocabulary Learning Strategies as Related to Individual Difference Variables. Unpublished doctoral dissertation, University of Alabama, USA.

Stone, R. 1985. 'Effects of English/Spanish language pattern differences on ESL learners' comprehension of English text'. ERIC Document Reproduction Service No. ED 266434.

Strage, A. 1998. 'Family context variables and the development of self-regulation in college students'. *Adolescence* 55: 17–31.

Strømsø, H. I., I. Bråten, and M. S. Samuelstuen. 2003. 'Students' strategic use of multiple sources during expository reading: A longitudinal think-aloud study'. *Cognition and Instruction* 21/2: 113–47.

Swain, M. 1985. 'Communicative competence: Some roles of comprehensible input and comprehensible output in its development' in Gass, S. M. and C. Madden (eds.): *Input in Second Language Acquisition.* Rowley, MA: Newbury House.

Taillefer, G. F. 2005. 'Foreign language reading and study abroad: Cross-cultural and cross-linguistic questions'. *Modern Language Journal* 89/4: 503–28.

Takagaki, T. 2003. 'The revision patterns and intentions in L1 and L2 by Japanese writers: A case study'. *TESL Canada Journal,* 21/1: 22–37.

Takeuchi, O. 1993. 'Language learning strategies and their relationship to achievement in English as a foreign language'. *Language Laboratory* 30: 17–34.

Takeuchi, O. 2003a. 'What can we learn from good language learners?: A qualitative study in the Japanese foreign language context'. *System* 31: 313–432.

Takeuchi, O. 2003b. *Yoriyoi gaikokugo gakushuho wo motomete* [Searching for better language learning strategies: Studies on good language learners in the Japanese FL context]. Tokyo: Shohakusha. http://www2.ipcku.kansai-u.ac.jp/~takeuchi/LLS.html.

Takeuchi, O. and N. Wakamoto. 2001. 'Language learning strategies used by Japanese college learners of English: A synthesis of four empirical studies'. *Language Education and Technology* 38: 21–44.

Tarone, E. 1978. 'Conscious communication strategies in interlanguage: A progress report' in Brown, H. D. and R. Crymes (eds.): *On TESOL '77: Teaching and Learning ESL.* Washington, DC: TESOL.

Tarone, E. 1980. 'Communication strategies, foreigner talk and repair in interlanguage'. *Language Learning* 30/2: 417–31.

Tarone, E., A. D. Cohen, and G. Dumas. 1976. 'A closer look at some interlanguage terminology'. *Working Papers in Bilingualism* 9: 76–90.

Tashakkori, A. and C. Teddlie. 1998. *Mixed Methodology: Combining the Qualitative and Quantitative Approaches.* Thousand Oaks, CA: Sage.

Tashakkori, A. and C. Teddlie (eds.). 2003. *Handbook of Mixed Methods in Social and Behavioral Research.* Thousand Oaks, CA: Sage.

Taylor, C. 1985. *Human Agency and Language.* New York: Cambridge University Press.

Teddlie, C. and A. Tashakkori. 2003. 'Major issues and controversies in the use of mixed methods in the social and behavioral sciences' in Tashakkori, A. and C. Teddlie (eds.): *Handbook of Mixed Methods in Social and Behavioral Research.* Thousand Oaks, CA: Sage.

Teichert, H. U. 1996. 'A comparative study using illustrations, brainstorming, and questions as advance organizers in intermediate college German conversation classes'. *Modern Language Journal* 80/4: 509–517.

Thompson, I. and J. Rubin. 1996. 'Can strategy instruction improve listening comprehension?'. *Foreign Language Annals* 29/3: 331–342.

Thornbury, S. 2002. *How to Teach Vocabulary*. Harlow: Longman.

Thumb, J. 2004. 'Dictionary look-up strategies and the bilingualized learners' dictionary'. (Lexicographica Series Maior 117). Tübingen, Germany: Niemeyer.

Tinkham, T. 1993. 'The effect of semantic clustering on the learning of second language vocabulary'. *System* 21/3: 371–380.

Tono, Y. 1984. On the Dictionary User's Reference Skills. Unpublished B.Ed. thesis, Tokyo Gakugei University.

Tono, Y. 1991. 'A good dictionary user: what makes the difference?' in Ito, K., K. Kanatani, and T. Noda *et al.* (eds.): *Recent Studies on English Language Teaching*. Tokyo: Yumi Press.

TRANSANA (n.d.). 2005–2006 University of Wisconsin. http://www.transana.org

Tripp, D. H. 1994. 'Teachers' lives, critical incidents and professional practice'. *Qualitative Studies in Education* 7: 65–76.

Tsui, A. B. M. and J. Fullilove. 1998. 'Bottom-up or top-down processing as a discriminator of L2 listening performance'. *Applied Linguistics* 19/4: 432–51.

Tucker, G. R., W. E. Lambert, and A. A. Rigault. 1977. *The French Speaker's Skill with Grammatical Gender: An Example of Rule-Governed Behavior*. The Hague: Mouton.

Ulitsky, H. 2000. 'Language learner strategies with technology'. *Journal of Educational Computing Research* 22/3: 285–322.

Upton, T. A. and L-C. Lee-Thompson. 2001. 'The role of the first language in second language reading'. *Studies in Second Language Acquisition* 23/4: 469–95.

Urquhart, S. and C. Weir. 1998. *Reading in a Second Language: Process, Product and Practice*. New York: Longman.

Uzawa, K. 1996. 'Second language learners' processes of L1 writing, L2 writing and translation from L1 into L2'. *Journal of Second Language Writing*, 5/3: 271–94.

Uzawa, K. and A. Cumming. 1989. 'Writing strategies in Japanese as a foreign language: Lowering or keeping up the standards'. *Canadian Modern Language Review* 46/1: 178–94.

Valdés, G., P. Haro, and M. Echevarriarza. 1992. 'The development of writing abilities in a foreign language: Contributions toward a general theory of L2 writing'. *Modern Language Journal* 76/3: 333–52.

Van Dijk, T. A. and W. Kintsch. 1983. *Strategies of Discourse Comprehension*. New York: Academic Press.

Van Hell, J. G. and A. C. Mahn. 1997. 'Keyword mnemonic versus rote rehearsal: Learning concrete and abstract foreign words by experienced and inexperience learners'. *Language Learning* 47/3: 507–546.

Van Parreren, C. F. and M. Schouten-van Parreren. 1981. 'Contextual guessing: a trainable reader strategy'. *System* 9/3: 235–241.

Vandergrift, L. 1997a. 'The Cinderella of communication strategies: Receptive strategies in interactive listening'. *Modern Language Journal* 81/4: 494–505.

Vandergrift, L. 1997b. 'The comprehension strategies of second language (French) listeners: A descriptive study'. *Foreign Language Annals* 30/3: 387–409.

Vandergrift, L. 1998a. 'Successful and less successful listeners in French: What are the strategy differences?' *The French Review* 71/3: 370–94.

Vandergrift, L. 1998b. 'La métacognition et la compréhension auditive en langue seconde'. *Canadian Journal of Applied Linguistics* 1: 83–105.

Vandergrift, L. 2003. 'Orchestrating strategy use: Toward a model of the skilled second language listener'. *Language Learning* 53/3: 463–96.

Vandergrift, L. 2004. 'Listening to learn or learning to listen?'. *Annual Review of Applied Linguistics* 24/1: 3–25.

Vandergrift, L. 2006. 'Second language listening: Listening ability or language proficiency?'. *Modern Language Journal* 90/1: 6–18.

Vandergrift, L., C.Goh, C. Mareschal, and M. H. Tafaghodtari. 2006. The Metacognitive Awareness Listening Questionnaire (MALQ): Development and validation'. *Language Learning*, 56/3: 431–62.

Vanderplank, R. 1988. 'Implications of differences in native and non-native speaker approaches to listening'. *British Journal of Language Teaching* (formerly *Audio-Visual Language Journal*) 26/1: 32–41.

Vann, J. R. and R. G. Abraham. 1990. 'Strategies of unsuccessful language learners'. *TESOL Quarterly* 24/2: 177–98.

Varonis, E. and S. M.Gass. 1985. 'Non-native/non-native conversations: A model for negotiation of meaning'. *Applied Linguistics* 6/1: 71–90.

Verplanck, W. S. 1962. 'Unaware of where's awareness: Some verbal operants—notates, monents, and notants' in Eriksen, C. W. (ed.): *Behavior and Awareness. A symposium of Research and Interpretation.* Durham, NC: Duke University Press.

Victori, M. 1995. EFL Writing Knowledge and Strategies: An Integrative Study. Unpublished doctoral thesis, Universidad Autónoma de Barcelona, Spain.

Victori, M. 1997. 'EFL composing skills and strategies: Four case studies'. *Revista Española de Lingüística Aplicada* 12: 163–84.

Victori, M. 1999. 'An analysis of written knowledge in EFL composing: A case study of two effective and two less effective writers'. *System* 27/4: 537–55.

Victori, M. and E. Tragant. 2003. 'Learner strategies: A cross-sectional and longitudinal study of primary and high-school EFL teachers' in Garcia Mayo, M. P. and M. L. Garcia Lecumberri (eds.): *Age and the Acquisition of English as a Foreign Language.* Clevedon: Multilingual Matters.

Vidal, K. 2003. 'Academic listening: A source of vocabulary acquisition?'. *Applied Linguistics* 4/1: 59–89.

Vieira, F. 2003. 'Addressing constraints on autonomy in school contexts: Lessons from working with teachers' in Palfreyman, D. and R. C. Smith (eds.): *Learner Autonomy across Cultures: Language Education Perspectives.* Basingstoke: Palgrave Macmillan.

Vogely, A. 1995. 'Perceived strategy use during performance on three authentic listening comprehension tasks'. *Modern Language Journal* 79/1: 41–56.

Vygotsky, L. S. 1978. *Mind in Society: The Development of Higher Psychological Processes.* Cambridge, MA: Harvard University Press.

Vygotsky, L. S. 1979. 'Consciousness as a problem of psychology of behavior'. *Soviet Psychology* 17: 29–30.

Vygotsky, L. S. and A. Kozulin (ed. and trans.). 1986. *Thought and Language.* Cambridge, MA: MIT Press.

Wakamoto, N. 2000. 'Language learning strategy and personality variables: Focusing on extroversion and introversion'. *International Review of Applied Linguistics* 38/1: 71–81.

Wang, A. Y. and M. H. Thomas. 1992. 'The Effect of imagery-based mnemonics on the long-term retention of Chinese characters'. *Language Learning* 42/3: 359–76.

Wang A.Y., M. H. Thomas, and J. A. Ouellette. 1992. 'Keyword mnemonic and retention of second-language vocabulary words'. *Journal of Educational Psychology* 84/4: 520–28.

Wang, L. 2003. 'Switching to first language among writers with differing second-language proficiency'. *Journal of Second Language Writing* 12/4: 347–75.

Wang, W. and Q. Wen. 2002. 'L1 use in the L2 composing process: An exploratory study of 16 Chinese EFL writers'. *Journal of Second Language Writing* 11/3: 225–46.

Waring, R. and M. T. Takaki. 2003 'At what rate do learners learn and retain new vocabulary from reading a graded reader?'. *Reading in a Foreign Language* 15/2: 130–63.

Watanabe, Y. 1990. External Variables Affecting Language Learner Strategies of Japanese EFL Learners: Effects of Entrance Examination, Years Spent at College/University, and Staying Overseas. Unpublished master's thesis, Lancaster University, Lancaster, UK.

Watson, J. B. 1930. *Behaviorism*. London: Kegan Paul, Trench, Trubner and Co.

Weaver, S. J. and A. D. Cohen. 1997. *Strategies-Based Instruction: A Teacher-Training Manual*. Minneapolis, MN: Center for Advanced Research on Language Acquisition, University of Minnesota.

Wegerif, F. R., N. Mercer, and L. Dawes. 1999. 'From social interaction to individual reasoning: An empirical investigation of a possible sociocultural model of cognitive development'. *Learning and Instruction* 9/6: 493–516.

Wenden, A. 1986. 'What do second language learners know about their language learning? A second look at retrospective accounts'. *Applied Linguistics* 7/2: 186–201.

Wenden, A. L. 1987 'Metacognition: An expanded view of the cognitive abilities of L2 learners'. *Language Learning* 37/4: 573–97.

Wenden, A. 1991. *Learner Strategies for Learner Autonomy*. Englewood Cliffs, NJ: Prentice Hall.

Wenden, A. 1995. 'Learner training in context: A knowledge-based approach' in Dickenson, L. and A. Wenden (eds.): Special Issue on Autonomy. *System* 23/2.

Wenden, A. 1999. 'Metacognitive knowledge and language learning'. *Applied Linguistics* 19/4: 515–37.

Wenden, A. 2001. 'Metacognitive Knowledge in SLA: The Neglected Variable' in M. P. Breen (ed.): *Learner Contributions to Language Learning. New Directions in Research*. Harlow: Pearson.

Wenden, A. and J. Rubin (eds.). 1987. *Learner Strategies and Language Learning*. Englewood Cliffs, NJ: Prentice Hall.

Wendt, M. 1993. *Strategien des fremdsprachlichen Handelns. Lerntheoretische Studien zur begrifflichen Systematik. Band 1: Die drei Dimensionen der Lernersprache.* [Strategies of foreign language action. Studies on conceptual systematicity from a learning theoretical perspective. Vol. 1: The three dimensions of learner language]. Tübingen, Germany: Narr.

Wendt, M. 1997. 'Strategien und Strategieebenen am Beispiel von Lernaktivitäten im Spanischunterricht' [Strategies and strategy levels. The example of learning acitivities in the Spanish classroom] in Rampillon, U. and G. Zimmermann (eds.): *Strategien und Techniken beim Erwerb fremder Sprachen*. Ismaning, Germany: Hueber.

Wenger, E. 1998. *Communities of Practice: Learning, Meaning and Identity*. Cambridge, UK: Cambridge University Press.

Wenger, E., R. McDermott, and W. Snyder. 2002. *Cultivating Communities of Practice: A Guide to Managing Knowledge*. Cambridge, MA: Harvard Business School Press.

Wesche, M. B. 1981. 'Language aptitude measures in streaming, matching students with methods, and diagnosis of learning problems' in Diller, K. C. (ed.): *Individual Differences and Universals in Language Learning Aptitude*. Rowley, MA: Newbury House.

Wesche, M. B. and T. S. Paribakht. 2000. 'Reading-based exercises in second language vocabulary learning: An introspective study'. *Modern Language Journal* 84/2: 196–213.

Whalen, K. 1993. 'A strategic approach to the development of second language written discourse competency: A comparison of mother tongue and second language written production processes' in Martin, J. F. B. and J. M. M. Morillas (eds.): *Proceedings of the International Conference of Applied Linguistics*. Granada, Spain: University of Granada Press.

Whalen, K. and N. Ménard. 1995. 'L1 and L2 writers' strategic and linguistic knowledge: A model of multiple-level discourse processing'. *Language Learning* 45/3: 381–418.

Wharton, G. 2000. 'Language learning strategy use of bilingual foreign language learners in Singapore'. *Language Learning* 50/2: 203–43.

White, C. J. 1995a. 'Notetaking strategies and traces of cognition'. *RELC Journal* 27/1: 89–102.

White, C. J. 1995b. 'Autonomy and strategy use in distance foreign language learning: Research findings'. *System* 23/2: 207–21.

White, C. J. 1997. 'Effects of mode of study on foreign language learning'. *Distance Education* 18/1: 178–96.

White, C. J. 2003. *Language Learning in Distance Education*. Cambridge: Cambridge University Press.

Williams, J., R. Inscoe, and T. Tasker. 1997. 'Communication strategies in an interactional context: The mutual achievement of comprehension' in Kasper, G. and E. Kellerman (eds.): *Communication Strategies, Psycholinguistic and Sociolinguistic Perspectives*. Harlow: Longman.

Williams, M. and R. L. Burden. 1979. *Psychology for language teachers*. Cambridge University Press.

Williams, M. and R. L. Burden. 1997. *Psychology for Language Teachers: A Social Cognitive Approach*. Cambridge: Cambridge University Press.

Willing, K. 1989. *Teaching How to Learn: Learning Strategies in ESL – Activity Worksheets*. California: Alta Book Center.

Winter, B. and A. S. Reber. 1994. 'Implicit learning and the acquisition of natural languages' in Ellis, N. C. (ed.): *Implicit and Explicit Learning of Languages*. San Diego, CA: Academic Press.

Witkin, H. A. 1962. *Psychological Differences*. New York: Wiley.

Wittgenstein, L. 1958/1971. *Philosophische Untersuchungen* [Philosophical investigations]. Frankfurt am Main, Germany: Suhrkamp.

Wolfersberger, M. 2003. 'L1 to L2 writing process and strategy transfer: A look at lower proficiency writers'. Retrieved May 6, 2006 from *TESL-EJ* 7/2: 1-12. http://www-writing. berkeley.edu/TESL-EJ/ej26/a6.html.

Wolters, C. 2003. 'Regulation of motivation: Evaluating an underemphasized aspect of self-regulated learning'. *Educational Psychologist* 38: 189–205.

Wong, A. T. Y. 2005. 'Writers' mental representations of the intended audience and of the rhetorical purpose for writing and the strategies they employed when they composed'. *System* 33/1: 29–47.

Wong-Fillmore, L. 1979. 'Individual differences in second language acquisition' in Fillmore, C. J., W. S. Y. Wang, and D. Kempler (eds.): *Individual Differences in Language Ability and Behaviour*. New York: Academic Press.

Wood, D., J. Bruner, and G. Ross. 1976. 'The role of tutoring in problem solving'. *Journal of Child Psychology and Psychiatry* 17/2: 89–100.

Woodall, B. R. 2002. 'Language-switching: Using the first language when writing in a second language'. *Journal of Second Language Writing* 11/1: 7–28.

Yamamori, K., T. Isoda, T. Hiromori, and R. L.Oxford. 2003. 'Using cluster analysis to uncover L2 learner differences in strategy use, will to learn, and achievement over time'. *International Review of Applied Linguistics and Language Teaching* 41/4: 381–409.

Yang, L., K. Baba, and A. Cumming. 2004. 'Activity systems for ESL writing improvement: Case studies of three Chinese and three Japanese adult learners of English' in Albrechtsen, D., K. Haastrup, and B. Henriksen (eds.): *Writing and Vocabulary in Foreign Language Acquisition, Special Issue of Angles on the English-Speaking World 4*. Copenhagen: Museum Tusculanum Press, University of Copenhagen.

Yang, N. D. 1992. Second Language Learners' Beliefs about Language Learning and their Role of Learning Strategies: A Study of College Students of English in Taiwan. Unpublished doctoral dissertation, The University of Texas at Austin, Texas, USA.

Yarmohammadi, L. and S. Seif. 1992. 'More on communicative strategies: Classification, resources, frequency and underlying processes'. *IRAL* 30/3: 223–32.

Yorio, C. A. 1971. 'Some sources of reading problems for foreign language learners'. *Language Learning* 21/1: 107–115.

Young, M.-Y. C. 1996. Listening Comprehension Strategies Used by University Level Chinese Students Learning English as a Second Language. Unpublished doctoral thesis, University of Essex, UK.

Young, M.-Y. C. 1997. 'A serial ordering of listening comprehension strategies used by advanced ESL learners in Hong Kong'. *Asian Journal of English Language Teaching* 7: 35–53.

Zainuddin, H. and R. A. Moore. 2003. 'Audience awareness in L1 and L2 composing of bilingual writers'. *TESL-EJ* 7/1: 1–19. Retrieved May 6, 2006 from http://www-writing.berkeley.edu/TESL-EJ/ej25/a2.html.

Zaki, H. and R. Ellis. 1999. 'Learning vocabulary through interacting with a written text' in Ellis, R., (ed.): *Learning a second language through interaction*. Amsterdam: John Benjamins.

Zamel, V. 1983. 'The composing processes of advanced ESL students: Six case studies'. *TESOL Quarterly* 17/2: 165–87.

Zhu, W. 2003. 'Performing argumentative writing in English: Difficulties, processes and strategies'. *TESL Canada Journal* 21/1: 34–50.

Zimmerman, B. J. 2000. 'Attaining self-regulation: A social cognitive perspective' in Boekaerts, M., P. R. Pintrich, and M. Zeidner (eds.): *Handbook of Self-Regulation*. San Diego, CA: Academic Press.

Zimmerman, B. J. 2001. 'Theories of self-regulated learning and academic achievement: An overview and analysis' in Zimmerman, B. J. and D. Schunk (eds.): *Self-Regulated Learning and Academic Achievement*. (2nd ed.). Mahwah, NJ: Erlbaum.

Zimmerman, B. J., S. Bonner, and R. Kovach. 1996. *Developing Self-Regulated Learners: Beyond Achievement to Self-Efficacy*. Washington, DC: American Psychological Association.

Zimmerman, B. J. and D. Schunk (eds.). 2001. *Self-Regulated Learning and Academic Achievement*. (2nd ed.). Mahwah, NJ: Erlbaum.

Zimmermann, R. 2000. 'L2 writing: Subprocesses, a model of formulating and empirical findings'. *Learning and Instruction* 10/1: 73–99.

Zuengler, J. and E. R. Miller. 2006. 'Cognitive and sociocultural perspectives: Two parallel SLA worlds?'. *TESOL Quarterly* 40/1: 35–58.

Index